Feminist Research
Recherche féministe

FEMINIST RESEARCH
PROSPECT AND RETROSPECT

RECHERCHE FÉMINISTE
BILAN ET PERSPECTIVES D'AVENIR

EDITED BY / RÉDIGÉ PAR PETA TANCRED-SHERIFF

Published for / publié pour
The Canadian Research Institute for the Advancement of Women
l'Institut canadien de recherches sur les femmes

by / par
McGill–Queen's University Press
Kingston and Montreal

Legal deposit fourth quarter 1988
Bibliothèque nationale du Québec

Printed in Canada on acid-free paper

Canadian Cataloguing in Publication Data

Main entry under title:
Feminist research: prospect and
retrospect =
Recherche féministe: bilan et perspectives
d'avenir
Text in English and French.
Bibliography: p.
ISBN 0-7735-0682-9 (bound) –
ISBN 0-7735-0686-1 (pbk.)
1. Women. 2. Women's studies. I.
Tancred-Sheriff, Peta. II. Canadian
Research Institute for the Advancement of
Women. III. Title: Recherche féministe.
HQ1206.F435 1988   305.4   c88-090278-7E

**Données de catalogage avant publication
(Canada)**

Vedette principale au titre:
Feminist research: prospect and
retrospect =
Recherche féministe: bilan et perspectives
d'avenir
Texte en anglais et en français.
Bibliographie: p.
ISBN 0-7735-0682-9 (bound) –
ISBN 0-7735-0686-1 (pbk.)
1. Femmes. 2. Études féministes. I.
Tancred-Sheriff, Peta. II. Institut canadien
de recherches sur les femmes. III. Titre:
Recherche féministe.
HQ1206.F435 1988   305.4   c88-090278-7F

Contents
Table des matières

Acknowledgments
Remerciements

I would like to express my warm appreciation to: Linda O'Neil, CRIAW Publications and Program Officer, for her extensive support during each stage of the publication process; the Simone de Beauvoir Institute, Concordia University, for the wide-ranging assistance provided by staff, and to Maïr Verthuy, in particular, for her collaboration in reviewing certain papers; the Canadian Research Institute for the Advancement of Women (CRIAW), and the Women's Program, Secretary of State, for financial assistance towards the cost of publishing this volume; and Isabelle McKee-Allain, Corinne Gallant, Marlène Carmel and their collaborators for their extensive work in organizing the 1986 CRIAW conference, held at l'Université de Moncton, from whose proceedings the collection was selected.

J'aimerais exprimer ici toute ma gratitude à Linda O'Neil, agente des publications et de programme à l'Institut canadien de recherches sur les femmes (ICREF), pour son constant appui tout au long de la préparation de ce volume; aux membres du personnel de l'Institut Simone de Beauvoir de l'Université Concordia pour l'aide généreuse qu'elles m'ont apportée, et à Maïr Verthuy en particulier pour sa collaboration dans l'évaluation de certains textes; à l'ICREF et au Programme de la promotion de la femme du Secrétariat d'État pour l'aide financière apportée en vue de la publication de ce volume; à Isabelle McKee-Allain, Corinne Gallant, Marlène Carmel et leurs collaboratrices pour le travail considérable qu'elles ont accompli en organisant en 1986 le colloque de l'ICREF, qui a eu lieu à l'Université de Moncton dont est tirée cette sélection d'articles.

Peta Tancred-Sheriff

Preface
Préface

In presenting this selection of papers from the 1986 CRIAW conference on "Feminist Research: Prospect and Retrospect," I am encouraged to reflect upon the ways in which the authors have chosen to treat this particular theme. While one clear avenue would have been to synthesize previous work and delineate parameters for future effort (and one or two authors have chosen this route), the majority of participants have opted to illustrate, through their own work, both the strength of previous research and the current tendencies. Thus, while they make reference to the relevant research for the specialized topic under review, it is frequently impossible to synthesize all the feminist research even within one particular subfield (as Marguerite Andersen suggests in her introductory paper). Instead, by locating their current research at a particular juncture in the literature – methodologically, contextually, and/or theoretically – the authors graphically illustrate both the retrospect of feminist research and its prospects for the future.

For example, Margrit Eichler opens the initial section, entitled "Reproduction and Maternity," with a hard-hitting analysis of the new reproductive technologies. In an ineluctably logical argument, she underlines the medicalization and judicialization of the whole reproductive process, and by using the powerful image of a woman wrapped around a foetus, she symbolizes the growing importance of the foetus to the denigration of the woman, a process that is in the interests of neither. Anne Quéniart and Jane Gordon take up the theme of the medicalization of reproduction in their complementary treatments of pregnancy and childbirth. They underline, with interviews and/or quantitative material, the way in which the medical definition of these female experiences has encouraged pregnant women to view the foetus as having priority during pregnancy,

and to see the birthing experience as "normal" – despite a high
degree of medical intervention. Martin Thomas completes this section with a synthetic approach to the question of gender distribution.
Drawing on a wide range of literature to develop a predictive model
of the effects of gender preselection, he concludes that only a minor
increase in male births is probable, and that concern on the subject
of gender maldistribution is unwarranted.

In the section entitled "Education: Pedagogy and Consequences,"
a dominant theme is the specificity of women's approaches in both
learning and pedagogy. Lanie Melamed and Irene Devine scrutinize
the Kolb Learning Style Inventory for gender bias and conclude that
women do have a preferred, more concrete style of learning. Angéline Martel and Linda Peterat outline the themes of a specifically
feminist ped-agogy and illustrate how these have been implemented
in their own teaching. Holly Devor reports on her personal experience in teaching women's studies to male prison inmates, concluding that despite differences between their reactions and those of all-
female classes, this population derived considerable benefit from the
course. Finally in this section, Roberta Mura undertakes the arduous
task of synthesizing international research on women and mathematics, indicating fruitful avenues for future efforts.

The third section, entitled "Women's Work in Historical and Developmental Perspective," starts with two historical studies of working women in the Maritimes, Ginette Lafleur's in Moncton in the
late nineteenth-century, and Nancy Forestell and Jessie Chisholm's
in St. John's in the period 1890–1920. The authors make astute use
of a variety of sources to illustrate resemblances to women's experience elsewhere in Canada in the same historical period. The remaining two articles examine the working experiences of women,
both domestic and waged, in two developmental contexts. Marie
France Labrecque and Maria Elisa Montejo argue that in Mexico,
waged work for women does not necessarily mean increased autonomy. Finally, in the last article in this section, Omer Chouinard
suggests that, in the Acadian peninsula, the extent of waged work
for women adapts itself to the necessities of their husbands' status
in the fishing industry, with the wives sometimes taking on a triple
day of domestic labour, supportive labour (for spouses), and wage
labour.

Women's well-being is the topic of the fourth section. Here Janet
Stoppard takes up the issue of women's higher rates of depression
and concludes that a synthesis of existing research supports the
feminist argument that such rates result from women's disadvantaged position within society. However, on a theme that is becoming

familiar, she adds that the impact of this perspective is unlikely to have much effect because of the dominant role of the medical (and particularly the psychiatric) profession in legitimating appropriate definitions. Linda Klimack applies a Grieving Model to the situation of battered women, outlining the dynamic process through which a woman arrives at some means of coping with an abusive relationship, and underlining that such "coping" might well take various concrete forms. Colleen Lundy examines the position of alcoholic women, emphasizing the importance of self-help groups in terms of both support and "empowerment."

In the section entitled "Women in Literature," Monique Genuist graphically illustrates the positive physical and moral strengths of aged and poverty-stricken women in the writings of Antonine Maillet, arguing that these symbolize women's future strength. Tracy Davis uses various interpretations of Ibsen's heroine Nora, of *A Doll's House*, to illustrate the changing priorities of the feminist movement over the past century.

The final five papers of the collection deal with women's political life in various arenas. Micheline de Sève argues that women's ambivalence toward power should be examined, for while the rejection of its oppressive nature can be justified, women's overwhelming desire for close affective relationships, as illustrated in the mother-son relationship, is very likely to perpetuate the domination of men as women refuse to "face the music." And, in fact, Marie-Andrée Bertrand illustrates one form of such domination in her account of a feminist analysis of criminal law. She argues that not only are women's interests frequently excluded from the legal framework, but its application, often by men, is discriminatory. Lorraine Code discusses the phenomenon of tokenism as one possible strategy, concluding that women who practise "identity politics" by recognizing their role within a collective endeavour may be able to realize the potential inherent in their position. The last two articles deal with the collective expression of women's interests in two very different forms. Dorothy Zaborszky provides a personal account of the founding of the Feminist Party of Canada, not only to put the experience on record, but also to draw out the full benefit of the events for any future efforts in this area. And Lorna Erwin presents data from a study of the rank-and-file of the pro-family movement, concluding that the characteristics of the members – particularly their isolation, religiosity and disaffection with the media – will make it difficult for the movement to extend its leverage. Nevertheless, she thinks that wide knowledge of such material is important for a detailed feminist understanding of the movement.

These, then, are the preoccupations of a wide range of feminist researchers, both inside and outside the university context, and they vividly symbolize the strengths of current research as it builds upon past efforts. It is pertinent that the final paper deals with the anti-feminist movement, for, as Marguerite Andersen indicates in her introductory paper, it is her opinion (and that of many feminists) that we are currently in a period of strong backlash. She goes on to argue that the "dynamite of research" will contribute to the erosion of opposition and to the construction of a positive route forward. Whether or not this current collection *proves* the existence of such research dynamite must be left to future judgement, but it surely illustrates both the accomplishments of feminist research, and its promise for the future.

Peta Tancred-Sheriff

Cette présentation est pour moi l'occasion de réfléchir sur les différentes façons dont les auteur-e-s des articles qui suivent ont choisi de traiter le thème du colloque 1986 de l'ICREF, « Recherche féministe: bilan et perspectives d'avenir. » Même si la voie la plus évidente était celle d'une synthèse des travaux déjà accomplis et de la mise en évidence des paramètres pertinents en vue des recherches futures, seules une ou deux auteures s'y sont engagées. La majorité des participant-e-s ont plutôt choisi d'utiliser leur propre travail pour illustrer à la fois la solidité de la recherche accomplie et les tendances de la recherche en cours. Situant leurs recherches actuelles dans une conjoncture particulière, sur les plans méthodologique, contextuel et/ou théorique, esquissant de ce fait un bilan de la recherche féministe et des perspectives d'avenir, leur réflexion ne permet pas, dans l'ensemble, d'effectuer une synthèse de la recherche féministe même à l'intérieur d'un sous-champ particulier – c'est ce que précise Marguerite Andersen dans son texte d'introduction.

La section intitulée « Reproduction et maternité » s'ouvre par une analyse implacable des nouvelles technologies de reproduction. Dans une argumentation d'une logique inéluctable, Margrit Eichler souligne la médicalisation et la judiciarisation du processus de reproduction; elle utilise l'image d'une femme enroulée autour d'un foetus pour symboliser l'importance grandissante accordée au foetus au détriment de la femme, dans un processus qui n'est dans l'intérêt ni de l'un ni de l'autre. Anne Quéniart et Jane Gordon s'intéressent également à cette question de la médicalisation de la reproduction. Basées sur des données d'entrevues et/ou quantitatives, leurs analy-

ses respectives de la grossesse et de la naissance montrent comment
les femmes ont été encouragées à considérer le foetus comme plus
important que leur propre personne au cours de la grossesse, et à
voir l'expérience de la naissance comme « normale » en dépit d'une
intervention médicale très poussée. Martin Thomas, enfin, applique
à la question de la distribution des genres une approche synthétique;
s'appuyant sur un vaste choix de textes pour évaluer les effets
qu'aurait une présélection du sexe, il conclut que l'augmentation,
prévisible, des naissances mâles est minime: les inquiétudes que l'on
pourrait avoir quant à un déséquilibre du ratio hommes-femmes ne
sont pas fondées.

Un des thèmes dominants de la section « Education: la pédagogie
et ses conséquences », est la spécificité de l'approche féminine aussi
bien en ce qui concerne l'apprentissage que la pédagogie. Un examen
approfondi des préjugés sexistes révélés par le « Kolb learning style
inventory » permet à Lanie Melamed et à Irene Devine de conclure
que les femmes préfèrent un mode d'apprentissage plus concret.
Angéline Martel et Linda Peterat, de leur côté, énumèrent les thèmes
propres à la pédagogie féministe et montrent comment elles les ont
intégrés à leur style d'enseignement. Holly Devor rapporte son expérience dans l'enseignement des études sur les femmes auprès de
détenus, et conclut que, bien que différent d'un auditoire exclusivement féminin, son groupe d'hommes a tiré un grand bénéfice du
cours suivi. Pour finir, Roberta Mura s'attaque à une tâche ardue:
synthétiser toutes les recherches concernant les rapports femmes-
mathématiques; elle en profite pour signaler un certain nombre de
pistes qui risquent de se révéler fécondes dans un proche avenir.

Les deux premiers articles de la section concernant « Le travail
des femmes: historique et développement économique » sont des
études historiques sur les travailleuses des Maritimes. Celui de Ginette Lafleur porte sur les femmes de Moncton à la fin du dix-
neuvième siècle, celui de Nancy Forestell et Jessie Chisholm sur les
femmes de St-Jean dans les trente années suivantes. Les auteures,
utilisant avec astuce une grande variété de sources, montrent que la
vie de ces femmes n'est guère différente de celle des autres Canadiennes vivant à la même époque. Les deux articles suivants relatent
l'expérience de travail des femmes – qu'il s'agisse de travail domestique ou de travail salarié – dans un contexte de développement
économique. Marie France Labrecque et Maria Elisa Montejo
observent que dans le cas du Mexique, le travail salarié n'entraîne
pas nécessairement pour les femmes une plus grande autonomie.
Omer Chouinard, quant à lui, montre que, dans la péninsule acadienne, la disponibilité des femmes pour le travail salarié est fonction

du statut de leur mari dans l'industrie de la pêche; aussi peuvent-
elles accomplir jusqu'à une triple journée de travail – tâches domestiques, participation aux activités professionnelles de l'homme
et travail salarié.

Le mieux-être des femmes fait l'objet de la quatrième section. Janet
Stoppard s'intéresse au taux élevé de dépression chez les femmes et
indique que les recherches actuelles rejoignent les analyses féministes
voulant que la situation défavorisée des femmes dans la société soit
en cause. Toutefois, ajoute-t-elle – et c'est là une remarque que nous
entendons de plus en plus – un tel point de vue restera sans doute
sans effet étant donné la position de force qu'occupe l'institution
médicale (en particulier psychiatrique) et grâce à quoi elle a la main
haute sur la légitimisation des définitions. Linda Klimack applique
le « Grieving Model » à la situation des femmes battues, soulignant
que le processus au terme duquel une femme arrive à faire face à
une relation abusive est un processus actif et qu'il peut, par ailleurs,
revêtir diverses formes dans la réalité. Colleen Lundy, étudiant la
situation des femmes alcooliques, met l'accent sur l'importance des
groupes d'appui mutuel aussi bien en ce qui a trait au support fourni
qu'aux pouvoirs qu'ils permettent de révéler.

Ouvrant la section « Les femmes et la littérature », Monique
Genuist illustre de façon vivante la force physique autant que morale
dont font preuve des femmes pauvres et âgées dans l'oeuvre
d'Antonine Maillet. Pour elle, ces caractéristiques symbolisent la
force à venir des femmes. Tracy Davis, pour sa part, illustre les
changements de priorités du mouvement féministe au cours du dernier siècle à partir des multiples interprétations qui sont faites de
Nora, l'héroïne de *La maison de poupée*, d'Ibsen.

Les cinq derniers textes du recueil portent sur la vie politique des
femmes, dans quelque arène que ce soit. Micheline de Sève pense
qu'il faudrait étudier soigneusement l'ambivalence des femmes par
rapport au pouvoir: le désir irrésistible qu'elles ont d'établir des
relations affectives très étroites, comme c'est le cas dans la relation
mère-fils, risque fort de perpétuer la domination des hommes, surtout si elles refusent de « faire face à la musique ». C'est justement
une des formes de cette domination qu'illustre Marie Andrée Bertrand dans l'analyse féministe qu'elle fait de la juridiction criminelle.
On voit que non seulement les femmes sont exclues du cadre légal
mais également que l'application même des lois (par des hommes)
est le plus souvent discriminatoire à leur endroit. Lorraine Code
parle du phénomène des femmes symboliques, et de la stratégie
qu'elles peuvent adopter, concluant que celles qui pratiquent la politique de l'identification en reconnaissant leur rôle au sein de l'effort

collectif sont peut-être en mesure d'utiliser le potentiel inhérent à leur position sociale. Les deux derniers articles traitent de l'expression collective des intérêts des femmes, sous deux formes très différentes. Dorothy Zaborszky nous explique comment a été fondé le Parti féministe du Canada, non seulement pour que l'acte en soit pris mais aussi pour que l'on puisse en retirer le meilleur profit en vue d'efforts futurs. Finalement, Lorna Erwin présente les données d'une étude portant sur les membres du mouvement pro-famille; elle conclut que leurs caractéristiques – particulièrement leur isolement, leur religiosité et leur mécontentement face aux médias – rendront difficile pour le mouvement une quelconque expansion de son influence. Il est important toutefois, affirme-t-elle, de bien connaître ces faits si l'on veut comprendre d'un point de vue féministe ce mouvement.

Telles sont, rapidement passées en revue, les préoccupations d'un large éventail de chercheur-e-s féministes qui poursuivent leurs travaux aussi bien à l'intérieur qu'à l'extérieur de l'institution universitaire. Elles témoignent des forces vives de la recherche en cours, patiemment édifiée sur les efforts du passé. Il me semble à propos de noter que le dernier texte porte sur le mouvement anti-féministe car, comme le souligne Marguerite Andersen dans son texte d'introduction (et cette opinion est partagée par un grand nombre de féministes), nous essuyons aujourd'hui les contrecoups de nos luttes. C'est la dynamite contenue dans la recherche qui nous servira à miner l'opposition et à construire la route où nous poserons nos pas. Seul le temps dira si le présent recueil est une preuve tangible de l'existence de la recherche en tant que matière explosive, mais je suis convaincue que déjà il témoigne de ce qu'est la recherche féministe, de ses richesses et de ses promesses pour l'avenir.

Peta Tancred-Sheriff

Introduction

MARGUERITE ANDERSEN

Women's Thought: The Road of Feminist Research in Canada

Three periods can be distinguished within the academic feminism of the last twenty years: in the beginning, a localized feminism during which the foundations for women's studies were laid; then a Canada-wide feminism which saw the creation of CRIAW and which managed to infiltrate other professional associations; and a third period we are now in, which is troubled by a serious antifeminist backlash, illustrated by books like Margaret Atwood's *The Handmaid's Tale* (1985). Yet, with the help of what Mary O'Brien calls "dynamite," namely feminism and feminist research, the boulders obstructing the female road to freedom will eventually be blown away.

La pensée des femmes: cheminement de la recherche féministe au Canada

Le féminisme universitaire des vingt dernières années peut être divisé en trois périodes: une première durant laquelle des féministes plus ou moins isolées ont créé les bases des études féministes au Canada; une deuxième qui a vu la création de l'ICREF et l'infiltration par les féministes des associations professionnelles; et une troisième, légitimée par la création de cinq chaires d'études sur la femme par le Secrétariat d'État, mais troublée par un sérieux *backlash*. Il est à prévoir toutefois que les recherches féministes finiront par débarrasser de ses obstacles la route des femmes vers la libération.

It would have been tempting to put together, for this overview of feminist research, an inventory of the most important studies published by Canadian feminists. Tempting, but impossible. The richness and the quantity of the available work is such that one person

alone could not possibly do it justice. A compilation by Carol Mazur
and Sheila Pepper (1984) listed seven thousand entries covering a
period of eighteen years of writings by and about Canadian women.
A critical evaluation of feminist research in Canada should be undertaken by an interdisciplinary team with considerable time to complete the task.

As an individual, however, I can reflect on what has happened to
me, a feminist in academia, over the last eighteen years. I distinguish
three different periods: the first five years, from the late sixties to
about 1973, were exciting and very creative, as we were laying the
foundations for feminist studies. We formed caucuses and attended
consciousness-raising seminars. But, in spite of all the meetings, these
first years of the feminist upsurge were somewhat lonely for the
individual academic. We were a relatively small number of women,
working mainly within our own institutions and our own cities, without many contacts elsewhere. We were creating new courses in a
new field, we were sensitizing students and colleagues to women's
issues, and we changed our perspectives as far as our research was
concerned. But what Frieda Forman, in a group interview with Melanie Randall, calls "sisterhood feminism," remained rather local
(1985, 3).

Of course, there were efforts to establish wider networks, Margrit
Eichler and Marylee Stephenson's *Canadian Newsletter of Research on
Women* being the most important and most successful. We tried to
establish an association for women in Canadian colleges and universities. Enthused by the idea of a powerful sisterhood, and under
the influence of the university politics of the time, we wanted this
association to be for students, staff, and faculty Canada-wide. It was
an ambitious project that vanished after a few years of interesting
annual meetings, but which nevertheless prompted the creation of
associations or women's caucuses within some universities.

American feminism was most important to us. I remember teaching, in 1970–1, an interdisciplinary course in women's studies at
Loyola/Concordia, in which I used a great deal of American material,
invited American speakers such as Mary Daly and Marlene Dixon,
and studied the outlines of courses given in American colleges and
bibliographies prepared in the USA. Today, the American model is
no longer necessary. While we might question the desirability or the
principle of an all-Canadian course, it would now be possible, in
most disciplines, to teach a women's studies course with only Canadian material. CRIAW has created a bank of researchers, the *KWIC
Index of Canadian Women's Periodicals*; the journal *Resources for Feminist
Research/Documentation sur la Recherche féministe* (RFR/DRF) (which is in

fact the daughter of the Eichler-Stephenson *Newsletter*)–a wealth of information has been accumulated over the past fifteen years. *Canadian Women's Studies* is a very readable teaching tool, and extensive women's studies collections are available in various institutions, such as the Women's Resource Centre at OISE. A great number of books have been published in the social sciences as well as in the arts, in English and in French. In 1983, RFR/DRF listed 180 books on women's issues published in Québec (Andersen 1983). Feminist publishing firms are solidly established in English Canada and in Québec.

We managed to do a tremendous lot of work during the first years of this feminist renewal, a period we might call preparatory. We continued in much the same way, as "filles studieuses," as Nicole Brossard would say, during the second period, which was richer in publications and concrete results such as policy changes.

The second period of recent feminism and feminist research began with the founding of our own professional association, the Canadian Research Institute for the Advancement of Women (CRIAW). It was a more collective period, a period during which we were able to make contact with each other and to bring feminism more aggressively into the academic forum.

We now could work without feeling too isolated; we were more closely connected with each other. This period made exchanges, contacts, and cooperation possible; it allowed us to create a family, so to speak, of feminists. We are separated, of course, by our famous linguistic and geographic boundaries, but we were nevertheless solidly united in a useful and efficient network.

In its beginnings, feminist research was essentially global in orientation, aimed at improving woman's status in general. Today, research tends to focus on much more specific problems. From "sisterhood feminism" we have moved to an "issue-oriented feminism" (Forman in Randall 1985, 3).

Currently, most universities offer women's studies courses. I believe that these courses are more widely accepted and therefore more solidly established in the social sciences and in history than they are in the liberal arts, where liberalism is said to reign but where feminism is often ignored or judged to be a passing fad. For example, a few years ago, during the deliberations of a committee in charge of deciding who, in a given field, will obtain government research grants, a colleague (quite a nice person and not particularly aggressive) asked me rather seriously how much longer it would be necessary to allocate funds to projects of a feminist nature!

In fact, women's studies has become a fairly respected field, as demonstrated by the financing of five women's studies chairs, at five

Canadian universities, through the office of the Secretary of State. This does not prevent antifeminist colleagues from maligning women who dare to give a feminist perspective to their courses. Professor Sheila McIntyre, in the Faculty of Law at Queen's University, is a case in point, and unfortunately not a unique one.

We see that, in spite of these many years of work, in spite of research, colloquia, and publications, all is not well. There is progress, yes, but not enough, and the progress we have made could quite easily be annihilated. Books such as *The Handmaid's Tale* and Suzette Haden Elgin's *The Native Tongue* (1984) point this out very clearly. And, during Melanie Randall's group interview, Margrit Eichler warned:

We have to start dealing with the backlash. We have to start taking it seriously and I am not sure what the appropriate way is. It's the one issue on which I think I am more profoundly pessimistic than other people because I see the danger as greater. That is why I consider it very important for feminists to get things into the so-called mainstream ... If you look at what the right wing movements here are trying to do, it is a real threat to women. What frightens me is fundamentalism and I don't care whether it's religious fundamentalism or political fundamentalism ... Several governments ... have been taken over by fundamentalists and we have strong right wing movements here and a fundamentalist movement which is both religious and political, and sometimes they conjoin (1985, 5).

In my opinion, we are in a third period in Canadian feminism, a period troubled by serious backlash. This backlash threatens our academic work as much as our lives and feminism in general. For a deeply disturbing analysis of right-wing women's aims in Canada, we must turn to two issues of the CRIAW publication *Feminist Perspectives* (Dubinsky 1985; Eichler 1986).

Eichler and I are of German background. Maybe it is the memory of Nazism that makes us realize how quickly any political or intellectual movement can be eradicated. When Hitler, in 1937, delivered his seventy-minute diatribe against modern art, which he qualified as being Jewish, Bolshevist, and decadent, he said that works of art which could not be understood by the average German would be destroyed, that artists or intellectuals who persisted in seeing the world in a way that contradicted National Socialist perceptions and ideas, ought to be dealt with by the Ministry of the Interior, where the sterilisation of the insane was being programmed, or else by criminal justice courts.

We know what happened to numerous artists and intellectuals under Nazi rule, and also under other totalitarian regimes: they were forbidden to write, to publish, to paint, to sculpt, and they were interned in concentration camps. Exile. Death. Any extremist regime could just as easily prohibit feminist research and teaching, burn feminist books, and erase feminist thought from the minds of future generations. We have only to read *The Handmaid's Tale* to understand what could happen should a rightwing, fundamentalist movement come to power.

Convinced that Canadians distrust extremes, Margaret Atwood does not situate *The Handmaid's Tale* in Canada. And indeed, if we examine the newsletter, *Reality Update*, published by REAL Women (a pro-family organization), we find that this group does not use extremist rhetoric. But it is precisely for this reason that REAL Women, and groups like it, represent a real threat to the continued improvement of the status of women in Canada. Atwood claims that her book does not harbour any particular warnings for Canadian political culture, yet she also maintains that vigilance is in order.

Offred, in *The Handmaid's Tale*, lives in a room "for ladies in re-duced circumstances" (18). She knows that in such circumstances "thoughts must be rationed" and that "there's a lot that doesn't bear thinking about" (17). As a young girl, she had, out of sheer frivolity, preferred not to think about certain political developments. A few years later – the Republic of Gilead has by now been proclaimed – she goes to buy cigarettes. The corner store's computer declares her credit card invalid. The same day she loses her job at at the library which, by a new law, must lay off all female employees. This is done within minutes, while men with machine guns look on. Take jobs and money away on the same day. What a clever thing, so much more efficient than what the Nazis did to their opponents and to the Jews in the early days of the Hitler regime when it was still possible to flee Germany – provided one had a passport, money, and the will to leave. Hitler had politically dangerous books burned. In Atwood's novel also, books and other feminist documents are burned; furthermore, women are forbidden to read and write. Girl-children are simply no longer taught these skills. Women like Offred must live for some time in institutions where so-called "Aunts," women at the service of the regime, proceed to brainwash them. The Republic of Gilead is the most intolerant theocracy a feminist can imagine. Feminists of the past, like Offred's mother, are classified as "Unwomen" and sent to labour colonies. It is said that they wasted time and government money on many silly projects such as "take-back-the-night" marches. In *The Handmaid's Tale*, women are again defined by biology, and subject to men's rulings. The "Aunts," like the ss women in concentration camps, torture other women. We are reminded here of what Mary Daly points out in *Gyn/Ecology* (1978): how cleverly men make arrangements to have women torture other women; European witchburning, Chinese foot-binding, and Indian widow-burning are her examples. In each case, it is women who prepare the victim for her execution or torture, exactly as in the Western world female nurses lead women to the gynecologist's table. And we can read in *Reality Update* how the unreal REAL Women of Canada malign the Women's Bureau of the Secretary of State, how they accuse feminists of immoral intentions, such as spreading lesbianism (a sin punishable by death in Atwood's Gilead), wanting daycare, or maybe even wanting childbearing choices. Who finances REAL Women, if not patriarchy?

The questions we must ask ourselves at all times are: Have women advanced and how much? What is threatening our future work, and what can we do to protect women's rights?

Allow me to connect the private and the political. I broke my leg twice during the summer of 1986 – walking in the street in full daylight and, I presumed, in total security. I stumbled, fell, and ended up in the operating room, in a cast, and finally in physiotherapy. A few months later, perfectly healed, I was again walking in the street, again in full daylight and apparent security. I stumbled again, fell, and the whole process started all over. Well, in my opinion, feminism is as fragile as bones; feminists may encounter obstacles, may stumble if they march forward without worrying too much about what awaits them. We must, in taking our stride, also take precautions, measure and evaluate possible obstacles, take seriously even that which appears somewhat ridiculous and unimportant, such as, for instance, the REAL [Un]Women of Canada.

I believe that the women's movement can suffer setbacks and accidents as easily as you and I. I am not saying that we should walk warily; I myself certainly do not intend to walk warily because of my two accidents. But vigilance is in order, we must look out for obstacles, and must not shrug off adversities that seem too ridiculous to be taken seriously. We cannot allow ourselves the luxury of ignoring opposition. In fact, the question of opposition to feminism among young women is extremely worrying. While I know a number of younger graduate students who are doing brilliant feminist work in their disciplines, I also see, mainly at the undergraduate level, a good number of young women who are afraid of social change. In 1984, for instance, when I taught a course on feminist literature and art at the University of Guelph, I asked one student whether she would like to present a seminar on Kathe Kollwitz (1867–1945), the German artist who was so greatly concerned with the plight of the oppressed, with the joys and sorrows of motherhood ... Well, the student was not sure; she took Kollwitz's biography home, I believe in order to show it to her parents, had her mother return the book to me, and dropped the course, which probably looked *radical*. She was only one out of about twenty students, but still it was a significant experience that made me realize how feminism and social change can frighten people into opposition. Then, there are those young women who believe that everything is for the best in the best of all possible worlds, that the last ten or twenty years have solved all problems, that the world will, thanks to all the good work feminists have done, treat them fairly, and that no further action is necessary.

Like Offred, they live by ignoring, ignoring that we are still making only sixty-five cents when men earn one dollar, that there still isn't enough childcare, that work continues to be segregated, that pornography is still good business, that violence against women is as rampant as ever, and that the choice in childbearing is not yet our own. We have achieved a lot, it is true, but we are safe neither in the political nor in the private spheres, and our work has changed only a fraction of what needs to be changed. To attend conferences is nurturing and informative, but older women continue to suffer from poverty; editing a feminist journal can be exciting, but women continue to occupy service positions; to teach a women's studies course tempts one to believe in a better future, but equal pay for work of equal value is not yet the rule. And new problems, such as those connected with reproductive technology, are being added to the existing ones.

Marion Colby names three essential processes for feminist research: "Consciousness-raising and awareness of self; acquisition of knowledge and formulation of theories, political action and social change" (1978). Right on. But these three steps must be taken again and again, awareness must constantly be renewed, new knowledge must be acquired, new theories formulated, and new action undertaken. In this sense, feminists can know no rest. We must watch out for antifeminist obstacles, and must, whatever the gentleman from the granting agency may have thought, constantly address new topics in our research. The ideal feminist, then, according to me, and not only because of my Prussian background, is vigilant and hardworking.

But a revolution, which is after all what we have here (in a non-violent form), is also an exercise in optimism. Why else would one engage in it? In *The Handmaid's Tale*, Atwood speaks of an under-ground "femaleroad" to freedom. In *The Native Tongue*, a science fiction novel set in the twenty-first century, women invent a new language, a new way of speaking with each other, which will even-tually allow them to distance themselves from men.

The road that we women scholars have decided to travel is that of research. Not the kind that men belligerently define as *pure*. No, our research is joyously impure, is action-oriented and issue-oriented – our theories include reflections of our life experiences. We live our feminism daily, and our work cannot be separated from it. It is with enthusiasm that we narrow the gap between theory and praxis.

Mary O'Brien said: "What we actually see feminism doing, in a partly coherent, sometimes inconsistent and often quick local way, is, on the one hand, challenging such institutions as the patriarchal family, and, on the other, challenging the veracity of patriarchal knowledge. And that's dynamite" (Randall 1985, 6). This dynamite – research – will, eventually, blow away the boulders obstructing the "femaleroad" to freedom.

Reproduction and Maternity
Reproduction et maternité

MARGRIT EICHLER

New Reproductive Technologies: Their Implications for Women[1]

This paper starts by briefly describing what are usually called new reproductive technologies, pointing out that not all of them are either new, or
technologies. It then discusses the following aspects which are of particular importance to women: that motherhood has irrevocably been redefined through these technologies; that some of the technologies are based
on the misrepresentation of social problems as medical problems; that
some of them turn children into commodities; that taken as a syndrome,
they tend to medicalize and judicialize pregnancy, and that they pit the
foetus against woman, man against woman and woman against woman.

Les nouvelles technologies de reproduction et leurs conséquences pour la femme

Nous commençons en donnant une brève description de ce qu'on appelle
généralement les nouvelles techniques de reproduction, en soulignant que
toutes ne sont pas nouvelles et toutes ne relèvent pas de la technologie.
Sont ensuite passés en revue sept points qui sont d'une particulière importance pour les femmes, notamment: la redéfinition irrévocable de la
maternité, l'ancrage dans un problème social faussement présenté comme
un problème médical, l'utilisation de l'enfant comme produit de base. Pri-
ses globalement, ces techniques entraînent la médicalisation et la « judiciarisation » de la maternité, opposant ainsi le foetus aux femmes, les
hommes aux femmes et les femmes aux femmes.

In her introductory paper in this collection, Marguerite Andersen
suggests the metaphor that the contemporary women's movement
is like a woman unconcernedly walking down the street, not thinking
that she might break her leg at any moment (this actually happened
to her). She meant this as a warning to the women's movement. I

will argue that we have already broken a leg, but that we are in such a state of shock that we have not yet noticed it. Our efforts must therefore be directed towards making it heal, and towards avoiding a second accident. I am referring to the new reproductive technologies (NRTS) and what they mean for women.

In the past few years, there has been a plethora of official commissions on some aspects of NRTS (for a comprehensive overview see Knoppers and Sloss, 1986). Looking at the composition of the various commissions which have been established to study the area, we find a predominance of legal and medical experts, with a sprinkling of social workers and philosophers/moral specialists. To the degree that one can judge from names, these committees tend to be overwhelmingly, or even exclusively, staffed by men. Women, who are the childbearers, have so far been largely excluded from the official discourse which is taking place in this area.

I will first look at what some of the new reproductive technologies are, and then discuss their importance for women.

REPRODUCTIVE TECHNOLOGIES

At least one of the reproductive technologies currently under discussion, *artificial insemination by donor (AID)*, is not new at all. Indeed, the first successful artificial insemination involving humans is reported to have occurred in 1884, when a medical doctor, without the knowledge and consent of the woman involved, artificially inseminated her with semen. Artificial insemination simply involves the fertilization of an egg by means other than sexual intercourse. Usually, it is done with a syringe. It is a simple procedure which can be done by the woman herself.

In vitro fertilization (IVF) involves the fertilization of an egg with semen outside the womb, in a Petri dish. Once an embryo has formed, and has been found to be nondefective, it is implanted in a woman's womb. The first baby to be conceived and born by this method was Louise Brown, in England in 1978. By 1987, there were well over two hundred *IVF* clinics worldwide, twelve of which are located in Canada.

In vitro fertilization involves, first, the removal of one or more eggs from the woman. Often, the woman's ovaries are induced to "superovulate" by drugs. The removal is a painful, costly, and lengthy process, usually involving full anesthesia (Murphy 1984; Pilon 1985; Victoria Committee 1983). The egg (or eggs) is (are) then fertilized in a Petri dish with the semen, and the embryo, sometimes after it has been frozen and stored for a while, is implanted in a womb.

One consequence of this procedure is that it makes it possible to separate the female's genetic contribution from her gestational contribution. In other words, an egg may be removed from a woman, be fertilized, and be reimplanted into her. On the other hand, the fertilized egg may be implanted into another woman, who will carry it to term, thus becoming its uterine mother, but without being genetically related to the child which she has carried for nine months, and to which she has given birth. In this latter case, we are dealing with an instance of *egg donation*, also sometimes referred to as *foetal adoption* or *intrauterine adoption*. The first child who was genetically unrelated to its uterine mother was born in 1984 (Ontario Law Reform Commission 1985, 2).

Another consequence of *IVF* techniques is that it is now possible to select the sex of the implanted embryo. Other techniques also permit the preselection of the sex of a child before conception. The *Toronto Star* ran a short article in September 1986, whose headline proclaimed: "Couple expects world's first sex-selected girl." This was, however, not the first sex-selected *child*, since it has been possible for a while to select for boys. In addition, there is a long-established tradition in many societies to select for a child's sex through infanticide, almost always by killing female babies. Corea has called this practice gynicide (1985, 188–212). Selective abortion provides another method of sex selection. What is new, then, is neither the desire to determine the sex of children, nor the actual practice of preferring one sex over the other, but simply the manner in which it is done, as well as the point in time, namely, before conception. In 1987, the first sex-selection clinic in Canada opened, in Toronto. It is a franchise of a U.S. company.

A particular form of reproductive arrangement involves preconception contracts for the production of a child, commonly called *surrogate motherhood*. This is an arrangement whereby a woman contracts to be artificially inseminated in order to carry a child for a person or couple, usually for a fee. This arrangement need *not* involve one of the truly new technologies; nonetheless, it is included here because it is a new social arrangement. If combined with *IVF*, it allows a woman to contract to carry the genetic child of a woman or couple who wish to become the social and biological parents of the child in question. At least one such child has already been born.

SOCIAL ARRANGEMENTS CONCERNING *NRT*'S

The new reproductive technologies are already established facts of life (literally). They open a Pandora's box of problems – medical, legal, social, and ethical problems. Rather than discuss the entire range of problems, I shall concentrate on the following issues, which are of particular importance to women:

1 the redefinition of motherhood;
2 the misrepresentation of social problems as medical problems;
3 the transformation of children into commodities;
4 the medicalization and judicialization of pregnancy;
5 the pitting of the foetus against the woman;
6 the pitting of men against women;
7 the pitting of women against women.

The Redefinition of Motherhood

The new reproductive technologies have already, irrevocably, redefined motherhood. There have always been three types of fathers – the social biological father (the traditional father); the social but *not* biological father (the stepfather or adoptive father); the biological but *not* social father (the natural father who is not involved in raising his child).

Until recently, there were also three types of mothers which corresponded to the three types of fathers. With the new technologies, being a mother has been subdivided into seven, rather than three, types:

1 the uterine, genetic and social mother (the traditional mother);
2 the social but neither uterine nor genetic mother (the adoptive mother or stepmother);
3 the uterine and genetic, but not social, mother (the birth mother who has given up her child or whose child has been taken from her, or surrogate mother);
4 the genetic, but not uterine or social, mother (the egg donor);[2]
5 the uterine and social, but not genetic, mother (the recipient of a donated fertilized egg);
6 the uterine, but not genetic or social, mother (the embryo carrier);
7 the genetic and social, but not uterine, mother (the user of an embryo carrier).

While types one to three have presumably always existed, types four to seven represent truly new forms of motherhood which were not previously possible. The egg donor (type four) is in an equivalent situation to the semen donor, except for the fact that egg donation and semen donation are in no way comparable, semen donation being a simple, quick, painless, and nonhazardous matter, while egg donation is neither simple, quick, painless nor nonhazardous for the woman involved.

The phenomenon of a uterine and social, but not genetic, mother (type five) already exists. That is, we now have instances in which a woman has given birth to a child to whom she is genetically unrelated. This was previously not possible.

Types six and seven represent the two aspects of one relationship. Technically, there is no difference in the last three types. The only difference between types five and six is that in type five the woman carries the child for herself, whereas in type six she carries it on behalf of somebody else who becomes the type seven mother in a surrogacy arrangement.

Overall, then, some very dramatic changes have taken place in what constitutes motherhood. We must now cope with the separation of gestational and genetic motherhood – an issue which simply did not exist a few years ago, as it was technically impossible for women to be genetic mothers without being gestational mothers and vice versa.

The Misrepresentation of Social Problems as Medical Problems

Most of the reports dealing with reproductive technologies suggest that such technologies or arrangements should be available on the basis of medical need only, and not for everybody. This is also true of the only published Canadian report on these issues, the Report of the Ontario Law Reform Commission (1985), which proposes that all forms of medical treatment for infertility be available for medical reasons only.[3]

However, there are problems with such statements, due to unclear thinking, and unclear definitions of what constitutes medical necessity. With *AID* or *IVF* technologies using donor gametes, as well as with pre-conception contracts for the production of children with the contracting mother's egg, it is not a case of an infertile patient who is being treated, but rather of a fertile woman who is bearing a child on behalf of an infertile woman, or a fertile woman who is bearing a child with a donor's sperm, either because her husband is infertile, or because she does not wish to be involved with a man.

The infertile person is not changed by the "treatment." In the case of *AID*, any fertile man could potentially fill the role of the *AID* donor. Instead, a family is medically and legally constructed as if it were something that it is not, namely a blood-related family. *AID* is kept as a shameful secret, rather than acknowledged as a different family form. This maintains the myth that there is more uniformity in family forms than in fact there is.

In the case of pre-conception contracts for the production of a child (surrogate motherhood), the child could be conceived through sexual intercourse with a woman and given to the father and his wife (where applicable) to rear. *There is, therefore, no need for medical involvement at all.* In other words, the physicians and medical personnel involved are reacting to a *social* problem. In the case of *AID* and surrogate motherhood, the infertile participants, as well as their spouses, want to avoid any semblance of adultery by removing sexual connotations from the process of conception.

This is sometimes almost – although not quite – admitted. For instance, the American Fertility Society states in its report: "For the husband of an infertile woman, the use of a surrogate may be the only way in which he can conceive and rear a child with a biologic tie to himself, short of divorcing his wife and remarrying only for that reason or having an adulterous union. Certainly, the use of a surrogate mother under the auspices of a medical practitioner seems far less destructive of the institution of the family than the latter two options." In other words, surrogacy does not constitute a medical treatment for a medical condition, but a medical/legal intervention to maintain "the institution of the family" (1986, 645).

Medical doctors, then, when employing artificial conception techniques that involve donor gametes, are sometimes engaged in upholding particular notions of appropriate sexual behaviour (married people should not engage in adultery in order to conceive a child if they are unable to conceive one with their partner) and a particular type of family (children should officially have only two parents rather than biological and social parents); they are not necessarily treating a medical condition with medical means.[4]

The other relevant issue often mentioned in this context is the principle that *AID* and pre-conception contracts should be available only where medically necessary. This is meant to avoid the use of contractual carrier mothers for "convenience reasons" by women who, for instance, do not wish to interrupt their careers and want a contractual carrier mother to bear their child for them.

As far as *AID* is concerned, the Ontario Law Reform Commission report recommends that it only be available where medically necessary, for example, if the husband has had an irreversible vasectomy. Now let us assume that the husband made a voluntary decision, compelled by no medical reason, to have a vasectomy in order to enjoy intercourse without worrying about pregnancy, and because he did not wish to have any (more) children. Later, he changed his mind (possibly because of remarriage) and wished to have a child.

Is the fact that his choice of a vasectomy was a lifestyle decision rather than a medically necessitated decision, irrelevant once it has happened? If not, a woman could let herself be stimulated to "su-perovulate," have her eggs removed, her tubes tied, have the eggs fertilized by her husband's semen and carried to term by a contrac-tual carrier mother. Is this, then, a lifestyle decision or a medical necessity? Possibly both? I am not suggesting that the motivations for voluntary infertility be probed, because this would probably de-velop into a process that would be neither fair, quick, nor cheap. I *am* pointing out that the concept of "medical necessity" is by no means as clear, unambiguous, and unproblematic as it may appear to be at first reading.

The Commodification of Children

Pre-conception contracts of children, when they involve payment, deal with the buying and selling of children.

Proponents who argue that pre-conception contracts for the pro-duction of children should be legalized argue strongly that, in cases where a fee is paid, this does *not* constitute a form of baby-selling, but is merely a payment for the services of a woman who lets herself be impregnated, carries the baby to term, and gives birth to it. Let us look at this in terms of the only extant legal decision which has been written on the issue in North America, the Baby M case. Judge Sorkow, who wrote the decision, states:

the money to be paid to the surrogate is not being paid for the surrender of the child to the father. And that is just the point – at birth, mother and father have equal rights to the child absent any other agreement. The bi-ological father pays the surrogate for her willingness to be impregnated and carry his child to term. At birth, the father does not purchase the child. It is his own biological genetically related child. He cannot purchase what is already his (In the Matter of Baby M, Superior Court of New Jersey, 70–1).

In another portion of his judgement, Judge Sorkow explicitly defines "a new rule of law," namely, that "once conception has occurred the parties [sic] rights are fixed, the terms of the contract are firm and performance will be anticipated with the joy that only a newborn can bring" (75). In other words, once the judge had explicitly de-clared pre-conception contracts as valid and enforceable under New Jersey law, the above passage has to be reinterpreted to mean:

At birth, mother and father have equal rights to the child unless they entered into a surrogate contract with each other. Having entered into such a con-tract, once conception has occurred, the terms are firm and the baby will belong to the father and be anticipated by him with the joy that only a newborn can bring.

Clearly, then, in cases where money changes hands, we *are* dealing with a contract to buy and sell a child, other declarations notwithstanding. If this were not so, and if the money were truly only for the woman's services of letting herself be impregnated, and carrying the baby to term, the contract would be fulfilled once the baby was born, even if the mother kept her child. I doubt that there would be many buyers if this were the case.

The Ontario Law Reform Commission report addresses this issue as follows:

In its most stark incarnation, this question reduces to whether, in the face of a refusal by the woman to transfer custody of the newborn infant, a court should be obliged to issue an order to surrender the infant, which could be enforced against her will by seizure of the child ... That a recalcitrant mother might be compelled through judicial process to surrender her newborn infant would seem to strike at the very heart of our shared values ... (249–50)

The report goes on to recommend that the baby be taken, with all the force the state can muster, from the mother and delivered to the social parents. If this were to become Canadian law, we would have, in fact, legalized the selling of babies.

The Medicalization and Judicialization of Pregnancy

Another aspect that is highly problematic with preconception contracts concerns the regulation of a pregnant woman's lifestyle. The Ontario Law Reform Commission report suggests that surrogate contracts specify "prenatal restriction upon the surrogate mother's activities before and after conception, including dietary obligations; and ... conditions under which prenatal screening of the child may be justified or required, for example, by ultrasound, fetoscopy or amniocentesis" (Ontario Law Reform Commission 1985, rec. 55[i], [f], and [g], 2: 284).

This raises some truly problematic questions. How will such regulations be enforced? Will whatever standards are agreed upon become standards of behaviour for *other* pregnant women, who are *not* involved in pre-conception contracts?

This is by no means an unrealistic fear. In the United States, there are already about fifteen cases in which mothers have been sued for failing to follow doctor's orders during their pregnancy.[5] In 1987, in two separate Canadian cases, foetuses were declared to be "children in need of protection." This issue will be picked up again in the next section.

Pitting Foetus Against Woman

Increasingly, the foetus is regarded as a patient in its own right. While this may lead to some advances in preventing defects in newborns, we also need to be concerned about what it means for the woman. If a particular treatment is considered beneficial to the foetus, but the pregnant woman either does not wish to undergo the treatment, or it is harmful to her, who should have the right to decide?

In Ontario, in the spring of 1987, a pregnant woman was apprehended and put into hospital by judicial decree, because her foetus had been declared a "child in need of protection." How does one apprehend a foetus? It happens to have a woman around it, and the only way to apprehend the foetus is by apprehending the woman.

In the second Canadian case, this time in BC, a doctor requested permission from a social worker to perform a Caesarian section on an unwilling woman, in order to save the foetus. The social worker advised the doctor "that he was apprehending the child and that the Doctor was to do what was required medically for the child but that he [the social worker] was not consenting to any medical procedure to be performed on the mother" (In the Matter of the Family and Child Service Act, 2). While the judge notes in his judgement that the woman subsequently agreed to the Caesarian section, one must wonder how freely such consent was given when she was already in labour and her doctor was pressuring her. The judge upheld the seizure of the unborn baby as being legal.

Coupling these independent legal developments with such prospective developments as legalization of pre-conception contracts for the production of children raises the spectre that third parties will set standards of behaviour and medical procedures for *all* pregnant women, which may be forced upon them against their will.

Pitting Man Against Woman

The issues we are discussing here are not sex-neutral. All baby carriers are obviously women; many of the buyers of babies will be men.

In the case of a pre-conception contract, in which a man contracts with a woman to bear his baby for him, his interests will be directly opposed to her interests, as was true in the Baby M case.

In such situations it is in the interests of men to push for stricter regulation of pregnant women's behaviour, and to ensure that in custody disputes, the baby goes to the contracting father rather than the mother.

However, the situation may also pit women against women.

Pitting Woman Against Woman

With the perfection of embryo transfers, we can expect more pre-conception contracts for the production of children to involve couples who contract to have their embryo, consisting of the wife's egg and the husband's sperm, carried to term by a contractual uterine mother. As has been mentioned, this has already happened.

With this type of technology, women of colour can carry white babies for white couples. The situation is clearly open to great exploitation of the carrying mother. In such instances, the interests of women who wish to avail themselves of the "services" of a uterine mother are opposed to those of the uterine mother.

We cannot expect all women to see the issue in the same manner, since some stand to gain individually from these new technologies, but it seems to me that collectively we all stand to lose.

This has been an extremely rapid view of some of the consequences of the new reproductive technologies. Many important issues have not been raised, such as the long-term effects of some of the extremely potent drugs that are routinely employed in certain techniques, the reasons for infertility, and the long-term psychological effects of continuous hope for pregnancy with eventual failure after a very protracted period of trying.

It should be clear, nonetheless, that this is an extremely important issue that must be addressed by the women's movement. If we fail to do so, we may find that technological and judicial developments have proceeded so rapidly that in the not-so-distant future, we will be in a society in which we have lost control over our own reproductive processes to a degree which seems quite impossible to most people at present. We may also find that the selling and buying of human beings has once more become legal. It is not a very pretty picture.

NOTES

1 More extensive treatment of these questions (partially overlapping with this text) can be found in chapter 8 of my book *Canadian Families Today: Recent Changes and their Policy Consequences*, 2nd rev. ed. (Toronto: Gage, 1988); and in my recent paper "Preconception Contracts for the Production of Children – What Are the Proper Legal Responses?" (*Sortir la maternité du laboratoire*. Actes du Forum international sur les nouvelles technologies de la reproduction humaine. Québec: Conseil du statut de la femme, 1988, 187–204).

2 With the new technology a woman might have a genetic child without ever being aware of it. Let us assume she had a hysterectomy and a doctor removed an egg, successfully fertilized it, and implanted it in another woman who eventually gave birth to a child. In this case the "donor" woman would be an unaware genetic mother.

3 There is currently a commission in Quebec looking into these issues. Their report is expected in 1988.

4 This is, of course, not true of *all* of these techniques. Some of them *do* constitute medical treatment for medical conditions.

5 Oral communication by Bernard Dickens.

ANNE QUÉNIART

De l'insécurité à la solitude: La médicalisation de la grossesse et ses effets sur le vécu des femmes

Par le biais de la médicalisation de la maternité – à l'heure des « sciences de la reproduction » – s'opère, dès le début de la grossesse, un « façonnement » médical du vécu des femmes qui va jusqu'à investir leur rapport au corps et à l'enfant à naître, et à les définir en termes de risques, d'anormalité, etc. L'intrusion de la médecine dans la vie des femmes est, aujourd'hui, plus diffuse mais aussi plus insidieuse: elle se fait au nom du foetus, lequel tend à devenir le sujet de la maternité au détriment des femmes. La solitude qu'éprouvent les futures mères tient à la centration excessive sur l'enfant et surtout, à l'évacuation des dimensions affectives et sociales de leur vécu.

From Insecurity to Loneliness: the Medicalization of Pregnancy and the Effects on Women's Experience

In the era of reproductive sciences, the medicalization of motherhood is a process by which a medical "reshaping" of a woman's life occurs from the very beginning of the pregnancy; this process goes to the point of limiting a woman's relationship with her body and her unborn child, leading her to define what she is experiencing in medical terms, that is in terms of risk factors, abnormalities, etc. The intrusion of medicine into women's lives is, today, more diffuse but also more insidious: it is carried out in the name of the foetus which has become the subject of motherhood at the expense of the woman. The loneliness which mothers feel stems from an excessive focus on the child and especially from the negation of the social and affective dimensions of their lived experience.

S'il est un moment de la vie des femmes fortement investi par le social dans nos sociétés occidentales modernes, c'est bien la maternité. En plus d'être prise en charge par l'institution médicale, cette expérience fait l'objet de diverses politiques sociales et économiques – calculs des budgets-temps, etc. – et surtout, se trouve au coeur de nombre de discours (théologiques, scientifiques, féministes) qui se proposent de la définir et de la modeler.

De façon surprenante, cependant, on sait peu de choses sur la façon dont les femmes vivent et pensent la maternité. En effet, malgré une imposante littérature sociologique, scientifique, et la vulgarisation des connaissances médicales sur la grossesse et l'accouchement – ce que l'on appelle, logique marchande oblige, le processus de la reproduction – on note un vide théorique quant à ce que vivent les premières concernées, les femmes: celles-ci font l'objet de nombreux écrits, certes, mais elles n'en sont jamais les sujets, elles restent une « matière à penser » (Mathieu 1985). À ce silence sur les perceptions et le vécu des femmes dans les champs de la recherche sociologique s'ajoute aujourd'hui, socialement, une remise en question de leur place et de leur rôle dans cet acte fondamental qu'est l'enfantement. En effet, à l'heure où se profile la possibilité de faire « évoluer » les embryons puis les foetus dans des utérus artificiels, ce qui est en jeu c'est l'expropriation des femmes de la gestation, doublée d'une appropriation matérielle concrète de leur corps et du produit de leur corps, l'enfant (Guillaumin 1978a, 1978b; Tabet 1985).

C'est de ce constat qu'est née l'idée d'entreprendre une étude qui, s'inscrivant contre ce courant d'effacement des femmes, visait à comprendre la maternité de l'intérieur, c'est-à-dire du point de vue des sujets mêmes de cette expérience. Comment les femmes d'aujourd'hui vivent-elles, dans leur corps, la grossesse? Sont-elles sensibles aux discours et pratiques concernant les nouvelles technologies associées au diagnostic prénatal? Quelle place font-elles à l'homme dans ce processus? Quel sens donnent-elles à cet évènement? Telles étaient les principales questions à la base de la recherche qualitative que j'ai menée à Montréal auprès d'une centaine de femmes qui donnaient naissance pour la première fois. [1]

Ce qui ressort fondamentalement de l'analyse de mes données empiriques, c'est la préséance des définitions sociales de la grossesse sur sa définition biologique et même, affective, psychologique. Ce n'est pas tant la fatalité de leur biologie qui pèse sur l'expérience des femmes que la puissance des idéologies et des normes sociales, et notamment de celles de la médecine.

Dans cet article, [2] je me propose de dégager les principales dimensions du vécu des femmes au cours des premiers mois de la grossesse. Mon objectif principal est de montrer que la médicalisation

de la maternité qui, historiquement, s'est traduite par l'hospitalisa-
tion des « accouchantes »[3] et par l'utilisation des techniques obsté-
tricales (Laurendeau 1983), prend aujourd'hui des formes nouvelles.
Je montrerai d'abord qu'elle opère comme processus de « façonnement » médical du vécu même des femmes, qui va jusqu'à investir
leur corps, leur rapport au corps et à l'enfant à naître. L'intrusion
de la médecine dans la vie des femmes se fait plus diffuse mais plus
insidieuse et on verra à cet égard que la légitimité de ses interventions
et discours, « qui s'est construite d'abord au nom de la science, vient
maintenant au nom du foetus » (De Koninck 1987, 241). Celui-ci
tend à devenir le sujet premier de la maternité. Pour leur part, les
femmes, si elles sont amenées à jeter un regard médical et médicalisé
sur leur grossesse, n'en souffrent pas moins, comme je ferai sortir
à la fin de mon texte, des limites de cette approche qui escamote les
dimensions affectives et sociales de leur vécu.

DE L'INTANGIBLE À L'OBSESSION DE LA NORMALITÉ

Les débuts de la grossesse se caractérisent par le fait qu'autrui (le
futur bébé) « est annoncé avant de s'annoncer » (Mottini-Coulon
1978): les femmes, certaines d'être enceintes grâce aux résultats du
test de grossesse et par les changements de leur corps (lourdeur des
seins, nausées, etc.) n'éprouvent ni saisie interne directe (absence de
mouvement du foetus) ni perception par observation (absence de
visibilité du ventre) de cette grossesse. Elles ont beau être assurées
de la présence de celle ou celui qui sera leur enfant, les signes de
son existence ne sont pas encore palpables ni tangibles. Cette
ignorance perceptive serait l'occasion, selon plusieurs auteur-e-s,
« d'une fusée d'imagination projective d'exceptionnelle richesse et
intensité » (Mottini-Coulon 1978, 70): ne sentant pas encore leur
enfant, les femmes tendraient à l'imaginer, à lui modeler un corps,
un visage. Pour ma part, les témoignages que j'ai recueillis ne con-
firment pas une telle interprétation et montrent que c'est plutôt
lorsque le « bébé » bouge et même, avant cela, lorqu'il devient « visible, » par l'échographie, que les femmes sont amenées à l'imaginer.
Au début de la gestation, on est plutôt portée à s'inquiéter. Ce qu'é-
prouvent fondamentalement mes répondantes, c'est en effet un sentiment d'insécurité. La notion d'insécurité est généralement définie
par son contraire, la sécurité, dont on dit, de façon presque tau-
tologique, qu'elle désigne l'état de celle ou celui qui est en sûreté,
« qui n'a rien à craindre pour ses biens et sa personne » (Moncomble
1985, 45). Dans le cas particulier des femmes enceintes, l'insécurité

« est moins de l'ordre du fait, de l'objet que du sentiment, de la représentation, voire de l'imaginaire » : elle renvoie « au champ des passions, » elle a partie liée avec les « multiples processus d'évitement de ce sentiment éternel: la peur » (Moncomble 1985, 46). En effet, c'est de peur qu'il s'agit en ce début de grossesse, une peur qui concerne d'abord le foetus, dont on se demande s'il est vivant et s'il le restera et surtout, s'il est « normal, » s'il se développe normalement:

On a peur un peu: est-ce qu'il est toujours là? Est-ce qu'il va rester? Est-ce qu'il ne va pas se décrocher? On a peur de faire une fausse-couche parce qu'on ne sent rien. Moi, j'ai eu beaucoup d'angoisses. Premièrement, est-ce qu'il sera normal, correct? Est-ce qu'il va être infirme? Va-t-il tout avoir? Puis est-ce qu'il serait normalement intelligent? S'il fallait que ce soit pas un vrai bébé? S'il fallait qu'il lui manque quelque chose?

Dans toutes les entrevues, on constate cette peur de l'anormalité et c'est là, selon moi, un effet de la médicalisation de la maternité que de ramener une bonne part de l'imaginaire des femmes à la distinction entre le normal et l'infirme, voire à faire de la normalité le principal paramètre de cet imaginaire. Comme je l'ai montré ailleurs (Quéniart 1987a, 1987b), la normalité devient le critère central d'évaluation, par les femmes, de leur vécu. On s'y réfère non seulement à propos du foetus, mais aussi pour décrire le déroulement de sa grossesse. L'anormal ne se situe plus strictement dans les frontières de ce qui est défini comme tel, mais envahit tout le champ de l'indéfini, de l'incertain. Tout se passe en fait comme si l'on ne tolérait plus l'incertitude. Ainsi, plusieurs femmes résument les débuts de leur grossesse en disant que « ça a été une phase à problèmes » et ce, parce que ce qu'elles vivaient ou ressentaient ne correspondait pas aux symptômes définis comme « normaux, » notamment dans la littérature destinée aux femmes enceintes qu'on consulte massivement. [4] Chez d'autres répondantes, la réalité corporelle importe moins que l'idéologie médicale; la notion de normalité en vient en effet à endiguer les signes d'alarme du corps lui-même: on se fie totalement au discours médical, même si ce que l'on vit semble inquiétant:

Je peux dire que j'ai eu un début de grossesse normal. J'ai eu des pertes de sang, mais il paraît que c'est normal. Enfin, j'avais lu que c'est les vaisseaux sanguins ... j'avais un peu peur de faire une fausse-couche, mais ça a tenu. On s'énerve beaucoup pour rien ... Mais si les médecins disent que c'est normal, c'est que c'est normal. C'est ça que je me disais.

LE PARADOXE DES RISQUES OU LA CERTITUDE À TOUT PRIX

La peur des femmes quant à la normalité de ce qu'elles vivent est telle qu'elle crée, chez beaucoup, un besoin d'être rassurées à tout prix, voire, paradoxalement, quel qu'en soit le prix ou le risque. Ainsi, si celles de nos répondantes qui ont passé une amniocentèse ont éprouvé quelques craintes quant aux risques, notamment de fausse-couche, que celle-ci comporte, elles estiment cependant que: « ça vaut la peine de prendre une chance pour être sûre que tout est correct, » « c'est un privilège de savoir avant la naissance si ton bébé est tout à fait normal. » Plus généralement, l'incertitude des débuts de la gestation semble si difficile à vivre que plusieurs femmes en viennent à prôner le recours aux nouvelles technologies, en particulier celles visant le diagnostic et le traitement du foetus in utero, comme la foetoscopie, l'amniocentèse, la biopsie du chorion, l'échographie, etc. En fait, reprenant à leur compte le discours dominant des média d'information, les femmes définissent les technologies de la reproduction comme des « signes de progrès » et n'y voient que des avantages: les unes, les plus « banales, » comme l'échographie, les rassurent sur la viabilité de leur « bébé » et même leur apportent « l'assurance du vrai »; les autres, telle la fécondation in vitro, « rendent heureux des gens qui ne pouvaient pas avoir d'enfants. » À cet égard, on entend souvent dire que l'un de leurs avantages est de permettre aux femmes de faire un choix. Cependant, on peut – et l'on doit – se demander de quels choix il s'agit: « d'avorter des enfants qui n'auront pas le bon sexe ou qui auront certaines malformations comme les becs de lièvre? » (Nadeau 1985, 41). Plus encore, s'agira-t-il vraiment d'un choix? Étant donné le nombre sans cesse grandissant des examens disponibles, « celles qui les refuseront ne seront-elles pas socialement culpabilisées, voire ostracisées? » (Hubbart citée dans Beaulieu 1985, 15). À l'inverse, l'État pourra-t-il obliger les femmes à subir un avortement dans le cas où elles porteraient un-e enfant handicapé-e? Comme l'écrivait Marcuse (1968, 35), « la liberté humaine ne se mesure pas selon le choix qui est offert à l'individu, le seul facteur décisif pour le déterminer c'est ce que peut choisir et ce que choisit l'individu ... » et, peut-on ajouter, la raison de ce choix.

LA FEMME PIÉGÉE: DU RISQUE À LA RESPONSABILITÉ

À cet égard, le vécu de mes répondantes est plus complexe qu'il n'y

paraît. Leur « perméabilité » face aux technologies de la reproduction, si elle est liée à leur insécurité, vient d'abord et surtout de la
prégnance, de plus en plus grande, de « l'idéologie du risque. » Cette
dernière consiste en un ensemble de doctrines qui visent non pas à
affronter un danger précis mais « à anticiper toutes les figures possibles d'irruption du danger ... pour en déduire de nouvelles modalités d'intervention » (Castel 1983, 123); infiltrée dans tous les
domaines de la vie sociale,[5] l'idéologie du risque appartient aux
nouvelles stratégies préventives qui se proposent de gérer l'incertitude, qui sont « surplombées par une grande rêverie technocratique,
rationalisatrice, du contrôle absolu de l'accident conçu comme irruption de l'imprévu » (Castel 1983, 123). En ce qui a trait à la
maternité, l'idéologie du risque se traduit par un ensemble de discours faisant de la grossesse un lieu de danger, ou plutôt, un moment
chargé de risques potentiels pour le foetus. En effet, à une époque
où, pourtant, « la mortalité maternelle et périnatale est au plus bas
et où on possède nombre de connaissances et d'outils aptes à contrôler la morbidité » (Renaud et al 1987, 199), on n'hésite pas, paradoxalement, à qualifier la maternité de phénomène risqué puis, par
un glissement de sens révélateur, on attribue l'entière responsabilité
du risque aux femmes. Ainsi, certaines se retrouvent étiquetées
« femmes à risques. » On véhicule donc l'idée que la grossesse constitue un phénomène « normal en soi, » mais que les modalités de sa
prise en charge (de sa gestion) par les femmes, elles, peuvent com-
porter ou entraîner des risques pour le développement du foetus et
l'état de santé futur de l'enfant nouveau-née. Cette insistance mise
sur le risque que court le foetus tout au long de sa vie utérine est
liée, bien sûr, aux développements de la médecine foetale et de la
néo-natalogie ainsi qu'aux progrès des techniques qui leur sont associées. Pour l'obstétrique moderne, « la santé foetale devient l'in-
dicateur clé de la qualité de la grossesse, laquelle est donc davantage
définie comme phénomène médical » (Renaud et al 1987, 198).

L'identification et le calcul des risques en question se font sur la
base de la mise en relation de différentes données d'ordre biologique,
physique, psychologique, etc. telles que les antécédents genétiques
des femmes, leur âge, leur poids, leur taille, leurs habitudes de vie,
leur profil psycho-social. Cependant, et c'est là un effet pernicieux
de ces stratégies préventives, si le risque est calculé en fonction de
corrélations statistiques établies entre diverses données, on ne men-
tionne généralement au grand public, dans les média ou la littérature
de vulgarisation médicale, qu'un type de facteur, celui d'ordre com-
portemental; on met ainsi les femmes enceintes en garde contre le
tabac, l'alcool, les « mauvaises » habitudes alimentaires, etc.[7] En

d'autres termes, on individualise la responsabilité: on se centre sur les effets potentiels des comportements individuels, occultant l'impact, tout aussi important, des structures sociales et médicales – conditions et rythmes de travail, salles d'accouchement traumatisantes – et des variables socioenvironnementales « lourdes » – pollution, etc. Les femmes, comme le montrent toutes mes entrevues, sont extrêmement sensibles à cette idéologie du risque: la plupart, dès qu'elles savent qu'elles sont enceintes, et parfois même avant la conception, choisissent de modifier leurs habitudes de vie, de les adapter à leur nouvel état:

Dès que j'ai su que j'étais enceinte, j'ai fait attention à tout: pu de café, pu de bière, bien manger, compter mes calories, bien dormir, pas faire trop d'efforts. Tu veux pas prendre de chances, surtout qu'on sait que c'est pendant les premiers mois que c'est dangereux pour le bébé.

Avec la médicalisation toujours plus poussée de la grossesse, il s'opère donc un renforcement du processus de responsabilisation exclusive des femmes dans la maternité, une accentuation de la mystique de la « bonne mère, » dont les intérêts et les besoins propres doivent passer après ceux de sa progéniture. Ce que la médecine suggère aux futures mères, c'est bien plus qu'un simple changement de comportement alimentaire: c'est en fait une nouvelle manière d'être. En effet, en les invitant à se conformer à certaines normes de conduites « pour le bébé, » on leur assigne en même temps un nouveau rôle social, celui d'une femme déjà mère, auquel est attachée une responsabilité: produire un enfant en bonne santé. Mes répondantes sont d'autant plus sensibles à ces discours qu'elles n'ont pas de prise sur eux: le champ normatif entourant la grossesse ne cessant de s'étendre, les conseils socio-sanitaires s'élargissant, les femmes ne savent plus trop où commencent et où s'arrêtent les risques encourus.

À cet égard, la logique médicale est insidieuse: en mettant l'accent sur les risques des trois premiers mois, on joue sur la peur des femmes à l'endroit d'un tiers, le « bébé, » dont on les rend et dont elles se sentent éminemment responsables, on alimente leur insécurité première; en présentant ensuite les techniques comme un moyen de mesurer voire d'éviter ces risques ou d'en corriger les effets, on est à peu près sûr qu'elles obtiendront la faveur des femmes. C'est en tout cas ce que laissent entrevoir mes entrevues à propos de l'amniocentèse et surtout de l'échographie. Celle-ci, conçue à l'origine comme un outil de dépistage réservé aux seuls cas où l'on soupçonne des anomalies de la grossesse, constitue aujourd'hui un examen de routine.[8] Certes, l'échographie n'est pas obligatoire et les femmes peuvent la refuser. Cependant, on peut se demander dans quelle mesure il s'agit d'un choix:

Mon médecin m'a dit, tu vas passer une échographie. Moi, j'avais des doutes sur les ultra-sons. Mais là, elle me dit: « on le fait pour voir si le placenta est bien placé et pour voir s'il n'y a pas de malformations chez le foetus. » Là je me suis dit: si j'en passe pas et qu'il y a des malformations, je m'en voudrai ... je me dirai toujours, j'aurais dû en passer une. Puis si j'en passe une et que tout est correct, je me dirai, bon, à quoi ça sert? Et puis, si j'en passe une et qu'il y a des malformations, qu'est-ce je fais? Est-ce que je vais garder un bébé tout croche?

Il semble difficile aux femmes, toutes imprégnées de l'idéologie du risque, de refuser sans angoisse un examen dont on leur dit qu'il peut dépister les malformations. Sans remettre en cause la capacité de l'échographie à repérer celles-ci, on peut s'interroger sur le fait qu'on ne semble pas informer adéquatement les femmes, par exemple sur les taux de malformation du foetus dans la population globale. Comment choisir si l'on n'a pas en main les différents paramètres, si l'on ne sait pas au nom de quoi faire un tel choix? L'échographie illustre bien cette façon qu'a la médecine de suggérer ou de canaliser des choix:[9] si on n'impose rien, en revanche, on propose « un méta-message qui est: malgré tout, il te faudra bien choisir » (Barel 1982: 220). À cet égard, on peut dire avec Katz Rothman (1984) qu'en se centrant presque exclusivement sur la santé foetale, en accordant une place de plus en plus grande au diagnostic prénatal, on a enlevé petit à petit aux femmes le choix de ne pas choisir.

LA SOLITUDE DES FEMMES: INDICE D'UNE RESTRICTION DU SENS DE LA NAISSANCE

Finalement, l'un des effets majeurs de la médicalisation de la maternité, c'est d'amener les femmes elles-mêmes à jeter, sur leur grossesse, un regard médical, c'est-à-dire « un regard qui y lit une potentialité de pathologie et qui propose la technique pour y remédier » (De Koninck 1987, 239). En même temps, elles souffrent des limites de cette approche qui escamote, évacue les dimensions sociales et affectives de leur vécu, qu'elles-mêmes ne peuvent ignorer. En effet, comme le montrent mes analyses, la maternité est loin de n'être, pour les femmes, qu'un phénomène biologique: elle représente une expérience globale et intense qui engendre la totalité de ce qu'elles sont, qui les transforme dans leur corps, dans leur

apparence et dans leur être.[10] À cet égard, si la médecine, par le
biais de l'amniocentèse, de l'échographie, etc. comble les craintes des
femmes quant au développement du foetus (craintes que cette même
médecine a contribué à créer ou à accentuer), elle ne peut par contre
dissoudre cette autre peur, plus diffuse mais très profonde, quant
à ce qu'implique de la venue d'un-e enfant dans leur vie. Leur insécurité, au début de la gestation, est aussi peur de l'inconnu; les
femmes sentent qu'elles entrent dans un processus de changement
social dont elles ne peuvent prévoir ou maîtriser les tenants et les
aboutissants. Ce changement social est, pour elles, « à la fois perte
d'identité et conquête ou promesse d'une identité nouvelle » (Barel
1985, 32), il est passage dans « le monde des mères » :

> T'as une peur parce que tu sais que ça va faire tout un changement dans
> ta vie, que peut-être ça sera pu jamais pareil avec ton « chum, » que peut-
> être t'aimeras pas ça, être mère. Puis aussi, t'as une peur pour ton enfant,
> quelle genre de vie il va avoir. Au début, tu te poses beaucoup de questions,
> t'as une certaine angoisse. Je me disais, ... est-ce que je serai une bonne
> mère? Est-ce que je vais l'aimer, mon bébé? Pis est-ce que je vais pouvoir
> l'éduquer comme il faut ... Pis tu penses aussi à toi, pis à ton mari: qu'est-
> ce qu'on va devenir, quelle sera notre vie, comme parents?

A travers leurs interrogations sur l'enfant à naître (perçu comme un
être en devenir et non seulement comme un foetus) et sur leur
propre rôle de futures mères, les femmes expriment un besoin d'être
à la fois rassurées et comprises dans leur décision de donner naissance:

> Une fois enceinte, tu veux que tout le monde le sache. T'as envie de crier:
> je vais avoir un bébé! Et tu voudrais que tout le monde te félicite et t'en-
> courage, qu'ils voient que c'est important pour toi, et que sans nous, y'en
> aurait pas de société.

Si toutes mes répondantes recherchent compréhension et reconnaissance sociales, beaucoup estiment ne recevoir pour l'essentiel
que des conseils d'ordre médical, même de la part des proches:
« Moi, ce qui m'a dérangée au début, c'est l'attitude des gens, comme
ma belle-mère pis mon mari: ‹ fais pas ci, fais pas ça ... c'est pas bon
pour le bébé. Tu vas le perdre si tu fais pas attention ... Faut penser
à lui, il est fragile. › »
    En reprenant à son compte l'idéologie du risque, l'entourage tend
à renforcer l'effacement des femmes comme sujets de la maternité
au profit du foetus. Tout au long de la grossesse, cette préoccupation

de l'enfant à naître se voit renforcée par le recours aux examens; ainsi l'échographie, qui tend à utiliser le corps des femmes comme un relais pour atteindre l'utérus et, à travers lui, le foetus. Il en va de même lors des visites médicales où ce qui est palpé, écouté, sondé, c'est le ventre, intermédiaire pour atteindre le foetus. Cette évacuation d'elles-mêmes au profit de celle ou celui qu'elles portent engendre, chez plusieurs de mes répondantes, le sentiment « de moins compter que le bébé, » d'être « ignorée, » voire de « n'être que la porteuse du bébé, » et explique en partie la solitude aiguë qu'elles ressentent:

Pendant toute ta grossesse, mais surtout au début, parce qu'après tu parles avec ton bébé, tu te sens seule. Seule avec tes problèmes, tes questions, seule aussi parce que tu es comme en dehors de la société: tu ne peux plus sortir comme avant, tu ne peux plus boire ou danser, tu fais moins de sport. C'est tout ça qui fait que tu te sens seule au monde.

Plus généralement, cette solitude des femmes semble tenir à la fois de la dé-collectivisation de cette expérience et de l'absence de prise en compte de sa globalité. En effet, parallèlement à la médicalisation de le grossesse, il s'est produit un renforcement de sa privatisation: tant concrètement que symboliquement, être enceinte (puis accoucher) devient de plus en plus une affaire privée, qui se passe d'abord entre la femme et le ou la médecin, cette relation étant en outre de plus en plus souvent médiatisée par la technique. Il s'opère ainsi une restriction du sens de la maternité, processus auquel nous participons, comme société et comme collectivité. En effet, en déléguant ce qui concerne la naissance aux expert-e-s, on contribue à la réduire à une dimension bio-médicale, et a laisser de côté les attentes et le vécu socio-affectif des femmes, autant que des hommes.

Par ailleurs, avec le développement des sciences de la reproduction, on transforme la grossesse en un véritable procès de travail, on l'instrumentalise: nous vivons déjà à l'heure des « mères porteuses, » terme qui traduit en fait « les débuts de la vente de la force de procréation et la salarisation de la maternité » (Vandelac 1985, 18). En outre, si les utérus artificiels (qui exclueront totalement les femmes de l'enfantement) relèvent encore de la spéculation, il n'en reste pas moins qu'on en parle comme d'une modalité nouvelle de « produire » la vie. Le recours fréquent à la technologie au cours de la grossesse accentue le morcellement du corps des femmes et surtout, renforce l'image même d'un corps « dissocié qui fonctionnerait comme une machine extérieure à la personne » (Thomas 1978, 189). S'il a été nécessaire – et s'il l'est toujours – de critiquer, comme le font nombre de féministes, les perspectives biologisantes, naturalistes de la maternité – lesquelles en évacuaient les aspects sociaux et les enjeux économiques – on doit aussi et en même temps interroger le traitement actuel dont elle fait l'objet et qui, lui aussi, tend à en nier le caractère éminemment socio-symbolique pour en faire un simple acte biomédical.

Pour terminer, on peut dire que les progrès actuel de la médecine et de la technique, en créant de pseudo-nouveaux choix, nous mettent, collectivement, devant de plus en plus de dilemmes: les droits du foetus ou les intérêts et droits de la femme qui le porte, la légitimité du désir d'un-e- enfant « parfait-e, » rendu de plus en plus possible par le diagnostic prénatal, avec en contrepartie la sélection des « bons » foetus et donc l'« extermination » des « mauvais. » Autant de dilemmes, de questions qui ne peuvent recevoir une réponse d'ordre simplement technique, car ils touchent à l'être, au devenir de l'être humain et à la place des femmes dans le processus de perpétuation de la vie. Il s'agit donc de choix de société, et ce qui est en question c'est de savoir qui fera ces choix et au nom de qui (de la femme, du foetus) et de quoi (du « respect » de la vie, de la « qualité » du foetus, des besoins de la mère) ...

NOTES

1 Cette recherche s'est déroulée à Montréal en 1983. J'ai réalisé des entrevues en profondeur avec une cinquantaine de femmes primipares, ayant accouché dans les quatre mois précédents. Elles ont entre dix-neuf et quarante ans, vivent toutes en couple et appartiennent à ce qu'on peut appeler la « classe moyenne. » La moitié d'entre elles travaillent à l'extérieur, dans des emplois de type col blanc, semi-professionnel et professionnel. En plus de ces entrevues, j'ai procédé à l'observation systématique de quatre groupes de rencontres prénatales, totalisant aussi une cinquantaine de femmes qui présentaient sensiblement les mêmes caractéristiques. L'analyse des données recueillies a donné lieu à la rédaction de ma thèse de doctorat (Quéniart 1987a).

2 Cet article est la synthèse d'une partie des analyses développées dans ma thèse. Je reprends par ailleurs certains éléments d'un article publié récemment dans un ouvrage collectif sur l'accouchement au Québec (Quéniart 1987b).

3 J'emprunte ce terme à Monique Cournoyer (1987).

4 La plupart de mes répondantes se sont de fait littéralement « jetées » sur la littérature de vulgarisation médicale concernant la grossesse et l'accouchement. Elles la consultent en fait non seulement pour s'informer, mais aussi et surtout pour comparer ce qu'elles y lisent avec ce qu'elles vivent.

5 Par exemple dans le domaine économique (secteurs ou investissements à risques) ou dans le champ de l'éducation (enfants à risques).

6 Marc Renaud et ses collaboratrices (1987) retracent ce déplacement des préoccupations médicales de la mère vers le foetus à partir de l'analyse des dix-sept éditions du Williams Obstetrics, le manuel d'obstétrique le plus utilisé en Amérique du Nord.

7 Il s'agit non pas de nier les effets nocifs du tabac ou de l'alcool sur l'état du foetus mais, dans la perspective sociologique qui est la mienne, de s'interroger sur la façon dont sont véhiculés ces discours sur le risque et de dégager leurs effets sur le vécu des femmes.

8 Parmi mes répondantes, six seulement ont dû passer cet examen en raison de complications dans le déroulement de leur grossesse ou d'antécédents génétiques. Toutes les autres ont eu une échographie « de routine. »

9 Même si on canalise leurs choix, cela n'empêche pas les femmes de donner du sens à ces technologies. Mes répondantes leur prêtent en fait de nombreuses vertus, notamment celles de leur apporter l'assurance qu'elles portent bien un-e enfant et que celle-ci ou celui-ci se développe normalement.

10 Je ne peux malheureusement pas, dans le cadre de cet article, dégager toute la richesse (mais aussi la complexité) du vécu des femmes, notamment de leur rapport au corps (définition et représentation de soi) et à l'enfant qu'elles portent, avec laquelle ou lequel elles tissent, petit à petit, ce qu'elles nomment « des liens du ventre, » terme qui traduit bien la relation unique et spécifique qu'elles vivent avec cet-te « autrui. »

JANE GORDON

Childbirth: The Mother's Perspective?

This paper discusses the experiences of a sample of women in prenatal care and during childbirth itself. In general the evidence suggests that although most of the women defined their childbirth experiences as "normal," there was a high degree of medical intervention. Most of the respondents did not find this extraordinary, and did not articulate dissatisfaction with the general patterns of childbirth available in Canada. They tended to assume personal responsibility if their own experience had been problematic, and believed that the difficulties arose from their individual pregnancy and birth, not from the way childbirth is managed.

The paper concludes by suggesting that it is the lack of an analytical framework which makes it difficult for women to criticize the way in which childbirth takes place.

La naissance: le point de vue de la mère

Cet article traite de l'expérience d'un échantillon de femmes au cours des soins prénatals et de l'accouchement. Dans l'ensemble, les données semblent indiquer que bien que la plupart des femmes définissent leur accouchement comme « normal », un très haut degré d'intervention médicale persiste. La plupart de nos répondantes n'en sont pas étonnées et n'expriment aucun mécontentement quant aux modes d'accouchement pratiqués au Canada. Elles ont tendance à se sentir personnellement responsables lorsqu'il y a eu problème et considèrent que leurs difficultés sont liées à leur grossesse et à leur accouchement comme tels, et non à la façon dont l'accouchement a été mené.

En terminant, nous suggérons que c'est un manque de modèle analytique qui rend difficile pour les femmes de critiquer la facon dont l'accouchement s'est déroulé.

The last decade has seen a tremendous proliferation of academic research and semipopular material on childbirth and related issues of prenatal care and the impact of maternity on women. To a large extent this concern with the issues surrounding childbirth reflects a coincidence of interests between the women's movement (especially the segment focused more narrowly on health issues) and the consumer movement, with its distinct emphasis on health care issues (Ruzek 1978). Birth has been recognized as a cultural and social phenomenon as well as a physiological process. It should, therefore, be subjected to the same critical analysis used to examine other institutionalized forms of social behavior.

Like most areas of social life in which women are involved, childbirth as a social process has been rendered invisible. Even when obstetrical and gynecological issues are discussed from a medical perspective, women's concerns are downgraded and problems are explained as failures of psychological adjustment (Scully and Bart 1973). Birth has been dealt with largely as a medical process controlled by high status physicians.

As in the case of domestic work and, to a lesser extent, voluntary work, the new focus on childbirth arises out of new feminist scholarship. Childbirth is seen as a form of social control (Arms 1975; Corea 1977; Ehrenreich and English 1978; Oakley 1976; Rothman 1982; Shaw 1974) and our present practices a consequence of power struggles within medicine (Barker-Banfield 1976; DeVries 1985; Donegan 1978; Donnison 1977; Ehrenreich and English 1973; Oakley 1984; Verlinghusen 1981; Wertz and Wertz 1979). The lack of power women have in childbirth has been amply described (Arms 1975; Corea 1977; Jordan 1983; Oakley 1979, 1980; Rothman 1982; Shaw 1974). Other areas examined are the way in which the social organization of medicine renders invisible, trivializes or devalues the past contribution of women as caregivers in birth, and how childbearing women are losing power over more and more aspects of reproduction, including the whole process of conception and prenatal care (Oakley 1976, 1980, 1984; Corea 1985; Rich 1977; Rothman 1986).[1]

Most of the new research on childbirth issues uses the traditional methodologies of mainstream disciplines. Oakley, however, suggests, on the basis of her research into childbirth (1979, 1981), that a different form of interviewing is required than is normally the case in sociology. Oakley's childbearing subjects asked as many questions as they answered, and demanded the interviewer share their experiences of pregnancy and birth. They were, in fact, insisting on a dialogue, not a monologue in the information gathering process. Jordan also raises questions about the way in which the focus of new work requires the researcher to make choices between traditional detachment and the need to help in a concrete way (1983).

In the new childbirth literature which focuses on the experiences of women with birth or motherhood, the longitudinal follow-up is limited. Both Oakley (1979) and Leifer (1980) conclude their studies at six months and six to eight weeks postpartum respectively. Other researchers have considered time periods up to the end of the infant's first year as appropriate terminal points for studying the impact of motherhood or assessing birth experiences.

The language of birthing, as Kelpin and Martel point out (1984), defines the woman as the passive participant in the birth process and the doctor as the active one. Both mothers and doctors agree on this redefinition of birth.

Common sense, numerous discussions with childbirth educators, and my own experience, suggest that one's experience with childbirth is something which undergoes (in varying degrees of activity and consciousness) reassessment over time. Women's perspectives on birth change during the time following the experience and are affected by subsequent (if any) birth experiences. They appear to follow certain stages.

The stages are as follows:

1 initial euphoria and joy;
2 physical recovery, adaptation and fatigue – the postnatal recovery;
3 strong emphasis/concentration on task learning – the mundane aspects of motherhood and consequent deemphasis of the childbirth experience itself;
4 reassessment, generally beginning at about the time the baby is six months old, when mothers begin to gain some detached perspective on what happened to them during childbirth. This may lead to a determination to "do it differently next time," or a surrender to the standard North American obstetrical model of childbirth ("I didn't like it but I can't change it so it's better to go along with it").

The initial euphoria stage is well substantiated in the vital statistics section of any newspaper. The birth announcement section is replete with heartfelt thanks to physicians and nurses who presided over or assisted at the delivery. The gratitude expressed to the medical staff involved in delivery only serves to emphasize the medical nature of the birth process and the appreciation of many new parents for what they see to be the important role of medical personnel in providing the desired outcome – a healthy and normal baby.

Longer-term follow-up on women's experiences with childbirth could find changes from the "doctor as baby-giver" appreciation expressed immediately following delivery. There is, however, very little information available on how women reevaluate their childbirth experiences months or years after the event.

In addition, our current normative practice of small families also ensures that each individual mother's experiences with birth are few enough so that she cannot begin to generalize about the nature of the birth process itself, but only sees her own few experiences. It also may be that forgetting the experience is the way in which mothers obviate the need to come to terms with the contradictions between what they have been told and what they feel.

This study was undertaken to find out how women felt about their experiences of childbirth long after the event.[2] The major criterion for being included in the study was having at least one child between one and ten years of age. The material was collected as part of a larger project designed to assess preferences and needs for maternity care facilities. Since, for that purpose, it was important to get respondents from a variety of geographic and socio-economic categories, it proved impossible to control also for the passage of time since birth. Fifty-one women were interviewed in depth for this project.

THE STUDY

In order to get the diversity of respondents desired for the study, a variety of residential areas or neighbourhoods, both in and surrounding the city of Halifax, Nova Scotia were sampled. Streets within these neighbourhoods were randomly chosen as target areas for the interviewer. Since we did not know the household composition of each dwelling unit on the street, the researchers left an introductory letter at all households on the selected street explaining the project and the criteria for inclusion. Households were then approached and those who were eligible asked if they would participate in the study. A convenient time was scheduled for the interview. Each street was canvassed in this way until the allocated number of respondents for that street was obtained.

Table 1 summarizes the distribution of the areas of residence of the respondents. This distribution reflects the population proportions of the region, and its mixture of urban, suburban, and transitional rural areas.

Lengthy interviews, ranging from 30 minutes to 2 1/2 hours were conducted with the 51 women interviewed. A standard interview

Table 1
Area of Residence

District	Number of Respondents
Major urban centre	12
Secondary urban centre	11
Outlying area of urban centre	6
Newly expanding suburb	7
Older village, now suburb	8
Semirural suburb	7
Total	51

schedule was used, containing both open-ended and closed questions. Each respondent was also encouraged to say whatever she wanted and talk as long as she wanted about her birthing experiences.

The women interviewed reflect the traditional values of the community selected. Forty-eight of 51 were currently married, one was divorced, and two had never been married. Their ages ranged from 21 to 40 with a mean of 30 years and 3 months. Twenty-three had only one child at the time of the study, 19 had two, and no information was available on 9 respondents. These are women who have not delayed or deferred childbearing, but appear to have had their babies within the conventional childbearing years, shortly following marriage. Judging from their ages, some of the women in the study have possibly not yet completed their families. Half of those who had children had an oldest child of five years or younger.

The women appear to reflect fairly traditional values in more ways than just marriage. Although over three-quarters of them (78.4% or 40) had had an income of their own before marriage, their occupations were conventional female ones. More than half of them did not have a university degree and had worked in the female occupational ghetto described by Armstrong and Armstrong (1984). Table 2 is a breakdown of their occupations prior to marriage.

Half of the women were employed at the time of the study. Of those working, almost half (45.2% or 12) had traditional female jobs, 42% or 11 had semiprofessional jobs with the requirement of a degree, and 7.7% or 2 had professional jobs. Husbands also worked at a variety of male occupations. Five husbands had professional jobs (2 or more degrees), 14 had semiprofessional jobs (1 degree) and 27 had no degree (2 unknown). Husbands had obtained higher educational levels and more qualifications than their wives. That, coupled with the fact that about half of the women were not em-

Table 2
Premarital Occupation of Respondents

Occupation	Number
Professional (2 degrees)	1
Semiprofessional (1 degree)	14
Traditional female job (no degree)	22
Nontraditional female job (no degree)	3
Other	3
Did not work prior to marriage	8
Total	51

ployed at present (and 11 or approximately 22% had never worked for pay outside the home at all), probably contributed to a traditional division of labour within the home.

ATTITUDES TOWARD BIRTH

Approximately one-quarter of the women had experienced a premature termination (miscarriage or abortion) of a pregnancy. Several had had two miscarriages in their childbearing history.

Most of the women had attended some form of prenatal classes. Only 5 respondents (9.8%) had not gone to any classes. Thirteen respondents or 25% had gone for all of their pregnancies, 62.7% or 32 had gone only for their first baby (1 unknown). Table 3 lists the reasons why women said they attended prenatal classes. (They were able to list all relevant reasons and usually gave more than one answer.)

Table 4 is equally revealing in describing the reasons the women did not attend prenatal classes. Bearing in mind that the table includes all *pregnancies* for which women did not attend prenatal classes, they have listed a variety of socially acceptable reasons for not going. Perhaps the pressures to attend such classes are so great that mothers-to-be do not feel they can avoid them unless they have a valid excuse. Just to skip attending because one didn't want to or was too tired appears to be thought unacceptable.

Prenatal classes offered by mainstream institutions (the local maternity hospital and the provincial Department of Health) were the most popular. Over 80% of the respondents attended a class offered by one of these two groups. Of the remaining 10% of the respondents who attended classes, two went to two different private organizations, only one of which was specifically oriented to childbirth education. Three others had attended prenatal classes outside the specific geo-

Table 3
Reasons for Attending Prenatal Classes

Reason	Number who Attended	
	No.	%
Wanted to learn more about birth	37	72.5
Recommended by doctor	18	35.3
Usual thing to do	13	25.5
Increased husband's role	7	13.7
Recommended by significant other	4	7.8
	N = 46	

graphic area and did not specify where or what types of classes.

The respondents' comments about the content of the prenatal classes appears at odds with their evaluation of the quality of the classes. Approximately 65% rated their classes as good or very good and only 4, or 8%, as unsatisfactory. Yet almost three-quarters of them said complications of pregnancy were not discussed in class, only 10% mentioned infant care as a topic, and less than 4% mentioned nutrition in pregnancy as a subject. Only 15 (29.4%) felt they had had an accurate and honest description of labor pain, and over 90% said they were inadequately informed on postnatal discomfort.

Most women felt their doctors gave them adequate prenatal care and they could talk to them. Most (86%) felt their concerns were taken seriously and attended to. On the other hand, 88% said they had questions they would have liked to ask, but could not or did not raise. Another new mother ranked first in the kind of person they would have preferred to query, and their own mothers came second. Health professionals other than their doctors ranked third.

From this apparently contradictory information it appears that women define in their own minds certain appropriate or legitimate concerns to raise with their doctors. They feel satisfied with the answers they get to these questions. However, their own sensitivity to the use of medical time may create an internal censoring mechanism. This may also define some areas of concern as unsuitable to be discussed with a doctor. Shyness and/or modesty may also affect the topics which are defined as medical. Women appear to have more questions than they are willing to ask their doctors, and prefer other women who have given birth as sources of information in these areas.

Most women described themselves as fairly relaxed in approaching labour. Perhaps this is a consequence of their confidence in the medical system, or of the reassurances they have received from their

Table 4
Reasons for Not Attending Prenatal Classes for Pregnancies

Reason	Number
Attended in previous pregnancy	18
Time conflict with class	6
Working	6
Inconvenient (babysitting problems)	2
Inconvenient location	2

physician about the availability of analgesics or anesthesia. Only 17 (33%) were worried about pain, only 9 (18%) about complications, and only 12 (24%) about the baby's health. Two (4%) were concerned about their own health. The absence of concern about infant or maternal health may be explained by the well-known low rate of maternity and infant mortality in childbirth. The absence of concern about complications may be a reflection of the information covered in prenatal classes, but it is also at odds with the high rate of obstetrical intervention in Canada today. Women may feel confident that their labour will proceed *normally*, but figures on obstetrical practices at the same maternity hospital where most of them delivered show a Caesarian section rate of 16.2% of all live births (Nova Scotia Department of Health 1983, quoted in Grace Maternity Hospital, *Role Study*). This raises the question of what it is that women define as normal labour.

The phenomenon to contemplate is whether or not women realistically understand the nature of contemporary obstetrical practices. Do the sources of information they rely on for information adequately inform them of these, or do doctors and prenatal classes convey an overly optimistic view of childbirth as painless and proceeding without intervention?

Most women approached labour optimistically. Neither the circumstances of the labour itself, nor external circumstances which might affect them, were sources of real concern to most of the respondents. Table 5 lists some of these.

This positive orientation seems to have been fostered by the combination of medical advice and the teaching of the prenatal classes. How well did their actual experiences in having babies compare with their expectations?

Most women had the doctor who gave them prenatal care present for the delivery of their babies. Two-thirds of them reported their doctor was present for all of their deliveries; an additional 16% had their doctor present for at least one of several deliveries. Nine women

Table 5
Worries Regarding Labour

Area of Concern	Number and Percent Who Cited Area as a Problem	
	No.	%
Pain	17	33.3
Complications	9	17.6
Baby's health	12	23.5
Own health	2	3.9
Bad weather conditions	4	7.8
Length of journey time	11	21.6
Coping when alone	8	15.7
Means of transportation	5	9.8
Care for other children	2	3.9
Absence of husband	2	3.9

(about 18%), however, did not have the physician who provided them with prenatal care with them at the delivery of their baby. Almost all (96%) of the respondents had their spouses with them (90% in all deliveries, 4% in at least one delivery). One person (2%) had her mother with her.

Research on North American childbirth practices suggests that isolation and strangeness is a difficult problem for women in labour (Arms 1975; Corea 1972; Jordan 1983; Shaw 1974). It appears as if the most superficial aspect of this problem has been addressed. The isolation women felt in an unfamiliar maternity ward has been diminished by the willingness of hospitals to allow the husband of the labouring woman to accompany her.

This band-aid solution, however, does not address the real issue of the woman brought into an unfamiliar environment at a critical and stressful point in her life. Short-term solutions *are* better than no solutions. However, we still have a situation where two outsiders are intimidated by contemporary obstetrical practices, but feel that they have won a major victory in the humanization of such facilities. And, if the attitude expressed below is typical, we have also a new culprit for some obstetrical intervention. For the chief of staff of a major obstetrical facility commented in an interview that one reason for the increase in the rate of Caesarian sections in Canada was the presence of husbands in the labour room. Husbands, he explained, were so distressed by the pain their wives were experiencing that they urged the doctor to do something. The obliging doctor responds with a Caesarian.

The breakdown of the numbers of women experiencing various

contemporary obstetrical practices is interesting. Table 6 summarizes this material.

The high prevalence of medical intervention almost belies the fact that 33 subjects (64.7%) defined their births as easy, and that an additional 7 women (for a cumulative 78.4%) defined their experiences as normal or usual. The extent to which such interventions are accepted as normal or usual by those to whom they are done is an indication of the successful incorporation of the medical definition of childbirth into the community at large.

DISCUSSION AND CONCLUSIONS

The respondents in this study, based on the aggregate statistical data alone, appear to be relatively satisfied with the current, medicalized definition of childbirth and the procedures which are a part of contemporary obstetrics. However, it is too facile an analysis of the data to use this as a final conclusion.

One of the most fascinating observations made in the collection of this material was the virtually universal comment by the women who were interviewed: "nobody ever talked to me about my experiences of childbirth before. I could never say anything to anybody about what it was like." (Another, more quantifiable way of documenting this need to talk is through responses to the question about whether they would like additional help in the immediate postnatal period. Over 60% said they would like some additional support from a support group, classes, more postnatal nursing visits or information and a helpline.) Women seem to put closure to their birth experiences by forgetting them, or just going on with their lives. But even up to a decade after a birth they are still eager to talk about their experiences to try to get some perspective on them.

The fact that women have not had a chance to talk about their birth experiences means that they have not been able to look at them critically. It is, therefore, not surprising that they have accepted the highly medical births they experienced as normal. They have not had a context in which to transcend their own personal childbirth experiences to look at how the medical environment shapes and controls birth. They are not aware of alternatives and options. They are grateful to be living in a twentieth-century North American, industrialized society in which they do not have to worry about "primitive" forms of childbirth, without technology, without hospitals, and without specialized medical practitioners like obstetricians and anesthesiologists. As an acquaintance told me, concerning the recent birth of her second child, "They like natural childbirth at the ...

Table 6
Frequency of Different Obstetrical Practices

Practice	Women Experiencing	
	No.	%
Amniocentesis	3	5.9
Caesarean section	7	13.7
Forceps	11	21.6
Internal foetal monitor	23	45.1
Intravenous solutions	33	64.7
Anaesthesia or analgesic	33	64.7
Enema	35	68.6
Episiotomy	38	74.5
Pubic shave	38	74.5
External foetal monitor	44	86.3
Ultrasound	47	92.2
Blood testing	51	100.0
Urine analysis	51	100.0

hospital ... but it is a painful process." When natural childbirth is defined as the absence of analgesics, but not as the absence of foetal monitoring, intravenous hookups, frequent internal examinations, no nourishment, inductions, rupturing of membranes, and other medical procedures, it is not surprising that it is "too painful, too hard."

Along with the surprise that someone was interested in their birth experiences, there was a virtually uninterrupted stream of descriptions, questions, and evaluative comments. These are not evident from the statistical data. However, the open-ended questions elicited a common response to the medical or hospital practice of a single pattern of childbirth. Women commented on the need for the individual's wishes and situation to be considered. They wanted to individualize and personalize the system of childbirth available to them, so that it would be more responsive to each of them as individuals. Significantly, none of the women expressed total dissatisfaction with their own experiences, yet most felt the system to be unresponsive and restrictive.

Women have only recently begun to question their treatment by the medical system. For most women, the medical system functions adequately as it is, and if they had a difficult time in childbirth it is because of *their* birth, and not the fault of the system. It is a case of blaming the victim. Women tend to believe that what is, is best. Cartwright (1979) has noted that women tend to choose things they have experienced. Porter and MacIntyre (1984) found in a study of innovation in antenatal (prenatal) care that pregnant women assumed that the arrangements they had experienced were the best possible arrangements. Shearer reports that childbirth educators suggest "patients develop a loyalty to their own births, a belief in the rightness or reasonableness of the way in which their births were managed" (1983, 77).

Women have not been given the perspective or framework within which to judge their childbirth experiences. They have internalized the medical definition of childbirth and do not have knowledge of other definitions or standards by which to evaluate their experiences. Therefore, the standards they use to assess their experiences have already eliminated the point of view that the system of childbirth is lacking. All that is left is to blame themselves, or their own experiences, if they have had problems with their births. They do not have the conceptual framework to examine the whole system. It is neither in their interests to see their experiences as invalid or problematic, nor to feel robbed of a unique aspect of the female role – the capacity to bear children.

That they are uncritical of our system of childbirth is not their fault. Many of them do not have the tools or the training to develop a critical perspective. The absence of this criticism should not be taken to mean that the system is a good one. Rather, it means there is need for a great deal more work in the analysis of medical-social control during childbirth and to bridge the gap between academic knowledge and its application in the lives of ordinary women.

NOTES

1 The new scholarship has examined the nature of childbirth, deeming it an appropriate topic of sociological research (although this does not guarantee its legitimacy). A report on women academics, which appeared in Ms. Magazine, describes the experiences of Nancy Stoller Shaw, author of *Forced Labor*, who was denied tenure on the basis that her work was not acceptable scholarship. Shaw's book was one of the first to describe the experiences of women in an obstetrical ward in a contemporary North American urban centre. Wertz and Wertz, two subsequent historians of childbirth, describe it as "the best sociological study of hospital maternity practice during the late 1960s" (Wertz and Wertz 1979, 255), and it is widely cited in later research on childbirth.

2 Here I would like to give thanks to those who contributed to this study and made it possible: Deborah Fiander, who carried out the actual interviewing and helped in many other ways; the Department of Employment and Im-

migration, which paid Deborah's salary under its summer student employment program; and Elizabeth Barker, a friend and colleague, who helped
in innumerable ways from start to finish.

MARTIN THOMAS

The Impact of Gender Preselection on Gender Maldistribution

It is widely assumed that the use of gender preselection will bring about gender maldistribution, and specifically, a surplus of males. Unfortunately, that assumption has not been tested effectively. This paper develops an elementary predictive model relating preselection to maldistribution by integrating empirical evidence from relevant research in the following areas: gender preferences, awareness of preselection techniques, willingness to use such techniques, reliability and gender bias of preselection techniques, and current birth gender ratio.

A slight proportional increase in male births is predicted. However, in part because the current adult population is predominantly female, and mortality among boys will continue to exceed mortality among girls, the assumption of impending adult gender maldistribution fostered by gender preselection appears to be unwarranted.

L'impact de la présélection sur la maldistribution des genres

On croit communément que l'usage de la présélection sexuelle mènera à une répartition inégale des sexes, et plus particulièrement, à un excédent d'hommes. Malheureusement, cette hypothèse n'a pas été vérifiée.Nous élaborerons, au cours de cet exposé, un modèle prévisionnel élémentaire qui rattachera la présélection à la répartition inégale des sexes en intégrant les données empiriques tirées des recherches pertinentes dans les domaines suivants: le penchant vers un sexe plutôt qu'un autre, l'information sur les techniques de présélection, la volonté d'utiliser ces techniques, la fiabilité de ces techniques et leur tendance à favoriser un sexe plutôt qu'un autre, et la proportion actuelle des sexes à la naissance. Une légère augmentation proportionnelle du taux des naissances masculines est prévue. Toutefois, soit parce que la population adulte actuelle est principalement féminine, soit parce que le taux de mortalité chez les gar-

çons continuera de dépasser celui des filles, l'hypothèse que la présélection des sexes entraînera une répartition inégale chez les adultes ne
semble aucunement justifiée.

This paper considers the probability of future gender imbalance as
a result of women and their partners having the opportunity to
preselect their children's gender. It is an issue of importance to all
those concerned with gender interrelationships, and one which is
especially salient to feminists. Preselection, as used here, does not
refer to identification of the foetus' gender and subsequent "veto"
choice by selective abortion, but to affecting the likelihood of conceiving either a female or male child. Techniques which accomplish
this are now available, and there is reason to believe that their use
will increase significantly in the near future.

Many scholars have speculated on the societal implications of gender imbalance resulting from preselection. But the logically prior
issue is the degree to which gender imbalance would be likely to
occur as a result of opportunities for preselection. It is that issue
which this paper addresses.

Demonstrating that the availability of gender preselection techniques will have some impact on the female-male ratio, and developing a specific prediction of the direction and magnitude of any
gender imbalance, requires answers to the following questions:

1 Will effective preselection techniques be available to potential
  users?
2 How large a portion of the population will have all three of the
  following characteristics: (a) gender preferences, such that if those
  preferences were realized, the gender mix would be different than
  it is currently; (b) awareness of the availability of preselection
  techniques; (c) willingness to use them?
3 To what extent will girl-preferring and boy-preferring adults differ with regard to either their knowledge of preselection, or their
  willingness to use it?
4 To what extent will the techniques used be inherently biased; that
  is, will the reliability rates of attempts to make children of each
  gender differ?
5 What is the birth gender ratio in the absence of preselection attempts?

This paper moves toward the development of a predictive model of
gender imbalance by evaluating available data pertinent to each of

these issues, and attempting to integrate the empirical and theoretical evidence.[1]

EFFECTIVENESS OF GENDER PRESELECTION TECHNIQUES

The gender of the foetus is determined by the characteristics of the sperm cell which fertilizes the egg; a sperm cell with an X chromosome creates a female, and one with a Y chromosome a male. (Men differ with regard to the relative proportions of X and Y sperm cells they carry.) All preselection techniques rely on physiological differences between these two types of cells. These differences include the following:

1 Hardiness: sperm cells with female characteristics, or gynosperms, are longer-lived, with significant numbers able to survive two days or more in a woman's body. Androsperms, with male characteristics, rarely last more than one day.
2 Size: gynosperms are much larger and heavier.
3 Mobility: the lighter androsperms move much more rapidly.
4 Biochemical characteristics: gynosperms prefer a relatively acidic environment; androsperms do better in a more alkaline environment.

Based on these differences, the available techniques employ one or more general approaches: timing of intercourse/ insemination; creating a favorable environment for one kind of cell or the other; or physically separating female and male sperm cells after ejaculation and prior to artificial insemination. These basic approaches are not mutually exclusive and are often used in combination. Since preselection techniques are detailed in the professional medical literature, as well as in popular publications, we briefly describe only the most prominent among them to simplify the subsequent discussion:

1 The Shettles, or "rhythm-douche" method, deals with both timing and control of the environment. Intercourse immediately after ovulation maximizes the probability of androsperms reaching the egg first; intercourse approximately two days prior to ovulation maximizes the probability that androsperms will be dead and gynosperms alive when ovulation does occur. With respect to control of the environment, douches which are mildly acidic or alkaline are used. Shettles also makes recommendations concerning position during and immediately after intercourse, although this has more to do with conception generally than with gender preselection (Rorvik and Shettles 1970).

2 The Ericsson technique, which has been patented, separates sperm
   cells by allowing them to pass through a thick medium, after which
   a sample rich in androsperms is collected (Ericsson et al. 1973).
   There are a number of variations on this approach, using different
   media and various methods of "skimming" the desired sample.
3 Electrophoresis involves separation of male and female sperm cells
   using electric current.

The Shettles technique, to which most of our attention will be devoted, has the longest history and largest data base. It has had a
success rate of approximately 85% for patients who used the technique under a physician's care (Rorvik and Shettles 1970). The technique is easily used without medical supervision, but effectiveness
data on this kind of use are not available. The lack of complexity of
the technique suggests that effectiveness would decline only slightly,
if at all, without the assistance of physicians.

Recent data on the Ericsson method used in attempts to create
males (n = 216), indicate a success rate just under 80%. More will be
said about effectiveness in the section on technique bias.

EVIDENCE OF GENDER PREFERENCE

Prior to the 1970s, when medical knowledge about gender preselection advanced rapidly, most of the social scientific research on
gender preference focused on fertility, and not on preselection. Gender preference was considered pertinent only with regard to pre-
dicting number of children. Beginning in the 1930s, a series of
research efforts in the United States, many with large samples, utilized "parity progression ratios," relating existing mixes/numbers of
children to decisions to have additional children. Of course, avoiding
pregnancy after having a child of the desired gender was the only
method of "selecting" which was generally available.[2] The behavioral
studies documented a male-female ratio for the last child which was
higher than for previous children, and, by inference, a preference
for male children.[3]

This body of research, although interesting, is flawed, in that the
decision to have additional children is constrained by a number of
factors unrelated to gender preference. Because these extraneous
factors have random effects on gender, we conclude that the infer-
ences about preference described in these papers underestimated
the extent of preference for males.

Recent research tends to focus directly on stated gender preference. This literature is largely consistent in its findings, including
the following:

1 There is a pervasive pattern of preference for male children. One
   review of more than fifty studies of gender preference revealed
   that the (male:female) preference ratio for all future children
   among all respondents ranged from 51.5:48.5 to 54:46 (Williamson 1976b).

2 Men and women differ somewhat in the degree to which they
   prefer male children. Men generally have strong pro-son preferences (Dinitz et al. 1954; Peterson and Peterson 1973; Williamson 1976b). Although the evidence is not entirely clear, the
   preferences of males may have become slightly less extreme in
   recent years (Gilroy and Steinbacher 1983, 675). Women also prefer sons, but not to the degree that men do. One study of childless
   couples found that the women had an overall preference ratio of
   approximately 52:48; the comparable figure for men was 54:46.
   Almost 70% of women consider it important to have at least one
   son; 60% consider it important to have one or more daughters
   (Pebley and Westoff 1982; Markle 1974).

3 For both men and women, the son-preference is markedly
   stronger for firstborn than for subsequent children. Among childless women, the mean preference ratio for firstborn is 65:35, and
   potential fathers' preferences are even more skewed. Similar attitudes exist with regard to the preferred gender of an only child.

4 Social class is weakly related to gender preference, with the middle
   class showing the least gender preference, the upper class showing
   slight male-preference, and those with low socio-economic status
   manifesting the greatest amount of promale bias. The correlation
   between parents' education level and boy-preference is generally
   negative, although the evidence is not entirely consistent.

5 A relationship appears to exist between religion and stated gender
   preference, with Catholics somewhat more interested in having
   boys than Protestants are. The data on Jews, derived from relatively small samples, is less compelling, but appears to indicate a
   strong preference for male children. Those with no religious preference showed the least bias (Dinitz et al. 1954).

   Needless to say, the variables social class, education, religion,
   and ethnicity are interrelated, confounding the relationship of
   each with the dependent variable, gender preference.

6 Nationality and culture are strongly related to gender preference
   (Williamson 1976a). The overwhelming preference for male children in some societies is well known to us. Female infanticide –
   especially in certain Asian countries – and a host of other practices
   only slightly less horrific, have been poignantly documented.

7 The stated gender preferences of those who are already parents
   is strongly affected by the current gender mix of their children.

That is, a strong tendency exists to express satisfaction with the gender(s) previously obtained, although that preference doesn't necessarily extend to future children. Women, more than men, display this response pattern. It may be that women are less strongly committed to one gender than the other, or that mothers develop closer bonds to their young children than fathers do.

PUBLIC AWARENESS OF GENDER PRESELECTION TECHNIQUES

Twenty years ago, Etzioni predicted the impending widespread use of gender preselection techniques (Etzioni 1968). This has not come to pass, and lack of public information is the reason. Public awareness of opportunities for gender preselection is still apparently negligible. This is so in spite of a lucid explication of the Shettles method in the obstetrical literature more than two decades ago (Shettles 1961), in popular literature a few years later (North 1969; Rorvik and Shettles 1970), and periodically since then.

There is one research effort which sought to measure public awareness of preselection opportunities, and the authors were sceptical of the results (Markle and Nam 1971). The authors asked respondents whether they had heard anything about opportunities to preselect the gender of their children, and, if they responded affirmatively, they were asked what the source of their information had been. Their responses and nonresponses to that follow-up question convinced the authors that a large proportion of those who claimed to have heard about preselection really had not.

Another measurement problem is the possible rapid change in the level of public awareness. Even recent studies risk being outdated, and accurate information on current awareness levels might not predict awareness a few years hence. With regard to the low level of public awareness, a number of contributing factors come to mind.

First of all, it appears that obstetricians have not been a wellspring of information. Some still claim loudly and publicly to be skeptical of gender preselection, even after decades of successes. Detail-poor caveats about "possible dangers to the health of the mother" somberly delivered by paragons of the medical establishment certainly have little to do with maternal health.

Perhaps some of the opposition, especially among obstetricians, is a result of speculation that widespread gender preselection could reduce the number of deliveries by 10%. But greed is not the only explanatory variable here. Physicians' lack of knowledge, or concerns about the ethics of preselection, may be factors in some cases. For whatever reasons, the medical community appears not to have been as informative as it could have been, although the data are admittedly impressionistic.

Second, social and natural scientists – even some who study gender preference or reproductive behavior – have been slow to get the message. For example, Dawkins, in his classic *The Selfish Gene*, states that "an individual cannot literally choose the sex of his [sic] children" (Dawkins 1976). And Gilroy and Steinbacher, writing in 1983, wonder about the potential use of a gender selection method "when it becomes widely available." Of course, it had been available for the previous twenty years to any couple with a thermometer and some patience. But even when scientists are well informed, we cannot, for a variety of reasons, expect them to provide mass education on the subject.

The mass media are the key. Until recently, their silence had been virtually complete, and public ignorance of the issue had been correspondingly complete. The inevitable discovery of the issue by the news media will bring gender preselection to the attention of the masses. During the past two years, gender preselection features appeared on the US Cable News network, the ABC network program "Nightline," and on the CBC's "The Journal." There were stories in *Newsweek* (Copeland and Hager 1986) and *Verve* (Anon. 1986), articles in the Montreal *Gazette* and the *Winnipeg Free Press* in 1986, and many in Toronto papers when, in November 1987, a "clinic" employing the Ericsson technique opened in that city. Sadly, most of the news stories to date have been careless, often creating the impression that preselection was possible only with the direct intervention of a physician. Inevitably, subsequent stories will be more informative. The knowledge breakthrough, and subsequent value breakthrough, will certainly follow.

In summary, the lack of current, reliable data on public awareness of gender preselection, and the inherent difficulties in extrapolating data of that type to make predictions of future awareness levels, makes this issue the weakest link in attempts to develop a predictive model; predictions of future levels of awareness will be highly speculative. Notwithstanding these difficulties, and Etzioni's unwarranted optimism, the speculation here is that public awareness will increase extremely rapidly over the next five years. What can be predicted confidently is that change in awareness will occur much more rapidly than change in the other relevant variables.

WILLINGNESS TO USE GENDER PRESELECTION

The next step is to evaluate the willingness of potential parents to

use gender preselection. Although this question has not been re-
searched as extensively or as effectively as the question of gender
preference, a few papers do deal with the issue. Most of the existing
works probably have significantly underestimated public willingness
to use gender preselection. This has occurred for two reasons: the
samples were nonrepresentative and the explanation of preselection
techniques given to the subjects was inadequate.

With regard to sampling problems, many of the works surveyed
the attitudes of those who were relatively young (usually students),
unattached, and with no immediate plans to have children. This is
a problem because both age and being married are positively correlated with willingness to use preselection. Furthermore, the middle
class, disproportionately represented among the student groups
from which most of the samples were drawn, tends to be less concerned with gender preselection.

For example, one pair of researchers included in their sample of
309 subjects 125 who had no intention of ever becoming parents
(again). That largely explains the authors' conclusion that only 35%
were willing to use preselection (Dixon and Levy 1985). In another
case, the subjects were disproportionately young and middle class;
only 25% were married. Asked whether they would be willing to use
gender preselection if their previous children had been the "wrong"
gender, 62% answered affirmatively (Markle and Nam 1971).

Two studies which asked couples, rather than individuals, about
their willingness to use preselection were gratifyingly consistent in
their findings. One study, with a relatively middle-class, well-edu-
cated sample, revealed that 60% were willing to use preselection for
the second child if the first wasn't of the preferred gender (Rosenzweig and Adelman 1976). (They didn't ask about subsequent children.) In the second study, with a more representative sample,
almost two-thirds of the 127 couples expressed willingness to use
preselection (Largey 1972).

The second factor biasing data on "willingness" is the inadequate
description of gender preselection techniques given to the respondents. The published papers often provide only sketchy outlines of
the explanations given to the subjects, but it appears that those explanations were, in many cases, confusing or nonexistent. Rosenzweig and Adelman (1976) clearly took pains to be accurate, explicit,
and informative. In contrast, another pair of researchers may have
left some respondents wondering whether the electrodes in electrophoresis are used before or after ejaculation. And in other research
projects, some subjects probably did not understand that the techniques were separate and independent. More to the point, some

subjects probably were not made to understand that gender preselection could be pursued without the intrusion of any healthcare
provider, and without side-effects, discomfort, danger, or significant
cost or inconvenience.

Not surprisingly, when different methods were described to respondents, their expressions of willingness to use preselection varied
greatly. Techniques requiring artificial insemination tended to be
regarded very unfavourably.

In conclusion, the best data we have suggest that roughly 65% of
all married respondents are willing to use preselection techniques.
But these data were collected from individuals, virtually all of whom
had no prior knowledge of preselection, in a cultural milieu in which
the acceptability of preselection was not yet clear. If our society
reaches a point where most potential parents know about preselection, and have some friends, neighbours, and relatives who have
used it, a large majority of those who have a gender preference
would be willing to use preselection. On the other hand, it is likely
that many of those who express a willingness to use preselection,
will not choose to use it.

RELATIONSHIP BETWEEN PREFERENCE AND WILLINGNESS TO USE PRESELECTION

In the previous section, we reviewed data on the proportion of the
population which had expressed willingness to use preselection. That
kind of data enables us to predict utilization rates, but it does not
enable us to predict the gender mix resulting from that utilization.
To accomplish that, we must obtain data on utilization willingness
for both girl-preferring and boy-preferring couples.

One researcher found that of those who were receptive to the idea
of using preselection, and who indicated a gender preference, approximately 80% preferred a male as their next child (Largey 1972).
Another paper reported that of those who indicated both a gender
preference and a willingness to use preselection, 86% sought a male
child. Women preferred sons by an 81:19 ratio; for men, the data
were 94:6 (Gilroy and Steinbacher 1983).

One problem with surveys that ask about preferences for the next
child is that many of the respondents are childless, with the result
that the question really asks about gender preference for the firstborn, for which pro-male bias is extreme. Markle and Nam avoid
this problem. Their data indicate overall gender preference and not
just preference concerning the next child. The mean number of
male and female children desired by those with favorable attitudes

toward preselection is 1.53 and 1.36 respectively, a modest 53:47 ratio.[4]

Unfortunately, there is also a bias in surveys which ask about overall gender preference. Many families are ultimately smaller than originally intended, because of divorce, separation, death, or resolutions formulated while changing diapers. The level of bias is difficult to estimate. Although there is a strong pro-male preference for the first child, preselection is less likely to be used for the firstborn. The research indicates that preselection is more likely to be used to end families than to begin them.

BIASES OF GENDER PRESELECTION METHODS

The next link in the causal chain concerns biases in gender preselection methods, where bias refers to differential success rates for attempts to create female and male children.

Because gender preselection methods have less than a 100% success rate, gender imbalances created by attempts to preselect gender will tend to be less extreme than the parents' mean gender preference ratio. For example, if 60% of all gender preselection attempts were to create males, and the techniques used were effective 80% of the time, only 56% of the babies would be boys. The calculation includes both successful attempts to create males and unsuccessful attempts to create females.[5]

But this "levelling" impact of technique ineffectiveness cannot reasonably be considered without reference to technique bias. Although there is an overt pro-male bias in the Ericsson method, it, and all of the other methods which require a physician's intervention, will probably have only a negligible impact on gender imbalance because they will represent a tiny proportion of total gender-preselected births.[6] On the other hand, the Shettles method is likely to gain widespread acceptance and popularity as a technique couples can use on their own. Does the Shettles method have an inherent gender bias? Although Shettles doesn't provide data on the subject, I infer that it does, and that the bias is pro-male.

With the Shettles method, creating a boy requires that insemination take place immediately after ovulation has occurred. There are reliable and easily used methods of determining when ovulation has occurred, including change in body temperature. But making a girl requires that insemination take place at least thirty-six hours prior to ovulation. Until recently, women were not able to do that with nearly as much reliability, having to rely primarily on observation of the opacity and elasticity of vaginal mucus. Now, however, there are simple chemical tests which give three or four days advance notice of ovulation; they are marketed over the counter and at low cost as a contraceptive aid. Notwithstanding these recent advances, the difficulty of anticipating ovulation precisely still exceeds the difficulty of noting its recent occurrence.

Unfortunately, we lack the kind of data necessary to precisely measure the extent of bias when the Shettles method is used privately by couples, as it most often will be. For the sake of the following discussion, it is estimated that preselection reliability will average .7 for females and .8 for males.[7]

GENDER RATIO IN THE ABSENCE OF PRESELECTION

One other relevant variable, which we have not yet discussed, is the proportion of babies of each gender born when no attempt at preselection is made. We know that during the past few decades in North America, the proportion of newborns who are girls is approximately .485. There are a number of explanations for the fact that the figure is not .5. For example, the ratio at conception (or primary sex ratio) is estimated to be 52:48 at minimum, but male foetus mortality is significantly higher. It may be that males carry a slightly higher proportion of androsperms; physical environmental as well as socio-economic factors have been shown to be relevant as a result of their impact on body biochemistry; and women may have acted on their gender preferences, either by use of preselection techniques, or by selective abortion.

Two points are important here. The first is that the ratio is not 50:50, and the second is that the deviation from that figure may be in part a result of action on pro-male preferences. Both of these facts are germane if one intends to predict future birth ratios as a function of preference.

DISCUSSION

This paper has reviewed some of the existing empirical data on variables which define the causal relationship between gender preselection opportunities and gender maldistribution:

1 the effectiveness of gender preselection techniques;
2 the gender preferences of those who intend to have children;
3 their awareness of opportunities for gender preselection;
4 their willingness to use gender preselection techniques;
5 the correlation between willingness and gender preference;
6 the biases of preselection techniques;

7 the gender birth ratio in the absence of preselection.

All have been expressed quantitatively, although values for the awareness and bias variables are estimates not directly supported by empirical research.

At first glance, the data we have reviewed portend extreme gender imbalance and probable adverse social consequences. Almost every relevant variable, when viewed independently, has promised a greater proportion of male births in the future. However, integration and thorough evaluation of the data suggest a different picture, one in which change is likely to be slight, incremental, and possibly even socially desirable.

Consider the fact that among respondents indicating a willingness to use preselection, the male:female preference ratio for all of their children would be approximately 53:47 (Markle and Nam 1971). We can interpret that as follows: if our preference for male children were to remain undiminished, and if all pregnancies were intended, and if everyone who intended to have a child had a gender preference, and was aware of the opportunity to preselect gender, and was willing to try to preselect, and did so, and if every preselection attempt was successful, then, and only then, would we have a birth ratio as extreme as 53:47. To the extent that these conditions are not satisfied, the male-female disparity would be diminished.

Needless to say, the willingness rate will never be 100%; it is not likely to be much more than 70% in the next quarter- century. The percentage of the population with clear gender preferences is, similarly, unlikely to exceed that figure. Assuming these 70% figures to be valid, the percentage of the population having both of these characteristics could range from 49 to 70, depending on the extent to which these variables are independent of each other.

With regard to public awareness of preselection, although a rapid and significant increase during the next few years is expected, the level of awareness will not approach 100%, or even 70%, in the near future. This compels us to further temper any predictions of increases in the proportion of newborns who are male.

Concerning effectiveness rates, the fact that they are less than 100% causes us to discount even further the effect of promale preferences. However, the disparity in effectiveness rates – the slight pro-male bias of the techniques – has the opposite effect.

What can we conclude from this mix of evidence and estimate? The implications of the data can be expressed as a prediction of the gender ratio of newborns in some future year, if certain assumptions are made concerning future utilization, etc. The following set of assumptions err – and deliberately so – in the direction of inflating the predicted disparity between male and female births. The intent is to describe the worst plausible scenario.

1 Seventy-five percent of all pregnancies will be intended.[8]
2 Thirty-five percent of intended pregnancies will involve preselection. The implication of these first two assumptions is that slightly more than one-quarter of all pregnancies will be attempts at preselection. Lower numbers for either of these two assumptions would lower the predicted number of males.
3 The overall preference ratio in preselection attempts will be 54:46, representing approximately 17% more males than females. Recall that Markle's figures were 53:47; even a correction for the "incomplete family" bias is unlikely to have brought the figures to 53.5:46.5.
4 For all attempts at preselection, the reliability of techniques used will average .8 for males and .7 for females.
5 The current birth ratio (51.5:48.5) has not been affected by either gender preselection or elective abortion.

Given these assumptions, the proportion of newborns who will be males can be calculated by summing four expressions, representing the proportion of all births which are male, and resulting from:
1 unplanned pregnancies;
2 planned pregnancies not involving preselection;
3 successful attempts to preselect males;
4 unsuccessful attempts to preselect females.
Or, symbolically,

$$M = (1 - I)(MN) + (I)(1 - P)(MN) + (I)(P)(MP)(MPS) + (I)(P)(FP)(1 - FPS)$$

where,

M = the proportion of newborns who are male,

I = the proportion of pregnancies which are intended,

MN = the proportion of male births when no preselection attempt is made,

P = the proportion of planned pregnancies which involve preselection,

MP = the proportion of preselection attempts intended to produce males,

MPS = the proportion of male preselection attempts which are successful,

FP = the proportion of preselection attempts intended to produce females, and

FPS = the proportion of female preselection attempts which are successful.

Inserting the appropriate values in the equation provides:

$$
\begin{aligned}
M &= (1-.75)(.515) + (.75)(1-.35)(.515) + (.75)(.35)(.54)(.8) + \\
&\quad (.75)(.35)(.46)(1-.7) \\
&= .129 + .251 + .113 + .036 \\
&= .529
\end{aligned}
$$

Thus, even if one makes these rather extreme assumptions, it appears that the proportion of newborns who are male is unlikely to exceed .53, regardless of changes in the level of public awareness. Of course, this "worst-case" ratio of 53:47 is still potentially serious. Its likelihood, and its implications, should be considered with reference to the following:

1 The predicted 53:47 ratio should be compared not to 50:50, but to the existing birth ratio of 51.5:48.5.
2 Any change in gender birth ratio will occur very slowly, because the various determinative factors will tend to change independently of each other, and incrementally, rather than suddenly.
3 Male preference for male children is diminishing, albeit slowly.
4 A number of scholars have argued that potential parents would react quickly to any apparent adult maldistribution by choosing to have children of the less prevalent gender. The empirical evidence is far from conclusive, but a variety of theoretical arguments have been presented (Dawkins 1976).[9]
5 Finally, the focus of this paper has been on the prospect of change in the birth gender ratio. But if one's intent is to understand the social consequences of maldistribution, ultimately the adult gender ratio will be of greater concern. Although a detailed discussion of the differences in demographic patterns between children and adults is beyond the scope of this paper, one or two points are worth mentioning.

Notwithstanding the fact that male births have outnumbered female births for generations, the adult female population currently is significantly larger than the adult male population. This can be attributed to higher male mortality rates, beginning in infancy and extending through adult life.[10] Recent Canadian census data reveal the impact of differential mortality rates. Every age category, expressed as ten-year intervals, had a higher proportion of males in 1971 than the next highest category (representing the same people) had a decade later.

The desirability or undesirability of this particular maldistribution is an issue on which feminists are likely to disagree. What some see as desirable, others will consider problematical. One of the problems created by this adult gender maldistribution is the difficulty faced by adult heterosexual women who attempt to find life partners. And the problem may be even more serious than the gender distribution data suggest, if the male homosexual population is larger than the lesbian population. Regardless of one's views on the optimal relative numbers of adult females and males in society, the possible shift in birth ratio from 51.5:48.5 to 53:47 must be viewed with reference to the proportionate number of adult females in our society currently.

Concerns have been expressed, sometimes passionately, about adverse consequences which would result from gender maldistribution, and specifically from a surplus of males. Those views may be entirely accurate, but their premise, concerning the serious effects of preselection on the adult gender ratio, is apparently false. What we can anticipate is a slight and gradual increase in the proportion of males born. That change is certain to ameliorate, not exacerbate, the existing gender maldistribution, especially among the adult heterosexual population.

The evidence, to this point, has been primarily empirical. But normative arguments were obviously implicit in the discussion of consequences of gender maldistribution. One other normative question deserves to be addressed. Reproductive freedom logically includes the freedom, on the part of women and their partners, to determine the gender mix of their children. It has not been viewed as such, partly because of lack of awareness or understanding of the methods of preselection, and partly because of fears that widespread exercise of this right would lead to a society in which a disproportionate number of adults are males. That fear, it now appears, was exaggerated, and perhaps entirely unfounded.

NOTES

1 Most of the research reviewed for this paper was conducted in the United States; two or three of the points made were derived from research in the Scandinavian countries. Although it was not my intent to address the problems of gender preselection only as they applied to Canadians, the approach

taken in the paper will allow the reader to substitute different values in the predictive model based on the perceived appropriateness of the research findings to the Canadian population.

2 Ironically, and paradoxically, the practice of continuing to have children until obtaining the desired gender, and then stopping, would not increase the proportion of children of that gender in society. On the contrary, it would result in the other gender occurring more frequently.

3 It has even been suggested that the change in body chemistry which occurs in women as they age increases the probability of conceiving a male child; since women will obviously be older during their last pregnancies than during earlier ones, it is possible that the relatively large proportion of males among lastborn may be attributable more to biochemistry than to gender preference. On the other hand, we know that the temporal gap between pregnancies is slightly greater if the first of the two pregnancies produced a male.

4 Interestingly, this research revealed that the gender preference of those who were less sympathetic to preselection was even more pro-male. The data presented by Markle and Nam (1971) suggest that surveys which include those not sympathetic to preselection probably overestimate preselection's impact on gender ratio. Religion may be an intervening variable here. Catholics tend to show a greater promale bias than Protestants do, as well as greater reluctance to use preselection.

5 Calculation of the proportion of males would be as follows: proportion = $(.8)(.6) + (1-.8)(1-.6) = .56$

6 Initially, the Ericsson method wasn't even used to create girls. Ericsson's recent claim that the technique can now be used to preselect either gender may be as much an attempt to deflect criticism of his clinics as it is an attempt to increase demand for the services his clinics provide. I am not aware of any data on the relative "purity" of the samples he derives, or his success rate on attempts to create girls.

7 Even accurate reliability figures exaggerate the effects of differences in reliability, because a preselection failure will generally bring about a subsequent effort to obtain the desired gender.
   Since reliability is measured as proportion of live births, we may ignore foetal mortality rates, which are significantly higher for males.

8 In 1976, married women in the United States claimed that 69% of the births they experienced during the previous year were planned (Anderson 1976). (Needless to say, respondents are likely to exaggerate somewhat the extent to which their pregnancies are planned.) Obviously, the corresponding percentage for unmarried women would be close to zero. At that time in the United States approximately 15% of births were out of wedlock (Anderson 1976). The corresponding datum for Canadian women today is probably less than 5%.

9 One implication of these arguments is that the current preference for males may be partly a result of potential parents perceptions that more (hetero-sexual) women than men are without partners. This may also be seen as a homophobic reaction.

10 Throughout childhood, a variety of often fatal diseases, notably cancers and kidney diseases, afflict males disproportionately. The higher mortality rates are a function of higher incidence levels among boys and/or their poorer responsiveness to treatment. In adolescence and early adulthood, accidents and suicides take a larger proportion of males. In middle age, a variety of diseases, especially cardiovascular and respiratory diseases, claim a greater number of males. Ingrid Waldron noted that the ratio of male to female mortality had increased steadily since 1920, reaching an incredible 1.6:1 (Waldron 1967). Although that trend lasted for approximately fifty years, I believe it may have begun to reverse itself in the years since her paper was published.

Education: Pedagogy and Consequences
Education: la pédagogie et ses conséquences

LANIE MELAMED AND IRENE DEVINE

Women and Learning Style: An Exploratory Study

A pilot study was undertaken to investigate potential gender biases in the Kolb Learning Style Inventory (1985), an indicator of individual preference and sense of self as a learner. The results indicate a significant difference in preferred learning styles for women and men. In the population studied, women showed a strong preference for concrete learning over abstract conceptualization. When women are subsumed into generalized categories without regard to gender, their particularity is obscured. The findings have implications for educational philosophy and practices in higher education.

Les femmes et leur style d'apprentissage: une étude exploratoire

Une étude pilote a été entreprise dans le but d'établir l'éventualité de préjugés sexuels dans le « Kolb Learning Style Inventory » (1985), un index des préférences individuelles et du sens du moi dans le processus d'apprentissage. Les résultats indiquent une différence marquée dans les préférences de styles d'apprentissage chez les femmes et chez les hommes. Dans la population étudiée, les femmes montraient une préférence pour le mode d'apprentissage concret plutôt que pour la conceptualisation abstraite. Si l'on fait entrer les femmes dans des catégories générales qui ne tiennent pas compte du genre, leur spécificité disparaît. Ces résultats ne sont pas sans retentir sur la philosophie et les pratiques pédagogiques au niveau des études supérieures.

These are exciting times for feminist scholarship. The world of women's cognition is just beginning to be re-discovered, re-visioned, and re-evaluated. We know, not only from our own experience, but from reading the works of others, that although men and women inhabit the same world, they experience it very differently (Bernard 1981; Rubin 1983). When new truths are applied to the field of education and women's way of knowing, a plethora of new questions arise. Is learning the same for men and women? What are women's learning strengths and how can these be made visible? Would women prefer different approaches to learning if they had the choice? And if distinguishable styles exist, how might teaching practices in institutions of higher learning be modified to make the climate less chilly for women (Hall and Sandler 1982)? This study explores some of these issues.

According to Sheriff (1977), approximately seventy percent of all research in psychology has been conducted by men on predominantly male sample populations. Bernard (1973) defines sociology as a "science of male society" and the prestigious methodologies which yield "hard" data as fundamentally a "machismo element" in research. When these majority culture standards, patterns, and norms are generalized to women and "others," the latter are generally found to be less than adequate, exhibiting impaired intellectual competence, morally inferior judgement, and undependable "emotional" responses (Belenky et al. 1986; Spender 1981). Once they are perceived as deficient, it does not take long for women (and other marginal groups) to come to believe in the perception, and to question their ability to think, learn, and act intelligently in the world. Rarely has it been recognized that women may experience themselves as outsiders, or "immigrants," struggling to function in a system which is alien to their reality (Franklin 1983).

The impact of male control of educational policy (97% in Britain) is pervasive, ranging from setting standards and determining what constitutes excellence, to decreeing which content is valued and which is not (Martin 1985; Spender 1981). When women enter "malestream" institutions, they receive an education equal to that of men, with little or no attention given to what constitutes their preferred aims and modes of learning. Sanford (1967) describes, with humorous overtones, aspects of masculine style in the university which are hostile to men as well as women: "stressing analysis, to the neglect of how things fit together; separating thought from feeling, inquiry from action, teaching from inquiry and action, work from play; abstracting functions for purposes of study, and then basing practice on the abstractions as if they were separate in reality ... the use of status competition as the motive force for keeping the machinery going; and engaging in grim, concentrated shop-talk relieved only by weekends of pro-football" (92–3).

Several studies have appeared in recent years which describe women's specificity in learning, knowing, and valuing, and which indicate the need to re-create theories in which women's experience is central (Belenky et al. 1986; Martin 1985; Gilligan 1982, 1979; Lyons 1983). Gilligan's challenge to Kohlberg's theory of moral development points clearly to the so-called "under achievement" of women when evaluated against male standards. Belenky et al. (1986) have expanded Perry's theory of cognitive development (1981) to include women at all stages of growth within and outside of formal learning environments. Based on women's theories, their work deepens our understanding of how a wide range of women develop a sense of self, voice, and mind.

When asked to describe their educational experiences, many women report being treated as stupid, feeling intimidated, being overwhelmed with information, and feeling less than competent to compete in an environment in which they are considered outsiders. Because they frequently use personal knowledge drawn from life experience to integrate institutional facts and ideas, women are likely to be alienated from educational methods which emphasize rationalism and the transmission of fragmented information (Belenky et al. 1986). Contexts which are neither hierarchical and stratified, nor competitive and judgemental, seem to be most supportive to the ways in which women learn (Spender 1981). Despite these findings, administrators and professors in higher education still argue against women's studies programs and avoid open debate on whether women's educational needs are different from men's.

Awareness of these issues motivated us to take another look at a learning style inventory which we had been using over the past years. The inventory was created by David Kolb (1976) and is based on the theory of experiential learning developed by John Dewey (1938) and Kurt Lewing (1951). Briefly, Kolb's model describes learning as a four-stage cycle, with each stage requiring different abilities and skills on the part of the learner. Immediate Concrete Experience (CE) leads us to Reflect and Observe what has occurred (RO). This reflection is assimilated into Abstract Concepts and generalizations (AC) which are then solidified through Active Experimentation (AE)(see figure 1). In turn, new experiences grow out of the old, and a repetition of the cycle ensues. The theory suggests that all four stages of the cycle must be integrated in order for learning or change to take place. An experience, for example, which is not reflected upon or is not tested in actual practice is not likely to result in effective learning.

The Learning Style Inventory (LSI) is a twelve-item questionnaire in which respondents rank-order their preferred ways of learning.

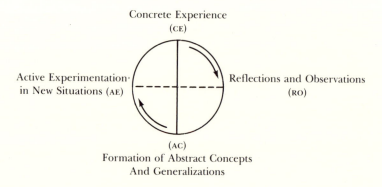

Figure 1. The Experiential Learning Cycle

The LSI measures an individual's relative emphasis on the four learning orientations; it also indicates the extent to which a person emphasizes concreteness or abstractness on one continuum and action or reflection on the other. It is important to remember that the LSI does not "objectively" measure learning style; rather it is an indicator of a learner's individual preference and sense of self at the time of completing the inventory.

When we look at the norms on which the LSI outcomes were originally based, we find a sample of 127 practicing managers, and 512 Harvard and MIT graduate students in management (Kolb 1973). A later study expanded the normative group to 1,933 college-educated adults, about two-thirds of whom were men (Kolb 1976). In the 1985 version, the sample consists of 638 men and 801 women who are "ethnically diverse and who represent a wide range of career fields." The original framework for Kolb's learning theory was therefore based on an all-male sample, expanded to include women in subsequent studies. While this may help us to understand aspects of the learning process, it does little to illuminate women's experiences. When the sample was expanded to include larger numbers of women, the latter were accommodated into an already existing conceptual performance grid.

The Kolb Learning Style Inventory is frequently used in teaching, faculty development, organizational development, and managerial education. Despite its success as a teaching and learning style indicator, the gender implications of the instrument have not yet been explored. Over seventy research studies have been based on the LSI; not one has explicitly considered gender as a variable (Kolb 1985). Cognizant of the significance of this omission, we conducted an exploratory study to identify possible gender bias in the instrument.

In addition, our interest was in increasing our understanding of women's particular learning needs.

METHODS

Two approaches were used to collect data: the LSI, and an open-ended questionnaire administered to a population of 124 persons (88 women and 36 men). Seven colleagues were interviewed as well. The breakdown of the population was as follows:

23 undergraduate students, Leisure Studies Department, Concordia University, Montreal

33 undergraduate students, Management Department, Concordia University, Montreal

23 students returning to college after spending time in the work force, Lesley College, Boston

25 library instructors enrolled in a continuing education workshop, Montreal

13 CEGEP teachers enrolled in a continuing education course, Dawson College, Montreal

7 colleagues from Canada and the US who were familiar with the LSI.

A The LSI was administered to each person in the population group and self-scored. A short lecture was given to elaborate the theory, followed by a small group exercise in which like-style groups met to discuss the results. A questionnaire was then distributed to collect individual opinions and reactions. The following three questions were asked:

(a) Thinking of yourself as a learner, how did it feel to take the Inventory?

(b) How well, and in what ways does it describe you as a learner?

(c) What's missing for you in this Inventory; i.e., what other words or descriptions would you use to describe how you learn best?

Data obtained were entered onto a D-Base computer program to facilitate analysis.

B Follow-up interviews were conducted with seven women students from the Leisure Studies Department, Concordia University. The student discussions added depth to our understanding of the learning needs of women undergraduates in the university setting. The interviews were taped, transcribed and analyzed for significant themes. Unfortunately, lack of times and funds prevented an in-depth analysis of these findings.

C Interviews were conducted with each of seven women colleagues (feminist scholars, psychologists, and teachers familiar with the

LSI or other learning inventories). The purpose of these interviews was to determine thoughts and opinions about the LSI in relation to women's epistemology.

ANALYSIS

Analysis of the data focused on four main questions. The central findings are reported below.

1 *Were there significant LSI variations according to gender?*
Results indicate a significant difference in preferred learning styles for women and men. On the concrete/abstract continuum, 64% of the women scored at the concrete end, compared with 36% at the abstract end (p – .005). Men rated higher at the abstract end of the continuum (69%) and lower at the concrete end (31%). It is important to note that the proportions of active and reflective learners (on the active experimentation/ reflective observation axis) is almost equal for males and females, in contrast to the significant differences between women and men on the abstract/concrete axis.

2 *Were there significant differences in the way men and women felt about taking the Inventory?*
Two-thirds expressed reservations about taking the instrument (64% women; 54% men). Those who had reservations commented that the instrument was repetitive; they felt they were answering the same question over and over again, and that it was too simplistic. Since the responses for each style were in the same columns on each question, it was easy to manipulate the instrument and to make it come out the way they wanted. Students said: "The responses were ambiguous"; "I found I could manipulate the responses"; "I took it three times and each time I came out differently"; "The four choices did not represent a response I could put down." Comments from the expert group were similar: "I couldn't distinguish between the questions. I kept feeling I had answered the same question before"; "It doesn't give the possibility of integrated learning as a choice"; "I found I could manipulate it to come out the way I wanted. When I saw that I was scoring too high on abstract thinking, I changed my answers so as to come out more well-rounded."

3 *Were there significant differences in how men and women thought the instrument described them as learners?*
Responses to the question of how well people thought the instrument/model described them as learners, revealed that 36% of the total population agreed that it described them well, while 64% of the total population had reservations. There were few differences

between male and female responses. It is interesting to note that the concrete learners (43% of the men and 36% of the women) were more dissatisfied with the instrument than those who scored on the abstract end of the continuum (17% of the males and 29% of the females). Comments on how well the LSI measured learning style revealed complaints about lack of context in the instrument. This was particularly significant for women, 33 of whom mentioned this, compared with only 3 of the men. Those who prefer learning which is connected to their experience (64% of the women) appear to have more difficulty with an instrument which does not situate the questions in context-based terms. Context was frequently defined as learning which is specialized according to time, place, purpose, pressure, and people. Some of the students commented: "Do I imagine myself learning ideas or how to become a waitress?"; "Are you talking about academic learning or learning about relationships?"; "If I took it again I would answer it in a different way"; "I am not a hands-on learner all the time"; "This needs to be answered with a specific situation in mind"; "I find that I adapt my learning style to fit the situation at hand." The experts said: "It should read: 'In thinking of myself as a learner of ... '"; "Different learning contexts require different styles." One teacher who has used the LSI frequently said: "When I take it (and Kolb would say it's because I'm a diverger), I always feel that there's no "there" there. It is Kolb's assumption that there is one way to learn everything."

4 *What was missing for people in the Inventory?*

Several women-centred issues emerged from the comments to this question. Of the 63 women and 23 men who responded, the following items were mentioned in descending order of frequency:

- the lack of a specific context in the questions. As noted above, this was the most disturbing item for many in taking the instrument. Thirty-three of the women mentioned the lack of context compared with three of the men.
- the need to share learning with others. Six females and two males noted this. All of the females who mentioned this scored on the *concrete* end of the scale. Some of the comments were: "Is the learning accomplished better alone or with others?"; "People-oriented needs to be added"; "The importance of relationships"; "When there is cooperation not competition."
- ways of knowing which are not primarily linear, logical or rational such as imagination, insight, and intuition. Six females and one male mentioned this. Of the seven, all were concrete learners. Some of the remarks were: "The final category only takes into

account one aspect of the learning personality. I'm far more intuitive, feeling, and less rational than the assimilator label would
suggest"; "They've only used one way of determining your style
on this – that's a very rational way. It should include essay questions. I like to poke and meander in my learning"; "It doesn't
measure all my learning, but no instrument does."

- the lack of any reference to motivation. "Not boring"; "variety";
  and "when the material is presented in an interesting way" were
  mentioned by seven females (all *concrete* learners) and one male.
- whether or not learning was fun. "Not serious"; "enjoyment"; and
  "idea play" were mentioned by four women and one man, all
  concrete learners.
- the nature of the environment. This included the need for a
  relaxed or informal atmosphere for learning. Four female respondents and one male mentioned this.
- the presence and absence of pressure. No males mentioned this
  while three females did. Two of the women said they learned best
  under pressure.

DISCUSSION

Several themes that contribute directly or indirectly to our understanding of women and learning emerged from the study. One was
the issue of generalizing research results without regard to gender
(or other minority culture) differences. Fifty-five percent of the total
population described themselves as concrete learners, in contrast
with 45% of the total population who preferred more abstract methods. This in itself is a significant finding, especially when we realize
that educational philosophy in most colleges and universities is an-
tithetical to learning from experience. When the data are analysed
according to gender, an even greater discrepancy emerges between
preferred style and compatibility with pedagogical practice (64% of
the women in the population preferred concrete over abstract learning). *When women are subsumed into generalized categories, their particularity is obscured.* This is one of the reasons it has been so difficult
over the centuries to isolate, recognize, and affirm women's particular ways of knowing.

Although the purpose of the research was not to compare the
scores of men and women, but to understand women's reactions to
the LSI, the findings regarding women's strong preference for concrete learning and the comfort of most men with abstract conceptualization provided serendipitous knowledge. The fact that we
mainly interviewed students and teachers who had chosen the hu-

manities as a career orientation indicates another feature of women's particular learning preferences. The disproportionate number of women in the classes and teacher groups we polled shows clearly the bias most women have for careers in areas such as business, recreation, teaching, library work. Had we included the minority of women enrolled in the male-dominated sciences we might have found different answers to our questions. We would expect to find many of these women engaged in learning the procedures necessary to succeed, and in many cases relinquishing their natural preferences and inclinations for the learning process (Belenky et al. 1986).

Franklin, in her attempt to understand the silencing of women engineering students, found they needed to deny their origins in order to adjust to the male technological order: "this often leads to feelings of, "I can't cope," "why can't I feel at home here?" and a lot of self-blaming. It must be recognized that it is not incompetence, lack of ability or stamina but the breaking of the ties with a natural community that is at the bottom of this malaise" (Franklin 1984, 86).

Four learning styles are described by Kolb. These are: diverger, converger, assimilator and accommodator. Women tend to fall into the accommodator quadrant. Use of the word "accommodator" to describe a predominantly female learning mode may in itself be an unfortunate decision. Although the word was taken from Piagetian cognitive psychology (1970), it seems to have a more pejorative image than "assimilator," at least in university settings. From our generalized experience, some women report being disappointed and even apologetic when learning that they are "accommodators," yet rarely are they uncomfortable with being called "assimilators." One woman teacher felt angry at the names used for each of the four quadrants; in her opinion none of them was easily accessible, or relevant to her experience.

It was the information from the expert informants which contributed most directly to articulating some of the less visible gender issues raised in the lsi. "The model," they said, "is good as far as it goes, but it does not go far enough. Women's strengths will not show up on this kind of scale." Because the lsi describes behaviour according to a cognitive model formulated by male theorists (Dewey 1938; Lewin 1951; Kolb 1984) and was developed in its original form from a primarily male university population, the picture of women's learning experience (and that of 31% of the men in our sample) is not adequately represented. By forcing choices to be made between either/or dichotomies, by viewing learning as an abstraction unrelated to context, by emphasizing the rational without also including the intuitive and the metaphoric, and by assuming that learning is an individual process rather than a collaborative one, women's preferred ways of knowing remain obscure. One respondent was concerned that the forced choice format is "biased against those who cannot 'fit' their self-concept into what appears to them as an abstraction."

The majority of women seem to be most comfortable in learning environments which value "relationships (working with others) over individualism; collaboration over competition, experience (the subjective) over abstraction (objectification), connectedness over separation, and wholistic over hierarchical approaches."

Women tend to be associated with knowledge which is primarily emotional, or body-based; yet valued knowing in our culture resides in the language of the mind. It is the knowledge which comes from seeing, and which originates in the "mind's eye," that characterizes accepted modes of knowing, rather than knowledge rooted in feeling, connectedness, and subjectivity. An adequate scale of the strengths derived from "tacit" and "intuitive" knowledge which exist primarily in women's spheres has not yet been conceptualized (McMillan 1982). One of the experts interviewed explained women's invisibility in the LSI in this way: "Most of the ways women learn best will not surface in the Inventory. Women in my classes seem to consistently score in one way ... The danger is that in no way does the LSI restructure what we know about learning. It reinforces the gender bias which has been maintained over the last century. It replicates old ways of knowing. It doesn't add anything new – a task which minority culture groups are actively engaged in at the present."

The use of the LSI and other male-generated frameworks to describe women's learning experiences places women in a double bind. They appear less capable when judged according to accepted educational standards, and their strengths remain invisible. The inventory expands our level of consciousness about learning by indicating that people learn in different ways, a concept which is especially useful to students and teachers alike. Despite opening the door to greater understanding about learning for the majority culture, the LSI merely brings women to the threshold. A concerted effort must be made to integrate the CE/AC RO/AE polarities, and to confront the tendency to judge one as superior to the other. Placing Concrete Experience and Abstract Conceptualization at opposite ends of the continuum reinforces the dualistic mind/body split. Competence in learning comes from integrating polarities, as well as from expanding the concept of learning itself. Opportunities must be created to document and validate the metaphoric, intuitive, collaborative, contextual, and relational components of learning and knowing, attributes which are not directly measured in the LSI.

What this pilot study suggests is that in order to understand the needs of silenced learners, it is necessary to begin with their experience, not to try to fit them in as an afterthought. Since more women than men seem to prefer a learning style which is concrete, connected, and experience-based, we need to better understand the consequences for women (and other minority groups) of being in educational settings where abstract conceptual learning styles are so highly rewarded. When the basic assumptions of educational philosophy and practice are expanded to include these perspectives, everybody's learning potential will be expanded.

ANGÉLINE MARTEL AND LINDA PETERAT

Feminist Ped-agogies: From Pedagogic Romanticism to the Success of Authenticity

While feminist pedagogy can, on the one hand, be regarded as a contradiction in terms, it can also point the way to change, grounded in an ideal of womanness reaching toward humanness. Four themes of feminist pedagogies are identified: (1) living and what matters, (2) participation and interaction, (3) collaboration and cooperation, and (4) teaching with a vision. Authenticity is claimed as a fundamental goal of feminist pedagogies, bilingualism as the praxeological mode. Humanness, made possible through authenticity, is the ultimate goal for women and men in education.

Les péd-agogies féministes: du romantisme pédagogique au succès de l'authenticité

Si une pédagogie féministe peut être perçue comme une contradiction dans les termes, elle peut par contre ouvrir la voie à un changement qui serait ancré dans une féminitude axée sur un humanisme. Quatre thèmes des péd-agogies féministes apparaissent: (1) la vie et ce qui compte, (2) participation et interaction, (3) collaboration et coopération, et (4) enseignement fortement motivé. Ces pédagogies féministes visent avant tout l'authenticité et voient le bilinguisme comme une modalité praxiologique. Leur but ultime est l'humanisme, rendu possible grâce à l'authenticité et éminemment souhaitable pour les éducateurs et éducatrices.

The phrase "feminist pedagogy" serves as a rallying term for many women educators living an increasingly conscious praxis in the classroom, that is, increasingly conscious of the link between theory and practice. The new discourse essentially transforms Paulo Freire's *Pedagogy of the Oppressed* (1970), for at the root of "feminist pedagogies" lies the recognition that women have been an oppressed group, and that emancipation from the power of the oppressor can only be attained by an educational process designed for, and by, women. We propose that such a process should be grounded in an ideal of womanness,[1] striving ultimately toward an ideal of humanness for both women and men. We shall look at the implications for women of feminist pedagogies as ways of being in the classroom, and as teaching styles contributing to the achievement of the general feminist goals of emancipation.

FEMINIST PEDAGOGY: A CONTRADICTION IN TERMS

"Feminist pedagogy" appears, at first, to be a contradiction in terms. The difficulty does not stem from the word "feminist" (even though the word itself represents many facets of women's beliefs and actions), as much as from its juxtaposition with the word "pedagogy." Pedagogy suggests education for entry *into* the patriarchal system, but education is problematic for women, as Mary O'Brien so aptly points out: "education is political in both the broad and the narrow sense of that word ... The notion of education as an objective uncovering of the truth and a subjective passing-on of knowledge obscures the fact that truth and knowledge are socially defined and legitimated, and that the power to define meanings and identify what is to be 'acceptable truth' is a very real power, exercised day by day in the bureaucracies and classrooms of educational systems everywhere" (1983, 3).

Women, she reminds us, have to be suspicious of the school hierarchies and curricula, for they are profoundly conservative bastions of male supremacy and ruling-class power. She brings to our attention the very concrete workings of the educational system.

At the same time, the word "pedagogy" serves as a reminder of a set of conventions and interactions within the educational field. Patriarchy has frozen ways of being in the classroom that it deems acceptable and appropriate. Let us call these particular practices "conventional pedagogical practices" in order to distinguish them from feminist and other so-called "marginal" pedagogies. As Adrienne Rich points out (1979), conventional pedagogy penalizes troublesome questioners as trouble-makers; lively, independent, and active students as disrupters; and curious students as misbehavors. Conventional pedagogical practices favour passivity and conformity in the learner.

Feminism makes it clear that women need to break out of conformity and passivity moulds. We can neither conform, nor be passive, and, as we discover the extent of our oppression, we refuse to let patriarchy do the thinking, talking, and naming for us. This sets

the stage for the two goals generally identified by feminist pedagogies. First, we need to understand how patriarchal ideology has
truncated and distorted our knowledge and experience of ourselves
and the world. Second, as thoughtful, expressive humans, we need
to explore actively our womanness and humanness. These two goals
make feminist pedagogy a special way of educating.

If we now return for a moment to the word "pedagogy"; the
contradiction between the word "pedagogy" and the word "feminist"
is manifest in two ways – education in patriarchy undermines feminist goals; and conventional pedagogical practices by encouraging
passivity and conformity, set up unacceptable conditions of education for women. The etymology of the word "pedagogy" is enlight-
ening. It is Greek, and means the leading (*agôgè*) of the child (*pais,
paidos*) to the traditional Greek master. The word "pedagog" came
later to mean the pedantic, narrow-minded school-master. The images conveyed by the etymology of the word adequately describe
patriarchal ideology of education with its rigid practices of conformity, passivity and conservatism.

There is, however, within the etymology of the word "pedagogy"
the possibility of transformation. The root *agôgè* (leading), provides
an alternative vision of classroom praxis. As for "ped," if we substitute
for the notion of child (*pais, paidon*) the notion of foot (*ped, pedis*),
we get a sense of "walking with one's own feet." We then restore to
the word "pedagogy" the meaning of leading, and acting on and for
our own, that expresses the goals of feminist pedagogies. We shall
also adopt the phrase "feminist ped-agogy," with a hyphen in "pedagogy" to remind us that we need to break with patriarchal traditions. In so doing, we transform and appropriate for ourselves the
images and language that so often exclude us.

A transformation of the word "pedagogy" also serves as a reminder
that we cannot engage in pedagogic romanticizing (nor in romantic
pedagogy). "Ped-agogy" tells us that transformations are difficult
and that the cleavage with patriarchal traditions is never clear, obvious, nor complete. As educators, we must work within a patriarchal
system, with the value judgments that this involves. Our marginal
and often marginalized efforts are fraught with the danger of what
the system calls "failures," a danger we must learn to daunt and
reverse. The word "ped-agogy" offers a hope of innovation and a
shelter against romanticism.

THE SUCCESS / FAILURE OF PRACTICE

In the institutions of learning where we dwell, the experience of success is always present with the surrounding tension of failure. Success and failure are issues because the patriarchal system labels the results of our life actions in these terms. First, we wish to express our vision of success, from a feminist point of view and with feminist goals in mind. Second, we wish to point out the necessity of being attentive to the patriarchy's definition of success. The first example of feminist success is described in Margo Culley's article, "Anger and Authority in the Introductory Women's Studies Classroom." When anger flares, women begin to see the bondage of ideology. She concludes: "Anger is a challenging and necessary part of life in the feminist classroom. Only when our anger has been felt and acknowledged, not denied, when it has been demonstrated to be grounded in a personal and collective sense of self-worth and not their opposite, can we hope that our students will join us in the remaining work to be done: a semester, and then a life-time, of affirmation and work for social change" (1985, 216).

We sense other successes in and with our students: new energy, self-direction, commitment, lively discussion, laughter, and the discovery of new, hidden interests of patriarchy. More explicit commentaries come to us from students through journals, notes, and thank-you cards:

I have more questions now than when I started this class. Actually, I didn't have any questions when I started the class ... I presented myself ready to be filled with knowledge. Ha! That was a misconception. I'm glad (Dorothy's journal, in a teacher education course, 1983).

The Ideas and activities we are generating in this class are incredible. What an experience – to get fourteen people together of all ages, experiences and backgrounds, as well as beliefs, teaching styles and opinions ... I'm finding out what I've been missing (Joan's journal, in a teacher education course, 1983).

Such words from students are indicators of the essential first measure of the success of our pedagogy: the unmasking of patriarchal ideology and the creation/discovery of our womanness/humanness. These are a few positive signs of women energizing and strengthening in their own becoming.

A fear of failure is also an experienced reality, however, when around us students (and some teachers) view education as a game played according to teachers' rules rather than as a step in personal and intellectual becoming. In this reality, the creation and discovery of our womanness and humanness, our foremost concern, is at risk of being marginalized to the goals of patriarchy's demands for conformity and passivity.[2]

We propose that, while we aim for success in our marginal domains as feminists with our marginalized goals of emancipation, we must also obtain a degree of success as it is defined by patriarchy. We propose a vision of bilingualism, that is, of living in two worlds, speaking the two languages of patriarchy and of feminism (and we can say the former, ironically, is our mother tongue). Bilingualism is difficult but necessary if we are to maintain, as individuals, the possibility of teaching. More importantly, however, and collectively so, feminist pedagogies need to succeed within patriarchy if they are to have a profound and lasting impact on the system that we want to challenge and change. We suggest, nevertheless, that success in feminist ped-agogy is not incompatible with some degree of success within patriarchal institutions.

The vision of bilingualism can restore a wholeness to education by reconciling objective and abstract knowledge with personal and lived experience. While the former is associated with patriarchy and the latter with women and other marginal groups, we must remind ourselves that most women teachers are bilingual. We have learned, memorized at times, the abstract lessons taught to us, but we can also dwell in and value the personal realm of experience. We frequently commute between the private and the public spheres of knowledge with amazing speed and are, as such, prime (if not some of the few available) agents of reconciliation. We can teach abstract knowledge, but we can also guide our students in examining its repercussions, and the value (if not truth) of their personal experience, as well as our own (Davis 1985). The dialectic between the two realms of knowledge is not only enriching but is a condition for success for feminist ped-agogies in patriarchal institutions.

While our notion of bilingualism is of and for women, we also suggest it is for men in our society. The feminist agenda naturally flows out of our stance as women, but in no way does it wish to exclude men students. Bilingualism also encourages men to see with other eyes, to examine the abstract through personal experiences, to claim their authentic space in the world. Transforming patriarchy is not a project that excludes men students and teachers. On the contrary, men also have a stake in fostering a better world.

THE NATURE OF FEMINIST PED-AGOGIES

In this section we focus on pedagogical praxis as we attempt to come to terms with our identity as women and teachers. As theoretical

writings on feminist ped-agogies emerge, we realize that our apparently lonely actions and reflections are paralleled by many
women. We have identified four themes which join together feminist
ped-agogies: (1) living and what matters; (2) participation and interaction; (3) collaboration and cooperation; and (4) teaching with
a vision.

Living and What Matters

A central feature of feminist ped-agogies is an enduring connectedness to the living, to the concrete. Either in beginning with the
concrete, in the sense of the perceptions and experiences of students
as the ground for formulating constructs and language, or in questioning language and theory by in-forming (forming within) experiences, feelings, and observations, the connection and relatedness
between thinking and experiencing is a dominant feature. From the
re-turn to experience, to living, arise questions such as: what does
this mean? What does this matter? This first feature of developing
personal meaning in relation to a problem is described by Dorothy
Buerk as allowing "each woman to make the problem meaningful
for herself and to clarify it both visually and verbally" (1986, 26).
One feature of conventional pedagogies, commonly described as set
induction or motivation, is a teacher activity. In feminist ped-agogies,
the questions of meaning and matter shift activity to the students,
permitting the women's own styles of learning to claim entry.

Re-storing the living and the context to the object of study, whether
it be a mathematical or a scientific concept, a word or an historical
event, is the first feature of the desired reversal of the relationship
between student and subject. The feminist ped-agogue desires that
students personalize the domain of study so that the object manip-
ulated and analyzed (in conventional pedagogies) is transformed into
a subject for their own becoming. Joan Countryman (1986) and
Dorothy Buerk (1986) describe this as restoring the "person-made"
quality to the domain of study. An historical perspective on knowledge enables students to recognize its human-made quality, and
encourages them to discover "their own personal and changing view
of the field" (Buerk 1986, 27). Such an invitation to enter any domain
of study encourages students not just to be consumers of pre-formed
knowledge, but to be active constructors of knowledge, appreciators
of the aesthetics of thinking, and discoverers of the part a domain
of study has in life.

In the re-turn to the living, to what matters, feminist pedagogies
risk being misinterpreted within the conventional pedagogical prac-

tices and structures of education. Traditionally, women's desire to alter the relationship between teacher and student and between student and subject, has been relegated to derivative and devalued forms of knowledge such as *applied* knowledge. This also has marginalized women's interests and practices (Peterat 1987, 31).

With the insistence on the connectedness, and on the relatedness between thinking and experiencing, the interpretation of knowledge by conventional pedagogical practices can be, and is being, demystified and unmasked. We are coming to see all knowledge in its human, social, and historical connections. Through such ped-agogical processes, students can claim a place within the domain of study and in society, opening up to new possibilities and to the hope of authenticity. With the living and the demand for connection, comes a restoring of community of self with others. Through this first feature of establishing individual relationship and meaning, arises the next, of participation and interaction.

Participation and Interaction

Participation and interaction have become themes of feminist pedagogies (Rich 1979; Maher 1985; Culley and Portugues 1985; Rosser 1986). As feminists, we struggle with the domination of classroom action and interaction by teachers and males. Although the problems of teacher authority and male student domination of class interaction arise from vastly different sources (the former stemming from an assigned role within an institution of learning, the latter from male socialization and legitimation by patriarchy), ultimately, they result in the same problem: domination of someone. Feminists undertake to praxeologically transform domination. In common parlance, the term "democratization" of ped-agogy would be used to describe this transformation. For feminists, it is democratization with a vision.

Gradually, we adopt a teaching style that favours participation and interaction by everyone. Through discussions, sharing of life and experiences is valued. Everyone's participation is important, and animation techniques allow the shyer, less expressive people to be drawn into the circle of sharing. Participation also means participation in decisionmaking; course outlines are presented as suggestions, and are open to negotiation. Periodic group evaluation allows a refocusing of course activities. Participation and interaction are also initiated at the very first class through an activity that requires the group as a whole to interpret one or two works which are central to the domain of study. This group work is then pooled in a class bank of definitions and interpretations; sections of particular interest are retained as part (if not all) of the course outline and class agenda. Through small group discussions, the students share their own lived experiences, and all students have the experience of leading these group discussions.

Class assignments are arranged so that students gain experience by teaching each other. They choose to research various topics, building on research done in previous years, and contribute to the growing classroom collection by leaving their work for students in succeeding years. Yet participation and interaction are not completely free-floating qualities in our classrooms. Since we believe that students should share the responsibilities for learning with the teacher, we must ensure that true sharing happens. We outline, sometimes in the first few meetings, a vision of supportive fairness where everyone assumes a responsibility to allow others to speak, to draw others in, and not to monopolize discussions. It is our responsibility as leaders to ensure, for example, that men, by virtue of their sex, do not reduce women to silence, as so often happens in social interaction. It is a very delicate task to ensure everyone their fair positive contribution, when we know that outside our classroom walls, rules that are contrary to participation, particularly women's participation, dominate. The key, perhaps, is to always be explicit about the vision of equity that guides us. We seldom encounter people who do not respond to the fairness of participation and interaction. On one occasion, a student brought this to our attention in her journal. Although she was one of the more talkative students in the class originally, she had clearly identified those who would dominate. She expressed in her journal why she found it so difficult to speak out in class. She was uncertain of her ability to form thoughts and to express them. Those who were dominating the class were those we had also identified as the strong, bright students. Unfortunately, this is often the case. We have found journal writing an important activity to encourage participation and confidence in students. Journal writing is another form of interaction, if we request to read them. Thoughts formed privately and reflectively by the students often enter the discussions in class. They become part of a continuing conversation which can be recalled and introduced either generally or specifically into the class discussion. Sharing our own writing with students, whether it be an article (in which case we would describe the context which gave rise to the article), or our own journal writing, is effective in establishing our equal positions as learners with our students.

Another obstacle to participation and interaction is viewing the teacher as an expert. One solution we choose is to value our own authentic searching. We realize that the answers we hold (experiential or theoretical knowledge) are only temporary answers. Before going into every class we affect a "cleaning of the slate" of knowledge (a *tabula rasa*). This allows us to truly hear what students are saying without posing as experts. Often we have been amazed at the knowledge emanating from them, and we ask ourselves why we need so many textbooks when each and everyone *is* an authentic text. Authenticity refers here to the "undisputed origin" (Morris 1980), the genuine authorship, of knowledge. Everyone becomes an authority, meaning that everyone can be the author of her or his own meanings. Along with the clearing of the slate, is the opening to multiple possibilities. The clearing of the slate is not forgetfulness, or denial, but rather an opening to the stories of students, and to various theories, in a clarifying and edifying process; a listening, communicating, translating process in which story informs theory, theory informs story, and story informs story. A "clean slate" attitude on the part of the feminist ped-agogue is also only part of the solution to the problem of domination by the teacher-asexpert. As we strive to transform social interactions in the classroom, we realize that we cannot at all times abdicate authority (in its conventional sense). Susan Stanford Friedman, in "Authority in the Feminist Classroom: A Contradiction in Terms?" remarks that: "As we attempt to move on to academic turf culturally defined as male, we need a theory that first recognizes the androcentric denial of *all* authority to women and, second, points out a way for us to speak with an authentic voice not based on tyranny" (1985, 207).

Perhaps we need to wonder if "authority" in its conventional sense is not the result of "authority" in its etymological sense of affirming author-ship. Just as students are author-ities when sharing their experiences, so is the feminist ped-agogue. The difference is the added "responsibility"; etymologically, an aptness to respond, a response-ability, to be assumed by the teacher. There is no need to pretend or to play a role. As our students participate and interact, we, the feminist ped-agogues, can be ourselves (as individuals), we can affect a "clean slate," listening anew to every experience, and we must see it as our responsibility to engage our response-ability. We are authorities in our personal and abstract knowledge and, as a result, authorities without tyranny. The basis is authenticity, not role play or pretence. The feminist ped-agogue finds gratification, not in having students accept her or others' stories, but rather in inspiring students in their own responseability and authenticity.

Collaboration and Cooperation

While interaction and participation aim at uprooting the tendency toward domination characteristic of patriarchy, a third focus of ped-agogy aims at changing its competitive features. Interaction and participation referred to activities; collaboration and cooperation name the attitude of connectedness that students and teachers adopt in a feminist classroom, cooperation being the stronger of the two. Collaboration and cooperation are found in a gradual blurring of boundaries between human beings; connections between individuals become a mode of understanding that restores the unity of human/kind, of a group.

This feature that we observe in feminist ped-agogies (Maher 1985; Culley and Portugues 1985; Friedman 1985) carries the danger of betrayal. It is interesting to note that women, having been oppressed for centuries, still wish to trust others, to make connections. It is as if our genes have not learned the lessons of history. Perhaps trust is one of the ingredients that leads to oppression. When placed opposite the drive to compete, trust appears as a weak alternative. For a child, though, trust is a precondition of maturity, and the time has perhaps come to hope that women can turn collaboration and cooperation into a positive force of interaction, a decision to trust oneself and others, but not to bow to oppression. Margo Culley relates how she sees the role of the feminist teacher: "In calling myself a feminist teacher, I take my charge from a statement made by Lucy Stone in 1885: 'In education, marriage, in religion, in everything, disappointment is the lot of women. It shall be the business of my life to deepen the disappointment in every woman's heart until she bows to it no longer'" (1985, 210). She indicates the moment when trust turns into a need for action.

We need to ponder further the word "betrayal," which comes from the Greek meaning "to give over" (Morris 1980, 1514). How often have we been disillusioned by a betrayal of our trust? How often have we realized that others do not work from ethics of collaboration/cooperation. For example, as one teacher says:

Part of the reality is that the notion of feminism is a very loose orientation – includes many in all stages and all kinds of beliefs. It is not cohesive. Women who you would expect to work from a feminist ethic don't, that is, trust, support other women. A petty incident with a senior member this week set me reeling – I no longer trust her. While we seemingly have similar goals re profession; our sense of politics, academics, etc. ... are worlds apart.

Women don't speak with the same voice. Trust is difficult to develop when some play according to masculist rules. Or are we self-deceiving to think it can be any other way? (Letter from a teacher, July 1986)

This teacher's words, along with Margo Culley's description of the mission of a feminist teacher, make clearly the point that tradition and treason are in fact related and have the same etymological root, and that patriarchal tradition has created a deeply engrained distrust that we live, even within our trust. The point of this discussion on trust is that, if trust is sometimes betrayed among feminists, then our classroom experiences will include a betrayal of trust. Cooperation will be an arduous task indeed, one in which discouragement will often breed.

But how else can competition be fought, other than with a perseverance of cooperation? We cannot oppose war with physical force, ask for peace by being violent, yell to a child to stop screaming. Can example not be the best teacher if, indeed, what we teach is how we teach? Despite the dangers and risks of betrayal, collaboration and cooperation are still the best means with which to overturn competition. The withdrawal from pedagogical romanticizing serves as a warning and as an encouragement. We must not be hurt by betrayal, but rather become stronger and more determined in the face of it.

Trust, collaboration, and cooperation allow a genuine understanding among individuals (Bordo 1986, 455). The authenticity of human interaction eradicates mistrust. Feminist ped-agogies favour specific approaches which rely on collaboration and cooperation. Some of these are:

Students can jointly write papers or prepare presentations.

Small discussion groups can rotate regularly so that everyone has, at some point, contact with everyone else in class.

Journal writings can be shared periodically.

Textbooks and other class materials can be shared when there are not enough for everyone.

Personal anecdotes can be shared, making the point that knowledge is social, not solitary.

Class desks can form a closed circle in the classroom.

Final exams can take the shape of group surveys, productions.

Drama techniques such as mime, improvisation, and playwriting can be employed, thus fostering small group projects and serving as class displays.

There is, however, no magic in these pedagogical examples, and feminists are not the only ones to incorporate them into their teaching. But the vision from which feminists work gives them specificity. Above all, however, cooperation/collaboration is an attitude that teachers communicate to their students. It transforms knowledge from a commodity into a construct, from a solitary activity to the social context. Success in this realm can only come when we, as teachers, enter the classroom with a desire to cooperate with our students.

We have come full circle, from ped-agogies to risks to a reformed notion of authenticity. But, full circle has reached a new plateau. Cooperation is normal in a feminist classroom because there is a common vision lurking on the horizon. We care and we hope for a better world.

Teaching with a Vision

Feminist ped-agogies convert praxeologically the abstract knowledge favored by patriarchy. To the abstract, rational, and distanced ideal of knowledge, feminist ped-agogies offer the passion of vision, our authentic heart-felt hopes for a better present and future.

There is a sense of urgency in feminist writings in general, and in feminist descriptions of ped-agogy in particular. Janice Raymond notes: "It is true that we must not preach. But we must passionately teach. Scholars of women's studies are models of a particular sort of mind – a feminist response to the world of learning. We are deeply involved in the things we study. We cannot pretend we do not care. We look at our subject with passion because we are our subject. The basic attitude of the feminist scholar is existential" (1985, 58). Janice Raymond's words can be extended to all feminist teaching. When the world of learning and teaching comes to be seen from a feminist point of view, there is no going back, and all subjects are touched, all knowledge is touched, even though our teaching sometimes seems like a subversive activity in deeply patriarchal domains.

Teaching with passion for change: that's what makes all the difference to feminist ped-agogies. This is called "passionate" pedagogy and scholarship by Barbara Dubois (1983), Janice Raymond (1985), and Jo Anne Pegano (1986). Restoring passion and a vision (of a better present/future) into our teaching affects an interesting transfiguration of the nature of valued knowledge in patriarchy. To abstraction, we bring the concreteness of the discovery of our oppressed, daily lived experience. To calm rationality, we bring emotions of revolt, of anger, of hope. To distance, we bring closeness and connectedness. The inversion could be called the authentication of knowledge, since the movement of questioning knowledge to the heart of our life revives the purpose of learning, its "raison d'être." Susan Bordo documents the historic masculinization of thought. She postulates that the Cartesian split between objectivity and subjectivity within Descartes' own life and within the seventeenth-century's flight from "the feminine" played an important part in women's exclusion from knowledge. The point is that, at this present moment in our history, valued knowledge ideologically excludes women and epistemologically favours the masculine. We know that "masculine" and "feminine" are social genderizations, and that:

The recent scholarly emergence and revaluation of epistemological and ethical perspectives that have been identified as feminine in classical as well as contemporary writing (as e.g., in the work of Carol Gilligan, Sarah Ruddick, and Nancy Chodorow) claim a natural foundation for knowledge not in detachment and distance, but in closeness, connectedness, and empathy ... An appreciation of the historical nature of the masculine model of knowledge to which this "different voice" is often contrasted helps to underscore that the embodiment of these gender-related perspectives in actual men and women is a cultural, not a biological phenomenon. (Bordo 1986, 455)

Bringing passion of vision to our teaching enables a welding of the knowledge of patriarchy with our own. Feminist pedagogies bring about the necessary transformation of knowledge. The valuing of concrete lived experiences, emotions, and connectedness is validated and legitimated by the most powerful force – our vision of a better present and a better future for women and men.

Jane Roland Martin gives a nice specificity to the inclusion of "feminine" traits into teaching. She speaks of the three C's – care, concern and connection. She concludes: "Masculinity and femininity do not have to be construed as polar opposites, but in fact they are. Thus, in seeking ways to promote generative love as well as rational mind in all students, educators will have to reckon not only with the phenomenon of trait genderization but with the underlying cultural construct of gender itself" (1986, 10). Our passionate vision within ped-agogy is fostered by care, concern, and connectedness. In turn, our vision within ped-agogy transforms the knowledge of patriarchy. We are witnessing another success of our pedagogies and again, that success emanates from a movement to authenticity of emotions and lived experiences as they become integrated within the curriculum.

On the one hand, the success we see in a vision that allows a transformation of valued knowledge cannot be claimed as success in patriarchal terms. Vision often isolates us from the established system, and understandably so; what interest does patriarchy have in the overthrowing of its own values? Patriarchy has built elaborate systems of protection and power in order to guard against such visions.

On the other hand, the authentic, passionate vision of feminist ped-agogies guarantees the strength of our marginality as a precondition for the development of women's knowledge as "feminine" knowledge. The difficulties here are enormous for ped-agogical concerns. Many who will accept and abide by the concepts of equity and fairness, will not wish women to foster the development of a "feminine" cultural identity. Yet, for "feminine" knowledge and culture to flourish, marginality has to be prized separation (Raymond 1985) so as not to be overpowered by masculinized thought, and yet be able to return to the system and transform it. Marginality, a dialectic between separateness and union (Martel and Peterat, forthcoming) allows a mutation of the patriarchal system. Susan Bordo concludes:

The historical identification of rationality and intelligence with the masculine modes of detachment, distance, and clarity has disclosed its limitations, and it is necessary (and inevitable) that feminized modes should now appear as revealing more innovative, more humane, and more hopeful perspectives. Clearly, the (unmythologizing) articulation of "the feminine" – and its potential contribution to ethics, epistemology, science, education, and politics – is one of the most important movements of the twentieth century. (1986, 456)

AUTHENTICITY IN PED-AGOGY

Authenticity, a word that we find echoed more and more frequently in feminist scholarship, expresses a vision of finding for ourselves grounds that are "worthy of trust, having an undisputed origin" (Morris 1980, 88–9; Martel 1986). It is a longing to raise our consciousness to the point where we eliminate false consciousness, a longing to reach our own primal grounds. What these grounds are, we don't know. What culture they will create, we cannot identify yet. We are undergoing a transition, a transformation (another word often used in this paper). Joan Roberts indicates the "emerging and changing phases" of women's culture, and the different conceptions that we all have of women's plight and of paradigm change. As for the future of this emerging culture, she says: "Despite the multiple problems in role change and role models, it is comforting for all women to know that their actions contribute to the larger scheme of things – a universal progression of morality away from geocentric, species-centric, ethnocentric, and androcentric world views toward a new social reality. In this new reality power is not based on "muscle as a measure of morality," or on the capacity of male culture to enforce its will by force of arms" (1985, 73). Authenticity, then, refers to authorship, to the creating, as authors, of a new world in which women are genuinely included as participants.

But authenticity is named with who in mind? We have spoken of "we" – "we as women," "we as teachers," "we as feminists," "we as feminist ped-agogues" – because we/I as individuals see ourselves in this way. For us, this naming – and the experience that stems from it – becomes an expression of authenticity. We are very much in this article, and it reflects a specific level of consciousness, our own. The word "we" was also an invitation for you as reader, as listener, male or female, to enter authentically into a sharing of consciousness with the option to acquiesce or disagree. Authenticity involves, then, first and foremost our author-ship, our author-ity, and the liberty of others to share with us.

We have, furthermore, indicated how authenticity as authorship can transform domination through participation and interaction. "Authenticity" replaced "empowerment" as a goal of our ped-agogies mainly because to speak of empowerment does not alter the system of domination, it mostly reverses who has power. Authenticity, in our ped-agogies, is not a case of presence or absence, but rather is a positive driving force of author-ship and author-ity that is attentive to context and to individuals, and is able to assume reponse-ability when the moment comes. Authenticity also allows us to live bilingually within our disciplines in order to succeed both on our grounds and on the grounds of patriarchy. It keeps the system from thinking: "Let the girls/women participate and collaborate as they wish but, when it comes to important and crucial matters, let the men put 'rigour'/efficiency back into the subject."

Authenticity was also contrasted with competition, through collaboration and cooperation. The attitude of authenticity values self and others. It is based on human possibility rather than on human denial. Collaboration and cooperation demand an attitude of trust, that is the only option if competition is to be altered and eventually eradicated. Trust is a dimension of authenticity because it is an effort to reach the genuineness of self and others.

Authenticity, as a vision, and as an attitude furthermore keeps us from romanticizing about our pedagogies. Authenticity requires that we remain attentive to every context, every individual, and every class; that we search for genuineness in ourselves, and in our way of being with students. It means that there is no such praxis as pedagogy but there are only pedagogies, multiple facets of being in the classroom.

This article is an effort to live the pedagogies we speak about in our research and writing projects. We describe feminist ped-agogies, our own, and reflections on others. We reach a certain realism in our praxis and proposals. We value the notion of marginality for the central tension it sustains betweeen being simultaneously a part of and not a part of conventional pedagogy. We hyphenate ped-agogy as a symbol of this marginality, a reminder that our individual ped-agogies flourish within broader institutional and social structures and meanings of ped-agogy. We are concerned that feminist ped-agogy not be patriarchy's present flirtation with progressivism, but rather that it be a fundamental influence toward a new education and humanness. We assert that feminist ped-agogies depart from other progressive pedagogies in that they are pedagogies with a vision, valuing difference. We hold a vision of the good and desirable life as a symphony orchestra rather than a military parade. Thus, we depart from the notion of empowerment, attempting to avoid a mere reversal of social power, choosing rather the notion of au-thenticity in the sense of author-ship. The extent that we succeed in being authentic in this work is the extent to which we contribute to the articulation of womanness and to a woman's culture. At the same time, the extent to which men can sympathize and empathize is the extent to which we have reached humanness.

NOTES

1 We developed the notion of womanness in an earlier paper, to describe the primordial knowing/being of women (Martel and Peterat, forthcoming). In this paper we retain the notion as essential to women forming an authentic identity, claiming difference when it matters and disclaiming difference when it doesn't matter, in a gender-sensitive ideal (Roland Martin 1986). It is also a notion essential to those who consider that one purpose of feminism is to counter the gendercentrism dominant in present society.

2 Martel and Peterat explore marginality as a social reality expressed through values and power relationships, by chronicling the ways that women, through schooling, lose the authority of their own being (forthcoming).

HOLLY DEVOR

Teaching Women's Studies to Male Inmates[1]

The author compares students in a first year introductory women's studies course, run at an all-male, medium security prison, with previous classes of exclusively female students in this course. The male inmate students were highly motivated and vocal. They expressed a similar level of stereotypical attitudes as on-campus students did, and appeared to be receptive to the ideas of the course to a comparable degree. Their written work was poorer, in many cases, than that done by on-campus students, while their participation rate in classroom discussions was noticeably higher. All in all, the male inmate students appeared to benefit from the course at least as much, in the shortterm, as any previous group of women's studies students.

L'enseignement des études féministes à des détenus masculins

La professeure compare les étudiants d'un cours de première année d'Introduction aux études sur les femmes, organisé pour des hommes dans un milieu carcéral à sécurité intermédiaire, avec un groupe d'un cours précédent composé presque exclusivement d'étudiantes. Les détenus masculins étaient très motivés et loquaces. Ils exprimaient les mêmes attitudes stéréotypées que les étudiants du campus universitaire, et étaient tout aussi réceptifs aux idées proposées dans le cours. Dans bien des cas, leur travail écrit était de qualité inférieur à celui des étudiants, mais leur degré de participation aux discussions en classe étaient sensiblement supérieur. Somme toute, les détenus semblaient, à court terme, avoir bénéficié du cours tout autant que les autres groupes d'étudiants qui avaient déjà suivi le cours d'Études sur les femmes.

Simon Fraser University, in conjunction with the Correctional Services of Canada, offers university credit courses in four federal penal institutions in southwestern British Columbia. This program is unique in that regular university courses are taught by university faculty within the confines of the prisons. Inmates involved in this program are enrolled at Simon Fraser University, usually as special-entry mature students. They may complete their BA degrees while incarcerated, or may continue their studies with no change of student status if they are released from prison before graduation. Most courses offered are drawn from a humanities program and may be combined with correspondence courses to complete degree requirements over a period of several years.

Matsqui Institution is one of the four institutions which hosts the university education program for inmates. Matsqui is located in a rural setting in southwestern British Columbia. It is a medium security institution housing an all-male population of approximately 350. Education is one of several work assignments that an inmate may choose. As a work assignment, education offers few advantages; it has a low rate of pay, and requires inmates to spend relatively long hours in the classroom and doing homework. One might assume that the thirty-five to forty inmates who choose and remain with this program each trimester do so for the rewards of education itself.

The Academic Centre is set off from other areas of the prison by the chain link fencing used throughout the prison. Entrance to the area is through a small guardhouse where there are ususally two guards on duty. Beyond that point, the student normally has no further contact with guards throughout his day. As a result, the atmosphere in the Academic Centre is considerably more relaxed than it is in other areas within the institution, and the spirit of free thought and lively inquiry is remarkably present in the university classrooms within the prison.

Each instructor is greeted by new students with a certain amount of wariness. Inmates seem to be concerned, rightly, that instructors not condescend to them, condemn them, or fear them. It is important for the inmates to know whether they can speak freely in the presence of an instructor, or whether they must fear that their remarks will find their way back to the prison administration. A successful student-instructor relationship must be based on easy communication. But in the prison environment, anyone who appears to be on easy and friendly terms with inmates is seen by the guards as suspect, and anyone who is on friendly terms with the guards, is seen by the inmates as suspect. As a result, relations between guards and instructors remain cool.

THE COURSE AND THE STUDENTS

I first offered "Perspectives on Women: An Introduction to Women's Studies as an elective at Matsqui Institution in the first trimester of 1986. This course had never been offered in any of the prisons before, nor had it ever been taught to an all-male class before. The course has been running more or less continually for ten years on the campus of Simon Fraser University with myself acting as teaching assistant during five of those ten years. The same course has also been offered by correspondence since late 1984 with a larger minority of men enrolled under those conditions.

The class began with an initial enrollment of twenty-six students. This number represented a little more than half of the entire university program population of forty-seven students and was the largest enrollment of any course that semester.[2] The number had dwindled to fifteen by the fourth week of class, the time when students had to pay their fees if they were to continue the course. A total of twelve students completed the thirteen-week course. Most of the men who took this class claimed to be there simply out of curiosity. One said that he came to women's studies to find out why his three marriages had failed. Another said that he was there because he thought that "women are a very hard subject."

The men who remained with the course past the final drop date ranged in age from twenty-two to fifty years, with most of them being in their thirties.[3] They came from diverse class, educational, ethnic, and racial backgrounds. Two identified themselves as coming from the middle class, while the rest of them came from less advantaged backgrounds. Several of the students had already completed a substantial number of university credits, while others had only recently completed their high school equivalency course.[4] Ten of the students were Caucasian, one was oriental, and one was Polynesian.

The inmates who attended this course were incarcerated for crimes against both person and property. The crimes that they were convicted of included assault with a deadly weapon, assault causing bodily harm, extortion, bank robbery, smuggling, living off the avails of prostitution, murder, and politically motivated destruction of property. Four students had been convicted of murder (two of whom admitted to having comitted the murder themselves) and were serving life sentences. Most of the men who took this course freely admitted that they had long histories of criminal activity (up to thirty years). Those who were imprisoned on first offenses were in the minority. This distribution may reflect the type of inmate who has the motivation to become a student. The women's studies students tended to be older individuals who had longer sentences and thus had longer expanses of time to fill.

The course was given in a lecture/seminar format supplemented by films and video tapes. Class time totalled four hours each week, for which students received four credits. The reading material for the course consisted almost entirely of reprints gathered from diverse sources. I varied the curriculum to reflect both my differences in philosophy from previous instructors and my perceptions of the needs of this particular student body. Where possible, reading material and general course contents were chosen which would encourage the personal emotional involvement of the students. The social and psychological aspects of women's lives was emphasized, and facts and figures were presented, along with evocative personal testimonials. The course differed from the one given on campus in that it was organized to be more emotionally demanding and to give more attention to a feminist perspective on masculinity.

"Perspectives on Women: An Introduction to Women's Studies," as taught at Matsqui Institution, consisted of six main sections. The course began with an exploration of the biological bases of sex and gender differences and similarities. This was followed by a brief look at evolutionary theories and the possible lessons to be gained from the study of technologically primitive societies. The second section covered psychological theories of the development of gender during early childhood, youth, and adolescence. This section also included a discussion of the physical and sexual abuse of children. The third section looked at the economic position of women, beginning with pre-industrial societies and ending with the status of women in unions and in nontraditional work. This was followed by several weeks of discussion on the institution of marriage, during which time economic, emotional, and psychological aspects of marriage for both men and women were examined. Subtopics included children and childcare, sexual relations, housework, and wife battering. The fifth section began with a look at the ways that women are portrayed in the arts, advertising, and the media. This led into a discussion of pornography, which was followed by classes devoted to the questions of rape and prostitution. The final weeks' classes were spent in study of a feminist utopian novel[5] and a history of some of the accomplishments of the women's rights movements in Canada, England, and the US.

Throughout the course I attempted to build in the students a sense of empathy with the experiences of women. It was helpful to call on similarities between the experiences of the students and the experiences of women. I therefore repeatedly made comparisons between sex/gender prejudice and class, racial, and ethnic discrimination. It also proved useful to call on their own experiences as powerless and disenfranchised people within the prison system. I felt that it was important that these students not feel personally blamed for the circumstances of women in general, but that they should be encouraged to examine their particular contributions to the social relations which they had experienced. It was also essential that they understood that feminist agendas offered increased freedom for both men and women, and that acceptance of the premises of the course would not lock them, as men, into losing and blame-filled situations.

It also proved necessary for me to be able to communicate with the students through the culture of men, from the perspective of women. This required that I be able to couch the messages of the course in terms that would be sufficiently familiar to the students to enable them to grasp the ideas easily, without obscuring the feminist nature of the material. The composition of the group, as both inmates and men, meant that they functioned within an extremely masculine social order which placed a high value on the concealment of emotions, on voracious sexuality, on toughness, and on a disregard for authority and middle-class social values. Thus, I had to find ways to evoke emotion and empathy in the students without myself appearing to be weak or emotionally involved. This meant that I was forced to validate larger portions of their masculine reality than I would otherwise have been inclined to do, in order to use their reality as a starting point in leading them to a feminist analysis of their experiences. It also meant that I tailored my style of delivery to be coarser and more hard hitting than I would normally use in a women's studies classroom. I also found it necessary to take a "one of the boys" attitude in the many discussions which alluded to sex, lest the classroom become infused with sexual tensions which would undermine my credibility as an instructor.

STUDENT RESPONSES TO THE COURSE

Overall, the response of the male inmate students to women's studies was enthusiastic. Attendance throughout the course remained unusually high and discussion was always spirited. I was continually surprised at the almost total absence of hostility and argument from the students. There seemed to be an exceptional willingness to hear, as one student put it, "the answers to the questions you never even thought to ask."

The information and analysis which I used was generally accepted, but there were times when the generalized information I offered did not match the personal experiences of the students. These occasions became excellent opportunities to explore class, ethnic, and regional differences in the roles of women, and to look at the ways that masculine and feminine roles sometimes cause individuals to perceive shared experiences very differently. It was usually possible, through discussion and exchange of ideas, to arrive at a confluence of opinions.

The greatest areas of contention centred around the romantic masculine notions of sexuality which surfaced during our discussions of marital relations, rape, pornography, and prostitution. The men in this course seemed to be strongly attached to the belief that women consistently derive satisfaction from sexual intercourse and therefore desire it as ardently as men do. They were very resistant to the idea that many women find their sexual relations with men disappointing, and that they often engage in them for reasons other than sexual release. They seemed to be unwilling, or unable, to dispassionately consider women's experiences of sexuality when they felt it reflected poorly on their own.

The most difficult ideas to convey were those concerned with the depth of the effects of feminine socialization to passivity, and the enforcement of passivity through structural barriers to female power. As men who had taken the masculine ideals of physical and emotional toughness and independence to extremes, they often found it difficult to understand why women would accept situations and conditions which they themselves would find humiliating and unbearable. Their life experiences told them that if a situation was unacceptable to them, they could force it to change or leave it behind. The idea that one's attachments to other adults or children, or the enormity of a social structure, might stop one from taking action, was foreign to them.

The students showed the least interest in any discussion which was entirely theoretical. They were curious about employment and income statistics for women but appeared to be uninterested in theoretical explanations of that situation. They were surprised to find how large the differences were between the earning powers of men and women, and especially surprised to find that increased education still left women in lower income brackets than men with similar training. Nonetheless, there was little support for the idea of gainful employment as a method of improving women's status. They seemed to hold the attitude that anyone who worked at a regular job was being foolishly exploited by his or her boss. As one man said: "Most of us wouldn't be here in the first place if we believed in working for a living."

The student's responses to me as the instructor varied during the course, and among individuals. At the beginning of the course, some students attempted to impress me with their civility, knowledge, and willingness to learn. They seemed to be concerned that I not see them as ignorant and dangerous criminals. Others took a more "wait and see" attitude, neither challenging me, nor putting forward any more than was minimally demanded of them. Still others seemed to be intent on testing my response to a thinly veiled display of sexualized machismo. This last group rapidly dropped out of the course when they realized that they would be unable to gain any control over the situation through such methods. Gradually the other two types relaxed into a group of individuals eager for the pleasures of learning.

The atmosphere in the classroom was generally free-flowing. Students appeared to feel free to initiate side discussions, and to ask questions or debate any topic which came to mind. As the course progressed, the students coalesced into a sort of working unit with a "team spirit" and an apparent faith in my leadership. Around the time that my testing by the students came to an end, the course material had accelerated in intensity, and the students had begun to show signs of feeling challenged by the content of the discussions and reading assignments. There were many hours of classroom time where the silence during lectures was intense and focussed, each man seeming to be inwardly reliving and reexamining his own experiences and the topic under discussion. Many classes ended with an almost palpable feeling in the room of the group having "gone through" something together. But, because the social code of extreme masculinity allows one the option of expressing only a very narrow range of emotions, it was rare for a student to do more than sigh and say, "that was a heavy class." Nevertheless, it was clear to me that the students were challenged, moved, and in some ways changed by what they were learning about themselves and about women.

The effects of this progression of consciousness could most clearly be seen in the nature of the interaction which took place after regular class time. I usually stayed after class to engage in informal conversation with students about anything that they chose to bring up. Over time, more and more students began staying for these social visits, which lasted longer and longer. As a rapport was established, topics became more personal, and students from other classes joined in. It was during this informal time that students began to speak about their emotional responses to the course, to exhibit their sense of camaraderie with me by disclosing personal information, and to include me in their inmate talk and social assumptions.

Students used this time with me to make revelations about themselves, both as criminals and as men. It was during such sessions that the stories of their past crimes and their times in court were related. It was also after class that they told me those things about their relations with their wives, girlfriends, and lovers that they would not admit in the public forum of the classroom. Even more telling were the stories that they related to me about the many times that they had transgressed their own understanding of the limits of the code of masculinity. Those were the times when they felt free enough, and safe enough, to speak about having experimented with wearing women's clothing, allowing a woman to take the lead in sexual relations, or finding a sexual thrill in the act of murder. They used the more casual time after class both to boast and confess; acts which court attention and intimacy, which display interest and trust.

At the conclusion of the course, an informal social was held and the students were asked to fill out course evaluation forms. Both of these provided opportunities for the students to express their feelings about the course. Overall the students expressed very positive feelings about the course. Five of the twelve men who completed the course felt that a similar course should be required of all students, two of them specifically stated that they thought the course should be required for university graduation, one suggested that every inmate in the prison should be required to take the course, and another man thought the course should be taught in elementary schools before young people had a chance to develop bad habits.

Three men said that they were saving their reading materials and passing them on to friends. One man had been giving them to his wife to read along with him as he progressed through the course, and another (twenty-odd year veteran of the criminal life) had been trying to get his nineteen-year-old daughter to read the course material in the hope that the information would help her to become better equipped to take care of herself as she made her way in the world. The third was saving his as a reference work on feminism. Eight of the twelve students completed course evaluation forms. In reply to one of the questions on the form, two of them said that they would like to minor in women's studies, and six students said that they might take another women's studies course if it fit into their course schedules.

At the end of the social, every student took the time to warmly thank me for my part in the course. They seemed genuinely pleased

to have had the opportunity to take this women's studies course and
made a point of making individual statements to that effect.

MALE INMATE STUDENTS COMPARED TO ON-CAMPUS STUDENTS

The inmate students differed from the usual on-campus students
on several counts. First, the major difference is the fact that they
were all men, unique for a women's studies class. Not only were the
inmate students men, but they were men who were more experienced generally, and more experienced in more marginal lifestyles
than the usual women's studies students. Previous classes on campus
had never drawn more than four male students in a lecture session
(less than ten percent) and it was not unusual for a class to be composed entirely of female students. Those male students who attended
women's studies courses on campus were mostly young, white, and
middle class, and in some way closely associated with at least one
feminist. The inmate students tended to be older than the on-campus
students, and to come from less privileged backgrounds. Thus, they
came to the course and the material with significantly different life
histories and perspectives from the customary groups of mostly
young, middle-class, female university students.

Introductory women's studies courses on campus have always
drawn more students than the Matsqui course did, so that campus
classes are larger and less intimate than the prison class. This may
have been a factor in the relatively high degree of student interaction
in the prison setting. It also seems likely that several of the students
in the prison were considerably more vocal as individuals, and would
have been so under any circumstances. The fact that the class was
comprised entirely of men who live closely together and who have
been collectively socialized to be more aggressive than a group of
young middle-class women, also contributed considerably to the
lively discussions which were a regular feature of the class. On a day-
by-day basis, a larger percentage of inmate students were more vo-
cally involved in classroom discussions than is normally the case on
campus.

The subject matter that the inmate students found most and least
interesting paralleled closely the pattern among on-campus students.
The male inmate students responded to the course in ways which
reflected their life experiences, which differed in many ways from
those of on-campus students, but they were interested and bored by
similar subjects. For example, "socialization" and "pornography" are
sections of the course which students usually find absorbing. The

male students found a feminist analysis of masculine socialization fascinating, and were able to use it to examine their own upbringing. Female women's studies students focus more heavily on feminine socialization, but in a similar way. The subject of pornography, on the other hand, while of equal interest to both types of students, had to be approached quite differently for the male group. When the subject is taught to a female class, because of women's general lack of exposure to the medium, the bulk of the time is spent in an introduction to the content of pornography. When discussing pornography with a group of male criminals, one can safely assume that they are already well acquainted with both the form and content of pornography, and proceed into a more sophisticated discussion.

Both inmate students and campus students seemed to be interested in all the topics studied, with the exception of psychological theories and theoretical analyses of women's economic position. The male students did not seem to be particularly attached to masculinist visions of either biology or evolution. They seemed to find the "woman the gatherer" theory of evolution as tenable as the "man the hunter" theory. Questions of psychological and socialization processes proved to be as fascinating to the male inmate students as they generally have been to female students on campus, but the male students were more involved in the problems of masculine socialization. The male inmate students also seemed to be somewhat shocked, but willing to learn, that women with training equal to that of men still earn far less than men do, while young female students on campus often resist believing that such is really the case. Women students usually enthusiastically embrace the idea that economic improvement for women can come through their efforts to enter into traditionally male, working-class jobs. The men said they had found the jobs they had done to be unrewarding and/or dangerous, and couldn't see why anyone would want to do that kind of work. They expressed the attitude that no one should have to do the "dirty work," no matter how well paid it was.

The topic of marriage was taught somewhat differently in the prison version of the course. I placed more emphasis on psychological aspects of long-term intimate unions, and the question of wife battering was dealt with in some detail. The course, as it is taught on campus, touches only lightly on intimacy and wife battering, and instead focuses more on housework. In the prison course, I attempted to impress upon the students the vast extent of the problem of wife battering and to explain, from a feminist perspective, some of the reasons men batter and women remain in battering relationships as long as they do. The men generally condemned wife batterers, but also tended to want to blame women for not leaving such relationships immediately. This section was very attentively received and prompted much spirited discussion. A similar unit on campus passes with less student involvement.

The weeks of the course which dealt with wife battering, pornography, rape, and prostitution followed closely on one another. The campus course follows a similar development, although it does not treat wife battering and prostitution as whole sections in their own right. In teaching about pornography, I took the approach that pornography acts as a form of sex education, and explored the messages that pornography teaches about sexual relations between men and women. I asked the men to remember how pornography had shaped their sexual appetites in their youth, and to consider whether they felt that the messages of pornography were healthy for men and women to learn. The men confirmed that pornography had influenced their sexuality and they condemned slasher, snuff, and kiddie porn. Although they were willing to state that it should not be freely available, they were not willing to endorse any measures which they perceived to be censorship of pornography.

In discussing rape, I explained how rape is tremendously underreported, and that it is unlikely that a man charged with rape will be convicted of it. I talked about the social message in the way rape is handled in our society and our criminal justice system. In explaining the differences between stranger rape, date rape, and soft rape, I concentrated on trying to get these men to understand that much of what they consider to be seduction is perceived as rape by women. The men started by being quite vocal in their condemnation of rapists, but when I started to explain about women acquiescing to unwanted sex out of fear of reprisals for refusing to cooperate, they grew quieter and more thoughtful. It seemed clear to me that they were coming to the realization that they had forced themselves on women whom they had thought of at the time as merely having succumbed to their superior powers of seduction. This was not an easy realization for many of them, and they tried to argue that women really wanted sex as ardently as they did. Nonetheless, I think that the message got through.

Prostitution had not been previously taught as part of introductory women's studies. I included it because it was a hotly debated issue in the local press at the time, and because I knew that most of my students had some experience with prostitution. I suspected that their opinions of women were infused with the madonna/whore dichotomy, so I wanted to address the question of what makes women into "whores." I explained prostitution as a job option which was usually turned to in desperation. I pointed out that many young women start out in prostitution after years of sexual abuse in their parental homes. I placed prostitution in the context of the limited economic options of most women, often in combination with the sole responsibility for young children and a history of abuse in the family home. Because these men often came from abusive homes themselves, and did not perceive themselves as having many economic options, I also had to explain that women turn to prostitution rather than bank robbery or drug dealing because of the particular pressures of female socialization.

Both campus and prison students responded similarly to these issues; they were depressed by the barrage of "bad news." But female students, especially the younger ones, tend to resist believing much of the material on wife battering, rape, and pornography; they seem to want to believe that the statistics are inflated and the case exaggerated. The inmate students, however, were willing to believe the severity of the situation, many of them having first-hand experience of wife battering, pornography, rape, and prostitution.

The inmate students were able to empathize sufficiently with the situation of women to independently recognize that life under such circumstances could easily result in women becoming fearful and/ or distrustful of men in general. Some of the men seemed to be hurt by this judgement by women but were able to see how it was a sensible response to a social structure which is dangerous to women. Not all of them, however, were able to make the leap from being outraged by the idea of men abusing women as an outlet for their own feelings, to the idea that patriarchal violence is not the solution to any conflict. One man commented that all of the men who beat up their wives "had better look out when us guys who have taken women's studies get out." He contended that the women's studies students would beat up the batterers, and that their grateful wives would fall in love with the men who had protected them and leave their abusive husbands for the arms of the enlightened and respectful ex-women's studies students.

The feminist novel studied in the prison course, Marge Piercy's *Woman on the Edge of Time* (1976), was not the one that is used on-campus. The inmates' response to a feminist vision of utopia was instructive. While they found the story interesting and the vision generally appealing, they were not able to suspend their experience of human nature sufficiently to accept the utopian vision. Their experience of human nature included an incorrigible dose of viol-

ence, brutality, and antisocial insanity. They were unwilling, or unable, to envision a human world without violent and dangerous
people in it.

The inmate students' responses to their instructor was, as a whole,
more enthusiastic than has been the case with on-campus students.
This may be, in part, a result of the smaller class size, but the almost
complete isolation of the inmate students from social contact with
people from outside the prison, and women in particular, probably
accounts for the greatest part of their openness, enthusiasm, and
eagerness to please. The student "testing" of their instructor, which
occurred at the beginning of the prison course, has never been
observed in on-campus classrooms, but the high level of enthusiasm
for the course and for me as the instructor was also exceptional.

All in all, the course can easily be said to have been as successful
as campus courses. The students were at least as receptive to feminist
analysis as any other group of women's studies students have been,
and were no more resistant to new concepts than any other group.
The classroom environment was more animated than in campus
classrooms and the level of inquiry was, at times, more probing than
on campus. The inmate students were more demanding than on-
campus students, but they gave of themselves as generously as they
asked.

SPECULATION AND SUGGESTIONS

The experience of teaching women's studies to a group of male
inmates proved to be both challenging and rewarding. The intense
interest and involvement of the students came as a pleasant and
exciting surprise to everyone associated with the course.[6] The students' reports of their willingness to withstand derogatory comments
from their peers, guards, and parole board members, and to stand
up for women's rights in front of other prisoners, revealed a commitment to the course and its contents which well surpassed all expectations.

Women's studies offered these students an exceptional opportunity in many ways. The course approached a topic which, it seemed,
had been a mystery to these men all their lives. Each man had his
own reasons for wanting to understand women better, but all shared
an ignorance of women. Extremely masculine people are not supposed to show any interest in femininity, except to control, possess,
and enjoy the people who most display it. This leaves "masculine
men" in a difficult position: they are supposed to be able to manipulate, control, and take pleasure in women without showing any

interest in understanding them. Women's studies offered these men an environment where it was legitimate and safe to ask questions and learn about women without losing face.

The inmate students came to the course in the rare condition of being almost entirely stripped of the usual male privileges. This, combined with the experiences of most of them as underprivileged people in the "outside" world, probably predisposed them to empathize with the experiences of women as powerless and disenfranchised people. When I introduced them to some of the realities of women's everyday experience, and made analogies to their own experiences within the prison system and in their upbringings, these men were able to see many of the similarities that are obscured for most men by their own power, and their self-interested attachment to the status quo. As prisoners, and as men who had rarely held any aspirations to success in mainstream society, they had few reasons to resist an analysis which attacked that system without directly attacking them.

The most senior and influential students also came to the course with a fairly well developed left-wing analysis of capitalism. They were vocal in their opinions and lent support, on many occasions, to the analysis I put forward. It was not a difficult adjustment for them to see the connections between the exploitation of workers' labour power and patriarchal capitalism's exploitation of women's productive and reproductive powers. They were mentally and emotionally prepared to understand the effects of such a system on the people whose lives are controlled by it. Unlike many of the young, middle-class women who take this course on campus, these men had been extensively exposed to the ugly underbelly of capitalism, and had few reasons to believe that the same socio-economic system that they had seen badly degrading and exploiting other human life would not control female lives in a similar way.

The few areas where they were resistant to the ideas put forward in the course might also have been, in part, a reflection of their circumstances as prisoners. As prisoners, they were constantly confronted with the reality that they could neither change the parameters of their everyday lives nor leave their situation at will. They seemed to be particularly attached to the idea that this is a condition of imprisonment, and that life outside prison is free from such restraints. Thus, the idea that such a dilemma could also exist for women who are "free" was a difficult one for them to accept.

Being imprisoned also seemed to affect their attitudes toward sexuality. Their access to female sexuality is extremely and carefully limited by forces almost entirely beyond their control, yet the social system within the prison places a heavy emphasis on the desirability of engaging in sexuality with women. Because of their restricted access to women, and a social code which encourages and rewards heterosexual activity, they seemed very attached to the myth that anyone who was not so restricted would be constantly eager for sex. Thus, prison conditions might explain their resistance to a feminist analysis of sexual experiences with men. On the other hand, this same social code probably contributed, at least initially, to the students' intense attention to me. It seemed evident that these students were very eager to please me and were starved for a positive female appraisal of them. It is possible that their desire to please was so strong that they made an effort to go beyond merely parroting the material, to understanding and accepting it.

On the basis of the positive outcome of this course, I strongly suggest that more courses of this nature be offered in the future. There are several elements in the success of this course which seemed to be particular to the prison setting, but there were a sufficient number of elements which would be common to any group of men to suggest that women's studies courses for men could also be successful in other environments. It is certainly true that prisoners have no monopoly on masculinity, and that most men are extremely curious to understand women better. Women's studies classes designed specifically for men would alleviate much of the stigma attached to asking questions and learning more about women and femininity. Men could come to such classes as part of their larger intellectual pursuits without making any particular commitments to feminism, or to changing themselves. Once in such classrooms, all-male groups of students would lend credibility to the masculine legitimacy of such an activity. Questioning masculine ethics and patriarchal myth and ideology would be easier in an environment made up entirely of gender peers. It would be essential to build into any women's studies classes for men the idea that feminism is not inimical to men, or even entirely so to masculinity. It would also be important for such courses to call heavily on those experiences of men which parallel women's experiences of powerlessness, external control and exploitation.

One of the major challenges of women's studies for men would be to encourage men to empathize with women. In a very real way, the success of such a course hinges on the ability of students to *emotionally* understand women. Course materials should therefore be chosen which include a large dose of personal testimonials and/or fictionalized accounts of the intimate emotional experiences of women's everyday lives. To the same end, a classroom ambiance which promotes emotional involvement and introspection should also be encouraged by the instructor.

Women's studies for men, if presented correctly, could prove popular with male students. Men are eager to share their most intimate moments with women; at the same time they disdain femininity. Few men feel that they understand women and most would like to. Women's studies for men could answer this need, while positively influencing men's attitudes both toward themselves and toward women.

NOTES

1 The complete version of this paper appeared in *Women's Studies International Forum* (11, no. 3, [1988]), following the presentation of a preliminary version at the 1986 CRIAW conference.

2 An English writing-skills course was almost as heavily enrolled, with twenty-five students, as was the "History of Psychology" course with twenty-one students. "Anthropological Concepts" started with sixteen students, "Introduction to Fiction" enrolled eleven, and "The Great War" initially attracted seven students. Four students also took directed readings courses.

3 Two men were in their twenties, seven were in their thirties, and three were between forty and fifty years old.

4 Seven men had earned sufficient credits to qualify them as first-year students, two were at the second-year level, and three were at the fourth-year level.

5 *Woman on the Edge of Time* was chosen because it deals with questions of poverty, discrimination against racial minorities, insanity, and incarceration, and presented feminist visions of a better world.

6 By people associated with the course, I mean university and prison administrators, other faculty, guest lecturers, myself, and the students themselves.

ROBERTA MURA

Recherche sur les femmes et la mathématique: bilan et perspectives d'avenir [1]

Dans cet article l'auteure donne un aperçu des travaux de recherche concernant les femmes et la mathématique. Ces travaux sont regroupés en quatre catégories, nommément: participation des filles aux cours de mathématique au secondaire, différences reliées au sex dans la performance, qualité des expériences scolaires, et niveau professionnel. L'auteure met en évidence des raisons qui ont contribué à susciter l'intérêt pour certaines questions. Des exemples des principaux résultats sont donnés ainsi que quelques directions dans lesquelles les travaux pourraient se poursuivre.

Women and Mathematics: Prospect and Retrospect

This article is a survey of research on women and mathematics. The field is subdivided into four areas: research on girls' participation in high school mathematics courses, research on sex-related differences in mathematics achievement, research on the quality of school experiences, and research concerning the professional level. The author examines some of the reasons which played a part in arousing interest in different kinds of questions, gives examples of the main results achieved, and identifies a few directions for future research.

Depuis quelques années, nous assistons à une production abondante de travaux qui semblent marquer la naissance d'un nouveau domaine de recherche, étiqueté parfois « femmes et mathématique, » d'autres fois « sexe et mathématique » ou encore « genre et mathématique. » [2] Le but de cet article est de faire le point sur les questions qui ont reçu le plus d'attention, sur leurs sources et sur les directions dans lesquelles les travaux pourraient se poursuivre. [3]

LA THÉORIE DU FILTRE MATHÉMATIQUE ET LA PARTICIPATION AUX COURS DE MATHÉMATIQUE AU SECONDAIRE

On a l'habitude de faire remonter l'origine de l'intérêt pour les femmes et la mathématique au début des années soixante-dix, et plus précisément à la parution d'une étude réalisée par la sociologue Lucy Sells (1973), auprès des étudiantes et des étudiants admis à l'Université de Californie à Berkeley. D'après cette étude, seulement 8 pour cent des filles, comparativement à 57 pour cent des garçons, avaient suivi suffisamment de cours de mathématique au secondaire pour pouvoir s'inscrire à n'importe quel programme d'études universitaires. Pour les autres, le choix était extrêmement restreint. Sells voyait ainsi dans la mathématique le « filtre critique » qui interdisait aux femmes l'accès à un grand nombre de carrières, notamment dans les domaines scientifique et technologique où les emplois étaient plus nombreux et mieux rémunérés.

À la suite de ce constat, la question qui se posait était de savoir pourquoi les filles ne s'inscrivaient pas autant que les garçons aux cours de mathématique au secondaire. La motivation de la recherche en ce sens était très pratique: il s'agissait pour les femmes d'obtenir le même pouvoir économique que les hommes, en se donnant la même liberté de choix professionnel. La mathématique étant considérée comme un moyen et non comme une fin en soi, l'attention qu'on lui portait découlait de l'analyse qu'on faisait de son rôle de filtre. Cette analyse est aujourd'hui remise en question puisqu'on s'aperçoit que l'augmentation de la participation des femmes en mathématique n'entraîne pas nécessairement une augmentation comparable dans les autres domaines visés, notamment dans ceux des sciences appliquées.

Toutefois, au début des années soixante-dix, la théorie du filtre mathématique était très majoritairement acceptée aux États-Unis. Il y avait alors convergence d'intérêts entre le mouvement féministe et la politique gouvernementale qui cherchait à orienter une plus grande partie de la population vers des emplois de type technologique.[4] Cette conjoncture a permis de lancer un véritable programme de recherches; toute une série de projets ont été subventionnés dans le but d'expliquer la sous-représentation des filles en mathématique au secondaire et d'identifier les mesures d'intervention les plus efficaces pour redresser la situation.

Ces études constituent un très bel exemple de concertation et d'articulation de projets de recherche dans le domaine des sciences sociales et de l'éducation. Elles ont été conçues et réalisées par des personnes oeuvrant dans les domaines de l'éducation, de la psychologie et de la sociologie. Souvent, ces personnes se sont regroupées en équipes multidisciplinaires et ont pris en considération un grand nombre de variables d'ordre cognitif et d'ordre affectif ainsi que l'influence de l'environnement social et scolaire.[5]

Avec toute l'imprécision inhérente à la volonté de résumer en quelques lignes des dizaines d'études, on peut dire que ce cycle de recherches a abouti à la conclusion suivante: si les filles étaient sous-représentées dans les cours de mathématique au secondaire, cela n'était dû ni à une moins bonne performance ni à un moindre intérêt de leur part. Les causes les plus probables étaient plutôt l'évaluation moins positive que les filles faisaient de l'utilité de la mathématique pour leur carrière future, et leur moindre confiance en leurs capacités dans cette matière.

Un examen plus approfondi du premier facteur a mis ensuite en évidence un point faible de la théorie du filtre: s'il est possible que les filles délaissent la mathématique par manque d'information sur son utilité dans certaines carrières, il est tout aussi possible qu'elles perçoivent la mathématique comme peu utile justement parce qu'elles ne s'intéressent pas à ces mêmes carrières.

Dernièrement, aux États-Unis, on s'est aperçu qu'il n'y avait presque plus de sous-représentation des filles en mathématique au secondaire. Mais cela n'a pas eu les effets escomptés sur la participation des filles en sciences et technologie. Aussi envisage-t-on maintenant de se pencher directement sur la façon dont se développe, chez les jeunes, l'intérêt pour les carrières scientifiques et technologiques.

Au Canada et au Royaume-Uni, la théorie du filtre mathématique n'a pas connu autant de succès qu'aux États-Unis, et les questions relatives à la participation, à la réussite des filles en sciences et à leurs attitudes ont toujours reçu autant, sinon plus, d'attention que les questions analogues relatives à la mathématique.

Récemment des féministes comme Sally Hacker (1983, 40, 50) et Dale Spender (1986) ont souligné les limites du cadre théorique qui sous-tend la plupart des recherches sur les filles et la mathématique: il ne tient pas compte de la notion de pouvoir. Le rôle de filtre joué par la mathématique est, disent-elles, en large partie artificiel et a pour objectif de garder le pouvoir dans les mains du groupe qui le détient. Au siècle passé, lorsque les langues classiques jouaient ce rôle de filtre, on prétendait que les filles n'avaient pas de talent dans ce domaine. Aujourd'hui que les langues ne servent plus d'instrument de sélection, on admet la capacité des filles dans ce champ, et elles sont nombreuses à y participer. La leçon que Hacker et Spender tirent du passé est que la pleine participation et la réussite des filles en mathématique ne feront que déplacer le rôle de filtre de cette discipline à une autre; il leur semble d'ailleurs que l'informatique et la technologie de pointe sont déjà en train de prendre la relève.

LA COMPARAISON DES PERFORMANCES

Lorsqu'on dit que l'intérêt pour les femmes et la mathématique a commencé au debut des années soixante-dix, il ne faut pas en inférer que des comparaisons entre les deux sexes concernant la mathématique n'avaient jamais été faites jusqu'alors. C'est plutôt que cela n'avait jamais été fait sur une si grande échelle, d'une façon aussi concertée, sur autant de dimensions et surtout en ayant à l'esprit l'intérêt des femmes.

A travers les époques et les pays, de nombreux philosophes, Aristote, Rousseau, et Kant, se sont prononcés soit sur l'incapacité naturelle des femmes à penser rationnellement soit sur les dangers auxquels elles se seraient exposées, ou auxquels elles auraient exposé la société, en poursuivant des études et, tout particulièrement, des études scientifiques et théoriques. Lorsque les arguments leur manquaient, ils n'hésitaient pas à brandir l'arme du ridicule.

La rareté des femmes dans l'histoire de la mathématique a été souvent citée pour mettre en doute le talent féminin dans ce domaine. Cet argument ne tient pas compte du fait que jusqu'à récemment les études supérieures étaient légalement fermées aux femmes. Aux États-Unis, les universités Princeton et Harvard ont refusé de décerner des doctorats aux femmes jusqu'aux années 1960 (Rossiter 1982, 29, 44). La soeur de Gauss aurait sans doute connu le sort que Virginia Woolf (1929) décrit à propos de la soeur de Shakespeare.

Si on se préoccupe depuis peu de la présence des femmes en mathématique, les comparaisons de performance, par contre, ont toujours suscité un certain intérêt, aussi bien dans le domaine de l'éducation que dans celui de la psychologie. Jusqu'au début des années soixante-dix, l'opinion prédominante voulait que la supériorité masculine en mathématique soit réelle et générale. Cette opinion se maintenait en dépit de certains résultats qui la contredisaient.

En Angleterre, par exemple, à l'examen d'admission à la *grammar school*, à onze ans, les garçons réussissaient habituellement moins bien que les filles. On attribuait çela à la maturation physique plus rapide chez les filles, et on fixait une note de passage plus haute pour les filles que pour les garçons afin d'éviter une trop grande proportion de filles dans ce type d'école (Isaacson 1982).

Dans la même veine, un rapport du Bureau de l'Éducation des États-Unis de 1911, après avoir fait état d'une supériorité féminine en mathématique au niveau collégial, recommandait de mettre l'accent sur des cours qui puissent « faire émerger cette différence convenable entre les sexes qui est si généralement reconnue » (Hacker 1983, 39).

Malgré l'existence de quelques données de ce genre, on continuait à croire que les filles s'inscrivaient aux cours de mathématique en moindre proportion que les garçons parce qu'elles y réussissaient moins bien. Elizabeth Fennema (1979) eut l'idée brillante de faire remarquer que l'on confondait cause et effet, et que si les filles réussissaient moins bien que les garçons dans certains tests de mathématique, c'était justement parce qu'elles avaient suivi moins de cours.

De fait, lorsqu'on choisit des échantillons homogènes du point de vue des cours suivis, les différences de performance entre les deux sexes diminuent de beaucoup – sans toutefois disparaître toujours complètement.[6]

Lorsqu'on mesure la performance au moyen des notes scolaires, habituellement, soit on ne trouve pas de différence, soit on constate que les filles ont l'avantage.[7] Par contre, les tests créés spécialement pour des fins de recherche ainsi que certains tests standardisés produisent des résultats variés. Jusqu'à la neuvième année environ, les différences sont rares; lorsqu'on en trouve, elles sont surtout en faveur des filles dans les tests de calcul et en faveur des garçons dans les tests de résolution de problèmes, d'applications et de raisonnement mathématique. Toutefois, quelques études ont révélé une meilleure performance des filles même dans ces derniers domaines. À partir de la dixième année, les différences sont plus fréquentes et le plus souvent en faveur des garçons. Cependant, même après la dixième année, on ne les retrouve pas toujours, ou, parfois, elles peuvent favoriser les filles.

Il faut souligner aussi que dans la plupart des études qui font état de différences de performance en mathématique entre les deux sexes, ces différences sont faibles.

Actuellement, les États-Unis investissent beaucoup de ressources dans l'étude de ces différences. Les noms les mieux connus sont ceux de Camilla Benbow et de Julian Stanley, qui travaillent sur la douance et ont publié, à partir de 1980, leurs résultats sur la supériorité masculine en mathématique: ils ont, pour les expliquer, ressuscité l'hypothèse d'un fondement biologique (1980).

Ce genre de propos a été repris par la presse populaire, avec des titres à sensation comme *Do males have a math gene?* ou *The gender factor in math: a new study says males may be naturally abler than females.* Les effets opposés que ce genre de reportage peut avoir sur la confiance des filles ou des garçons en leurs capacités en mathématique me semblent évidents.[8]

LA QUALITÉ DES EXPÉRIENCES SCOLAIRES

Le débat sur l'aptitude, ou l'inaptitude, mathématique des femmes aura eu au moins une conséquence positive: mettre en évidence la non-scientificité du concept d'aptitude avec la connotation d'aptitude innée. En effet, tout test mesure toujours des apprentissages, qu'il s'agisse d'apprentissages formels ou informels. Le fait que les filles et les garçons dont on veut comparer la performance aient suivi les mêmes cours de mathématique ne garantit pas qu'ils et elles aient effectué les mêmes apprentissages à l'extérieur aussi bien qu'à l'intérieur de ces cours.

De nouvelles recherches ont été alors entreprises pour mettre en évidence les inégalités de chances d'apprentissage possibles entre des filles et des garçons qui bénéficient des mêmes cours de mathématique. Par exemple, le nombre et la qualité des interactions élèves/enseignant-e peuvent varier selon le sexe des élèves. Les filles ont moins d'occasions que les garçons de développer des comportements autonomes face à leur apprentissage mathématique. Enseignantes et enseignants semblent renforcer davantage chez elles des attitudes de dépendance intellectuelle, et la conviction que leur succès est dû à leur assiduité au travail et à leur capacité de suivre des règles. Croyant que les filles souffrent d'anxiété et de manque de confiance, les enseignantes et les enseignants adoptent parfois à leur égard des comportements protecteurs qui ne feraient qu'aggraver le problème.

Même lorsqu'on traite les filles et les garçons exactement de la même manière, il est possible que les effets soient différents chez l'un et l'autre sexe. Le style d'apprentissage ou la vision de la mathématique imposés à l'école conviennent peut-être mieux à un sexe qu'à l'autre. Par exemple, un style d'apprentissage axé sur la compétition pourrait favoriser les garçons.

Cette nouvelle orientation de la recherche est en train de prendre de l'importance dans plusieurs pays, en particulier au Royaume-Uni où, à cause du caractère obligatoire des cours de mathématique au secondaire, on n'a pas connu le phénomène de la sous-représentation des filles dans ces cours. Par contre, on y a constaté leur sous-performance aux examens terminaux (seize ans et plus) et on en recherche l'explication surtout à l'intérieur du système scolaire.[9]

L'étude de la qualité des expériences scolaires enrichit la problématique un peu étroite à laquelle on s'était cantonné pendant une dizaine d'années, lorsque la question de la sous-représentation occupait le devant de la scène. L'accent est mis de nos jours sur la présence et les expériences des filles dans les cours de mathématique, plutôt que sur leur absence, on s'intéresse aux niveaux primaire et préscolaire autant sinon plus qu'au niveau secondaire, et l'on attache de l'importance à l'étude de la mathématique comme une fin en soi et non seulement comme un outil pour entreprendre d'autres études.

LA PROFESSION DE MATHÉMATICIENNE

La situation des femmes en mathématique au niveau postsecondaire a été étudiée de façon moins systématique et moins soutenue. Cela est dû d'une part au fait que l'on croyait pouvoir expliquer la sous-représentation des femmes en mathématique à l'université par leur sous-représentation au niveau secondaire, et d'autre part, au fait que l'on s'intéressait à la mathématique surtout en tant que moyen d'accès à d'autres disciplines: l'attention était tournée beaucoup plus vers la profession d'ingénieure que vers celle de mathématicienne.

Les quelques travaux disponibles (sondages, entrevues, témoignages spontanés) visent trois objectifs principaux: identifier les facteurs qui ont facilité l'accès de certaines femmes aux études supérieures et aux carrières en mathématique, décrire les difficultés d'insertion auxquelles elles ont été confrontées et analyser leur relation à la mathématique.

Pour ce qui est du premier objectif, on n'a pas obtenu jusqu'ici de résultats qui aient suffisamment de généralité et qui puissent être utilisés dans des programmes d'intervention auprès des jeunes. Le résultat le plus intéressant est peut-être d'avoir établi que la présence de femmes qui servent de modèle n'a pas l'importance qu'on lui avait attribuée intuitivement. Par contre, celle de l'appui du milieu familial a été confirmée.

On a connu davantage de succès avec le deuxième objectif. Les sondages ont mis en évidence le poids des stéréotypes et ont révélé que le succès ne suffit pas à combler l'écart entre les mathématiciennes et leurs collègues masculins en ce qui concerne la confiance en soi. Les témoignages, recueillis lors d'entrevues ou donnés spontanément, illustrent bien comment le sexisme du milieu réussit parfois à éloigner de leur profession des femmes qui avaient pourtant franchi tous les obstacles de la formation.

Le troisième objectif appelle à une réflexion sur la façon de concevoir et de créer la mathématique ainsi que sur le rôle que joue cette dernière dans le psychisme conscient et inconscient des individus. Ces questions rejoignent celle de la possibilité d'une critique féministe de la mathématique elle-même, c'est-à-dire de la recherche des traces que l'androcentrisme culturel ambiant a pu laisser sur les théories, les concepts et les méthodes mathématiques.

Cette problématique, qui s'éloigne de la psychologie et de la sociologie pour se rapprocher de la psychanalyse et de l'épistémologie, a suscité jusqu'à présent davantage d'intérêt en France qu'ailleurs.[10]

L'importance des nuances dans ce genre de discours rend la présentation rapide des écrits situés dans ce courant particulièrement délicate. En voici quand même quelques exemples. Brigitte Sénéchal (1982) a identifié cetaines sources possibles de la difficulté des femmes à prendre leur place en mathématique. Elle a mis en évidence le conflit entre l'image de la mathématique comme plaisir et le conditionnement des femmes à ne pas s'accorder de droit au plaisir. Mais la mathématique n'est pas que plaisir, et « les difficultés éprouvées par les femmes à s'approprier un registre conceptuel traditionnellement mâle » pourraient témoigner « de l'angoisse à utiliser les armes du maître ». Enfin, la psychanalyse classique oppose « féminité » à « refoulement » et associe ce dernier à toute symbolisation et représentation ...

Du côté de l'épistémologie, un groupe d'étude interdisciplinaire féministe, le *Séminaire limites-frontières*, s'est formé autour d'un intérêt pour la manifestation de l'idéologie sexiste et de la subjectivité dans les théories scientifiques. En mathématique, le formalisme des textes pose à ce genre d'analyse un obstacle supplémentaire qui n'a pas encore été franchi. C'est pourquoi le Séminaire a porté une attention particulière à la question du formalisme et lui a déjà consacré deux publications (Frougny et Peiffer 1984; *Femmes et formalismes* 1985).

L'hisoire de la mathématique semble offrir un matériel plus accessible. Par exemple, Jeanne Peiffer (1986, 125–6), membre du Séminaire, a fait des observations intéressantes au sujet des oppositions pythagoriciennes et de la démonstration déductive. Cette dernière – remarque-t-elle – a pris naissance dans les joutes oratoires dans lesquelles les citoyens grecs s'affrontaient, se provoquaient mutuellement, tentaient de faire sortir l'adversaire de sa réserve, de le pousser dans des positions extrêmes, d'avoir prise sur lui. La forme déductive s'est donc forgée dans le contexte de rivalité, de défi et de combat de l'agora, c'est-à-dire dans un lieu où les femmes n'étaient pas acceptées.

Les oppositions pythagoriciennes illustrent l'influence d'éléments idéologiques sur le développement de la mathématique. Peiffer rappelle la table de ces oppositions, selon Aristote: Défini-Indéfini, Limité-Illimité, Impair-Pair, Un-Multiple, Droit-Gauche, Mâle-Femelle, Repos-Mouvement, Droit-Courbe, Lumière-Obscurité,

Bon-Mauvais, Carré-Hétéromèque. Elle constate que cette table
« conjugue au féminin tout ce qui est exclu des mathématiques grec-
ques: le mouvement, l'infini, le courbe qui est sans cesse ramené au
droit. »

Les recherches dans cette direction avancent lentement, en partie
à cause de la difficulté extrême de repérer la subjectivité dans le
discours mathématique, mais aussi à cause du caractère très théorique des questions et du petit nombre de personnes qui s'y intéressent.
Dans les pays anglo-saxons, sauf quelques exceptions, les chercheuses
qui se rattachent à cette problématique ont traité plutôt des sciences
expérimentales, ou encore de la mathématique scolaire.[11]

Aux États-Unis aussi bien qu'en France, ce courant de pensée a
été contesté par des mathématiciennes qui voient dans l'évocation
de la possibilité d'une relation particulière des femmes à la mathématique et d'une « masculinité » inhérente à cette discipline, le danger d'un retour aux théories de l'inégalité des sexes face à la
mathématique, inégalité qui est toujours interprétée comme in-
fériorité féminine. (Par exemple, Comparat 1981, Ruskai 1986).[12]
Au-delà de certains malentendus de part et d'autre, on peut voir ici
le reflet des débats sur l'altérité, qui ont toujours été au coeur du
mouvement féministe.

Si la situation actuelle des femmes en mathématique n'a pas fait
l'objet de beaucoup d'études, les recherches historiques, par contre,
sont en train de prendre une ampleur considérable. Ces travaux ont
été en partie initiés, ou tout au moins inspirés, par des mathématiciennes désireuses de connaître et de rendre hommage à leurs pré-
décesseures, ainsi que par des pédagogues soucieuses de présenter
aux filles des figures historiques de mathématiciennes. On peut en
voir une conséquence dans le fait que les ouvrages de vulgarisation
destinés aux jeunes, tels que celui de Perl (1978), ont eu autant
d'importance que les publications savantes.

Nous disposons déjà des biographies détaillées de quelques-unes
des mathématiciennes les plus illustres, par exemple celles de Sofia
Kovalevskaia par Koblitz (1983), de Mary Sommerville par Patterson
(1983) et de Ada Byron Lovelace par Stein (1985), mais ce qui a été
accompli n'est qu'une mince partie du travail à faire. Les recherches
historiques sont particulièrement difficiles du fait que, dans le passé,
les femmes en mathématique n'apparaissaient qu'à titre d'assistantes
ou de collaboratrices souvent anonymes. Mais l'examen minutieux
de sources primaires jusqu'ici négligées par l'histoire des sciences
permet de redécouvrir certaines de ces femmes et de leur redonner
leur juste place.

Au delà des portaits individuels, le livre de Margaret Rossiter

(1982) constitue une contribution importante à l'histoire de l'accès des femmes aux sciences aux États-Unis. Il reste à poursuivre le travail entrepris et à l'étendre aux autres pays.

Quelle évolution de la recherche peut-on prévoir ou souhaiter dans le domaine « femmes et mathématique » ?

La participation aux cours

Sans doute une partie des ressources investies dans l'étude de la participation des filles aux cours de mathématique sera-t-elle redistribuée en faveur d'autres disciplines, en particulier des sciences appliquées. Il serait important de situer ces nouvelles recherches dans un cadre plus vaste, qui tienne compte de la ségrégation sexuelle des programmes d'étude et du marché du travail en général, de façon à pouvoir surveiller comment, d'une discipline à une autre, se déplace le rôle d'instrument de sélection.

La performance

À cause du caractère fondamental des aptitudes de type mathématique, celles des femmes dans ce domaine sont probablement destinées à être périodiquement remises en question. Au-delà des travaux nécessaires pour contrecarrer ce genre d'attaque, il serait utile et intéressant de constituer une histoire des opinions et des recherches sur les aptitudes des femmes en mathématique et sur l'éducation qu'il convient de leur donner dans ce domaine.

Les expériences scolaires

Malgré que la mathématique ait un peu perdu de son importance en ce qui concerne l'étude de l'orientation scolaire des jeunes, l'intérêt pour la qualité des expériences scolaires en ce domaine est probablement appelé à croître dans les prochaines années; aux études descriptives succéderont sans doute des études expérimentales, puis viendront des recommandations sur les méthodes d'enseignement les plus aptes à favoriser l'apprentissage de tous et toutes les élèves. Une partie de la problématique qui sous-tend ce type de recherche est susceptible de critiques analogues à celles que l'on a adressées à l'hypothèse d'une relation différente des femmes à la mathématique: si filles et garçons réagissent différemment à certaines méthodes d'enseignement, faut-il adapter celles-ci aux préférences des filles, ou faut-il plutôt chercher les raisons de ces différences afin de les effacer?

La profession

La recherche historique sur les femmes en sciences semble être en expansion. Aux travaux de redécouverte des mathématiciennes du passé, il faudra ajouter les recherches nécessaires pour situer la participation des femmes à la mathématique à travers l'histoire en relation avec leur accès à l'instruction, avec leur condition sociale et avec l'évolution de l'idéologie sur les différences entre les deux sexes.

La situation des mathématiciennes contemporaines fera probablement aussi l'objet d'études dans le but d'appuyer la mise en place de programmes d'accès à l'égalité dans l'enseignement supérieur et dans l'industrie.

Par contre, le progrès étant moins prévisible pour ce qui concerne l'épistémologie de la mathématique, il est à espérer que la difficulté évidente de cette problématique ne découragera pas la poursuite de la réflexion. Il faudra aussi s'assurer que les tentatives éventuelles de critique féministe de la mathématique ne puissent pas être interprétées comme un argument pour éloigner davantage les femmes de cette discipline.

NOTES

1 Cet article a été publié aussi dans le *Bulletin de l'Association mathématique du Québec* 27, no. 4 (Déc. 1987):40–5; cette version comprend une bibliographie plus complète que celle qui est présentée ici.

2 On n'utilise pas l'expression « hommes et mathématique. » Faut-il en déduire qu'encore une fois « femmes » = « sexe »? A ce sujet, voir Dumais (1987).

3 Pour des bilans plus détaillés voir Schildkamp-Kündiger (1982) et Peiffer (1986).

4 On connaît une situation semblable aujourd'hui au Québec, comme en témoigne un document du Conseil de la science et de la technologie (1986, 1) où il est bien dit que l'intérêt que l'on porte à la participation des femmes dans les sciences et les technologies est, au premier chef, fonction des besoins du système scientifique et technologique du Québec en ressources humaines.

5 Un compte rendu de plusieurs de ces études se trouve dans Chipman, Brush, et Wilson (1985).

6 Une excellente recension des écrits sur ce sujet se trouve dans Kimball (manuscrit non publié). Les remarques qui suivent en sont largement inspirées.

7 Au Québec, également, la réussite des filles en mathématique, au secondaire comme au CEGEP, est aussi bonne que celle des garçons sinon meilleure (Guilbert 1985).

8 Les titres cités sont ceux d'articles parus respectivement dans *Newsweek*, 15 décembre 1980, et dans *Time*, 15 décembre 1980. Jacobs et Eccles (1985) ont étudié certains effets de ces reportages. Il est vraisemblable d'ailleurs que tout discours sur « le problème » des femmes en mathématique, quelles qu'en soient les intentions et la teneur, contribue à aggraver le problème.

9 L'ouvrage collectif *Girls into Math Can Go* (Burton 1986) fournit une excellente vue d'ensemble des travaux réalisés au Royaume-Uni. En 1986, la Société Royale de Grande Bretagne a produit un rapport dans lequel elle écarte l'éventuelle différence d'aptitude innée entre les sexes comme explication de la moins bonne réussite des filles en mathématique. Elle voit plutôt les causes principales de ce manque de performance dans les attitudes des parents, des enseignant-e-s et des commissions d'examen. Pour un bref aperçu du rapport, voir Dickson (1986).

10 En France, Jacques Nimier (1976) avait déjà étudié la relation des élèves du secondaire à la mathématique dans une perspective psychanalytique pour les années soixante-dix. Bien qu'il ait établi des comparaisons entre les filles et les garçons, ces comparaisons n'étaient pas l'objectif principal de son travail, et les résultats n'ont pas été mis en relation avec la sous-représentation des filles dans les sections scientifiques, sous-représentation qui existe encore aujourd'hui.

11 Pour une revue plus détaillée des travaux concernant directement ou indirectement la critique du discours mathématique dans une perspective féministe, voir Mura (1986).

12 Un indice de l'ampleur de cette inquiétude chez les mathématiciennes peut se voir dans les propos de Carol Wood, candidate à un poste d'administration de l'American Mathematical Society, et qui, appelée à décrire sa position par l'Association for Women in Mathematics, a déclaré que l'une de ses préoccupations principales concernait « le malentendu presque universel sur la nature de la mathématique, malentendu particulièrement alarmant lorsqu'il provient de certaines de nos collègues féministes dans les sciences sociales » (*Association for Women in Mathematics Newsletter* 16, no. 5 [1986]:4). En 1987 ce genre de préoccupation s'est poursuivi et a donné lieu à plusieurs panels et débats publics (*Association for Women in Mathematics* 17, no. 5:10–12; 17, no. 6:5–16).

Women's Work in Historical and Developmental Perspective
Le travail des femmes: historique et développement économique

GINETTE LAFLEUR

L'industrialisation et le travail rémunéré des femmes, Moncton, 1881–91

Cet article traite de la participation des femmes au travail rémunéré entre 1881 et 1891, période qui correspond aux débuts d'industrialisation de la petite ville de Moncton, dans le sud-est du Nouveau-Brunswick. Nous avons retrouvé, dans les recensements manuscrits de 1881 et de 1891, la trace des travailleuses de Moncton, soit avant et après l'ouverture de plusieurs manufactures ou fabriques dans cette ville. Les renseignements supplémentaires accessibles dans les rapports d'enquête gouvernementale nous ont permis de pénétrer dans un monde du travail où règnait la discrimination.

En 1881, la femme qui oeuvre à l'extérieur de son foyer est le plus souvent jeune, célibataire et domestique. En 1891, malgré une augmentation considérable de la main-d'oeuvre féminine, les travailleuses sont encore généralement jeunes, célibataires et cantonnées dans quelques emplois. Par contre, on en retrouve plus fréquemment dans l'industrie légère qui, en cette fin du dix-neuvième siècle, fait un usage assez marqué de cette main-d'oeuvre à bon marché.

Industrialization and Women's Wage Labour in Moncton, 1881–1891

This article deals with the participation of women in the paid labour force between 1881 and 1891, that is, during the period of industrialization in the small town of Moncton in south-east New Brunswick. We follow Moncton's female workers through the handwritten censuses of 1881 and 1891, that is, before and after the introduction of several factories and mills in the town. Additional information from government survey reports allows us to penetrate a working community where discrimination against women prevails.

In 1881, the typical woman working outside the home was usually young, single and a domestic worker. In 1891, although there was a substantial increase in the size of the female workforce, female workers were still for the most part young, single and confined to few occupational choices. On the other hand, toward the end of the nineteenth century, we frequently found women being used extensively as cheap labour in light industry.

Au cours des années 1880, la ville de Moncton vit une période de mutation. Elle s'engage sur la voie de l'industrialisation. On assiste à une croissance du secteur manufacturier due, principalement, à la hausse des tarifs protecteurs résultant de l'application de la Politique Nationale du gouvernement de John A. Macdonald et à la construction du chemin de fer Intercolonial (Hickey 1986, 1). Le visage urbain de Moncton prend corps. Dans ce dernier quart du dix-neuvième siècle, les gens de la campagne se dirigent vers les villes et y constituent un réservoir de main-d'oeuvre pour les diverses entreprises. On constate une augmentation démographique de 74 pour cent durant la décennie 1881–91, alors que dans l'ensemble de la province, la population stagne (Recensement du Canada 1880–81a, tableau 1; Recensement du Canada 1890–91a, tableau 3). L'expansion de Moncton est signalée, en 1885, dans un rapport sur les industries manufacturières des provinces maritimes. On y lit: « Moncton ... is second only to St. John, in the Province of New Brunswick, in industrial and commercial importance; and it enjoys the advantage of being the central point of the Intercolonial Railway system. The progress of Moncton ... has been very rapid – more so than that of any town in New Brunswick, or, indeed, in the Maritime Provinces » (« Report on Manufacturing Industries, » 1885, 54).

Toutefois, les industries de Moncton n'atteignent pas la dimension de celles de grands centres urbains comme Montréal, Toronto ou Hamilton. Par comparaison, Moncton n'est qu'une petite cité et obtient un pointage bien moyen dans la course à l'industrialisation, mais celle-ci modifie tout de même le travail dans cette communauté.

Plusieurs recherches montrent que, dans un premier temps, l'industrialisation est grandement tributaire du travail féminin (Bradbury 1983, 291–2; Cross 1977, 34–59; Harvey 1978, 136–7; Lavigne 1983, 18). Madeleine Guilbert souligne particulièrement bien ce phénomène: « si la grande industrie n'a pas créé le travail des femmes, elle a peuplé de femmes – et d'enfants – les premiers ateliers, tel semble être le fait nouveau qui caractérise, en ce qui concerne les femmes, les premiers développements de l'industrialisation » (1966, 39–40). Nous avons voulu savoir si, au cours de ces premiers balbutiements du capitalisme industriel à Moncton, on a eu largement recours à la main-d'oeuvre féminine, comme cela s'est produit en d'autres lieux d'Amérique ou d'Europe. Ces débuts d'industrialisation ont-ils revêtu un caractère particulier? Ont-ils effacé les formes de travail préindustrielles? Est-ce que le capital industriel a attiré beaucoup de filles à la ville? Les travailleuses sont-elles célibataires? En fait, nous voulons clarifier les incidences de l'industrialisation sur le travail rémunéré des femmes.

GAGNER SA VIE À LA FIN DU 19e SIÈCLE

À Moncton, en 1881, bien peu d'entreprises manufacturières existent, les femmes devant gagner ou aider à gagner le pain familial n'ont pas un choix d'emploi très varié. Dans le recensement manuscrit (« New Brunswick, 1881 »), nous avons relevé 198 femmes avec indication de profession, occupation ou métier.[1] Le groupe des domestiques domine largement les autres, constituant 43 pour cent des travailleuses. Il est suivi du groupe des couturières avec 22 pour cent, des tailleuses avec 12 pour cent, et des institutrices avec 9 pour cent des effectifs féminins. Jusqu'ici point de surprise, les femmes se retrouvent majoritairement dans les services domestiques et personnels (53 pour cent) et dans les manufactures et industries mécaniques (36 pour cent). La totalité des travailleuses de ce dernier secteur est dans l'industrie du vêtement. Ce sont des « emplois » que les femmes assuraient déjà à l'intérieur du cadre domestique. Depuis longtemps, ils ont été identifiés comme des « ghettos » de main-d'oeuvre féminine. Le secteur professionnel se compose essentiellement d'un personnel enseignant; il attire 11 pour cent des travailleuses.

En 1881, 198 femmes sont entrées sur le marché du travail, en 1891 (« New Brunswick, 1891 »), on en identifie 577 dans différents secteurs. Il y a donc croissance des effectifs féminins de 191 pour cent. Au cours de la même période, l'augmentation de la population n'est que de 74 pour cent. On peut déceler d'une part, l'arrivée à Moncton de jeunes filles des campagnes environnantes.[2] Le développement de Moncton provoque leur mobilité géographique, d'autant plus que « le marché du travail dans les régions rurales est encore plus fermé aux jeunes filles qu'aux jeunes hommes » (Cross 1977, 33). Le taux élevé de travailleuses en pension (59 pour cent), en 1891, fournit un autre indice de déplacements concernant des femmes seules et non accompagnées de leur famille. D'autre part, la grande croissance de la main-d'oeuvre féminine peut signifier de meilleures possibilités d'emploi en raison de la création de nouvelles industries. En ce cas, nous devrions retrouver un grand nombre d'ouvrières de manufactures en 1891, d'autant plus qu'un certain transfert doit s'opérer du « service domestique et personnel » vers les « manufactures et industries mécaniques. » En effet, plusieurs auteur-e-s soutiennent qu'en dépit de conditions de travail et pécuniaires déplorables dans les ateliers, manufactures ou fabriques, les ouvrières préfèrent une place en usine à une place servile en maison privée (Leslie 1974, 71–125; Johnson 1974, 29–30; Collectif Clio 1982, 201; Cross 1977, 41; « Rapport des Commissaires, » 1882, 4).

À Moncton, en 1891, les domestiques sont encore les plus nombreuses: 39 pour cent de la main-d'oeuvre féminine. Ce taux élevé, constaté également en d'autres lieux au Canada, peut signifier, comme le fait remarquer Claudette Lacelle, que le service domestique conserve certains attraits: « En dépit de ces fatigues et contraintes, on s'engageait néanmoins en grand nombre dans le service parce qu'on y voyait certains avantages, notamment ceux du gîte et du couvert, du vivre et de l'entretien » (1982, 194).

Ce fort pourcentage de domestiques à Moncton peut aussi refléter certaines déficiences de la structure industrielle, celle-ci n'étant peut-être pas assez développée pour absorber les nouvelles demandeuses d'emploi. Si nous comparons les effectifs en 1881 et en 1891, nous remarquons une hausse de 173 pour cent dans le secteur du service domestique et personnel, de 190 pour cent dans les manufactures et industries mécaniques, et de 114 pour cent dans les professions. Le secteur manufacturier connaît donc la plus forte progression, quoique suivi de près par le service domestique et personnel.

En comparant la part qu'occupe chaque secteur d'activité des femmes, nous observons que la portion du service domestique et personnel, tout comme celle des professions diminue quelque peu de 1881 à 1891 (53 pour cent à 50 pour cent et 11 pour cent à 8 pour cent des travailleuses). À l'intérieur du premier groupe, les servantes font un recul de 4 pour cent. Le secteur manufacturier se maintient (36 pour cent des travailleuses) et on voit apparaître une nouvelle tranche nommée « commerce et transport » (6 pour cent de la main-d'oeuvre féminine). Le secteur agricole accapare moins de un pour cent des travailleuses. La section « commerce et transport » semble avoir pris naissance au détriment des secteurs professionnel et domestique. Cette entrée d'un nouveau domaine générateur d'emplois pour les femmes, à la fin du 19e siècle, a été notée également par Madeleine Guilbert (1966, 59) pour la France.

Nous avons constaté toutefois qu'en 1891, la majorité des commis de toutes sortes est de sexe masculin. Cette occupation n'est pas encore féminisée. Ainsi, un des plus gros employeurs de Moncton, l'Intercolonial, n'engage pratiquement pas de femmes. Devant la Commission royale sur les relations du travail avec le capital, le 13 avril 1888, D. Pottinger, chef de gare du chemin de fer Intercolonial, affirme que seulement deux femmes sont employées comme télégraphistes (*Report of the Royal Commission* 1889a, 317).

À Moncton, nous avons vu que 36 pour cent des travailleuses sont classées dans le secteur manufacturier en 1891. Au cours de la décennie précédente un important employeur féminin a fait irruption: la filature de coton. Les ouvrières du coton relevées dans le recensement nominatif de 1891 sont au nombre de 54 et regroupent 9 pour cent des femmes sur le marché du travail. Ce chiffre reste cependant en deçà de la quantité d'ouvrières requise par la filature. Dans le recensement imprimé (1890–91c, 119), on indique un total de 97 femmes et filles employées à la fabrique de coton (voir tableau 1). Quarante-trois ouvrières n'ont donc pas été retenues par le recenseur parce que leur emploi devait être temporaire: « Mais il ne faut pas oublier qu'il ne saurait y avoir un accord parfait entre les deux exposés [sur la main-d'oeuvre dans l'industrie et sur les occupations], vu qu'ils ont rapport à deux états de choses différents, l'un donnant le nombre de mains employées dans diverses industries à la semaine, au mois ou à l'année, l'autre mentionnant l'occupation à laquelle telle personne donne la plus grande partie de son temps (*Recensement du Canada*, 1890–91b, ix; voir aussi *Recensement du Canada*, 1880–81b, vii) ».

Les statistiques sur les emplois sous-estiment la présence féminine sur le marché du travail. Ainsi, elles ne permettent pas d'évaluer le nombre de travailleuses occasionnelles devant venir en aide à la famille lors de périodes difficiles (Cross 1977, 59): « Ces rapports ... ne donnent pas le nombre de celles qui ne sont employées que temporairement dans des industries rémunératives [sic], leurs principales occupations étant de voir au soin de leurs maisons. De ces dernières on en compte un grand nombre » (*Recensement du Canada*, 1890–91b, ix).

Selon différentes sources, la filature de coton fonctionne tout de même avec une moyenne de 90 à 100 femmes et filles, entre 1884 et 1891, comme le montre le tableau 1. La main-d'oeuvre féminine oscille entre 53 pour cent et 58 pour cent à la Moncton Cotton Manufacturing Co. Elle constitue une fraction très importante de la population ouvrière de la filature. Le travail des enfants est aussi à souligner. Dans l'industrie textile, il relève d'une longue tradition, qui débute avec l'apparition même des fabriques en Angleterre (Rouillard 1974, 54).

Si les relevés effectués à partir des recensements manuscrits sous-

Tableau 1
Composition de la main-d'oeuvre, filature de coton, Moncton,
Nombre et Pourcentage

	Hommes No.	%	Garçons No.	%	Filles No.	%	Femmes No.	%	Total No.	%
1884	57	33	14	8	—	—	100	58	171	100
1888	45	26	35	21	30	18	60	35	170	100
1891	58	32	24	13	29	16	68	38	179	100

Source: « Report on Manufacturing Industries, » 1885, 55; Report of the Royal Commission, 1889, 298; Recensement du Canada, 1890–91c. 119.

estiment la participation féminine à la filature, nous pouvons présumer qu'ils font de même pour les travailleuses salariées dans d'autres entreprises. Nous allons nous tourner vers une autre source (« Report on Manufacturing Industries, » 1885) pour essayer de mieux cerner les incidences de l'industrialisation à Moncton sur le sexe féminin.

Le tableau 2 montre qu'en 1884, 904 ouvriers(ères) travaillent dans le secteur manufacturier, alors qu'en 1878, on y compte seulement 140 personnes. La force de travail féminine s'est accrue relativement à celle des hommes et des garçons, ce qui peut supposer la création d'entreprises basées sur la main-d'oeuvre féminine au cours de ces années. Les femmes passent de 16 pour cent à 27 pour cent de la main-d'oeuvre manufacturière. Nous avons recensé 198 travailleuses en 1881, nous en retrouvons 242 uniquement sur la route de la manufacture en 1884.

À Montréal, où déjà à partir des années 1840-50, le capital industriel donne un nouveau profil à la ville, les femmes représentent, en 1871, 33 pour cent de la force de travail industrielle (Bradbury 1983, 292). En 1881, le nombre de femmes y oeuvrant dans l'industrie atteint son maximum; le travail en manufacture a surclassé le service domestique, le premier occupe presque 16 pour cent de la population féminine comparativement à 8 pour cent pour le second (Cross 1977, 59). Dans une ville de textile comme Lowell au Massachusetts, les femmes constituent 56 pour cent de la force de travail en cette fin du dix-neuvième siècle (Bradbury 1983, 292). Plus l'économie d'une région repose sur l'industrie légère, plus la dépendance envers le travail des femmes et des enfants peut être notable. Comme le souligne Bettina Bradbury (1983, 292), la présence de femmes et d'enfants dans les manufactures est une particularité des débuts du capitalisme, mais elle est très inégale selon les lieux.

Tableau 2
Composition de la main-d'oeuvre, secteur manufacturier, Moncton, 1878 et 1884,
Nombre et Pourcentage

	Hommes No.	%	Garçons No.	%	Femmes No.	%	Total No.
1878	108	77	9	6	23	16	140
1884	625	69	37	4	242	27	904

Source: « Report on Manufacturing Industries, » 1885, 55.

De 1878 à 1884, le nombre d'entreprises de Moncton s'appuyant sur la main-d'oeuvre féminine s'est accru. En 1878, les ouvrières sont embauchées uniquement dans le « vêtement » (confection et tailleurs). Elles y constituent le gros de la main-d'oeuvre (85 pour cent dans la confection et 75 pour cent chez les tailleurs) (« Report on Manufacturing Industries, » 1885, 55–6). En 1884, sur un total de 34 formes d'industrie dénombrées par Edward Willis, 9 engagent des femmes comme le révèle le tableau 3. Mais 97 pour cent des ouvrières besognent dans les textiles et le vêtement, industries moyennes et petites requérant une forte proportion de travail par rapport au capital et où s'applique la division du travail. Dans ce cas, les femmes font les tâches inférieures ou jugées inférieures. Ainsi, dans le métier fragmenté de tailleur, les hommes font la conception, la coupe, et les femmes l'exécution, la couture (« Report of the Royal Commission, » 1889b, 174–5). Par ailleurs, la mécanisation de certaines tâches à la filature de coton permet de passer outre les qualifications, de réduire l'effort physique et par conséquent d'utiliser une main-d'oeuvre non-qualifiée, les femmes. On fait alors appel à la rapidité et aux gestes répétitifs. Les travailleuses forment de 50 à 100 pour cent de la force de travail de ces industries des textiles et du vêtement. À Montréal, en 1871, trois types de production dominent: la fabrication du cuir et des chaussures, la confection de vêtements, et l'industrie reliée au matériel de transport et au travail du métal. Dans les deux premiers, la proportion du nombre de femmes est respectivement de 50 pour cent et de 80 pour cent (Bradbury 1983, 291–2).

De façon générale, l'industrialisation à Moncton présente un caractère « universel »: développement d'une industrie légère fondée sur le travail des femmes. De façon spécifique, on ne retrouve dans cette branche qu'un seul gros employeur, la filature de coton.[3] On ne distingue, par exemple, aucune grande entreprise de confection ou de fabrication de chaussures. Il y a eu une importante croissance du secteur industriel de 1878 à 1884, mais elle ne semble pas avoir été

Tableau 3
Industries qui emploient les femmes, Moncton, 1884

	Hommes No.	%	Garçons No.	%	Femmes No.	%	Année de Fondation des entreprises
Filature							
de coton	57	33	14	8	100	58	1882
Tailleurs	19	26	—	—	53	74	1877,79,81,82,83
Fabrication							
des tricots	1	3	—	—	35	97	1882
Modistes	—	—	—	—	20	100	1880,83
Confection	3	15	—	—	17	85	1868
Fabrication							
de lainage	10	50	—	—	10	50	1882
Buanderies	1	20	—	—	4	80	1884
Fabrication							
Prod.chimiques							
Pharmac.	3	75	—	—	1	25	1882
Tapissiers	1	33	—	—	2	67	1881

Source: "Report on Manufacturing Industries," 1885, 55–6

assez forte pour laisser paraître un transfert du service domestique et personnel vers les manufactures. Et on décèle encore 226 domestiques en 1891 (39 pour cent de la main-d'oeuvre féminine) ...

Il est à noter également que Moncton ne semble pas avoir connu la « crise domestique » signalée à la fin du siècle à Montréal et en d'autres points du Canada. Le recrutement de plus en plus difficile de domestiques oblige à faire appel aux immigrantes; de nombreuses sociétés se consacrent à l'accueil de jeunes filles venant des Iles britanniques (Lavigne 1983, 20; Roberts 1979, 185–202; Parr 1980). À Moncton, en 1881, 93 pour cent de la main-d'oeuvre féminine est née dans les provinces maritimes, dont 77 pour cent au Nouveau-Brunswick; seulement 7 pour cent ont comme pays de naissance l'Angleterre, l'Écosse, l'Irlande et les États-Unis. En 1891, 92 pour cent des femmes au travail sont natives des Maritimes, dont 79 pour cent du Nouveau-Brunswick; 94 pour cent ont comme lieu de naissance une province canadienne. Les autres sont nées en Angleterre, en Australie, en Écosse, aux États-Unis, en Irlande et à Terre-Neuve. Les travailleuses étrangères ne semblent pas avoir eu d'attrait particulier pour Moncton. Les jeunes filles en provenance des campagnes environnantes peuvent sans doute suffire et à la demande d'ouvrières de manufacture et à la demande de domestiques. De plus, dans les villes du Nouveau-Brunswick, le travail est insuffisant pour retenir un grand nombre de femmes qui vont servir les intérêts du capitalisme industriel en Nouvelle-Angleterre, c'est du moins ce que nous rapporte Henri d'Entremont, dans un numéro de l'*Évangéline* de 1888: « Et combien y en a-t-il de ses [sic] pauvres jeunes filles qui travaillent ainsi dans la cité de Boston, et qui ne gagnent pour tout salaire que $2,50 à $3,50 par semaine? Mme Charlotte Smith qui travaille dans l'intérêt de cette classe de jeunes filles nous informe qu'il n'y en a pas moins de 20,000. Beaucoup de ces filles du métier viennent de la Nouvelle-Écosse, du Nouveau-Brunswick, et nulle [sic] doute un grand nombre sont d'origine acadienne » (1888, 2).

Nous ne percevons pas d'immigration notable de jeunes filles d'Europe vers Moncton. Nous avons constaté par contre de 1881 à 1891, une grande croissance de la main-d'oeuvre féminine d'origine ethnique française. La ville de Moncton a attiré les jeunes rurales francophones. Jean-Roch Cyr (1982, 3–4), auteur d'une thèse sur les Acadien-ne-s de Moncton de 1698 à 1881, note qu'à la fin de la période étudiée, on commence à voir bouger les Acadienne-s. L'essor de Moncton entraîne leur mobilité géographique, à un rythme lent, au début, mais plus accéléré au 20e siècle. Voyons ce qu'il en est pour les Acadiennes spécifiquement.

QUELQUES ASPECTS DU PROFIL DE LA TRAVAILLEUSE

Origine ethnique

En 1881, les femmes d'origine irlandaise forment le groupe le plus important parmi la main-d'oeuvre féminine (37 pour cent). Ce pourcentage est très supérieur au poids démographique des Irlandais-e-s à Moncton (19 pour cent).[4] Ce taux peut signifier que les Irlandaises exercent un métier, relativement, en beaucoup plus grand nombre que les femmes des autres ethnies. Si nous prenons comme hypothèse que la femme besogne par nécessité au dix-neuvième siècle, la communauté irlandaise est de fait une des plus défavorisées de la société « monctonienne. »

Les femmes de souche anglaise et écossaise suivent avec 27 pour cent et 22 pour cent des effectifs féminins en 1881. Alors que la présence des travailleuses écossaises est à peu près représentative de la communauté écossaise dans la ville (23 pour cent), les Anglaises sont nettement sous-représentées par rapport au pourcentage des gens d'origine anglaise à Moncton (45 pour cent). Moins de femmes de cette ethnie travaillent ou ont besoin de travailler.

Les derniers 14 pour cent de la main-d'oeuvre féminine sont partagés entre les travailleuses d'origine française, hollandaise et allemande. Leur proportion est sensiblement la même que celle de leur groupe ethnique par rapport à le population générale de la ville (7 pour cent et 7 pour cent, 4 pour cent et 2 pour cent, 3 pour cent et 3 pour cent).

Le recensement de 1891 ne procure plus les données relatives aux différentes origines ethniques. On fait toutefois une mention spéciale pour les Canadien-ne-s français-es. Des modifications importantes se produisent, de 1881 à 1891, dans la composition de la main-d'oeuvre féminine; la portion occupée par les femmes francophones passe de 7 pour cent à 21 pour cent, leurs effectifs haussent de 846 pour cent. L'augmentation démographique de la population francophone durant la même période est de 251 pour cent (*Recensement du Canada* 1880–81a, tableau 3; *Recensement du Canada* 1890–91a, tableau 3). Nous retraçons 21 pour cent de travailleuses canadiennes-françaises à Moncton alors que le groupe canadien- français constitue 15 pour cent des habitant-e-s de la cité. Les Acadien-ne-s se sont déplacé-e-s de 1881 à 1891, mais le pourcentage de travailleuses canadiennes-françaises montre que les Acadiennes ont bougé encore plus que les hommes, ou travaillent en plus grand nombre que les femmes non francophones.

Les Acadiennes venues à Moncton représentent, avec d'autres, la force de travail de la filature de coton. Elles constituent le principal groupe ethnique à l'intérieur de la filature.[5] On retrouve 41 pour cent des travailleuses francophones dans le secteur manufacturier. Elles sont également en grand nombre dans le « service domestique et personnel » (54 pour cent des travailleuses francophones).

Les francophones sont peu présentes dans le secteur « commerce et transport » (0,8 pour cent) et dans les services professionnels (4 pour cent). Plusieurs des occupations dans ces secteurs requièrent un minimum d'instruction et sont, de ce fait, accessibles à une portion plus privilégiée de la population. Des critères de classe doublés de critères linguistiques ont pu défavoriser les Acadiennes dans leur accès aux différents emplois.

La principale profession pour les femmes est l'enseignement. Nous savons que l'accès à l'école normale est semé d'embûches pour les francophones; le principal obstacle à franchir est, selon Elspeth Tulloch, la langue:

Très peu d'étudiants francophones s'inscrivent à l'école normale. Pour l'année scolaire 1877–8, l'école normale, alors établie en permanence à Fredericton, compte 229 étudiants; de ce nombre, seulement deux sont francophones, dont une femme. En 1878, l'école normale crée un cours préparatoire en français pour permettre aux étudiants francophones de suivre l'enseignement régulier dispensé en anglais ... En 1883, on améliore quelque peu les choses en permettant aux étudiants francophones d'obtenir un brevet d'enseignement permanent par l'intermédiaire d'un nouveau « French Department » qui dispense des cours en anglais et en français. Mais le brevet d'enseignement est toujours de troisième classe, la moins bien payée et la moins prestigieuse. (1985, 98)

Jusqu'en 1943, selon Elspeth Tulloch (Ibid.), les cours de l'école normale et les cours de sciences infirmières sont les seules formes d'enseignement supérieur offertes en français (et encore seulement en partie) aux femmes francophones du Nouveau-Brunswick. Il n'y a pas à s'étonner qu'on les retrouve moins dans les « professions » et dans des emplois de bureau exigeant un certain degré d'instruction.

Age et état civil

Nous découvrons pour 1881 et 1891 une population de travailleuses composée majoritairement de jeunes célibataires. L'âge moyen est de 25 ans en 1881 et de 26 ans en 1891. Nous retrouvons 82 pour cent de célibataires, 4 pour cent de femmes mariées et 14 pour cent de veuves, en 1881. La répartition des travailleuses selon l'état civil est presque identique en 1891, 82 pour cent, 5 pour cent, 11 pour cent.

Le nombre de femmes mariées au travail est très faible au cours des deux périodes. Cet état de choses peut s'interpréter de diverses façons. Nous savons que les recenseurs ne prennent pas en considération les femmes ayant un travail occasionnel. La non-comptabilisation des emplois temporaires explique peut-être notre faible pourcentage de femmes mariées car celles-ci, pour des raisons de grossesse ou parce que « leurs principales occupations sont de voir au soin de leurs maisons » (*Recensement du Canada* 1890–91, ix) sont sans doute les plus oubliées dans les recensements. Bettina Bradbury (1983, 306), lors de son analyse de l'économie familiale des quartiers St-Jacques et Ste-Anne à Montréal, n'a retracé également, dans le recensement de 1871, que 2,5 pour cent de femmes mariées exerçant un emploi.

Toutefois, si nous jetons un coup d'oeil sur le nombre de femmes mariées trouvé par les commissaires qui ont enquêté sur la main-d'oeuvre (temporaire et régulière) des moulins et fabriques en 1881, nous ne décelons que 2 pour cent d'épouses ou de mères.[6] Nous en concluons qu'il n'y a pas seulement sous-évaluation par les recenseurs de la présence féminine dans l'univers du salariat. Des modèles idéologiques ou des pressions sociales entrent en ligne de compte lorsqu'il s'agit de travail féminin. G.C. Brandt (1981, 119) le signale, après avoir interviewé d'anciennes ouvrières de la filature de coton de Valleyfield, au Québec. Le travail de la mère de famille est particulièrement condamné. Dans le rapport d'enquête sur la main-d'oeuvre des moulins et fabriques en 1881, on peut lire: « cependant il nous fait peine d'avoir à dire que nous avons découvert dans deux ou trois occasions que des maris, à rebours des usages du monde civilisé, envoyaient leurs épouses et mères de famille aux manufactures et voyaient eux aux travaux de la maison » (« Rapport des commissaires, » 1882, 4).

La place de la femme mariée est à la maison et, comme le travail se déplace de plus en plus vers les fabriques, celle-ci ne peut guère contribuer à la production marchande. En ce sens, l'industrialisation et l'urbanisation, en transférant le travail à l'extérieur du domicile, contribuent à exclure une partie de la population féminine de la main-d'oeuvre active: les femmes mariées.

L'image idéale de la femme, véhiculée dans la société peut cependant aller à l'encontre des besoins du capital industriel en main-d'oeuvre à bon marché ou de la réalité des familles nécessiteuses. Des femmes ont besoin de travailler pour augmenter le revenu familial. La présence d'enfants leur rend la situation encore plus difficile. A Moncton, il ne semble pas y avoir de salles d'asile où les femmes puissent laisser leurs enfants et vaquer à des activités extérieures.[7]

En 1881 et en 1891, à Moncton, seul un petit nombre de femmes ayant des enfants à la maison déclare exercer un emploi régulier, soit 11 pour cent. Elles sont le plus souvent veuves, 68 pour cent en 1881 et 63 pour cent en 1891. Ces travailleuses ont peu d'enfants en bas âge, ce qui leur facilite la tâche pour un emploi à l'extérieur du foyer, et on les retrouve principalement dans les services domestiques et personnels ne requérant généralement pas beaucoup de qualifications (68 pour cent en 1881 et 58 pour cent en 1891).

À Moncton, en 1881, les choix de gagne-pain offerts à la gent féminine sont très limités. Le service domestique procure le plus de travail. Les activités de couture occupent un nombre assez considérable d'ouvrières. En 1891, les formes de travail rémunéré ne sont guère plus diversifiées. Bien que nous retrouvions beaucoup plus de femmes sur le marché de l'emploi, elles ne sont apparentes que dans des couloirs bien spécifiques: services domestiques et personnels, industries du vêtement et des textiles.

Reléguée dans un éventail d'emplois plutôt restreint, la main-d'oeuvre féminine constitue tout de même un important facteur de production, spécialement dans l'industrie légère. Des entreprises dont les coûts de production sont pour l'essentiel la main-d'oeuvre, vont s'appuyer largement sur les femmes au cours de cette décennie, car cette force de travail est bon marché. Le mouvement de participation des femmes au marché du travail s'inscrit dans une demande de main-d'oeuvre sous-qualifiée et sous-payée, et dans des secteurs précis de l'économie. Comme le rapportent les commissaires enquêtant sur les relations entre le travail et le capital en 1889: « Les femmes et les enfants peuvent être obtenus à meilleur marché, l'on peut les soumettre à de nombreuses petites exactions et les faire travailler sans se plaindre pendant de longues heures. Tels sont les avantages offerts par l'emploi de cette classe de travaillants qui est si largement employée. » (« Report of Royal Commission, » 1889b, 87). En cette fin du dix-neuvième siècle, les industriels n'ont aucune préoccupation de la reproduction de la force de travail et du développement d'un marché de consommation. Les familles sont perçues comme des unités de production et non comme des unités potentielles de consommation. La main-d'oeuvre est payée au plus bas prix possible et on l'utilise au maximum; si la femme répond aux attentes, on l'engage.

À Moncton toutefois, en 1891, les femmes s'engagent encore en grand nombre comme domestiques, car les industries ne sont pas assez développées pour absorber toutes les nouvelles demandeuses d'emploi.

Il y a une grande croissance des effectifs féminins de 1881 à 1891, mais la femme qui se lance dans le monde du travail demeure généralement célibataire et assez jeune. Toutefois, il se produit un changement au niveau de l'ethnie de 1881 à 1891; la femme au travail est plus souvent canadienne-française en 1891 qu'en 1881. Le développement industriel de Moncton l'a éloignée des campagnes et attirée en ville.

S'il est vrai qu'en Europe et en Amérique un déclin du travail féminin en manufacture s'amorce à la fin du 19e siècle (Cross 1977, 59; Rouillard 1974, 53–4), il ne faut pas oublier qu'à l'époque de la surexploitation de la main-d'oeuvre, cette période du capitalisme qu'on a appelé « sauvage, » c'est à la main-d'oeuvre féminine sous-payée qu'on a eu recours.

NOTES

1 Toutes les statistiques contenues dans cet article sont établies à partir des recensements manuscrits (« New Brunswick, » 1881; New Brunswick, » 1891), à moins d'indication contraire. Nous avons tiré des séries de données de ces recensements et les avons traitées avec le système PFS sur micro-ordinateur. Par ailleurs, nous ne pouvons pas évaluer le pourcentage de main-d'oeuvre féminine parmi la population active, car dans le recensement imprimé, on ne distingue pas les sexes, « en faire mention séparée prendrait trop de place » (*Recensement du Canada* 1880–81b, vii).

2 Une recherche de l'auteure sur la provenance des travailleuses de Moncton en 1891 indique que la majorité a pour origine les comtés ruraux alentour de Moncton.

3 La « Moncton Cotton Manufacturing Co, » quoique employeur important (179 ouvriers(ères) en 1891), est une petite filature en regard de celles situées au Canada central. Au cours de la période 1888–90, par exemple, 1040 personnes travaillent à la « Montreal Cotton Co » de Valleyfield (Ferland 1982, 87).

4 Les pourcentages de personnes de diverses origines ethniques sont calculés d'après Recensement du Canada 1880–81a, tableau 3.

5 Sur les cinquante-quatre ouvrières du coton retrouvées dans le recensement manuscrit en 1891, vingt-sept sont Canadiennes françaises, ce qui veut dire que 50 pour cent des travailleuses régulières sont acadiennes.

6 Les commissaires W. Luckes et A.H. Blackeby ont visité 465 moulins ou fabriques au Canada en 1881. La main-d'oeuvre de plus de quatorze ans comprenait 13,059 femmes et de ce nombre, 324 étaient mariées (« Rapport des commissaires » 1882, 11).

7 Elspeth Tulloch (1985, 104) a découvert l'existence d'une garderie à St-Jean, à la fin du 19e siècle; un genre de réseau de garderies existe à Montréal au dix-neuvième siècle, voir Micheline Dumont (1983, 264).

NANCY FORESTELL AND JESSIE CHISHOLM

Working-Class Women as Wage Earners in St. John's, Newfoundland, 1890–1921 [1]

Our essay surveys working-class women of St. John's as waged labour between the years 1890 and 1921. Drawing extensively from primary sources, we trace the general outlines of a working-class women's history in St. John's. The themes which emerge parallel those in the Canadian literature, illustrating that urban women in Newfoundland were not isolated from economic and social developments elsewhere.

Les ouvrières de St-Jean, T.-N., de 1890 à 1921

Exploitant des sources en grande partie originales, nous essayons dans notre article de brosser les grandes lignes d'une histoire des femmes de la classe ouvrière de St-Jean, T.-N., de 1890 à 1921. Les principaux traits qui les caractérisent en tant que main d'oeuvre salariée rappellent ceux qui ont été mis en lumiére par les autres travaux canadiens, montrant ainsi que les femmes des milieux urbains de Terre-Neuve n'étaient pas isolées des progrès économiques et sociaux qui se produisaient ailleurs à la même époque.

By 1890, many women in St. John's were wage earners, employed as domestics, retail clerks, office workers and teachers; hundreds of female operatives were working in local factories, in the boot and shoe firms, the clothing industry, the cordage enterprise and the confectionery and bakery business. Yet the work experience of urban women in the capital has gone unnoticed by historians and social scientists.

Our essay is a collaborative effort. Our methodologies and emphases differ, reflecting variations in available sources. Section 1 covers the period 1890 to 1914, and is based on an intensive reading of the daily press.[2] Section 2 traces working-class women through the war years and the postwar depression, drawing extensively from data in enumerator lists for the 1921 census, and supplemented by a range of newspaper and archival sources.[3] The study is based on a common conviction that working-class women were a significant portion of the St. John's labour force, and that their history is an integral part of Newfoundland's social experience.

Historians familiar with the history of women's employment in Canada will note the emergence of similar themes: the employment of female workers as cheap factory labour; the tensions between poorly paid female help and skilled male workers; the expanding employment opportunities for women during wartime; and the patterns of women's resistance, strike activity, and mobility which belied contemporary images of women as passive and timid. Historians may be puzzled, however, by the absence of conventional documentary sources, particularly for the period 1890 to 1914. Sources for Newfoundland women's history vary considerably from those available to Canadian scholars, as noted in the bibliographical comments.

The difficulty in reconstructing working-class women's experience in St. John's lies in piecing detail unto detail to reveal a complex and vivid female past. Rediscovering working-class women in Newfoundland history is a provocative and challenging process; a process which has only just begun.

1890 – 1914

In 1890, St. John's was a commercial and maritime centre with a population of 30,000 and an economy centered on the waterfront. As in other seaports, employment was seasonal for many craftsmen and labourers. Perhaps the most explicit description of the household economy of the working poor is contained in a conversation recorded in a local newspaper in 1890. A reporter had questioned an aged dock worker: how had he supported a family on less than $100 a year? The longshoreman replied that "then the seal fisheries were good ... This, with nurse-tending by my wife got me through till some of the family were grown up. I have two sons in the States ... and they send money occasionally. A daughter who lives with us is a tailoress and her addition to our income makes us fairly comfortable" (*DC* 19/9/1890).

It is probable that many women who worked outside the home in St. John's were young, childless, and single, while married women with dependents sought employment compatible with childtending and housekeeping. Certainly, at the turn of the century many married women in the city were home workers, employed at piece-rates by local factories. Perhaps as many as 350 girls and women worked in such a fashion for the two largest concerns, the Colonial Cordage Company (the Ropewalk) and the Newfoundland Clothing Company. They sewed and finished garments, knitted nets, and made twine. Contracting and subcontracting were also standard practices among many marginal tailoring and clothing firms. Piecework completed at home was commonly done at rates far below factory scales, and the wages paid women in these factories were very small indeed, averaging $1.75 to $3.00 weekly.[4] There are indications that home work declined through the decades as businesses consolidated production within their factory gates. In 1914, the manager of the Newfoundland Clothing Company testified that company work "is now all done in the factories ... for some years, we gave out trousers to be done, ... now ... all work is done in the factory."[5]

In 1903, the number of female factory workers in the city was estimated at six hundred; these girls and women were employed in clothing, boot and shoe, cordage, and confectionery firms. A 1905 figure indicated fifteen hundred working women, an estimate which included retail clerks and office workers (*ET* 14/10/1903; *TR* 20/5/1905). Unfortunately, the Newfoundland census for the prewar period did not record urban occupational data by gender. Without information on the marital status and age of working women, it is almost impossible to recreate a lifecycle for St. John's female wage-earners in this period. Although statistics are elusive, evidence compiled from government documents, city directories, and newspapers allows certain generalizations about women's work in prewar St. John's. The first is the continued significance of traditional female occupations – domestic service remained the largest single employer of women. The second is the importance of female operatives in the manufacture of consumer goods.

Servants were the largest group of female wage-earners in St. John's. It was the conventional wisdom of the day that the most agreeable domestic servant was an outport girl; oral evidence indicates that it was common practice for rural Newfoundland girls to enter service with families in neighboring villages, to assist with domestic duties, and to aid in the fishery.[6] If this was true in the nineteenth century as well, outport women employed as servants in St. John's were simply expanding traditional rural practices. Domestic service remained unattractive to many women, because of the long hours, small wages, and almost constant supervision. In the 1890's general servants expected $3 per month; by 1914, this had increased to $5 or $6 monthly. In St. John's, there was the familiar "domestic problem," as girls were reluctant to enter or remain in service; the newspapers constantly carried advertisements for general servants, housemaids, and cooks.

While domestic service was a traditional female occupation, factory work for women in St. John's was relatively recent. The Newfoundland government encouraged the establishment of a secondary manufacturing sector through preferential tariffs, subsidies, and special legislation, as part of a diversification strategy to lessen Newfoundland's dependence on the fishery. During the period 1870 to 1900 there was a visible shift from primary manufacturing to the production of consumer goods;[7] it was in these latter industries that women operatives were employed as cheap labour.

Local factories employed large numbers of working-class women. Archibald's Tobacco works hired 100 girls and women in 1886 (80 percent of their labour force), who removed stems from tobacco leaf and wrapped plugs; 120 females worked in the Harvey's Tobacco Works in 1898, and 70 in 1903, this latter number remaining somewhat constant until 1914 (*DC* 1/4/1886; *ET* 31/8/1898; *TR* 16/5/1903). The Ropewalk had traditionally employed women and girls in the manufacture of nets and twine. Following a fire, the factory was rebuilt and enlarged in 1886; it accommodated 100 to 300 employees, the divergent numbers reflecting seasonal and yearly fluctuations. The Ropewalk frequently advertised for family labour, promising employment "for the entire family ... new and commodious houses ... good school convenient." But girls ten years of age and upwards and women were hired at the Ropewalk under conditions which the press termed "sweating," and at wages which were subsistent: 25 cents per day, $1.60 weekly (*ET* 15/3/1892; 15/9/1906). Women were also employed in smaller numbers in bakery and confectionery firms, boot and shoe factories, and in steam laundries. But it was in the clothing industry that female labour was predominant. The five clothing factories in St. John's employed three hundred workers in 1914, 80 percent of whom were women (Dominions Royal Commission 1915, 106).

In the larger factories, work was segregated by skill, and, apparently, by sex. Although women were numerous on the factory floor, they seldom secured well-paying or supervisory jobs; these skilled positions were held predominantly by males, frequently foreign. Hours were long, wages small, and employment erratic; factories frequently closed because of mechanical difficulties, inventory shortages, and labour problems. Although the majority of women operatives worked in large factories, a sizeable number were employed in the middling and small enterprises, marginal businesses which averaged fewer than five employees, and where conditions were even less satisfactory (Joy 1977, 41 – 2).

Women employed in factories and small firms struck on a number of occasions. In 1899, girls employed in Ropewalk refused to work overtime without pay; they were fired and replaced. In 1902, wrapping girls at Harvey's struck for higher wages; the strike collapsed when management refused concessions. There were two strikes by women employees in 1904; in one case the strikers secured an extra 50 cents per week (*ET* 9/5/1902; 14/3/1904; 12/4/1904). The most dramatic involvement of women in labour protest occurred in 1913 when women operatives at Parker and Monroe walked off their jobs in support of striking male workers. St. John's unions were sympathetic to the plight of the women and donated monies to sustain their sympathy strike (*EH* 24/4/1913; 1/5/1913).

The St. John's female factory worker was particularly vulnerable, as she was not protected by minimum wage legislation or factory inspection acts. Perhaps nowhere was that vulnerability as pronounced as at the Newfoundland Clothing Company. In January 1912, female operatives in the pants department struck, protesting a reduction in piece-rates. Some of the strikers obtained employment in other St. John's factories; others were forced to resume work without obtaining any concessions. Yet evidence presented to the Dominions Royal Commission in 1914 suggests the persistence of worker discontent and the extraordinary measures adopted by management to dispel it: "Three years ago we had some labour difficulties, with the result that we sent out our manager to Leeds and set up a factory to make clothing and brought in a large quantity of goods for two years. We overcame the labour difficulty and ceased to bring manufactured clothing into the Colony" (*ET* 22/2/1912; Dominions Royal Commission 1915, 107).

The employment of women as cheap labour created tensions among male craftsmen; journeymen tailors viewed with alarm the increasing employment of women in the smaller tailoring shops.[8] These female assistants were hired at piece-rates far below craft schedules. Although they seldom threatened the most competent and experienced of employees – the cutters and the fitters – they frequently displaced journeymen tailors on the floor, especially during the dull seasons. Journeymen tailors in St. John's were a small but highly skilled group of tradesmen with a long tradition of collective action and organization. In 1904, they had affiliated with the Journeymen Tailors Union of America (JTU) as Local 410, the first international affiliate in Newfoundland.[9] Their response to the employment of women was threefold: first, to insist that women hired

as cheap labour be restricted to unskilled jobs; second, to demand
equal wages be paid women performing the same work as their male
counterparts; and third, to actively recruit women as members of
Local 410.

Tension in the tailoring firms became open conflict in 1911 when
Local 410 struck the city firm of Mark Chaplin ("King of the Tailors"). It was reported that the union had demanded the prohibition
of female labour. This was vigorously denied by the union president
in a strong letter which defined the position of the union on female
workers and reiterated the demand of equal wages for equal work:
"[Union men] refused to work on a premises [sic] where cheap labour
is employed, that is, female labour ... The Union would like most
emphatically to state that it does not want the services of female help
... dispensed with. What it does object to is females ... being paid
very much less than the journeymen on a similar job. When female
help is able to do equally as good work as the male, there is no
justification for that class being paid less than the other ... " The
strike was settled to the satisfaction of the union (*EC* 18/5/1911; *DN*
26/5/1911).

Local 410 actively recruited tailoresses as members. In September
1910, Hugh Robinson, international organizer for the JTU, visited
St. John's. Sensitive to the organizing potential of women workers,
he underlined the advantages to females of trade unionism; a subsequent issue of the JTU journal, *The Tailor*, listed the first women
in St. John's to join Local 410 (*The Tailor* Nov. 1910, 31). Yet the
protection afforded by unionism covered only a small segment of
the needle trades and an even smaller proportion of women workers.
By the outbreak of the war in 1914, more female hands were employed by the Newfoundland Clothing Company than by union tailor
shops.

In 1907, the largest single group of female workers listed in the
city directory was retail clerks.[10] The increasing number of women
employed in local stores reflects dramatic alterations in the retail
business and marks the demise of the shop assistant as a skilled male
occupation (Holcombe 1973, ch. 4). In 1890, a discouraged draper
urged parents not to apprentice their sons as shop assistants: "The
trade is such an effeminate one that girls learn it quickly and by
working for smaller wages they take the place of the male drapers."
As in factory work, hours were long; assistants were required to
work after hours, often until midnight. Women stood the entire day:
"in all the shops the lady assistants are not permitted to seat themselves at any time between regular business hours." Premises were
ill-ventilated and unheated. (*DC* 14/2/1887; 4/3/1890; *EH* 6/9/1907;

24/4/1893; 26/11/1898). These conditions were not peculiar to New-foundland; however no protective legislation for shop girls was enacted in the colony until the passage of a Shop Closing Act in 1936. The St. John's Retail Clerks Union (1907–1912) expressed interest in the organization of female shop girls. Throughout 1908, enthusiastic meetings were convened and proposals adopted for the admission of women and the establishment of a Ladies' Branch. It is unclear why the movement to organize women stalled; however, by 1911 the Retail Clerks union in St. John's had collapsed as a viable labour organization (*ET* 14/1/1908/; *EH* 4/10/1909; *Fishermen's Advocate* 19/11/1910).

Many women, discouraged by job prospects at home, emigrated. The patterns of female emigration were twofold: the immigration of outport girls to St. John's, and the emigration of outport and city women alike to Canada and New England. Contemporaries were alarmed by the extent of female mobility. Outport representatives complained that the scarcity of female labour disrupted the fishery; Archbishop Howley preached against emigration, warning that young girls "that had gone away ... had become the victims of the White Slave Traffic." Newfoundland girls were recruited as operatives and domestic servants. Factory agents, frequently local men employed with the steamship or railroad lines, advanced passage monies, arranged travel schedules and secured lodgings for prospective employees. Advertisements for domestic service in Canada were common in all Newfoundland newspapers. A local enterprise, the Newfoundland Employment Agency, operated by a Mrs George Walsh, was highly visible throughout the period 1906 to 1914, recruiting women as cooks, housemaids and general servants for the genteel classes in the city, as well as for positions in Maritime Canada (*EC* 621/9/1909; *ET* 2/5/1907; *EH* 3/5/1905).

Statistics are not available for Newfoundland women who left the Colony under the sponsorship of Maritime factories or employment agencies; we do not know the numbers who followed family and kin to labour in distant cities, nor can we state with certainty why they left.[11] Yet to an outport girl with few opportunities for remunerative employment, to a domestic employed in St. John's at $3 per month, or to the city factory worker surviving on a couple of dollars a week, the prospect of higher wages and easier working conditions may have been compelling. An outport girl en route to Montreal as a domestic was interviewed in 1912 by a local correspondent. She reported that she had been offered a position in a St. John's stationery shop at $6.50 a month. "If that is all St. John's can offer me, then I must make my future elsewhere" (*ET* 16/5/1912).

1914–1921

World War I revitalized the sagging Newfoundland economy, which
had been crippled by the recession of 1913 and 1914 and by British
embargoes on salt fish shipments to Mediterranean areas. Wartime
demands dramatically expanded Newfoundland markets, stimulated
local economic activity – particularly in the secondary manufacturing
sector in St. John's – and increased job opportunities for the city's
working women. Women filled positions vacated by men who had
volunteered for military service; by 1918 almost twenty-six hundred
men from St. John's had enlisted, 30 percent of the city's male population seventeen years of age and over.[12] Although conventional
mores regarding suitable jobs for women prevented their employment in many "male" occupations, such as waterfront labour, the
war broadened economic prospects for the city's female workers. An
article in the St. John's *Daily News* commented: "By means of this
war thousands of the best of the manhood of the nation have been
killed and wounded and woman ... has been thrust into service so
that now she is prepared to occupy a new role in the industrial and
economic work of the world" (15/4/1918).

During the war years, the demand for female factory workers
intensified as city manufacturers expanded existing production facilities and established new firms. In the fall of 1915, a munitions
factory commenced operation, providing steady employment for
over one hundred workers (Smallwood 1937, 1:344). Two clothing
factories and a woollen mill were opened, and existing clothing concerns were renovated to allow the employment of additional operatives. Almost the entire work force in these sectors was female. The
number of female workers in St John's during this period aroused
much comment; a visitor to the city in 1918 observed: "In our early
walks in the morning have we not been struck with the multitude
of young girls – some of them hardly old enough to be away from
school – all hurrying away to the factories and other places of employment (*DN* 15/7/1918). Because of increased employment opportunities for women, there are indications that the "domestic
problem," which already existed in the city, worsened; in St. John's,
as elsewhere, girls were reluctant to enter service when other jobs
were available. One woman commented critically that the ladies of
the local Current Events Club devoted a great deal of discussion to
the domestic question and concluded wryly that there were more
pressing issues among working women than the servant crisis (*DN*
22/2/1919).

As has been mentioned, prior to the war, working women in St.

John's had initiated a number of strikes and had been involved in several trade unions. Yet the actual number of unionized female workers was small, and their influence marginal; no women had served as union delegates or sat on union executives. In 1918, however, an autonomous labour organization, composed exclusively of female workers, was established. Although intended as a branch of the Newfoundland Industrial Workers Association (NIWA), an all-male industrial union formed in 1917, this new body had complete control over its own activities, handling its own finances and drafting its own by-laws. The organizing effort commenced on 8 August 1918 when the following invitation was circulated: "At the request of a large number of those interested, there will be a meeting of the girl workers of all city factories in the British Hall at 8 o'clock this Thursday night, for the purpose of forming a Ladies' Branch of the New-foundland Industrial Workers Association. All those ladies who are wage earners in any capacity are also invited to be present" (*DN* 18/8/1918).

The response to the notice was overwhelming; within five weeks, the NIWA Ladies' Branch had over four hundred members. Although the vast majority of members were factory workers, women in other occupations, notably domestics, also joined.[13]

Under the energetic direction of its president, Julia Salter Earle, the Ladies' Branch attempted to alleviate the difficulties of working women, especially female factory workers. In a letter to the *Daily News*, Salter Earle described the plight of many women operatives: "There are those who toil so hard all day, sometimes having to stand from 7 a.m. until 6 p.m. with no words of sympathy, working nearly in every case for a wage which cannot give anything but bread, butter and tea." She noted that some members of the Ladies' Branch received as little as $1.60 to $3.50 a week. In another article, she commented "I stood outside one of our factories the other night about 9:30 p.m. and waited as the girls lined out. With very little strength they wandered home, too tired in many cases to even enjoy the rest that nature craves to enable them to start again the next day" (*DN* 22/2/1919).

Committed to the cause of female workers, the NIWA Ladies' Branch pressed for shorter working hours, better factory conditions and higher wages for women. The Ladies' Branch intervened on more than one occasion to have a fired worker reinstated, and to present employees' grievances to management. In the fall of 1918, women members of the NIWA struck two local factories. The first strike occurred at a bakery and confectionery firm, when employees demanded higher wages. The second walkout was initiated by union members at the cordage company who objected to the employment of non-union labour. Although the strike at the bakery failed, strikers at the Ropewalk won concessions. If the Ladies' Branch was not successful in attaining all its objectives, some gains were made, particularly in the improvement of working conditions. Perhaps because the Ladies' Branch was effective in addressing the special interests of female workers, proposals for the formation of a ladies' branch of the retail clerks' union were seriously considered in June 1919. The plans were abandoned, however, as the postwar slump deepened into a severe economic depression (*DN* 30/8/1918; *ET* 30/11/ 1918; 27/6/1919).

Economic growth in many nations slackened after World War I, but as the London *Times* noted, "in few countries has the change from prosperity to adversity following the aftermath of the war been so marked as in Newfoundland." The St. John's economy suffered directly; in the fall of 1920 the Governor of Newfoundland, Alexander Harris, described business in the city as extremely restricted. Many city companies became insolvent and factories closed. Those factories which survived frequently operated on short-time. Retail outlets were also affected. It was announced in the *Evening Telegram* that "one store in particular has had to give notice to its entire staff as it is going out of business at the end of the month."[14]

What impact did the postwar depression have on the employment of women in St. John's? Government officials, church leaders, businessmen, and labour leaders earnestly discussed the increasing unemployment in the city, but little concern was expressed for the unemployed working woman except as the daughters or wives of unemployed men. Although women workers were doubly vulnerable, threatened by the contraction of limited job options, and the competition of returned soldiers, their plight went unnoticed by most contemporaries. This silence can largely be explained by the prevailing ideology of the "male breadwinner," which held that an adult male ought to be the primary, and ideally the only, wage-earner in the family. This ideology actively discouraged the employment of married women, and undermined the economic value of all women's waged labour, as it was assumed that female wages merely supplemented those of the male head of household. Few in St. John's, then, voiced distress about unemployed women, because presumably they had fathers or husbands to support them; it was perceived to be more crucial to secure work for men, as they were the "breadwinners" (Barrett and McIntosh 1980).

It was the lone voice of Julia Salter Earle who reminded the public that large numbers of working women were without jobs. In a letter to the Newfoundland House of Assembly, she appealed: "Do not forget the hundreds of girls also out of work on account of the factories closing." She explained in another letter that unemployed women were "girls supporting their little brothers and sisters ... girls boarding without father or mother or friends ... girls supporting widowed mothers" *ET* 14/6/1921, 31/1/1921). Those working as factory operatives appeared to be the largest group of female workers to suffer the consequences of the economic depression. Yet women working in other sectors were undoubtedly affected as well; female office workers lost their jobs when businesses failed and retail saleswomen were laid off or retained only part-time as purchasing power declined.

A review of job advertisements in several St. John's dailies from the fall of 1920 to the end of 1921 effectively illustrates the restricted job prospects for some. The vast majority of advertisements called for domestics, although employers commonly stated a preference for outport girls over their city counterparts. Domestic work outside the country remained available, although not at the volume recorded in the prewar period. While emigration to Canada and the United States became quite restricted for Newfoundland men, women emigrating as servants met few barriers. A Canadian government official explained that "the Canadian Immigration Act will allow women to land in Canada provided they are in good health and have assured employment or are such persons, as in the opinions of officials could easily secure work as domestics" (*ET* 26/06/1922). American immigration regulations were similar to those in Canada. Many young women may have been enticed to go to Montreal or Boston, especially as wages promised were twice the amount they could hope to secure in St. John's. During the war there had been daily advertisements for female workers in many of the larger plants; in the postwar period, no advertisements for manufacturing work appeared, aside from employment notices for bottlers at an aerated-water factory. There were scattered, but consistent advertisements for saleswomen and typists, while those for bookkeepers, tailoresses and teachers appeared only infrequently (*ET* 15/8/1921; *DN* 5/11/1918).

In 1921, how many women retained jobs or secured new employment in the city? Data compiled from the enumerators' lists – the manuscript records for the 1921 census – indicated that 2,829 women in St. John's were wage-earners.[15] These working women comprised 21.4 percent of the urban work force, significant statistics, although slightly less than those recorded in neighboring Maritime cities – comparable figures for working women in Halifax, Nova

Scotia, and Saint John, New Brunswick, were 25.5 and 23.8 percent respectively. Unfortunately these numbers tell us little about the rate of unemployment among women seeking work. Published census figures, however, reveal a disproportionate number of women in the city, particularly between the ages of fifteen and twenty-four; in these age cohorts, there were over fifteen hundred more females than men. This imbalance in the sex ratio caused by the influx of outport girls to the capital, and the heavy fatalities among the city's war recruits, was similar to demographic patterns in Canadian cities at this time. As a result of this imbalance, there was a large pool of young women in St. John's who had limited opportunities of marriage. Therefore, the actual number of women seeking employment was high, and those already in the work force tended to remain longer than usual.

In 1921 the largest proportion of working women in St. John's– 34 percent – was employed in domestic service. This figure is quite high when compared with other Canadian cities; in Halifax, for example, domestics represented only 20 percent of the employed female labour force. Retail and clerical employees comprised the next largest occupational groupings for female workers; saleswomen made up 14.7 percent of the female work force, while typists and stenographers represented 10.1 percent. Women in these occupations alone – domestic service, retail and clerical work – constituted nearly 60 percent of the city's women workers. Although the number of women employed in individual manufacturing categories was not large, the manufacturing sector as a whole accounted for 17.9 percent of female wage earners. The numbers of professional women were small, constituting only 10 percent of the women workers. Of course, professionals were concentrated in "female" professions such as teaching, nursing, and librarianship; in 1921, there was only a single woman doctor in the city.

With some exceptions, the patterns of women's paid work in St. John's paralleled those found in other urban centres in Canada. Women who worked tended to be young and single. Wage employment for many women was a relatively brief stage in their lives between leaving school and getting married. Women were concentrated into a small number of "female" occupations. Although domestic service continued to be the largest field of employment, clerical and retail work became increasingly important as suitable occupations for women. Employment in manufacturing had slackened during the postwar economic depression, but this sector still employed a significant number of women.

General conditions in the city threatened many women's jobs in

1921, and evidence indicates that some female workers were laid off. Yet, women's presence in the city's labour force remained intact; in fact, their participation increased over the next decade. Contrary to popular impressions, women were not passive and docile workers; when conditions were favourable, they demonstrated their willingness to organize and to strike. Women workers in St. John's were vulnerable because of larger economic determinants, particularly the limited job opportunities for urban female wage workers and the precarious nature of the city's economy.

NOTE ON SOURCES

There are no reliable secondary accounts of working-class women in St. John's for this period; Newfoundland lacks many of the sources utilized by Canadian historians of other regions. Census data usually provide a beginning point for a description of wage-earning women and the nature of their labour. Published data indicate the level of female participation in the labour force over time; they frequently allow analysis of female employment patterns by age, marital status, occupation, industry, region, and less often, by earnings. The Newfoundland census for 1891, 1901, 1911, and 1921 permits no equivalent examination. The occupational classifications are too broad to be useful for an urban labour force, and more critically, they exclude gender as a variable.

In Canada and the United States, census data are often supplemented by statistical material on women workers compiled by government investigators – Department of Labour reports and archival files, official government publications, factory inspection reports, minimum-wage board investigations and decisions, Royal Commission reports or Senate hearings. There are no Newfoundland equivalents. Although evidence presented to the Newfoundland Tariff Commission (1898) and the Dominions Royal Commission (1914) touched briefly on the lives of working women, particularly factory operatives and needlewomen, it did so only incidentally; no women workers testified. Although the establishment of a Labour Bureau was promised in 1910, government files on labour matters remained sporadic and scattered through a series of archival holdings. There are no government publications equivalent to the Canadian *Labour Gazette*, with its wealth of statistics on unemployment, wage schedules, industry conditions, and labour disputes. Elsewhere, reformers or interested observers left rich and detailed accounts of the working poor and labouring women. Visitors to Newfoundland were drawn to the social conditions and culture of the outports; few commented on the working-class people of St. John's.

Ironically, empirical data for Newfoundland women between the wars is much richer than that of Canada; enumerator lists for the 1921, 1935, and 1945 census are available on microfilm at the Centre for Newfoundland Studies, Memorial University of Newfoundland, and at the Provincial Archives of Newfoundland and Labrador. Similar data from the Canadian census will not be open to the public for some time. The urban daily press remains a rich and colorful source for women's history in the capital, providing us with rare and fragmented glimpses of working-class women. Given the minimum amount of other contextual evidence, it is a valuable source.

NOTES

1 Abbreviations for newspapers cited are as follows:
   DC Daily Colonist (St. John's)
   TR Trade Review (St. John's)
   DN Daily News (St. John's)
   ET Evening Telegram (St. John's)
   EH Evening Herald (St. John's)
   EC Evening Chronicle (St. John's)
   Other newspapers cited but not abbreviated include the *Times* (St. John's), *The Tailor* (Chicago), the *Fishermen's Advocate* (St. John's) and the *Times* (London).

2 A more detailed version of this paper was presented to the History Graduate Seminar 689/700 at Memorial University of Newfoundland. See Chisholm, 1986.

3 The period included in the research was subsequently extended to 1939. See Forestell 1987.

4 For factory work, see *TR* 26/3/1910; *DN* 27/3/1896; *Times* 5/10/1892. On contracting, see testimony by W.J. Clouston, quoted in *Evidence as to a Revision* (St John's, 1898), 29–30.

5 See testimony by Mr. Bishop to *Royal Commission on the Natural Resources* (England 1915), 108.

6 On domestic service in rural Newfoundland, see Antler 1983; on general literature, see Katzman 1978; Barber 1985.

7 For government encouragement of Newfoundland industry, see Joy 1977.

8 For a detailed description of the employment of women in the tailoring trade, see Chisholm 1986, 16–24.

9 For tailors' organizations in St. John's, see *EH* 1, 7, 21/10/1896; *The Tailor* July 1904, 17; August 1904, 14.

10 Calculations from *McAlpine's* 1907–8.

11 For an overview of Newfoundland migration patterns, see Thornton 1985; the *Fisherman's Advocate* 19/11/1910; *EH* 9/5/1906; *ET* 3/3/1910.

12 For the impact of the war, see O'Brien 1982. Enlistment statistics were compiled by Christopher Sharpe and Jessie Chisholm for volume 3 of the *Historical Atlas of Canada* (Toronto: University of Toronto Press, forthcoming).

13 For a detailed history of the NIWA, see McInnis 1987; on the formation of the Ladies' Branch, see *DN* 18/8/1918 and 17/9/1918.

14 The *Times* (London) 8/7/1921, reprinted in *ET* 8/8/1921; Dispatch, Harris to Milner, 30 September 1920, CO Series 194, volume 229; *ET* 22/11/1920, 17/12/1920.

15 *Sixth Census of Canada* 1921, vol. 14 (Canada, 1929): occupations. Newfoundland printed returns in the *Census of Newfoundland and Labrador, 1921*, vol. 1 (England, 1923). For a detailed analysis, see Forestell, 1987.

MARIE FRANCE LABRECQUE ET MARIA ELISA
MONTEJO

Travail salarié dans la campagne mexicaine: dépendance ou autonomie?

Partant d'une expérience récente sur le terrain, au Yucatán (Mexique), nous examinons ce que représente pour les femmes l'introduction du travail salarié à la campagne, dans le cadre d'un programme gouvernemental d'intégration des femmes au développement dans un contexte de crise économique.

Les activités des femmes participant à ce programme sont variées. En comparant deux types d'activité salariée dont l'une se déroule à la maison et l'autre à l'extérieur, nous voulons nuancer la corrélation qui a été établie entre travail salarié et autonomie des femmes.

Waged Work in Rural Mexico: Dependence or Autonomy?

Following recent fieldwork in Yucatan, Mexico, we examine the implications of the introduction of remunerated work for peasant women within the framework of a governmental program designed to integrate women into development during an economic crisis.

The activities of women within this program are varied. The comparison of two types of remunerated activities performed by these women, one within the home, the other outside, leads us to reexamine the correlation that has been made between remunerated work and the autonomy of women.

Notre but est de comprendre davantage le lien contradictoire qui existe entre l'intégration des femmes des campagnes mexicaines au travail salarié d'une part et la dépendance idéologique qui continue de les caractériser d'autre part. Nous n'avons pas l'intention de revenir sur la critique féministe à l'endroit d'Engels (e.g., Deere 1982, Beechey 1982, Roldan 1983). Il est en effet relativement bien établi que le travail salarié des femmes ne suffit pas à mettre fin à leur subordination sociale et idéologique. Cette constatation s'appuie sur de nombreuses études de cas dans pratiquement toutes les parties du monde (BIT 1982, Buvinic et al. 1983, Nash et Safa 1986, Leacock et Safa 1986).

Il est entendu que le travail salarié des femmes varie à l'infini et qu'elles peuvent être actives dans différents secteurs de la production. Pour un même secteur, que ce soit le secteur industriel, le secteur agraire ou celui des services, les conditions de travail sont également très variables. Or, même si les chercheures décrivent bien les conditions de travail, elles les utilisent rarement pour raffiner l'analyse de la subordination liée à ces conditions. En d'autres termes, on fait comme si la subordination idéologique des femmes était relativement homogène et indépendante des conditions ambiantes de travail.

Il ne s'agit pas de nier non plus que la subordination des femmes est la résultante du patriarcat ou de la domination masculine, selon le cas. Cependant, cette généralisation tend à masquer les variations possibles de l'idéologie et des mécanismes par lesquels elle s'impose. Notre recherche récente au Mexique nous a donné l'occasion d'examiner différentes formes de travail salarié des femmes paysannes au sein d'un projet de développement promu par l'État et destiné spécifiquement à ces dernières.

On ne discutera pas ici du bien-fondé de ce type de projet puisqu'il existe sur le sujet un corpus important de littérature critique avec lequel nous sommes d'accord (Rogers 1980, Mignot–Lefebvre 1985, Staudt 1985). Il demeure que des milliers de femmes sont enrégimentées dans ces projets de développement et qu'elles doivent s'accommoder de leurs conséquences. Or, comme dans toute expérience, ces conséquences sont contradictoires. Tout n'est pas que négatif. Par l'observation et l'analyse du contenu matériel des projets, il est possible d'identifier les conditions de travail qui renforcent ou affaiblissent la subordination idéologique. L'état d'avancement de nos travaux ne nous permet pas de tirer de conclusions définitives sur le rapport entre conditions matérielles et reproduction idéologique. Pour cette raison, nous nous pencherons surtout pour le moment sur les conditions matérielles du travail des femmes.

La recherche sur laquelle se base notre étude s'est déroulée dans le Nord du Yucatán. Le projet de développement qui nous intéresse, appelé Unité agricoles et industrielles pour les femmes, a été conçu en 1971, activé en 1975 lors de l'Année internationale de la Femme, et enfin mis en oeuvre en 1979. En 1986, il avait atteint sa vitesse de croisière. Il a pour objectifs de retenir les familles paysannes à

la campagne, de relever le revenu paysan et de diminuer le taux de
natalité. En le comparant à d'autres projets pour les femmes, on
constate qu'il s'agit d'un projet tout à fait classique.

Il y a une centaine d'unités agricoles et industrielles de ce genre
au Yucatán. En compagnie d'une équipe d'assistantes, nous en avons
étudié six en profondeur dans une sous-région sélectionnée pour
son homogénéité à différents points de vue: économique, social et
idéologique. Les activités de production de ces unités sont variées et
leur étude nous permet justement de comparer des conditions de
travail fort différentes les unes des autres. Une unité particulière
peut s'adonner à l'une ou l'autre des activités suivantes: la couture,
le tissage de hamac, la broderie, l'horticulture, l'élevage de porcs et
de poulets, la floriculture, la récupération de rebuts de fibres de
sisal, et la confection de paniers.

Les femmes qui font partie des unités n'exercent aucun contrôle
sur le procès de production. L'État est à l'origine de l'ensemble du
programme et l'encadre étroitement par plusieurs institutions. La
plupart du temps, les unités qui reçoivent un crédit de fonctionnement n'arrivent pas à le rembourser totalement, ce qui a pour
conséquence d'accroître leur dépendance vis-à-vis de l'État. Bien que
ce problème mériterait qu'on s'y arrête longuement, nous nous en
tiendrons aux conditions actuelles de travail dans les unités. Dans
une démarche que nous voulons dialectique, nous considérerons ces
conditions à la fois comme résultant de la subordination historique
des femmes et comme engendrant de nouvelles formes de subordination ou éventuellement d'émancipation.

Nous nous proposons dans les lignes qui suivent de présenter les
similarités et les différences caractérisant deux des unités étudiées.
Les femmes qui font partie de la première unité tissent des hamacs
et les autres pratiquent l'horticulture. Dans les deux cas, les femmes
reçoivent un salaire à la pièce.

LA CONFECTION DE HAMACS À NOLO, AU YUCATÁN

La première unité est située dans le village de Nolo qui compte
environ 1500 habitants. A partir de Mérida, capitale de l'État du
Yucatán, il faut compter environ une trentaine de minutes pour se
rendre à Nolo en automobile (28 km, direction est). Quatre-vingt-
deux femmes font partie de l'unité, mais une soixantaine seulement
confectionnent des hamacs. Cette activité traditionelle s'exerce à la
maison. Elle nécessite des instruments de travail comme un *bastidor*
(métier à tisser) et des navettes en bois de fabrication artisanale. Il
faut aussi la matière première, les fils, que l'unité achète en utilisant
le crédit accordé par la Banque agraire.

La confection de hamacs se faisant à la maison, les femmes ont la possibilité de s'acquitter de plusieurs tâches à la fois. Tout en travaillant, elles surveillent les enfants, jettent un coup d'oeil aux aliments durant la cuisson ou, simplement, regardent la télévision ou encore écoutent la radio. En fait, le tissage de hamacs pour l'Unité agricole et industrielle de Nolo ne change pas l'organisation du travail domestique. Notons d'ailleurs qu'à Nolo ces deux activités ont de tout temps été associées.

Si l'on examine la manière dont se fait l'apprentissage de la confection de hamacs, on s'aperçoit qu'il est intégré, comme les autres tâches domestiques, au processus d'éducation des enfants. Cette formation suppose qu'une personne expérimentée, en l'occurence la mère, supervise l'enfant, lequel apprend surtout en observant les gestes des adultes. On fait en sorte que la fille ou le garçon aprenne à tisser rapidement, c'est-à-dire que le tissage devienne une activité exercée de façon machinale, une fois compris le procès de travail.

En ce qui a trait aux gestes exécutés lors de la confection du hamac, certaines qualités sont indispensables. Ainsi, l'artisane doit faire preuve de dextérité pour séparer les fils d'une main et faufiler la navette de l'autre. Cette tâche nécessite aussi de l'endurance, même dans le cas d'une artisane expérimentée car le tissage s'effectue debout et il faut en moyenne une soixantaine d'heures pour fabriquer un hamac. En outre, la patience devient essentielle puisque la répétition systématique des gestes est fastidieuse et que l'artisane a souvent l'impression de ne pas progresser dans son travail.

Le tissage de hamacs comprend trois étapes: la bordure (*orilla*), la partie centrale (*cuerpo*) et les extrémités (*brazos*). Toutes les artisanes savent les deux premières mais la confection des extrémités est confiée à certains hommes du village qui, selon les témoignages de membres de l'unité, sont experts en la matière. Les femmes payent les hommes en leur versant de 7 à 10 pour cent du salaire qu'elles reçoivent pour un hamac.

L'artisane est maîtresse du temps qu'elle consacre à son ouvrage. Une femme peut s'y donner une fois par jour pendant deux heures alors qu'une autre tissera quatre fois par jour et arrivera à un total de six heures, selon l'organisation des tâches à l'extérieur de la maison. L'achèvement du produit n'est pas compromis même si les femmes ne tissent pas pendant une ou plusieurs journées. Si les femmes contrôlent les deux premières étapes de la confection, il leur faut toutefois prévoir la disponibilité de l'homme qui sera chargé du tissage des extrémités. Il faut en effet être en mesure de remettre le produit fini à la date fixée par la Banque agraire au moment où le prêt est consenti à l'unité. C'est là la première contrainte qui s'exerce sur l'artisane, contrainte venant de l'extérieur.

La Banque agraire se réservant le droit de refuser les produits qui ne correspondent pas à ses normes, le contrôle de la qualité incombe entièrement à l'artisane. C'est elle qui juge si les fils sont en bon état, si les dimensions du hamac, le nombre de mailles, la combinaison de couleurs, etc. sont adéquates; en plus, elle s'assurera que celui qui sera chargé des extrémités du hamac peut accomplir un travail satisfaisant.

Par ailleurs, les événements communautaires ne doivent pas entrer en conflit avec la production. Les femmes participant à des festivités, religieuses ou autres, s'assurent qu'une autre artisane tisse à leur place, ou alors elles prennent de l'avance. Lorsqu'une artisane est en retard, il lui faut parfois tisser une ou deux nuits sans arrêt pour remettre le produit à temps.

Quant au revenu des artisanes de l'unité de Nolo, il est très bas si l'on considère le nombre d'heures investies et les qualités exigées des productrices. En moyenne, une artisane confectionne un hamac par mois et gagne un salaire équivalent au quart du revenu moyen des hommes pour une même période. Le salaire des femmes ne peut suffire à payer les aliments, souvent achetés à crédit. Il est important de noter qu'avant la présente crise économique aiguë, la confection traditionnelle des hamacs assurait aux artisanes un revenu qu'elles pouvaient utiliser à des fins personnelles. Toutefois, le revenu des femmes reste toujours inférieur à celui des hommes.

Qu'est-ce qui pousse les femmes à accepter de travailler dans de telles conditions? D'une part, c'est un métier qu'elles connaissent bien. En outre, elles possèdent déjà les outils de production et ne sont pas obligées de sortir du village pour se procurer la matière première. D'autre part, elles sont assurées d'un revenu mensuel.

En somme, si l'on examine les rapports hommes-femmes, avant et après l'instauration de l'unité de production à Nolo, on constate qu'ils sont essentiellement les mêmes. Les hommes ne se sont jamais opposés à l'artisanat des femmes. Dans le contexte économique difficile qui prévaut actuellement au Mexique, ils ne peuvent pas nier la contribution importante du revenu des femmes au budget familial. Nous l'avons vu, il n'y a pas vraiment de réorganisation des tâches domestiques. Par contre, à cause de la crise économique et du chômage, les hommes commencent à tisser des hamacs. Les femmes, qui dépendaient du travail des artisans pour la confection des extrémités, pourraient éventuellement être remplacées par des hommes. Actuellement, il arrive qu'un homme fabrique des hamacs pour l'unité de production; c'est alors une femme, membre de l'unité qui livre le produit mais elle remet l'argent qui lui est versé à l'artisan, perdant ainsi un revenu traditionnellement réservé aux femmes.

LE CAS DE L'HORTICULTURE À LEPAN, YUCATÁN

La deuxième unité se trouve dans le village de Lepan, qui compte
à peu près 1000 habitants. Il est situé à environ quarante minutes
de route de Mérida, les communications s'effectuant fort bien. Sept
femmes font partie de l'unité et comme il s'agit d'horticulture, leurs
activités se déroulent hors de chez elles, sur un terrain qui leur a été
concédé. Les femmes doivent donc se déplacer entre leur maison et
le terrain. Comme le village est petit, aucune d'entre elles ne vit à
plus de 800 mètres de ce terrain. Elles s'y rendent en général le
matin, pendant que le repas de midi est en train de cuire. Celui-ci
est essentiellement composé de haricots noirs pouvant bouillir sans
surveillance. En général, un autre membre de la maisonnée se charge
d'acheter les tortillas, sorte de crêpe de maïs accompagnant tous les
repas. Les femmes quittent le terrain vers midi et y reviennent en
fin d'après-midi, surtout si les légumes, à cause de leur étape de
croissance et de la température, doivent être arrosés. Les productrices n'échappent pas à la règle implicite selon laquelle une femme
ne se déplace jamais seule. Elles se rendent au terrain avec un enfant,
leur mari ou une autre productrice. S'il arrive qu'une femme mariée
fasse un saut au terrain en solitaire, les célibataires par contre n'y
vont jamais seules.

Bref, le procès immédiat de travail de l'horticulture requiert de
la mobilité; il y a une séparation radicale entre la réalisation du procès
de travail et l'exécution des tâches domestiques. Le fait que les femmes aient à se déplacer nous montre clairement les limites de leur
autonomie physique.

La connaissance du procès de travail ne fait pas normalement
partie de la socialisation des femmes. Des techniciens du ministère
de l'Agriculture ont enseigné à quelques femmes certaines notions
d'horticulture; les autres membres de l'unité apprennent en observant les premières. Cependant, de l'avis de toutes les femmes de
l'unité, l'apprentissage du travail se fait par tâtonnements. Les témoignages montrent d'ailleurs qu'une unité d'horticulture fait plusieurs erreurs avant d'atteindre une bonne production. Les
connaissances techniques que l'on doit posséder pour mener à bien
ce procès de travail sont énormes. En fait, il ne s'agit pas d'un seul
procès de travail mais bien de plusieurs, les modalités de culture
variant selon qu'il s'agit de radis, de laitue, d'échalottes, de piments,
de tomates, de persil, etc. Dans chaque cas, l'irrigation, la vapori-
sation d'insecticides et d'herbicides, le degré d'exposition au soleil
varient considérablement. De plus, les produits chimiques ne sont
pas toujours les mêmes de sorte que les productrices doivent s'a-

dapter vaille que vaille à l'utilisation de nouveaux insecticides ou herbicides. En somme, toutes les étapes sont critiques: une seule erreur, une seule négligence, et la récolte est perdue. On ne sera pas surpris de savoir que l'État encadre étroitement tout ce procès de travail par l'intermédiaire de ses techniciens en agronomie qui doivent, en principe, se rendre une fois par semaine sur le terrain. Notons que tous les techniciens sont des hommes. L'horticulture comprend donc plusieurs procès de travail; chacun est complexe, assez spécialisé et aussi contrôlé pour assurer un bon volume de production et une bonne qualité du produit.

Ces procès de travail sont exécutés durant les heures les plus chaudes de la journée et sur un terrain qui, aux fins de son utilisation, doit être bien exposé au soleil. L'ensemble des tâches requiert par conséquent de l'endurance. Pour certains aspects du travail comme le sarclage, il faut aussi de la patience; de plus, une certaine force physique est nécessaire, notamment pour transporter les sacs de terre engraissée. Cette dernière exigence ouvre la porte à l'intervention du mari, du père ou d'un frère d'une productrice; toutefois, les femmes de l'unité, ne reculant nullement devant l'effort, sont tout à fait capables d'exécuter cette tâche.

En horticulture, la nature, bien que relativement domestiquée par l'utilisation d'insecticides et d'herbicides, dicte son rythme à l'intervention humaine. Si l'on veut réussir à produire, certaines opérations doivent être menées à bien à des moments précis et, dans ce cas, les décisions ne dépendent pas de l'initiative des productrices mais s'imposent à elles. En somme, les femmes ont peu de contrôle sur le procès de travail.

La qualité des produits dépend très peu des productrices même si les techniciens en agronomie estiment généralement que les femmes pourraient exercer un meilleur contrôle sur les différentes étapes de la culture. Ainsi, les facteurs climatiques peuvent avoir des effets négatifs sur la récolte. Des facteurs sociaux interviennent également. Par exemple, quelques éleveurs n'arrivent pas à empêcher leur bétail d'envahir le terrain, des voleurs s'introduisent parfois la nuit alors que le terrain n'est pas surveillé. L'horticulture baigne donc dans une certaine ambiance de fatalité.

Les événements communautaires influent également sur la production et, en ce sens, font aussi partie des conditions de production. Ainsi, les productrices n'hésiteront pas à abandonner momentanément leurs activités horticoles pour participer aux festivités qui ponctuent l'année. Cette relâche peut signifier la perte d'une partie de la récolte ou une production de moindre qualité.

Il faut dire que les revenus tirés de l'horticulture n'incitent guère les productrices à la ponctualité et à la constance. Par ailleurs, divers facteurs ont contribué à l'endettement de l'unité par le passé. Bien qu'assurée par les productrices, la vente des produits sert à rembourser l'institution de crédit et les sommes qu'elles consacrent à cette fin sont insuffisantes, ce qui a pour conséquence de ralentir le rythme du paiement de la dette.

Le revenu global des femmes est inférieur à celui de leur conjoint. Cependant, le sous-emploi chronique touchant les hommes et l'irrégularité de leurs revenus font en sorte que les femmes, malgré leur bas salaire, assurent le maintien et la reproduction de leur maisonnée pendant certaines périodes de l'année. Le salaire versé aux femmes est loin de leur procurer d'emblée l'autonomie économique; jamais elles n'utilisent, à des fins personnelles, l'argent gagné par leur travail. Toutefois, il arrive que les productrices et leurs enfants ne dépendent plus de façon absolue de leur mari ou de leur père. À l'opposé, ceux-ci se retrouvent parfois, provisoirement, en état de dépendance.

Dans la conjoncture actuelle de crise économique et de sous-développement, les hommes ne sont pas en position d'exiger de leur conjointe ou de leur fille qu'elles abandonnent leur emploi, lequel de plus, n'est accessible qu'à quelques femmes. Toutes proportions gardées, les hommes bénéficient de l'apport économique, même modeste, des femmes.

Si les hommes se gardent bien d'intervenir négativement sur le front économique, ils se permettront par contre de s'y manifester positivement. Ainsi, après avoir constaté qu'ils bénéficiaient des revenus générés par leur femme, ils n'hésitent pas à prêter main-forte et à participer au procès de travail. Comme ils ont en général un peu plus d'instruction et d'expérience que les femmes, ils s'immiscent même dans les tâches administratives que l'organisme de crédit confie aux membres de l'unité. Dernièrement, les productrices ont exprimé le désir que l'unité soit transformée en coopérative afin que les hommes aient le droit de s'y joindre officiellement, privilège qu'ils n'ont pas actuellement. D'une participation complaisante au procès de travail, les hommes semblent vouloir, avec l'accord des femmes, prendre le contrôle d'une bonne partie du procès de production.

Il nous semble qu'il s'agit là d'un effort implicite des hommes pour réaffirmer leur autorité sur les femmes. Cette autorité, au premier abord, paraît leur échapper parce que le procès de travail se déroule à l'extérieur de la maison et que les femmes sont sous la surveillance de techniciens, des hommes, ne l'oublions pas, mais des hommes de l'extérieur de la communauté. De plus, les hommes perçoivent l'horticulture comme une source de revenus toujours bas mais réguliers.

Ils souhaitent donc contrôler cette activité pour récupérer leur autorité basée traditionnellement sur leur contribution exclusive au revenu familial. Nous avons, dans ce cas, affaire à une détérioration des rapports hommes-femmes puisque les productrices ont potentiellement accès à l'autonomie, mais que celle-ci leur est déniée par un mécanisme de récupération.

Après avoir comparé deux unités (activités) de production différentes, à la fois par le lieu où elles se réalisent et par le procès même de travail, on constate que l'autonomie économique des femmes n'a pas augmenté. Dans le programme gouvernemental des unités de production, aucun mécanisme n'est prévu qui favoriserait une plus grande autonomie des femmes. Dans le cas de la confection des hamacs, on pourrait montrer aux artisanes la façon d'en tisser les extrémités. Il y aurait ainsi transfert de savoir-faire des hommes aux femmes qui pourraient se rendre compte qu'elles sont parfaitement capables d'exécuter cette étape de travail.

Dans le cas de l'horticulture, il conviendrait d'améliorer les techniques dans le but de permettre aux femmes de l'unité d'assumer toutes les tâches du procès de travail. De plus, la coopération entre les femmes favoriserait leur autonomie en éliminant leur dépendance des hommes pour l'exécution de certaines tâches.

En définitive, alors même que les femmes ont la possibilité d'exercer une activité rémunérée grace à la mise en oeuvre du programme gouvernemental *Unités agricoles et industrielles pour les femmes*, leurs conditions économiques ne se sont pas améliorées; au contraire, elles se sont détériorées. En fait, le travail salarié, qu'il soit accompli au domicile ou à l'extérieur, peut dans certains cas, comme ceux que nous avons étudiés, aller à l'encontre de l'autonomie des femmes. La crise économique pousse les femmes à chercher du travail mais le fait d'être salariées n'entraîne pas nécessairement pour elles une plus grande autonomie, que ce soit par rapport aux hommes ou par rapport à la société.

OMER CHOUINARD

Petite production et production domestique dans la péninsule acadienne

Les plans de modernisation de l'activité de pêche dans les années 1960–70, dans le nord-est du Nouveau-Brunswick, visaient à transformer le pêcheur-artisan en pêcheur-entrepreneur. L'État voulait alors accroître la productivité en séparant la main-d'oeuvre familiale du métier de pêcheur.

Cet article montre dans un premier temps la contribution du travail, tant domestique que salarié, des femmes de pêcheurs de la péninsule acadienne au maintien ou au support du métier de leur mari.

Deuxièmement, il fait ressortir que la disponibilité des femmes s'adapte aux nouvelles réalités: si le travail des femmes à l'extérieur est nécessaire au maintien du statut du pêcheur côtier en tant que producteur dépendant, il en va autrement pour les pêcheurs semi-hauturiers et leur statut de producteurs indépendants. Cependant, pour les deux catégories de pêcheurs, le travail domestique est le lot des épouses.

Petty Commodity and Domestic Production in the Acadian Peninsula

Plans for the modernization of the fishing industry over the period 1960–70 in north-east New Brunswick were designed to transform small-scale fishermen into entrepreneurs. The state wished to increase production by separating family labour power from the fishing industry.

The current article demonstrates, first of all, the contribution of the wage and domestic labour of fishermen's wives in the Acadian peninsula to the maintenance and support of their husbands' occupations. Second, it underlines that the availability of women's labour power adapts itself to new realities; while the wage labour of wives is necessary for the maintenance of the coastal fishermen as dependent producers, the situation is quite different for the wives of the semi-ocean fisherman and their status as independent producers. However, domestic labour is the responsibility of the wives of both types of fishermen.

Au début des années soixante, la petite production, dont le niveau de subsistance était relativement élevé, représentait un frein pour le développement de la société de consommation en région et particulièrement au Nouveau-Brunswick où 54 pour cent de la population vivait en milieu rural. Les programmes de modernisation visaient l'élimination du petit producteur indépendant au profit du pêcheur entrepreneur, afin de briser le cercle de l'auto-subsistance lié à la production domestique, et d'accroître la productivité des régions rurales. Ceci nécessitait l'aide de l'État. À cette destructuration de la petite production s'ajoutait un ensemble de programmes qui avaient pour but de socialiser la reproduction de la force de travail, tant au niveau régional que national, autour de la santé, de l'éducation, du bien-être, et de la culture.

Cette présentation vise à cerner la déstructuration-reconstruction de la petite production et de la production indépendante dans le secteur de la pêche au Nouveau-Brunswick, ainsi que le rôle de l'État, de la production domestique et plus particulièrement du travail des femmes au sein du foyer comme lieu de transfert de valeur vers le mode de production dominant. Ce travail gratuit permet la survivance du petit producteur pêcheur et contribue par ailleurs à la stabilité du producteur indépendant dans ce secteur.

PETITE PRODUCTION ET PRODUCTION MARCHANDE DANS LE SECTEUR DE LA PÊCHE AU NOUVEAU-BRUNSWICK

La petite production dont nous parlons ici possède un capital relativement limité. Le petit producteur pêcheur contrôle ses moyens de production; il est donc à la fois travailleur et propriétaire de ses moyens de production. De façon générale, il y a peu d'exploitation économique parce qu'on utilise de la main-d'oeuvre familiale ainsi qu'une quantité limitée de main-d'oeuvre payée, qui varie en fonction des espèces de poisson pêchées. C'est cette catégorie que nous appellerons pêcheur côtier. Elle comprend des bateaux de moins de 25 tonnes (– de 50 pieds).

D'autre part, il y a le producteur indépendant. D'après nos estimations faites sur le terrain à l'été de 1986 au moyen d'un questionnaire, les quantités produites sont généralement au moins dix fois plus élevées que celles produites par le pêcheur côtier. Le capital utilisé et le coût de la technologie sont environ vingt fois plus élevés. Le producteur indépendant est propriétaire de ses moyens de production et la nature des opérations de pêche nécessite une quantité de main-d'oeuvre plus élevée et une division du travail plus poussée entre les membres de l'équipage. Il y a aussi des différences avec la pêche côtière dans le type de rémunération. On voit se creuser ici la différence de rapports sociaux entre le travail et le capital.

La petite production et la production indépendante se comparent également du fait qu'on doit échanger le surplus de production de biens, ce qui constitue les bases objectives d'une accumulation privée. Le producteur indépendant sera appelé pêcheur semi-hauturier pour les fins de cet exposé. Cette catégorie comprend des bateaux de 25 à 100 tonnes, c'est-à-dire de 50 à 65 pieds environ.

Disons cependant que la pêche côtière et semi-hauturière diffère de la production capitaliste au sens strict du terme. Celle-ci sépare le capital du travail, et la propriété des moyens de production repose sur la circulation des biens, particulièrement celle de la force de travail, pour en extraire la plus-value. C'est à cette catégorie qu'appartient la pêche hauturière; bateaux de 100 tonnes et plus, soit approximativement ceux qui ont plus de 65 pieds.

EFFET DES PROGRAMMES DE MODERNISATION

Avec la modernisation du secteur pêche on assiste, sur une période de vingt ans, à une restructuration des diverses catégories de la flotte de pêche.

Alors que les plus petites unités des catégories des côtiers et semi-hauturiers ont accusé des diminutions importantes, les plus grandes unités de ces mêmes catégories ont connu une hausse importante. En effet, les côtiers de moins de 10 tonnes (35 pieds) ont chuté de 65.5 pour cent alors que ceux de 10 à 24.9 (de 35 à 50 pieds) ont grimpé de 92.4 pour cent. Ces bateaux valent environ \$50,000 à \$60,000. De plus, les semi-hauturiers de 25 à 49.9 tonnes (50 à 60 pieds) ont diminué de 30.3 pour cent alors que les semi-hauturiers de 50 à 99.9 tonnes (de 60 à 65 pieds environ) ont connu une hausse de 161.8 pour cent. Cette catégorie de bateaux est évaluée à environ 1,0 million de dollars.

Quant aux hauturiers, les catégories de 100 à 149.9 tonnes et celle de 150 tonnes et plus ont connu des augmentations respectives de 283.3 pour cent et 116.7 pour cent. Ces bateaux valent plus de 2.0 millions de dollars l'unité.

168   Omer Chouinard

Tableau
Changement du tonnage de la flotte de pêche du Nouveau-Brunswick
de 1964 à 1984

Catégorie de tonnage		Nombre de bateaux 1964	1984	Variation de tonnage en %
Côtiers	− 10 tonnes	3,578	1,272	− 65.5
	10 à 24.9 tonnes	674	1,297	+ 92.4
Semi-	25 à 49.9 tonnes	122	82	− 30.3
hauturiers	50 à 99.9 tonnes	34	95	+ 161.8
Hauturiers	100 à 149.9 tonnes	6	22	+ 283.3
	150 et + tonnes	6	14	+ 116.7

Source: Canada, *Revue statistique annuelle des pêches canadiennes*, Pêches et Océans Canada, 1975–84, No. 9–16.

Même s'il y a eu une diminution importante des plus petites unités, côtières en particulier, on peut se demander pourquoi la petite production, elle, s'est maintenue.

CONSERVATION DE LA PETITE PRODUCTION ET DE LA PRODUCTION INDÉPENDANTE

Breton (1977) montre que la modernisation provoquée par l'État encourage les nouveaux investisseurs à contrôler les moyens de production, en particulier les transports, la transformation, la mise en marché et la circulation du capital. Il restera alors aux petits producteurs un piètre pouvoir de négociation et un faible contrôle sur leurs moyens de production. Ils seront guettés par la prolétarisation ou, s'il gardent leur statut, verront leur autonomie se réduire. Pour perdurer, la petite production devra consentir à l'allongement du temps de travail (Mollard 1978). Dans cette foulée, Sinclair (1985) montre que le rôle de l'État a contribué à maintenir la petite production et la production indépendante grâce à des paiements de transfert, plus particulièrement à l'assurance chômage. Cependant, à la suite des recommandations des Commissions MacDonald (Canada 1985) et Forget (Canada 1986) sur la supervision des programmes de l'assurance-chômage, le statut du producteur indépendant et surtout de la petite production dans le secteur de la pêche est menacé.

Toutefois, la littérature récente reconnaît que c'est le travail domestique qui a joué le rôle principal dans la conservation de la petite production. Passons en revue les principaux arguments avancés.

RÔLE DU TRAVAIL DOMESTIQUE DANS LA SURVIVANCE DE LA PETITE PRODUCTION ET DE LA PRODUCTION INDÉPENDANTE

Des théoricien-ne-s de la question du sous-développement qui ont étudié le lien entre le mode de production domestique et le mode de production capitaliste disent que l'on assiste à un transfert gratuit des valeurs de la production domestique vers l'économie capitaliste (Meillassoux 1980, 149 et 159). Sans équivoque, Meillassoux nous dit que c'est dans la famille, lieu de la production domestique, qu'est produit, grâce au travail gratuit des femmes, le travailleur libre (1980, 214). Donc le travail gratuit des femmes est essentiel au mode de production capitaliste. Au Canada, en se basant sur le cas des Maritimes, Sacouman (1980, 236) fut un des premiers à montrer que l'articulation du mode de production capitalistes avec les autres modes de production non spécifiquement capitaliste constitue l'une des principales formes d'appropriation du surplus et de transfert de valeurs, ceci entraînant une surexploitation de la famille du petit producteur et avant tout des femmes et des jeunes. Ainsi, pour maintenir l'indépendance du petit producteur, femme et enfants sont forcé-e-s d'aller travailler à l'extérieur pour des salaires de subsistance.

Dans les communautés acadiennes du Nouveau-Brunswick, N. Davis (1981) dira que le petit producteur pêcheur survit grâce à la production domestique et au travail des femmes. Pour des féministes cependant, l'organisation structurale de la famille dans les sociétés capitalistes a pour fonction d'extorquer du travail gratuit, et on considère la famille comme un système de classe (Delphy 1983, 12). De plus, le mariage viendrait officialiser le cercle de l'exploitation familiale « comme unité de production où le mari apparaît de toute façon comme l'interlocuteur privilégié dans son rôle de chef d'exploitation-coexploitante ». Ainsi, on arrive à des classes de sexe où « le travail productif serait masculin et le travail improductif féminin » (Barthez 1983, 36, 42).

Enfin pour Andrée Michel (1983), l'exploitation des femmes en milieu rural repose d'abord sur l'accumulation réalisée à partir du temps de travail domestique des femmes dans la famille, i.e., travail non payé, un temps de travail nécessaire à la reproduction de la force de travail du mari, des enfants et des femmes elles-mêmes et qui contribue indirectement à la formation de la plus-value du travail marchand. C'est donc grâce au travail domestique, qui est le lot des femmes, que s'opèrent en même temps la production de la subsistance familiale et la reproduction de la force de travail.

Puisque nous n'avons pas encore terminé l'analyse de nos questionnaires sur la pêche dans la péninsule acadienne, nous illustrerons l'importance de la part du travail domestique dans les familles de pêcheurs à partir de l'enquête de Suzan Ilcan (1986), enquête menée auprès d'une communauté de pêcheurs en Nouvelle-Écosse. Nous complèterons avec nos observations préliminaires.

Selon Ilcan, les deux-tiers du revenu provient du pêcheur, le tiers des autres membres des familles de producteurs indépendants (Ilcan 1986, 21). Qui plus est, 39 pour cent des conjoints de pêcheurs propriétaires de bateaux travaillent en dehors de la maison, et leur revenu contribue pour 15 à 25 pour cent au revenu total du ménage. Cette tendance apparaît à la première lecture de nos résultats (péninsule acadienne). Toutefois, elle serait aux environs de 25 pour cent chez les pêcheurs côtiers et inférieure à 5 pour cent chez les semi-hauturiers.

Sur un plan qualitatif, la contribution des femmes aux opérations de pêche de leur mari est souvent équivalente au temps que les maris consacrent au travail rémunéré, et ce, tant en Nouvelle-Écosse que dans le nord-est du Nouveau-Brunswick. Ce qui fait dire à Ilcan que la contribution des femmes est perçue comme une part de leur devoir dans la famille.

Sa recherche, ainsi que nos observations, démontrent que non seulement les femmes connaissent le travail de leur mari (durée des opérations de pêche, etc.), mais qu'en plus, elles prennent une part active à ce travail, particulièrement à la gestion des opérations de pêche. Cette dernière tâche est sous-estimée par les femmes.

De par notre expérience d'intervenant, nous avons été en mesure de noter pendant la période de 1975 à 1985 que les femmes des communautés traditionnelles de pêcheurs acadiens ont joué un rôle actif dans les revendications de leur mari, que ce soit lors des manifestations, lignes de piquetage pour le droit à la syndicalisation des pêcheurs côtiers, ou dans des rassemblements populaires pour revendiquer une meilleure gestion des ressources halieutiques.

Arrivé à ce point, nous aimerions faire part de quelques conclusions provisoires de notre travail de terrain (entrepris à l'été de 1986 dans la péninsule acadienne). Même si les conditions générales des femmes de pêcheurs côtiers et semi-hauturiers se ressemblent, les conditions matérielles de chacune des catégories de pêcheurs entraînent, pour les femmes de chacune de ces catégories, des contraintes spécifiques.

Au niveau du petit producteur pêcheur, c'est-à-dire du pêcheur côtier, le travail des femmes à l'extérieur est considéré comme nécessaire pour maintenir un mode de vie, une qualité de vie. C'est principalement dans les usines de transformation de poisson qu'il leur faudra travailler. Ces femmes cumulent travail domestique, travail en usine et gestion des opérations de leur mari. Elles considèrent que, sans leur travail à l'extérieur, il aurait été difficile de bénéficier des avantages de la société de consommation (équipements ménagers, vacances annuelles, etc.). Il faut cependant souligner que les conditions de travail de ces femmes en usine sont généralement médiocres (travail sur un plancher en ciment, humidité constante, froid, etc.). Selon les témoignages recueillis, bon nombre d'entre elles sont atteintes d'arthrite ou de rhumatisme à l'âge de trente-cinq ans. À cela s'ajoute la pénétration des nouvelles technologies dans ces usines. Ces femmes voient donc leur travail menacé et doivent livrer de dures luttes pour conserver des droits acquis: l'ancienneté par exemple.

Quant aux femmes de producteurs indépendants, c'est-à-dire les pêcheurs semi-hauturiers, généralement le revenu élevé de leur mari leur permet de ne pas travailler à l'extérieur. « On est sur le ‹ stand-by › vingt-quatre heures sur vingt-quatre. » Elles se font un devoir de rester à la maison pendant la durée d'un voyage de pêche et de répondre aux demandes de leur mari au moyen de la radio, qu'il s'agisse de contacter le mécanicien, l'acheteur de poisson, etc. Leur vie est axée sur la réussite professionnelle de leur mari. Ces femmes ne connaissent pas la précarité des conditions de travail en usine ni l'incertitude de l'avenir du pêcheur côtier. Cependant, le travail gratuit qu'elles effectuent pour leur mari n'a aucune valeur marchande. En cas de séparation ou de divorce, quelle sera leur situation? Elles n'ont, le plus souvent, pas de métier reconnu socialement et elles devront rebâtir leur vie.

Nous avons voulu mettre en évidence certains des facteurs qui permettent au petit producteur et au producteur indépendant du secteur primaire de l'industrie de la pêche de se maintenir.

D'une part, nous savons que l'État joue, par l'assurance-chômage, un rôle crucial dans le maintien du statut du petit producteur marchand et du producteur indépendant. D'autre part, la production domestique, le travail domestique des membres de la famille, et en particulier le travail des femmes, jouent un rôle clé dans le maintien de cette « indépendance. » Il convient toutefois de souligner l'apport différencié du travail des femmes selon les catégories de pêcheurs. Alors que le travail des femmes à l'extérieur est nécessaire pour le maintien du petit producteur pêcheur, forçant ainsi la femme à un

double travail, la professionnalisation du métier de pêcheur, c'est-
à-dire le statut de producteur indépendant du pêcheur semi-hauturier, ne rend plus obligatoire le travail des femmes de cette catégorie à l'extérieur.

Comme l'a souligné L. Vandelac, le travail domestique s'adapte
aux nouvelles conditions et « la femme devient disponible comme
jamais auparavant » (1985, 171); cette disponibilité est essentielle au
maintien du statut du pêcheur.

Women and Well-Being
Les femmes et le mieux-être

JANET M. STOPPARD

Depression in Women: Psychological Disorder or Social Problem? [1]

Rates of depression are found to be consistently higher in women than in men. Feminist analyses emphasize the disadvantaged position of women in society to account for the higher rates of depression among women. Mainstream theories of depression emphasize intraindividual factors. An evaluation of the research on depression supports the conclusion that its findings are more consistent with feminist than with mainstream formulations. A feminist perspective on depression, however, is unlikely to have much impact on mental health practices and policies, because of the dominant position of the psychiatric profession in legitimating clinical definitions of depression.

La dépression chez les femmes: dérangement psychologique ou problème social?

Le taux de dépression est constamment plus élevé chez la femme que chez l'homme. Les analyses des féministes incriminent la situation défavorisée des femmes dans la société. Les théories actuelles sur la dépression mettent l'accent sur les facteurs biologiques et internes. En faisant la revue des recherches faites sur la dépression, on constate que les conclusions viennent beaucoup plus confirmer les vues des féministes que les interprétations dominantes. Il est toutefois peu probable que le point de vue féministe ait un impact significatif sur le pratique et les lignes de conduite en santé mentale car la psychiatrie professionnelle, seule habilitée à définir la dépression sur le plan clinique, est en situation de dominance.

Surveys of mental health in the general population as well as statistics on use of psychiatric treatment services indicate that depression is one of the most frequent forms of psychological disorder among women (cf., Guttentag et al. 1980). A consistent finding in Western countries is that depression rates are significantly higher among women than men (Nolen-Hoeksema 1987), the sex ratio generally being placed at around 2:1 or higher (Weissman et al. 1984).

Despite evidence that there is a sex difference in rates of depression, the status of these findings is the subject of debate among researchers. While some accept the findings as valid (e.g., Guttentag et al. 1980; Nolen-Hoeksama 1987), others question whether there is a "true" sex difference in depression (e.g., Angst and Dobler-Mikola 1984; Hammen 1982).

To understand why some researchers are reluctant to accept the validity of the sex difference findings, the nature of current theories of depression needs to be considered. In psychiatry, biological theories currently hold sway (Maxmen 1986) and are consistent with the use of somatic treatments such as electroconvulsive therapy (ECT) and antidepressant drugs for depression. Psychological theories emphasize the role of intrapsychic factors, such as negative thoughts and irrational beliefs, and therapies derived from these theories involve the modification of the psychological deficits presumed to underlie depression (Beck et al. 1979).

Theories of depression which emphasize the role of biological or intrapsychic factors cannot easily account for a sex difference in depression. Attempts to explain women's higher rates of depression in terms of genetic or hormonal influences have not received consistent empirical support (Nolen-Hoeksema 1987). Also, available findings contradict the idea that women are more likely than men to have the psychological deficits thought to underlie depression (Stoppard 1987). Therefore, if the finding of a sex difference in depression is proved to be valid, then it would present a serious challenge to current theoretical formulations, as well as to the modes of treatment they serve to justify. Higher rates of depression among women imply that social conditions need to be considered in accounting for depression in women, and also that intervention strategies need to incorporate social factors in addition to, or instead of, bio-psychological processes. Alternatively, the lack of strong evidence for a sex difference in depression fits more closely with conceptions of depression which emphasize intraindividual factors.

In contrast to mainstream positions, the finding that rates of depression are higher among women than men is quite compatible with a feminist perspective. In broad terms, feminist analyses point to a link between the socially oppressive conditions experienced by women and their high rates of depression (Oakley 1986), and conceptualize depression in women as a psychological consequence of their disadvantaged social status (Kaplan 1986).

From a feminist perspective, the relevance of this debate lies in its implications for treatment strategies and mental health policies which deal with depression in women. Feminist analyses imply that increased allocation of public resources for programs aimed at improving social conditions for women would be an important part of any strategy for decreasing the high rates of depression in women.

In the remainder of this paper, I will first provide a brief overview of the findings on sex differences in depression and then examine some of the explanations put forward to account for higher rates of depression in women. Next, I will discuss why mainstream researchers are reluctant to accept the validity of the sex difference findings. I will conclude that while the available evidence is entirely consistent with feminist formulations of depression, the powerful role of the mental health professions – especially psychiatry – in legitimizing definitions of depression, is an obstacle to any changes in mental health policy which would have beneficial effects on the well-being of women.

EVIDENCE FOR SEX DIFFERENCES IN DEPRESSION

To understand research on depression, it is necessary to know something about the way depression is defined and assessed. Depression is generally defined as a disorder of mood or, more technically, as an "affective disorder" (American Psychiatric Association [APA] 1980) in which a person's mood is characterized by feelings of sadness. For a depressed mood to be indicative of depression, however, it has to be more persistent (usually lasting two weeks or more) than the fairly fleeting "low" moods experienced by most people from time to time (APA 1980). To be diagnosed as depression, a depressed mood has to be accompanied by several other "symptoms" such as sleep disturbance, appetite loss, impaired concentration, fatigue, or suicidal ideas (APA 1980). In practice, depression is usually diagnosed by the pattern of symptoms observed in, or reported by, a person. Self-report questionnaires have been developed to assess depressed mood and other depressive symptoms, although a formal diagnosis of depression would not be made solely on the basis of questionnaire responses.

A crucial issue in the interpretation of findings on sex differences in depression is the validity of diagnostic procedures used to assess depression. In a widely cited paper published in 1977, the psychiatric epidemiologists Myrna Weissman and Gerald Klerman reviewed research on the prevalence of depression and concluded that there is a "true" sex difference in rates of depression. Subsequently, however, their conclusion has been challenged on the grounds that a number of the studies they reviewed used diagnostic procedures of questionable validity (e.g., Hammen 1982).

More recent epidemiological studies are less vulnerable to criticism on diagnostic grounds because they involve the use of procedures which incorporate criteria for diagnosing depression that are officially sanctioned by the psychiatric profession. Studies carried out more recently have been consistent in finding a significant sex difference in depression in general population samples in England (Bebbington et al. 1981), Australia (Henderson et al. 1979) and the United States (Myers et al. 1984). The findings of studies using self-report questionnaires to assess depression have also consistently shown a sex difference (e.g., Frerichs et al. 1981).

Although self-report questionnaires are widely used in research, the findings of studies using such measures are viewed by psychiatric epidemiologists as providing less convincing evidence than those in which diagnostic criteria are used to assess depression. In line with this view, a leading group of epidemiologists has taken the position that self-report measures of depression actually assess a non-clinical condition, one for which the label "demoralization" would be more appropriate (Link and Dohrenwend 1980, 115). Given such views, it is hardly surprising that researchers tend to dismiss the findings of studies using self-report measures as largely irrelevant to the issue of whether there is a sex difference in rates of depression (e.g., Hammen 1982).

Sex difference findings in studies using the diagnostic procedures considered valid by mainstream psychiatry would seem less easy to dismiss. There are signs, however, that such a discounting process is beginning to occur. In a recent study by Angst and Dobler-Mikola (1984), rates of depression were found to be higher in women. After observing that women were more depressed than men at similar levels of self-reported occupational impairment, these investigators proposed that the diagnostic criteria be modified so that fewer symptoms are required in men than in women in order to diagnose depression. When these modified criteria were applied to the original data, the sex difference in depression was considerably reduced.

The diagnostic strategy advocated by Angst and Dobler-Mikola (1984) assumes that women are no more likely than men to be depressed – women simply report more depressive symptoms. More generally, this study shows that even the procedure considered most valid for diagnosing depression is not immune from attempts to discount sex difference findings.

EXPLANATIONS FOR SEX DIFFERENCES IN DEPRESSION

Space does not permit a review of all explanations offered to account for sex differences in depression. Response bias and social explanations will be considered here because they are particularly relevant to the debate surrounding the existence of sex differences in depression.

Response Bias Explanations

The proposal by Angst and Dobler-Mikola (1984) that depression rates in men are underestimated because men tend to report fewer depressive symptoms than do women is an example of a response bias explanation for sex differences in depression. According to response bias explanations, a "true" sex difference in depression does not exist; rather, findings of higher rates of depression in women are due to the influence of biases in the reporting of depressive symptoms, which results in the underestimation of the rates in men.

For instance, Warren (1983) has suggested that lower rates of depression in men can be explained in terms of men's avoidance of expressing feelings – such as depression – that conflict with a "masculine" self-image. In a similar vein, Hammen and Peters (1977) have hypothesized that men are motivated to avoid expression of depressive feelings because they are more likely than women to meet with social rejection if they appear to be depressed. Support for Hammen and Peters' hypothesis is quite mixed, however, and so far there have been no studies examining reactions to depressed individuals in real-life situations.

Presumably, the hypothesis that sex differences in depression arise because of women's greater willingness to disclose depressive feelings derives from the stereotypical belief that women are more emotionally expressive than men. Gender role prescriptions also include the expectation that women are warm, friendly, and supportive in interactions with others – behaviours that are hardly consistent with depression. An equally plausible possibility, therefore, is that expression of depressive feelings is proscribed for women as well as men. Moreover, it could be argued that women may have to be *more* depressed than men before they will disclose their feelings. Expression of depressive feelings conflicts with expectations that women are available to nurture others, so that such disclosure by a woman may be especially likely to result in rejection.

Another response bias explanation is that depression in men is

often unrecognized because it is "masked" by symptoms of other
disorders, such as alcoholism. If rates of depression in men are
underestimated because of failure to recognize masked depression,
then elevated rates of drinking problems and other symptoms
thought to mask depression might be expected in married men, the
group consistently found to have the lowest rate of depression. It is
not the case, however, that higher rates of problems thought to mask
depression are found in married men. Symptoms considered signs
of masked depression occur at higher rates in those men having
social characteristics – such as being unmarried or unemployed –
known to be associated with increased risk for depression (e.g., Klerman and Weissman 1980). Moreover, recent findings on interge-
nerational patterns of alcoholism and depression are inconsistent
with the idea that the two disorders are different forms of the same
underlying disorder (Merikangas et al. 1985).

   In conclusion, despite the lack of empirical support for response
bias explanations, mainstream investigators continue to hold the view
that such influences cannot be precluded as a possible source of sex
differences in rates of depression (cf., Hammen 1982). At the same
time, the possibility that reported rates of depression in women may
underestimate their actual rates has not been explored.

Social Explanations

Studies reporting higher rates of depression in women have been
criticized on the grounds that investigators have failed to control for
background social factors that are correlated with both sex and
depression. For instance, in a review of research on sex differences
in depression, Hammen concluded that "whether women show an
excess of depression compared with men in similar role situations
or whether the sexes are similar under similar circumstances remains
unclear at this time" (1982, 146). Hammen seems to be saying that
if men and women were found to have equal depression rates under
identical social conditions, then social explanations for sex differences in depression could be ruled out.

   Hammen implies that sex differences in rates of depression are
artifactual, arising from the failure of investigators to include appropriate methodological controls for "extraneous" social variables.
This position, however, sidesteps the issue of systemic discrimination
against women and ignores the extensive documentation of women's
disadvantaged status on socio-economic indicators. Feminist analyses
(e.g., Oakley 1986) identify inequalities in the status of women as a
crucial starting point in accounting for higher rates of depression

in women. Thus, the finding that sex differences in depression are eliminated when background social factors are taken into account would be quite consistent with feminist explanations for higher rates of depression in women.

Evidence from a number of studies indicates that when various demographic and socio-economic factors (e.g., education, marital status, income, and employment status) are statistically controlled, an existing sex difference in depression is either reduced (e.g., Amenson and Lewinsohn 1981) or eliminated entirely (e.g., Gore and Mangione 1983). Finding that the sexes have comparable rates of depression when men and women are specifically selected to have similar background social characteristics would also be consistent with feminist analyses. For instance, a sex difference in depression has not been found in studies involving college students (e.g., Padesky and Hammen 1981) or young adults employed in the same job category (Jenkins 1985). These findings, rather than being interpreted as arguments against a sex difference in depression, as has been suggested by mainstream researchers, should be interpreted as showing that in homogeneous samples of young, unmarried adults, levels of depression in women and men tend to be comparable.

Further support for the role of social factors is provided by the results of a recent study by Repetti and Crosby (1984) in which levels of depression were examined in women and men whose occupations were either high or low in prestige (professional vs. sales/service). Within levels of occupational prestige, there was no sex difference in depression; however, men and women in high prestige occupations were less depressed than those in low prestige occupations. Repetti and Crosby's findings (1984) are particularly significant because women are much more likely than men to be in low prestige (and low paying) jobs.

In conclusion, the findings reviewed above appear to be entirely consistent with feminist formulations that link higher rates of depression in women to their disadvantaged social status. Other approaches to explaining sex differences in depression which emphasize biological factors or psychological processes related to gender cannot readily account for such findings.

MAINSTREAM RESISTANCE TO SEX DIFFERENCE FINDINGS

Despite the growing body of evidence consistent with social explanations for sex differences in depression, such findings have had little impact on mainstream views about links between sex and depression, or on prevailing modes of treatment. Instead, as I have tried to show, evidence indicating higher rates of depression in women has been discounted on various grounds. Researchers have downplayed sex difference findings by proposing that criteria for diagnosis of depression in men and women be defined differently (Angst and Dobler-Mikola 1984). It has even been suggested that depression which is associated with adverse social conditions, or which does not lead to inpatient treatment, should not be viewed as "true" clinical depression (i.e., the kind of depression diagnosed by psychiatrists [Bebbington et al. 1984, 361]). Given these indicators of trends in the field of depression research, further work within current paradigms appears to offer little promise of increasing our understanding of depression in either sex, and especially in women.

It is important, however, to analyse the reasons underlying mainstream resistance to findings that link the disadvantaged social status of women to their increased vulnerability to depression. It is necessary to identify the sources of this resistance if strategies are to be devised for advocating the development of mental health policies that better serve the needs of women. Sources of mainstream resistance can be located in both the theoretical and practice domains.

At the theoretical level, findings of sex differences in depression represent a threat to the integrity of the medical model of mental illness, because such findings cannot easily be accommodated without acknowledging the role of social factors in psychiatric disorders. Since the medical model informs much of psychiatric practice, theoretical challenges also undermine the dominant position of psychiatry in the mental health field. Thus, one source of resistance to findings of sex differences in depression may be the threat posed to the theoretical hegemony of the medical model of mental illness.

Historically, an important function within psychiatry has been the definition of mental illness for diagnostic purposes, a role which also provides a means of defending the medical model against contradictory evidence. Through the promulgation of diagnostic manuals such as DSM-III (APA 1980), the psychiatric profession plays an important gate-keeping role in legitimating definitions of disorders, such as depression, for research purposes. Nonpsychiatric researchers have to conform to psychiatric definitions of depression if their work is to have credibility. In this way, findings such as those showing sex differences on self-report measures of depression can be dismissed as irrelevant to psychiatric definitions of depression.

In recent years, there has been a reassertion of the primacy of biological modes of treatment in the practice of psychiatry (cf., Maxmen 1986). This retrenchment appears to have occurred at a time when claims to therapeutic expertise by other mental health professions (psychology, social work, nursing, etc.) have increased in scope. One strategy available to psychiatry for retaining its dominant position is to emphasize treatment methods whose use is restricted to those with medical training. Only physicians are qualified to prescribe antidepressant drugs and ECT, and within psychiatry these are considered the treatments of choice for depression.

The treatment of depressed patients represents a significant portion of psychiatric practice, so the lack of credence given to evidence which contradicts prevailing views of depression is hardly surprising. Resistance to alternative formulations, therefore, may stem from fears within psychiatry that other mental health professionals may gain a larger role in the treatment of depression.

My analysis leads me to the conclusion that a feminist position on depression in women will have little impact within the mental health establishment, given the extent of investment in psychiatric formulations of depression. Nevertheless, available findings do provide a basis for recommending policy changes in directions that would benefit women's mental health. The finding that, in women, depression occurs at a high rate in comparison to rates for other types of mental health problems provides justification for calls for increased funding for research on depression in women. In Canada, research on mental health problems specific to women has been underfunded (Stark-Adamec 1981), and women's mental health problems are perceived by clinicians as being less serious than mental health problems in men (Page 1987). The sex bias in allocation of research resources and the general lack of attention to women's mental health problems can be identified as appropriate targets for feminist efforts.

More broadly, the conclusion that research has yielded findings in support of social explanations for higher rates of depresssion in women is also consistent with efforts to achieve greater equality for women in such areas as education, childcare, and employment. Overall, current findings imply that mental health policy needs to be more consistent with the position that depression in women is a social problem rather than a psychological disorder.

NOTE

1 An extended version of this paper with additional references is to appear in *Atlantis: A Women's Studies Journal* (Autumn 1988).

LINDA J. KLIMACK

Coping with Abuse: Applying the Grieving Model to Battered Women [1]

To date, most of the research which examines a woman's propensity to stay in an abusive relationship has been based on models in which the woman becomes progressively more entangled until there is little likelihood of her escaping. These models fail to account for the women who do alter the relationship. The Grieving Process corrects this by categorizing the battered woman's psychological states from the first incident of abuse to the point where she realizes violence is a part of her conjugal relationship and chooses a course of action based on this realization. The Grieving Process explains what keeps the woman in the relationship, when she accepts the violence as a recurring phenomenon, and when she takes steps either to leave, or to alter the situation.

La confrontation de la violence: application du « Grieving Model » aux femmes battues

Jusqu'à présent, presque toutes les recherches qui ont cherché à comprendre pourquoi les femmes tendent à demeurer dans une relation, alors qu'elles subissent des sévices, utilisent des modèles dans lesquels la femme s'empêtre de plus en plus jusqu'à ne plus jamais pouvoir s'en sortir. Or, ces modèles ne tiennent pas compte des femmes qui réussissent à modifier la relation qu'elles entretiennent avec leur conjoint. Le « Grieving Process » apporte un éclaircissement nouveau, en classant les états psychologiques de la femme battue par catégories à partir du premier incident agressif, jusqu'au moment où elle se rend compte que la violence est une partie intégrante de sa relation conjugale et où elle choisit une ligne de conduite en fonction de cette prise de conscience. Le « Grieving Process » explique pourquoi la femme reste dans une telle relation, identifie le moment où elle accepte la violence comme un phénomène devant se répéter, et celui où elle pourra prendre les mesures nécessaires soit pour partir, soit pour modifier la situation.

Our society has seized upon the problem of wife assault as though it were yet another by-product of technology. Wife beating is not a new phenomenon; it is society's awareness of it as a problem which is new. Because of the relatively recent attention given to wife assault, researchers have tried to align this area of study with victimology or criminology. Victims of wife assault have been treated as equivalent to other victims of violent crimes, such as rape or robbery (Loseke and Cahill 1984). This focus on the violence ignores the conjugal relationship as a significant factor distinguishing wife assault from other crimes; which leads to the highlighting of the question "Why does she stay?"

Inherent in this question are several assumptions about the woman and her situation. Asking the question assumes that leaving is the only response to an abusive relationship (Loseke and Berk 1982). Focusing on why she stays assumes it is only the woman's decision to leave. This ignores the fact that a batterer frequently continues to abuse the woman after she has left (Okun 1984). Asking why she stays or leaves assumes that the woman can engage in either one behaviour or the other and creates two artificial categories of women – those who stay and those who leave. Asking why she stays assumes that leaving is the normal thing to do. It also assumes that many women do stay and that they are more in need of help than women who have left (Loseke and Cahill 1984). Focusing on why she stays promotes the view that the battered woman chooses victimization (Loseke and Berk 1982). Finally, focusing on the woman's response to the violence has created a new category of deviants – women who stay – and in the process has excused the batterer for his crime (Walker 1979).

Existing theories that seek to explain why a woman stays in an abusive relationship concentrate on the passive, dependent behaviour of the woman, and spend only minimal time discussing the sequence of events which brings her to that point (Walker 1979). Attention on the outcome focuses attention away from the process which gets her there, and trivializes her prior behaviour. It distorts the time frame of the relationship, leading the reader to believe that very quickly the woman becomes helpless. It also leads to the view that the woman is in a spiral situation – the longer she remains in the situation, the less likely she is to escape.

Thus, the major problem with past researchers has been their preoccupation with the question "Why does she stay?" Focusing on the woman's ultimate response to the violence ignores her reaction to the violence from the first incident, to the point where she realizes she must respond to the situation. It also fails to recognize the many coping techniques she uses, as she attempts to preserve her marriage while stopping the abuse. Finally, the question itself assumes there is only one alternative for a woman once the violence has begun – to leave. In reality there are a variety of alternative outcomes – to stay and accept the violence; to stay and force change; to leave; or in extreme cases to kill the batterer.

This paper will develop a descriptive model which answers the following questions: (a) what keeps the woman in the relationship? (b) when does she accept the violence as a recurring phenomenon? and (c) and when does she take steps to leave or alter the situation? It must be understood that the Grieving Process is not based on empirical research, but is supported by existing literature. It can be regarded as a starting point for future research.

Researchers trying to understand why a woman stays in the relationship have placed their emphasis on the presence of the violence, rather than on the nature of the marriage as maintaining the abusive relationship. This emphasis assumes that when the woman leaves, she feels relief and ignores the loss she also feels. Applying the grieving model will do what no other models have done: consider the importance of the marriage in the abusive relationship, recognize the positive features of the marriage, and legitimize the grief the woman feels.

Kubler-Ross (1969) identified five stages of grieving which terminally ill patients pass through before accepting the impending death. The grieving stages were not designed to be a precise description of the psychological states an individual passes through; rather, they were developed to assist the medical profession in understanding the coping mechanisms a person will employ.

In stage one, denial and isolation: the patient disbelieves the news, rationalizing that there has either been a mistake in the test results, or the results have been muddled with those of another patient. In stage two, anger: the patient displays anger, rage, envy, and resentment over the fact that he or she is going to die as opposed to other "less worthy" people. In stage three, bargaining: the individual attempts to enter into some sort of agreement in the hope of postponing the inevitable. In stage four, depression: the person becomes aware of death and is in a state of mourning for everything and everyone he or she has loved. In the last stage, acceptance: the patient no longer fights the inevitable. The struggle is over and death is seen as a welcome relief from the pain and suffering.

Several authors have applied the grieving model to wife assault (Campbell 1984; Flynn and Whitcomb 1981; Silverman 1981; Weingourt 1979). The focus of these authors is on intervention, and as such they establish a "how-to" guide, rather than more fully developing insight into the woman's emotions and behaviour in response to the violence. They do, however, point the way to using the Kubler-Ross (1969) model as a means of understanding the behaviour of abused women. In the Grieving Process their work will be carried further.

To the five stages described by Kubler-Ross one additional stage, triggering mechanisms, has been added. While reading case studies I realized that many battered women mention "something" which made them aware they could no longer tolerate the violence and forced them into a stage of action. Triggering mechanisms looks more thoroughly at what triggers a woman out of depression and into some form of acceptance.

Unlike the terminally ill, battered women have alternatives in the acceptance stage. Realizing this, I included four alternative outcomes: staying and resigning oneself to the violent relationship, staying and forcing change on the batterer, leaving, or killing the batterer.

THE GRIEVING PROCESS

Stage One: Denial

The first stage of the Grieving Process is denial. This is the reaction to the initial occurrence of the violence, as either an attack on the woman, or psychological abuse.

The violence begins early in the relationship, for most, within the first year (Walker 1979). This is usually the time corresponding to pregnancy or the arrival of the first child (Flitcraft 1977); the period when the woman is most dependent and most isolated.

The woman's initial reaction to the first few abusive acts is shock, confusion, numbness, and disbelief (Silverman 1981). The first incidents leave the woman feeling betrayed (D. Sinclair 1985), and contradict her feelings of love (Ferraro 1983). She rarely redefines the relationship as dangerous, and considers the incident an isolated event (Silverman 1981) which has no connection with other aspects of her life.

Kubler-Ross describes the function of denial as "a buffer after unexpected shocking news, [which] allows the patient to collect himself [or herself]" (1969, 39). Like a person grieving a death, the battered woman uses this time to collect herself, to protect herself from experiencing the full impact of her fears (Weingourt 1979).

The most extensive defence mechanism employed by the battered woman is rationalization. This is the woman's continual adjustment to the situation, where she attributes the abuse to external forces, denies the injuries, or believes she is the cause of the attacks (Ferraro 1983).

Social isolation typifies these women; many are without close friends of relatives to whom they can turn for help (Smith 1984). The woman's isolation is augmented by her husband's control over their social life. This, in turn, increases the battered woman's dependence on her husband (Sinclair 1985) and the likelihood of her remaining in the abusive relationship (Nielsen et al. 1979).

Isolation creates a situation where the woman loses touch with those who could offer realistic feedback on abuse (Sinclair 1985). Without this, the woman begins to rely on the batterer's definition of the violence, quickly losing track of the gravity of the situation. Because the batterer's perceptions of the abuse are incongruous with the woman's own thoughts, the woman's self-concept is eroded, and she begins to question her sanity.

Stage Two: Anger

The second stage is anger. The woman has moved from the protective stage of denial, where she felt nothing, to the point where she is experiencing emotions – the predominant one being anger. Few women remain totally in this stage; instead they vacillate between the first two stages, encouraged by the intermittent nature of the abuse (Campbell 1984).

The woman's initial reaction to her anger is to reciprocate the violence. Only fifty percent of battered women actually fight back (Dobash and Dobash 1979). The result is usually an escalation of the batterer's violence (Bowker 1983). The woman soon learns to repress her anger, choosing to express it indirectly in the form of sarcasm or unkept promises (Walker 1984), to project it onto others (Campbell 1984), or to keep it inside, which can lead to the development of depression or somatic symptoms (Weingourt 1979). The woman then becomes passive, in the mistaken belief that it will decrease the violence, but the reverse often occurs; nonresistance may precipitate the violence and be just as dangerous as fighting back.

Researchers agree overwhelmingly that as time progresses, the violence increases both in frequency and severity (Johnston 1984). It is during the anger stage that one can expect the violence to increase to the point where the woman requires medical treatment for injuries sustained during the beatings.

The batterer quickly becomes adept at inflicting injuries that are not noticeable, or are the most humiliating to the woman. The focal point is usually her head, in particular her face, and her chest and abdomen (Flitcraft 1977).

The attacks to the abdomen do not stop when the woman is pregnant. In fact they may intensify. About half of all abused women are battered while they are pregnant (Walker 1984), increasing the risk of injury and miscarriage (Flitcraft 1977).

With the escalation in violence comes the increased risk of sexual assault. Between thirty-five and sixty percent of battered women say they have experienced marital rape (Finkelhor and Yllo 1984). Marital rape does not occur in isolation, but is present with other forms of violence, and may just be an escalation of physical abuse to a new level.

Thus, the second stage is characterized by anger. To an outsider, the woman may look passive, as if she has given up the fight, but in reality this is a coping mechanism which is intended to preserve the woman from further abuse.

Stage Three: Bargaining

In the bargaining stage of Kubler-Ross's (1969) model, the dying patient attempts to bargain away death with the promise of good behaviour or some other sacrifice. Similarly, the abused woman attempts to strike a bargain, the prize being the discontinuance of the violence.

This is the first point where the woman acknowledges that violence is a part of the relationship. She does not regard the abuse as an important part of the marriage, and continues to believe that with minor changes the violence will be eradicated. Her efforts are aimed at ending the abuse, not the marriage.

With the acknowledgment that the violence is a part of the relationship, the woman is able to anticipate future attacks. It is the stress from the actual abuse, and the anticipated attacks, as well as the repressed anger, that begin to physically take a toll on the woman. The list of somatic symptoms includes headaches, insomnia, allergies, choking sensations, hyperventilation, chest, pelvic and back pains, and eating disorders (Ferraro and Johnson 1983).

To bargain implies a compromise between the actors (Weingourt 1979). First, the batterer must be willing to negotiate (Flynn and Whitcomb 1981). This usually occurs after an episode when he is feeling remorse and believes he will not be violent again. Second, the woman must have something that the batterer wants and with which she is willing to bargain. In this case it is the woman's freedom, which she gives up either by remaining in the abusive relationship, or by suppressing portions of her personality in order to become her husband's ideal wife (Campbell 1984).

Battered women try many techniques in an effort to end the violence (Smith and Chalmers 1984). This belies the myth that the woman passively reconciles herself to the violence. A normal progression of help-seeking transpires as the battered woman first tries to make changes within the relationship, then turns to friends and relatives, and finally to social agencies (Bowker 1983).

In the beginning, almost all women remain in the relationship and try to bring about change (Pagelow 1981). When this does not stop the abuse, they adopt the coping technique of separation. Eighty to ninety percent of women think of leaving or threaten divorce at some time (e.g., Smith 1984). The actual number of women who separate, as opposed to those who remain, is unknown. We do know that 80 percent of women separate at some point in the relationship (Johnston 1984). Smith and Chalmers refer to this process as a technique, with the goal being "a change in the partner's behaviour or avoidance of the behaviour on the temporary basis" (1984, 25).

There are a variety of practical reasons why the woman returns, but the main reason is the batterer has repented and has promised to cease his violent behaviour (D. Sinclair 1985). Thus, the woman separates in the hope the batterer will reform and returns when he promises to do so (Smith and Chalmers 1984). Some women return to the batterer involuntarily, either under his threats of further violence and death to herself or those helping her, or due to physical force or kidnapping (Pagelow 1981).

Once they have acknowledged that they are in abusive relationships, and get a glimpse of the uncertain future, not all women move forward to the depression stage. Some women, after making the comparison, may decide that their situation is tolerable, and retreat to the denial stage by minimizing the violence. Only when a woman realizes that no reasonable change will stop the abuse, is she forced to admit the futility of the situation and move into the depression stage.

Stage Four: Depression

For battered women, depression is the single most diagnosed response (Walker 1984), a result of unexpressed anger, grief, and fear

(Rounsaville 1978). This depression is manifested in a variety of self-destructive behaviors – alcohol and drug abuse, and suicide attempts (Sinclair 1985).

Compared with nonbattered women, battered women receive three-quarters of the prescriptions for tranquilizers, antidepressants, and pain-killers. The medication may help a woman overcome her feelings of hopelessness, but it also reduces her ability to respond to the situation (Okun 1984).

Half of battered women consider suicide at some point (Pagelow 1981), and about one-quarter of all battered women actually attempt suicide (Sinclair 1985). Many women use the drugs prescribed by their doctors as a weapon.

As a result of the depression, the alcohol and drug abuse, or the suicide attempts, many women find themselves in the mental health system, either under the care of a psychiatrist or in hospital (Stark et al. 1979).

The battered woman is in a period of "emotional dormancy" as she ceases to struggle to reform the marriage, surviving each day with depression and a lack of enthusiasm (Ferraro and Johnson 1983). Her feelings of strong dependency and commitment to marriage lead to the grieving reaction (Campbell 1984). The battered woman experiences reactive grief, mourning the losses which have occurred, and anticipatory grief, mourning the losses she expects to occur. Compared to other grieving persons, battered women do not bury their husbands, they bury their hopes and dreams (Silverman 1981).

One source of reactive grief which deserves special mention is the loss of the vague optimism which has shielded the woman from the admission that the violence is a major part of the relationship (Weingourt 1979). It is this denial which has enabled her to continue to pour her energy into the marriage. To admit that there is no hope is to admit that the violence is not a minor aberration, and that her husband has a problem with violence.

Fear is the other predominant emotion the woman feels (Sinclair 1985). She fears losing the children, losing her sanity, attacks by the abuser on those close to her, and the unknown. She also fears being killed, or losing control and killing the batterer.

The woman is now at the point of no return, where she appreciates the reality of the relationship, but is unable to forgive herself for choosing the wrong partner (Sinclair 1985), to express her anger openly, and to sort out her love for her husband and for herself. The task ahead of the woman is to break existing roles and go on to develop self-worth, the ability to be assertive, and a renewed sense of trust in her own judgment (Sinclair 1985).

Stage Five: Triggering Mechanisms

Between the depression stage and acceptance stage a transition in the battered woman occurs, which is very brief but extremely important. Something happens to her which brings about a sudden change in her attitude to the abusive relationship, marking a clear separation between the earlier stages and acceptance, from which there can be no retreat. Researchers in the area of wife assault have not identified a triggering mechanism as important, but they have mentioned several significant events.

Triggering mechanisms may be the result of a change in the level of abuse, such as the introduction of a weapon (Ferraro and Johnson 1983); the abuse reaching a point where the woman can no longer tolerate it; or the woman recognizing the lethal potential of the situation (Johnston 1984).

For some women marital rape only occurs near the end of the relationship (Finkelhor and Yllo 1982), and may act as a triggering mechanism by being more devastating than other forms of abuse, or may erode the last barrier of communication and tenderness between the couple.

The abuse can also create a crisis if it begins to erupt in public. To the woman the battering is no longer a private degradation, but has become a public humiliation (Ferraro and Johnson 1983).

The triggering mechanism mentioned most often by researchers is the woman seeking help after children have become involved in the abuse (Langley and Levy 1977). The children's involvement can either be attempting to intervene on their mother's behalf, or becoming victims of child or sexual abuse.

Another triggering mechanism may be a change in the woman's resources such as receiving a sum of money, gaining education or job skills, or obtaining outside employment. These can give the woman the financial means to flee the situation (Ferraro and Johnson 1983).

The important change that transpires in the woman is a shift from self-blame or blaming external factors, to holding the husband solely responsible for the abuse (Shields and Hanneke 1983). This shift both represents an emotional break in the relationship and signifies a change as the woman no longer regards the abuse as a variable characteristic which has the potential for change (Shields and Hanneke 1983).

Up to this point I have been writing on the assumption that all battered women are beaten more than once. For a small group of women, an estimated 10 percent (Stark et al. 1979), there is only a single beating. One beating can be the basis of ongoing psychological abuse, it can maintain male dominance in the family, it can cause serious injury, and it can be lethal. It can also be a trigger for the woman to put an end to the violence either by leaving the abusive relationship (Smith and Chalmers 1984), or by forcing her husband to stop beating her (Bowker 1983). For this latter group of women, the first abusive incident acts as a triggering mechanism and propels them from denial to the end of the Grieving Process.

Thus, the triggering mechanism is a significant event which breaks through the denial, anger, rationalization, and isolation. It is the transition point where the woman realizes she can tolerate no more abuse. The woman's activity level right after an incident is the best predictor of whether of not she has moved into the acceptance stage (Nielsen et al. 1979).

Stage Six: Acceptance

For the battered woman, as for the dying patient, the acceptance stage signifies the end of the struggle. It is the time when the dying patient accepts that death is inevitable. The battered woman does not accept the violence itself, but rather accepts that it is an integral part of the conjugal relationship, and that only with major structural changes will it stop. No longer is she taking full or partial responsibility for the abuse; she has come to redefine it as her husband's problem.

In the acceptance stage the woman must draw on strengths she may not know exist. The woman takes command of her life and no longer spends all her energy trying to placate her husband; instead she expends it making decisions concerning herself (Silverman 1981).

Unlike dying persons, who must accept their death, battered women have a variety of alternative outcomes from which to select. Not all women consider the alternatives in depth; in some cases a decision is made in a crisis situation, quickly following the triggering mechanism.

Resigning Herself to the Abuse. The woman who resigns herself to the abuse, for a variety of reasons, does not regard leaving her husband as an option (Stacey and Shupe 1983). She differs from women in other stages of the Grieving Process in that she has realized the abuse is a major part of the marriage and has adjusted her idealized version of marriage to include the violence, just as other women might accept an undesirable characteristic in their husband. This woman does not stay because of the violence in the relationship, she stays because of the relationship.

Researchers have suggested that three groups of women are more likely to be resigned to the abuse: women with a strong traditional ideology (Pagelow 1981), women who have strong religious beliefs (Stacey and Shupe 1983), and older battered women who were raised when emphasis was placed on traditional values and keeping the family together.

Most researchers have ignored this alternative. In the literature, only passing reference is made to these women, and even then it is done with overtones of "some day they will do the right thing and leave."

Forcing the Abuser to Change. After accepting the abuse many women take a problem-solving approach to the violence (Weingourt 1979). The same techniques that were tried during the bargaining stage are also used in the acceptance stage, the difference being that now they are successful in stopping the abuse.

If these techniques prove to be only fairly effective, then what differentiates between those that work and those that do not? Bowker concludes that no one personal strategy or help source is the most effective; rather, in different situations, different factors are effective. "What really matters," says Bowker, "is the woman's showing her determination the violence *must stop now*. Once the batterers ... become convinced of their wives' determination to end the violence, they usually reassess their position in the marriage and decide to reform" (1983, 131). It is the strong character of the woman, the development of inner strength, and an increase in her power, which aid her in making a change in her life. In some cases, the woman is so changed by having overcome the violence, that she is no longer willing to stay in the relationship (Bowker 1983).

Leaving the Abusive Relationship. The decision to leave an abusive relationship generally occurs after a history of beatings and reconciliations. Leaving is a signal that the woman can no longer believe her husband's promises of no more violence, nor forgive past episodes of violence. It is also a signal that the woman has lost hope that things will get better (Langley and Levy 1977).

Smith and Chalmers' (1984) second concept, the strategy of leaving, describes what occurs in the acceptance stage, where the goal in leaving is leaving itself. Similar to the cases where women force their husbands to change, in this case commitment and determination are the important factors.

There are two final notes I would like to add to this section. First, rarely does the batterer abandon the family home. In most cases the woman leaves, partly because she has no choice, and partly because hiding may be the only way she can escape further violence. Second, one other way a battered woman can leave the relationship is to commit a crime and be imprisoned. Estimates are that 50 to 90 percent of female inmates in prisons are battered women (Jones 1980). Some of these women may see incarceration as the only way they can be safe from the abuser.

It is important to remember that leaving does not automatically stop the abuse. Approximately one quarter of battered women continue to be threatened or abused by their former husbands (Okun 1986). The risk of abuse for these women only drops when they become widows (Flitcraft 1977). In the short run, leaving may be the most dangerous thing a woman can do (Okun 1986), provoking further abuse or an escalation to more severe forms of violence, or murder.

Killing the Batterer. In the most extreme cases of abuse, either inside or outside the relationship, murder can be seen as the logical consequence of wife assault. Many women consider killing the batterer at some point, but few carry through with their plans (Stacey and Shupe 1983).

Compared with spousal abuse, where the woman is overwhelmingly the victim, in homicide the woman is equally likely to be either the victim or the perpetrator (Chegwidden, et al. 1981). There are major differences between husbands and wives who kill. Husbands who kill have a history of being abusers, while wives who kill have a history of being abused; while husbands kill during a beating, wives kill in self-defence (Walker 1984).

Is this fourth alternative based on a rational choice, or is it the result of temporary insanity, in which case the woman may be at another stage in the Grieving Process, possibly depression? I have chosen to place it in the acceptance stage because, like the other alternative outcomes, it often occurs after a triggering mechanism. But unlike the other alternative outcomes, it is not a well thought out decision; it may simply be an emotional reaction or a survival instinct.

In the acceptance stage, the battered woman accepts the violence as a major part of her relationship, and takes responsibility for the actions that follow. To reach this point the woman has undertaken many coping mechanisms in an effort to stop the abuse and keep her marriage. It is her determination and effort which produce a change in the relationship and in her life.

Before concluding, let me clarify the difference between the woman "acknowledging" the violence and the woman "accepting" that her conjugal relationship is abusive. This difference is similar to the difference between women who are in the bargaining stage, and those who choose to stay and resign themselves to the situation.

In the bargaining stage, the woman acknowledges the violence as existing in the relationship, but assumes it plays only a minor role in an essentially good marriage. She blames herself or external factors for provoking that abuse, and hopes that without her involvement, small changes will end the violence.

In the acceptance stage, the woman no longer sees herself as playing a role in provoking the abuse; she now considers it as her husband's problem. She sees the violence as a major portion of the relationship, and believes that only with restructuring will the abuse end. The woman also accepts that if change is to occur, she must take responsibility for initiating it.

The Grieving Process presents initial work toward an understanding of the defense mechanisms a battered woman employs to cope with abuse in a conjugal relationship. The model is based on the work of Kubler-Ross (1969) and follows the woman from the first incidents of abuse to the point where she realizes the violence is a major portion of the relationship, and that if any change is to occur, she will have to assume responsibility for initiating it.

The Grieving Process is not proposed as the final word on battered women. It is just the beginning. It lays out the framework for an alternative way of viewing battered women, and even if it is found not to be empirically supported, several underlying concepts remain important in reshaping our view of battered women.

First, rather than being viewed in a negative light, as a helpless victim, the battered woman is seen as an active person trying various techniques to cope with the extraordinary situation. Second, the model does not regard leaving as the only alternative outcome open to a battered woman. Third, the Grieving Process does not view the violent couple as locked in a spiral situation which further entraps the partners over time. It views the woman's reactions to the situation, and the behaviour of the abusive couple, as a progression moving towards a realization of the abuse. Finally, the model recognizes that there is an event in the woman's abusive relationship which triggers her realization that things will not get better, and that she can tolerate no more violence.

It is these four points which will help to redefine the view of battered women in existing research, and which are as important as the Grieving Process.

NOTE

1 Readers who feel that they would like to explore the ideas set out in this article more fully can refer to the author's master's thesis (Carleton University, 1987) from which this article was drawn. The thesis and the complete bibliography can be obtained on request from the author.

COLLEEN LUNDY

Empowerment of Alcoholic Women: The Importance of Self-Help

Although the oppressive condition of many aspects of women's lives is well documented, debate and research about alcoholic women is still in its infant stage, and thus far has taken place primarily within a biological-psychological framework that views the problem as a result of inherent deficiencies of the individual woman. This paper addresses the oppression experienced by alcoholic women, and the importance of self-help groups in their recovery. It draws heavily on the results of a study of alcoholic women, their social roles, and their alcohol dependence conducted by the author.

La révélation du pouvoir chez les femmes alcooliques:
l'importance de l'appui mutuel

Même si la situation d'oppression dont témoignent plusieurs aspects de la vie des femmes a été bien étudiée, les débats et les recherches sur les femmes alcooliques en sont encore à leurs débuts, et jusqu'ici a prévalu une interprétation biologique/psychologique du problème – lequel apparaît comme lié à des déficiences inhérentes à la femme elle-même. Cet article porte sur l'oppression vécue par la femme alcoolique et sur l'importance des groupes de conscience dans le processus de guérison. Il repose en grande partie sur les résultats d'une enquête menée par l'auteure auprès de femmes alcooliques, leur rôle social, et leur dépendance à l'alcool.

Powerlessness, the real or perceived loss of control over one's life, and the devastating sense of alienation which usually accompanies it, are problems that have faced members of all oppressed groups at one time or another. However, through a critical examination of their situations, and the development of an awareness of their oppression, some people have become empowered and changed their life circumstances. [1] Although the oppressive condition of many aspects of women's lives is well documented, [2] debate and research about alcoholic women is still in its infant stage, and thus far has taken place primarily within a biological-psychological framework that views the problem as a result of inherent deficiencies of the individual woman. [3] This paper addresses the oppression experienced by alcoholic women and the importance of self-help groups in their recovery. It draws heavily on the results of a study of alcoholic women, their social roles, and their alcohol dependence conducted by the author.

THE RESEARCH PROCESS

Upon consideration of the research on drinking women, and the restricted form it has taken, I became interested in looking at women's social roles and their relationship to the alcohol dependency process. My purpose was to attempt to understand, through a phenomenological approach, the drinking experiences of women, as they related to other aspects of their lives, rather than to seek the causal factors of drinking. Using intensive biographical interviewing, the lives of 50 women were traced over the course of the process of alcohol dependence. Two groups of women were studied; one which had been alcohol free for at least one year and one which continued to drink. The nondrinking women were self-referred or referred by a women's counselling centre, and the drinking women were referred by a local detoxification unit. The selection and interviewing took place over a five-month period. The interviews were taped and transcribed, and a thematic analysis was performed on them. While it is recognized that the respondents selected were not necessarily representative of a larger population, their responses indicate fruitful research avenues.

PROFILE OF THE WOMEN

The women interviewed were a diverse group. Although this study was conducted in the southern United States, half of the women in both groups were originally from the Northern States, or other countries. The ages of the women (again, similar in both groups) ranged from 16 to 67, with an average age of 33. All the nondrinking women were white, whereas five of the drinking women were black. Four of the women (three in the nondrinking group) stated their emo-

tional and sexual preferences to be other women. The women in
the drinking group were less educated than the nondrinking women
and more likely to be unemployed. Of the drinking group, 64% of
the women were not working, compared to 24% of the nondrinking
women. Approximately 60% of the women in both groups had been
divorced, and 22% were currently married.

THE SOCIAL CONDITIONS OF THE WOMEN

The extent and forms of oppression experienced by the women, as
children and later as adults, is striking. The most startling finding
is the violence to which the women were exposed (see table 1). Of
the 50 women, 76% reported some form of parental abuse. An
astonishing 36% of the women reported a daughter-father/ stepfather relationship that included at least one episode of incestuous
activity, from fondling to forced entry.[4] Most of the father-daughter
incest occurred from the ages of 10 to 16. Two women related sexual
abuse by brothers as well. One woman was, at the age of seven,
forced to perform fellatio on her brother, and at age 13 raped by
another brother and regularly fondled by her father.

Physical abuse in childhood occured in 42% of the women. The
beatings were administered with switches, cords, broom sticks,
leather straps, crow bars, belts, or directly with fists and open hands.
The welts and bruises in visible areas were not uncommonly a source
of shame and embarrassment when the victims were questioned by
friends.

Emotional abuse was experienced by 64% of the women. These
women felt belittled and ignored as children. For some, the message
was communicated indirectly by neglect and lack of attention ("didn't
listen to me," "no time for me") while for others it took the form of
verbal abuse ("I wish you were gone," "stupid," "fuck-up"). Not surprisingly, sexual abuse was invariably accompanied by emotional
abuse.

A significant number of the women continued to experience violence into adulthood. Sixteen of the 50 women (32%) were victims
of physical and verbal abuse from their partners. The abuse was
twice as prevalent in the drinking group as it was in the nondrinking
group. Another striking finding is that all the women who experienced abuse in a partner relationship had been abused either emotionally, physically, or sexually as children.

A number of the women had dropped out of school before completing the twelfth grade (68% of the drinking women and 16% of
the nondrinking women). This early cessation of formal education

Table
Abuse of Women During Childhood

	Nondrinking No. = 25	Drinking No. = 25
	%	%
Physical Abuse	32	52
Emotional Abuse	64	64
Sexual Abuse	32	40
One Form of Abuse	36	28
Two Forms of Abuse	28	16
Three Forms of Abuse	12	32
No Abuse	24	24

does not appear to be related to academic inability or failure. The majority of the women felt that they had been good students. The primary reason for leaving was marriage and/or pregnancy. Many women viewed marriage as an opportunity to flee the disturbing conditions within their homes, as well as a hope for the love and affection so often absent in their own families.

Later, as mothers and partners, the women often felt a sense of powerlessness due to limitations and roles imposed on them. This attitude is clearly expressed by a twenty-six-year-old woman who had left school in the seventh grade: "I was mechanical. I had my baby. I had to do what society planned for me to do as a wife. It was all mechanical ... I never had an outlet for me."

THE ROLE OF ALCOHOL

The personal accounts of the women attest to their use of alcohol as a means of escape from the alienation, loneliness and physical and emotional pain, or a source of solace and support. "When I drank I could make everything I wanted to be, and escape from the reality of my situation," commented one woman. Such statements were representative of the alcoholic women in the study.

In this context, alcoholism can be viewed as merely one of the manifestations of the oppression experienced by these women. Alcohol dependence, although commonly viewed as a personal affliction, is essentially socially constructed. My central argument is that a clear connection can be made between the drinking behaviour of women and the conditions under which they function.

Marian Sandmaier, who supports this view, states:

A woman's experience with alcoholism cannot be separated from the realities of sexism in our culture. Every dimension of a woman's addiction – its causes, its consequences, its subversive hidden quality, its treatment – are shaped by her subordinate and devalued status. To a large degree, the depth of this connection stems from the sheer pervasiveness of sexism. Women are driven to all kinds of self-destructive escapes from their powerlessness and their conflicted visions of themselves: depression, compulsive eating, other drug addiction, obsessive housekeeping, suicide ... alcohol is only one escape of many (1982, 232).

The oppressive conditions faced by the women influenced not only the onset and progression of their alcoholism, but their opportunities for recovery as well.[5] The drinking women in this study were characterized by their easy entry, nonprofessional jobs, by the increased prevalence among them of abuse as children and later as partners, by their considerably less education and more frequent periods of unemployment, and by the greater likelihood of their having non-supportive, troubled families. All of these factors can be seen as obstacles to recovery. The oppressive nature of the women's lives, coupled with an allconsuming reliance and dependence on alcohol, created a joyless, lonely, despair-filled existence which often produced feelings of self-hatred. The sense of hopelessness was reinforced by their lack of external support.

LIFE WITHOUT ALCOHOL

The reasons why an alcohol-dependent person stops drinking are complex. The concept of "hitting bottom," put forward by Alcoholics Anonymous, is based on the premise that people stop drinking when they reach their "bottom" – an individual level of existence that is viewed as intolerable and which motivates them to stop. However, the fact that an alcoholic perceives her situation to be intolerable does not mean that she has alternatives. Many women reach "bottom" and remain there indefinitely, a fact that is reflected in this study. The potential or feasibility of attaining sobriety will depend very much on factors other than subjective or psychological ones. Decent employment, education or training, and a dependable support network increase the chance of recovery from alcoholism.

For those women who had stopped drinking the recovery process was a distressing, difficult time. Sobriety, in and of itself, did not remove the problems, or the feeling of low selfworth: "The only thing that happened was that I sobered up. I had to take a look at my life, I hated what I saw and I couldn't cover it up with alcohol ... There was a lot of despair, a lot of denial and all those things ...

I think some of the worst times have been since I sobered up."

The despondency and depression experienced during the period of problem drinking often continued after drinking stopped. For some of the women there were thoughts of suicide: "I just couldn't picture letting my kids find me dead somewhere. That would be too horrible. In fact, if I had been assured that they wouldn't find me I probably would have done it. But until I was sober for about six months I still felt suicidal because it was real difficult. In recovery it's very difficult because all the issues were still there. There just was no alcohol." Another woman comments on her emotional health: "I'm working on it, that's all I can say. It has been the pits. I've wanted to commit suicide, even now, you know I still think about it. Just a quick way out you know."

Sobriety was not always positively acknowledged by others, particularly employers and partners. During problem drinking bouts the women were frequently able to function adequately at their jobs. In fact, at times they overcompensated by working long hours. This pattern changed with sobriety: "I was overcommitted in that area for so long that I think for some period of time they may have felt cheated when I decided to just have a better balance for myself. I was not quite willing for that to be my whole life and I think at first they felt cheated. It was wonderful when I was drinking. I came early. I stayed late, made up for all my other deficiencies and now I work eight hours."

For some women, alcohol had made an unsatisfying job more tolerable. This dissatisfaction became more acute with sobriety: "After I sobered up I got much worse at my job. After you got sober your emotions went to shit and you really started messing up on the job. It was just that, it was something mindless, something I could do from eight to five. When I sobered up I continued to do my job but I was restless."

Most women were without partners during their recovery. In fact, only seven were in live-in relationships and two of those women were unhappy and considering leaving. For one woman, her sobriety was threatening to her husband: "he couldn't handle the fact that I didn't have to completely depend on him anymore. He didn't mind it (the drinking) at all because, like I said I was totally dependent on him at that time – totally. When I went into treatment he got very upset."

SELF-HELP AND TRANSFORMATION: FROM
ALCOHOLICS ANONYMOUS TO FEMINIST SELF-HELP

An analysis of the research findings reveals two important and re-

lated factors in achieving sobriety: first, the importance of participation in a self-help, mutual-aid group, and second, the need to
understand and acquire a degree of control over one's situation.[6] I
call the latter empowerment.

The transition from drinking to sobriety is a wrenching experience. Support is essential. The most salient feature of the lives of
the alcoholic women during this period of recovery was their involvement in a self-help group, Alcoholics Anonymous (AA). Of the
25 nondrinking women, all but four were active members. In contrast, only four of the women in the drinking group were attending
AA meetings.

As a support group, Alcoholics Anonymous offered the women
an opportunity to be connected with others and combat the loneliness
and alienation that had been such a large part of their existence
while drinking. Some of the women referred to AA as a family: "I
feel estranged from my family. I don't really feel that I have any
close family that I can share my problems with. AA is the closest thing
to a family I have ... by the end of the meeting I knew I was at home.
I belonged there. Someone told their story and more than anything
I felt connected to people again that I hadn't done in so long. I felt
all this warmth and love that I hadn't been able to feel in so long."

And as one woman stated: "I'd get one hour where I wouldn't be
afraid." Alcoholics Anonymous was of paramount importance to
these women.

It has been stated that "one of the most significant characteristics
of mutual-aid groups is the fact that they are empowering and thus
delineating" (Reissman 1976, 41). The AA program is seen as presenting a guideline with which alcoholics can transform their con-
sciousnesses and change their lives (Whitfield 1984, 1–53). Members
are encouraged to see alcoholism as a disease and to gain strength
and support from the group in order to achieve personal growth
and maintain sobriety. The philosophy and life-structuring function
of AA, combined with the ever-present fellowship, offer new coping
strategies for day to day living.

Despite its proven success in aiding alcoholics, AA's empowerment
process has definite limitations for women. First, the focus is on
individual change, not change in social conditions. The emphasis is
on biological abnormality with little recognition of underlying social
causes. Second, AA is a one issue movement, but alcoholism in women
involves more than just drinking. Third, although women comprise
approximately one-third of the members of AA, and AA guidelines
now accommodate the formation of groups just for women, the

question still needs to be raised as to what opportunity women have to address the issues specific to them.[7]

I suggest that given the nature of the oppression encountered by women, a self-help approach based on a feminist ideology and praxis has greater potential in aiding recovery. The ideology, beliefs, attitudes, and values of self-help groups, guide the members in defining the nature and causes of their problem and the course of action for its alleviation (Suler 1984, 29–36). The efficacy of a critical consciousness for oppressed groups in the empowerment process has been convincingly argued.[8] Critically examining our lives and the social forces that dominate us is the first step to becoming empowered. A feminist ideology recognizes inequalities, domination, and exploitation in society as sources of difficulties for women and as obstacles to overcome. The personal experience of women is connected to the larger political context. In this way the problem of alcohol dependence is shifted away from the individual to the social structure and ideology that oppresses women.

Although feminist self-help which centred on a number of health concerns was an early component of the women's movement, feminist groups specifically for alcohol-dependent women were not formally organized. The feminist traditions of self-help, consciousness-raising, and social action provide rich experience and a valuable framework with which to begin to address the problems of alcohol-dependent women. Through such an approach these women can take the first step in the direction of living an alcohol-free existence, and moreover, begin to work at changing the ideologies and structures which oppress all women.

NOTES

1 See, for example, the works of Paulo Freire (1970) and Charles Kieffer (1981).

2 See, for example, the writings of Michelle Barrett (1985) and Christine Delphy (1984).

3 For the most part, the research narrowly examines conflict between conscious and unconscious levels of sexrole identification in women. The findings have been ambiguous and inconclusive, undoubtedly as a result of a methodology which uses highly questionable psychometric measures (Lundy 1987, 69–78). It is also a product of a theory which fails to deal with the material conditions of women's lives.

4 This finding is considerably higher than the 14.9% reported in one study

(Beckman 1984, 101–13). However, it is in closer agreement with the findings of Covington and Kohen. They report that from their sample of 35 alcoholic women, 74% reported at least one instance of sexual abuse, and that incest accounted for 34% of these cases (Covington and Kohen 1984, 50). The reported incidence of father-daughter incest in the general population varies from 1.3% (Finkelhor 1979, 121) to 4.5% (Russell 1984, 186).

5 Although progression of alcohol use was similar for both groups, the women in the drinking group indicated that they had been drinking excessively for longer periods of time, ranging from 3 to 41 years ($\bar{x} = 14$) as compared to the nondrinking women who had been drinking problematically for periods ranging from 2 to 22 years ($\bar{x} = 8$) prior to stopping.

6 Many of the women had received a variety of professional services prior to or at the time of stopping drinking. The self-help/mutual-aid experience was viewed as being vital to staying sober and surviving in the difficult period of recovery.

7 Dr Jean Kirkpatrick, a sociologist and an alcoholic, believed that AA was not responding to women's concerns so she organized an alternative support group called Women for Sobriety (1978). The focus is on overcoming alcohol dependence by regaining a positive self-image. Both AA and Women for Sobriety are apolitical and do not engage in advocacy; the focus is on individual change (adaptation and adjustment) rather than social change.

8 Again, the work of Paulo Freire (1970) is critical here.

Women and Literature
Les femmes et la littérature

MONIQUE GENUIST

La vieille femme chez Antonine Maillet: héritage et avenir

J'analyse ici le personnage de la vieille femme chez Antonine Maillet et sa signification en me basant principalement sur *La Sagouine* (1971) et *Évangéline Deusse* (1975). Je montre comment ces femmes assurent la continuité des valeurs civilisatrices, porteuses qu'elles sont de tout un héritage culturel et linguistique. Par leur étonnante résistance physique et l'ensemble de leurs qualités morales (bon sens pratique, lucidité sans amertume, appréciation des éléments naturels, courage dans les épreuves, attachement passionné à toute forme de vie), ces femmes, vieilles et pauvres, sont aussi garantes de l'avenir possible des femmes.

The Old Woman in the Work of Antonine Maillet:
Her Legacy for Women's Future

My study analyzes the character of the old woman in Antonine Maillet's work, and its meaning, based primarily on *La Sagouine* (1971) and *Évangéline Deusse* (1975). I show how these women ensure the continuity of civilizing values, while they are also the bearers of an entire cultural and linguistic heritage to be preserved and passed on. Because of their incredible stamina and their numerous moral qualities (good practical sense, clearheadedness without bitterness, appreciation of nature, courage through hardships, and passionate attachment to all forms of life), these old and poor women are also the keepers of women's potential future.

Lorsque *La Sagouine* (1971) a été jouée (une quarantaine de fois) dans les Maritimes en 1972, le public acadien a spontanément rebaptisé la Sagouine, Évangéline deusse (Royer 1972). Quatre ans plus tard, en 1976, le Rideau vert présentait une nouvelle pièce de Maillet, intitulée *Évangéline deusse* (1975). Ces prénoms qui riment,

Sagouine, Évangéline, soulignent la parenté entre les deux personnages, même si leurs significations sont complètement différentes.
Une sagouine, en acadien, est une femme sale, au sens physique
d'abord, puis au sens moral, c'est à peu près un synonyme du mot
salope; alors que dans Évangéline se trouve la racine « ange » avec
tout ce que cela implique de propreté morale et de foi religieuse.

Dotées de prénoms antithétiques mais qui riment, ces deux femmes sont proches parentes. Toutes deux sont des Acadiennes pauvres, filles de pêcheurs, vivant ou ayant vécu au bord de la mer,
probablement originaires de la région de Richibouctou. La Sagouine
a mis au monde douze enfants, Évangéline, onze garçons. Toutes
deux arrivent à la fin de leur existence: la Sagouine a soixante-douze
ans, Évangéline « fesse » ses quatre-vingts ans, et elles parlent au
nom d'une longue expérience de vie de femme et de misère. La
Sagouine est seule en scène, Évangéline est accompagnée de trois
hommes qu'elle domine de sa vigueur et de sa faconde, si bien que
les personnages masculins semblent être surtout là pour lui donner
la réplique.

Ces deux personnages féminins sont nés de l'expérience concrète
de leur créatrice:

Quand j'étais enfant, raconte Antonine Maillet, j'ai connu des femmes de
mon pays qui étaient des Sagouine. Les gens d'en bas venaient souvent pour
vendre des palourdes, des huîtres. Et pour chercher du linge, demander la
charité, en somme le contact que nous avions avec ces gens étaient comme
une coupure entre deux mondes. C'était un contact au niveau du donner-
recevoir ...

La vie m'a fait approfondir le personnage ... Et je suis allée rencontrer
une sagouine que je connaissais. Elle était vraiment typique. À la fois sa-
voureusement « forlaque » un peu mauvaise fille et profondément intelli-
gente ... Après deux heures de conversation, j'étais bouleversée. Je n'aurais
pas parlé avec De Gaulle avec plus de profit qu'avec cette Sagouine ... Puis
un jour, j'avais un texte à écrire pour la radio. J'ai voulu laisser parler mes
entrailles. Voir ce qui viendrait du fond de moi-même. C'est cette Sagouine
qui m'est venue. (Royer 1972)

La Sagouine et Évangéline parlent la langue acadienne et emploient,
comme les paysan-ne-s des pièces de Molière, le je suivi du verbe à
la première personne du pluriel: « Par chus nous, j'appelons ça des
coques parce que j'avons point appris à parler en grandeur » dit
Évangéline (Maillet 1975, 25); « Je parlons avec les mots que j'avons
dans la bouche et j'allons pas les charcher ben loin. Je les tenons de
nos péres qui les avions reçus de leurs aïeux. De goule en oreille

comme qui dirait, » explique la Sagouine (Maillet 1971, 40). Leur je
est aussi un nous et représente la collectivité acadienne.

Les deux vieilles femmes sont porteuses de tout un héritage linguistique : le français d'Acadie, resté jusqu'à Antonine Maillet une
langue essentiellement orale, cette langue des aïeux qui a gardé des
formes de prononciation remontant au haut moyen âge, par exemple
la palatalisation des consonnes, cotchiner pour coquin, tchas pour
tas, inchéter pour inquiéter, ou le *er* prononcé *ar* dans parsoune,
avartie, sartain. Comme au dix-septième siècle, la voyelle o est fermée
dans coume (comme), grous (gros), houme (homme), chouse (chose)
et le son *oir* est prononcé *ouère* dans avouère (avoir), voulouère
(vouloir). De nombreux mots du vocabulaire viennent de Norman-
die, de Bretagne, de Vendée, du Poitou, qu'ri pour chercher, espérer
pour attendre, ersoudre pour sortir, etc. Évangéline tombe
amoureuse du Breton en partie parce qu'elle découvre qu'il parle
la même langue qu'elle :

Le Breton : ... Et si j'étais le Cyprien de la dernière heure, hein ? Un Cyprien
qui vous aurait espérée septante ans ... Évangéline : Septante ans ! ... j'ai
point entendu ce mot-là depuis que j'ai quitté le pays. Le Breton : La Bretagne était pleine de vieux mots acadiens. Si je m'y mets, je parviendrai à
les déniger tous. (Maillet 1975, 88–9)

Cette langue, dit Maillet, ce n'est ni le chiac qui est parlé surtout
dans les milieux urbains, ni le français international mais :

En fait c'est de l'acadien. Et l'acadien, c'est une intonation et un accent local
greffés sur un langage ancien qui était le langage du xviᵉ et du xviiᵉ siècle.
Dans *La Sagouine*, je n'ai pas inventé un seul mot.
    Cette langue ... est encore en usage chez les vieux et dans les campagnes
assez reculées ou encore chez les enfants qui n'ont pas encore été à l'école.
Les personnes jeunes ou d'âge moyen et surtout les citadins n'en usent guère.
Par contre, en Nouvelle-Écosse, tous les habitants d'origine acadienne qui
parlent encore français s'expriment toujours comme la sagouine. (Dassylva
1972)

De même que Michel Tremblay donnait la parole aux femmes qué-
bécoises des quartiers pauvres de Montréal avec ses *Belles-soeurs* en
1968, de même Antonine Maillet donne voix aux femmes acadiennes
dans les années soixante-dix avec les monologues de la Sagouine ou
les dialogues d'Évangéline. Ces femmes racontent l'expérience qu'elles ont vécue, assez différente toutefois de celle écrite dans l'histoire
officielle.

L'Américain Henry W. Longfellow propose en 1847, sous forme d'une épopée romantique dans son poème *Évangéline*, une image mythique de la vie des Acadien-ne-s avant la déportation de 1755, et une image mythique de la femme acadienne. Paroissien-ne-s fidèles groupé-e-s autour de leur prêtre et de leur église, les Acadienne-s auraient alors, selon lui, connu une sorte d'âge d'or dans la paix, la prospérité, l'angélisme – le bonheur parfait pour ainsi dire. En 1902, dans la préface au poème traduit par Pamphile Le May, se retrouve cette même vision: « La vie des Acadiens ... avait été une idylle de paix et de bonheur et de douce simplicité » (1912, 14). En 1978, Michel Roy, dans son essai *L'Acadie perdue*, conteste la vérité historique de cette version et affirme que les Acadien-ne-s n'avaient pas eu la vie facile: « Dix attaques anglaises en moins de cent ans, dix-huit ou vingt-deux enfants. » Comment un historien tel que Rameau de Saint-Père osait-il alors arriver à cette conclusion: « la femme et les enfants heureux et gais, se berçaient sans souci » (1978, 90)?

Quant à l'héroïne de Longfellow, Évangéline Bellefontaine, c'est la jeune fille idéale, belle, pure, soumise à Dieu et au prêtre, fidèle jusqu'à la mort à son fiancé Gabriel dont elle a été séparée au moment de la déportation. Dans sa préface au poème, Édouard Richard déclare: « Il convenait que l'héroïne choisie pour fixer dans les esprits les péripéties douloureuses du ‹grand dérangement› restât la *douce* et *pieuse* fille qu'était l'Acadienne; que ses souffrances fussent supportées avec cette *muette résignation* particulière aux âmes simples et droites » (1912, 14; c'est nous qui soulignons).

À l'image mythique de la Vierge d'Acadie décrite par Longfellow en ces termes,

À l'église, souvent, les gars du voisinage
Tenaient ouvert leur livre, ou priaient à genoux,
En reposant sur elle un oeil un peu jaloux
Comme si, dans un nimbe, elle eût été la sainte
Qu'ils venaient invoquer en la pieuse enceinte
Heureux qui par hasard touchait sa blanche main,
Voyait sourire un peu ses lèvres de carmin! (1912, 28)

Antonine Maillet oppose la réalité de ses deux vieilles femmes qui ne sont ni douces, ni pures, ni surtout muettes ou résignées.

En contraste avec Évangéline Bellefontaine, Évangéline deusse n'est pas vierge, loin de là; avant son mariage avec Noré elle était amoureuse de Cyprien qui fut sans doute le père de son premier enfant, « Ben mon plus vieux, je l'ai nommé Cyprien, Joseph-Ernest

Cyprien. Noré a jamais parmis que je l'appelions d'autre chouse qu'Ernest, ben sus son baptistère, j'ai fait écrire Cyprien. Et ce que Noré a jamais su ... » (67); à quatre-vingts ans, elle tombe encore amoureuse du Breton. La Sagouine, elle, a été une fille à matelots tout en étant mariée et mère de famille.

Loin de rester silencieuses, les deux vieilles femmes donnent ouvertement leur avis sur tout, « Et pis ce qu'elle a dans sa caboche, elle l'a jamais caché à parsoune » (Maillet 1971, 14), dit la Sagouine à propos d'elle-même. Aucune des deux n'abdique devant le malheur. Quand le Breton raconte à Évangéline deusse l'histoire des Acadiens, prisonniers dans l'église avant d'être déportés et écoutant sagement le message de résignation de leur prêtre, celle-ci s'exclame, « Il leu manquait une femme ou deux à nos houmes, pour les organiser, pis les fouetter, pis leur faire honte » (Maillet 1975, 45). Et quand elle apprend que tout ce qu'Évangéline Bellefontaine a su faire dans cette situation, c'était de pleurer dans son tablier, elle s'indigne et cite en contraste le courage des femmes acadiennes lors du naufrage de la dune, « vous ariez point trouvé une femme du Fond de la Baie assise sur la côte, la face dans son devanteau. Non! J'étions au goulet, c'te jour-là, à garrocher des câbles pis des boueyes à l'eau; à pousser les hommes à la mer, en doré de sauvetage » (ibid). À l'image de l'héroïne unique, fiancée vierge, modèle de souffrance dans la passivité et les larmes, se substitue la présence de femmes nombreuses, décidées, solides qui agissent à côté des hommes. Évangéline, la sainte, descend de sa statue à Grandpré et s'incarne dans Évangéline deusse tandis que le mythe romantique et statique s'estompe dans le passé et fait place à une réalité dynamique.

De son côté, la Sagouine, qui pourrait être totalement accablée par son lot de servitude et de pauvreté où, comme elle le répète souvent, « c'est malaisé, » n'est ni amère, ni acariâtre. Tranquillement, du fond de sa misère et tout en gardant toujours un brin d'espoir et de gaieté, elle peint avec perspicacité et lucidité ses pairs et son milieu. Nullement résignée, elle dénonce, sans en avoir l'air, cette société qui divise le monde entre riches, puissants, forts, d'un côté, et de l'autre, faibles, guenilloux, crasseux, dont elle fait partie. Elle a pourtant l'impression qu'au commencement toutes les humaines sont d'égale valeur. À la naissance, elle a été baptisée comme n'importe quel-le autre enfant, « Ondoyée, baptisée, emmaillotée, j'ai passé par toute la sarémonie avant d'aouère les yeux rouverts. C'est pour dire, hein? Je sons tout du monde pareil, à c't âge-là. C'est plus tard que ... » (Maillet 1971, 92). Les points de suspension indiquent que la Sagouine s'interroge sur ce qui s'est passé entre cette égalité qu'elle constate à la naissance et aussi à la mort, « Moi je me figure qu'un corps ouvert ça doit ressembler à tous les autres corps ouverts » (Maillet 1971, 14). À la naissance et sur leur lit de mourant-e, les humain-e-s se ressemblent. Entre les deux pourtant, l'une deviendra bourgeoise et l'autre sagouine, « j'étais rien qu'une femme après toute, et une femme d'en bas ... Une femme d'en bas, ça quasiment rien qu'un choix ... Tu t'attoques sur le poteau de téléphône ... ou ben tu te promènes d'un bout à l'autre du chemin du roi ... Pis tu guettes » (Maillet 1971, 16–17).

Mine de rien, prenant des précautions pour ne pas s'attirer les foudres du ciel et mettant parfois cette responsabilité sur le dos de Gapi, son mari, la Sagouine raille les institutions qui favorisent et permettent ces inégalités et injustices sociales. Ce sont les gouvernements, qui s'intéressent aux Acadiens seulement quand le Canada a besoin d'hommes pour la guerre. C'est aussi et surtout l'église réservée aux riches, « une église de dimanche » (Maillet 1971, 12), soutenue par les bourgeois-es qui se donnent bonne conscience en pratiquant une charité à bon marché, payant leurs serviteurs et servantes de leurs vieux habits démodés ou de leurs jouets cassés; le jour de Noël, « y avait un petit prône du curé qui finissait tout le temps par: ‹Aimez-vous les uns les autres!› pis la chicane prenait. Vous compornez ces enfants qui receviont un aroplane qui vole plus ou ben une petite catin-qui-pisse qui pisse pas, ils se mettiont à brailler et ça finissait en jeu de chiens » (Maillet 1971, 24).

L'église catholique en Acadie a en effet largement contribué à favoriser cette hiérarchie des êtres humains, le haut et le bas de l'humanité. Témoin ce que dit Michel Roy à propos des collèges classiques où étaient formés les futurs prêtres et les membres de la bourgeoisie acadienne: « Le collège a été une usine à roitelets. Un sens strict de la hiérarchie s'y élaborait. On faisait vite la distinction entre le Père recteur, devant qui on crevait de peur, et un préposé à l'entretien, auprès de qui on sentait monter en soi les ivresses du sentiment dominateur. » (Roy 1978, 50) Et il ajoute: « Au seuil du collège, le péché était en nous comme une maladie. Sous à peu près toutes ses formes. Il est cependant notoire que jamais allusion n'a été faite au plus grand péché de tous, celui de l'exploitation de l'homme par l'homme » (Roy 1978, 51).

Justement la Sagouine est une préposée à l'entretien, une femme de ménage, qui se trouve tout au bas de l'échelle, qui n'a rien, ne possède rien, ne domine personne. Ce dénuement complet lui confère une certaine liberté de regarder le monde autour d'elle, de réfléchir, de penser à haute voix sur cette société qui l'entoure, ses vices, ses injustices. Selon Mgr Richard cité par Michel Roy, « l'Acadie n'a vu aucun des siens occuper un rang honorable dans la société.

Privés d'éducation, ils se sont livrés à la colonisation, à l'agriculture, à la pêche, ne pouvant prétendre à d'autres professions. » (1978, 56) Aux yeux d'un tel Monseigneur, la Sagouine, à genoux sur le plancher à « forbir, » ou assise avec son grand tablier bleu à peler les pommes de terre, n'occuperait certainement pas non plus un rang honorable. Pourtant Maillet lui confère la dignité et la clairvoyance qu'on attribue d'habitude aux maîtres à penser. Nous assistons à une contestation sociale par le biais d'un renversement des valeurs où celle qui est le plus bas conteste la supériorité de ceux qui sont le plus haut et paraît beaucoup plus respectable que ces derniers. La Sagouine pose sur le monde un regard candide, observe, remet en question la hiérarchie sociale avec finesse, bon sens et humour. Les spectatrices et spectateurs l'écoutent et sont amené-e-s à reconnaître que sagesse et intelligence ne sont pas nécessairement l'apanage des puissants, des riches ou des gens instruits, mais que ces qualités peuvent aussi bien appartenir aux plus humbles, et même aux femmes.

Pour Antonine Maillet, l'héritage culturel ne sera pas transmis par les collèges classiques, où l'on apprend surtout à reproduire des schèmes d'oppression mais plutôt par la voix de la sagesse populaire, ici celle de cette femme pauvre, lucide devant ceux qui l'oppriment mais qui en même temps reste confiante et optimiste. La Sagouine et Évangéline, malgré leur grand âge et leur pauvreté, sont en effet du côté de l'espoir, par leur attachement au réel et leur respect de la vie en elles, dans la nature et autour d'elles.

C'est le sens du réel qui amène la Sagouine à voir clairement l'hypocrisie de l'église et des bourgeois prêchant la générosité mais pratiquant l'égoïsme, et qui fait rejeter par Évangéline deusse l'image fausse de l'héroïne acadienne, créée par le poète américain, et adoptée par l'église pour servir son idéologie. Ces femmes ne sont plus dupes de ces idéologies, même si elles continuent à en être les victimes. L'une dénonce l'oppression, l'autre le mythe de la sainteté féminine. Ni aveugles, ni soumises, ni muettes, elles ont les qualités de courage, de détermination des résistantes. Elles ont réussi à garder la tête haute à travers les indignités que leur condition de femme pauvre leur a fait traverser. Elles ont conservé le respect d'elles-mêmes; par exemple la Sagouine se présente comme ayant « la face nouère pis la peau craquée » (Maillet 1971, 11), mais aussi les mains blanches. Elle sait que la noirceur n'est qu'une façade et elle est fière de ses mains, plus blanches que celles de n'importe quelle bourgeoise, parce qu'elles sont le signe de sa valeur, de son travail, de son honnêteté, de sa franchise.

Quant à Évangéline, elle est forte de sa longue expérience, « D'abord j'ai appris à me défendre. Quand c'est que t'en as quatre-vingts dans le dos, des hivers, tu finis par saouère par quel boute le prendre. La meilleure façon [de prendre la vie] c'est de la prendre à brasse-corps » (Maillet 1975, 30) et elle estime que cela lui assure une certaine supériorité, « j'suis d'une race, ça s'adoune, qui peut encore recoumencer sa vie à l'heure que les autres achevont d'achever la leur » (Maillet 1975, 36).

Les deux femmes sont profondément liées à la terre par leur sens du concret et leur amour de la nature. Dans sa magnifique ode au printemps (Maillet 1971, 75–80), la Sagouine s'émerveille d'entendre les outardes remonter vers les terres, de voir l'eau se remettre à couler, de sentir les premières odeurs qui montent du sol. Cela lui donne envie de « subler pis de turluter » (Maillet 1971, 80). Évangéline prend soin du petit sapin que son fils lui a envoyé de la côte; elle le transplante, l'arrose, lui parle, si bien qu'il reprend vie et que les goélands sont même venus de la mer lui tenir compagnie, « Et asteur, mon petit sapin naissant, tu seras pu tout seul pour grandir à l'étrange. Le cri du pays est arrivé » (Maillet 1975, 108).

Les deux femmes ont le culte de cette vie qu'elles possèdent encore. La Sagouine, vieille et souffrante, imagine un paradis très terrestre où elle pourrait se rendre, « si les anges pouvions nous sarvir du fricot au petit-noir et de la tarte au coconut faite au magasin et si Djeu-le-Pére en parsoune pouvait s'en venir câler la danse le samedi souère, ça serait point de refus » (Maillet 1971, 97). Évangéline, elle aussi, aime encore la danse et y entraîne ses compagnons. Pleine d'une extraordinaire vitalité, elle ne renoncera pas à la terre avant la dernière minute et elle encourage les autres à l'imiter, à ne pas se laisser aller, « Quand c'est qu'un bon matin, une parsoune se réveille, et qu'a s'aperçoit qu'a' slaque, a' s'aperçoit du même coup qu'a vieillzit. C'est ça qui fait mourir les vieux : i' slaquont. Faut point slaquer, point s'arrêter pour prendre son souffle avant d'être rendu, d'être ben sûr d'être rendu » (Maillet 1975, 65).

Antonine Maillet met ces femmes en contraste avec les hommes qui les accompagnent, Gapi, le mari absent dont la Sagouine parle beaucoup, et le Breton, l'amoureux d'Évangéline. Dans les deux cas, les hommes manquent de confiance et d'espoir, ils sont inquiets, pessimistes. Cette opposition dans le couple se retrouve aussi avec Pélagie qui entraîne la charrette de la vie dans sa remontée vers l'Acadie tandis que son compagnon, Bélonie, lui, hale la charrette de la mort.

Contrairement à l'image traditionnelle de la vieille femme faible, devenue stérile, laide, acariâtre et inutile, Antonine Maillet présente des vieilles femmes attachantes, énergiques, porteuses d'un message

de vie et d'espoir. Ces personnages s'inscrivent dans une lignée lit-
téraire où se rejoignent les créations de romancières aussi différentes
que Gabrielle Roy, avec sa vieille Martha veillant jusqu'à sa mort sur
son jardin de fleurs dans la nouvelle, *Un jardin au bout du monde*,
Marie-Claire Blais, dressant le portrait de Grand-mère Antoinette
qui défend avec acharnement ses petits-enfants, Jean-le-Maigre puis
Emmanuel, contre la tyrannie destructrice du père, ou encore Anne
Hébert donnant, dans *Les fous de Bassan*, l'exemple de Felicity Jones
« qui aborde l'âge d'être grand-mère comme quelqu'un qui commence à vivre » (1982, 36). Ces vieilles femmes avec leur grande
vitalité, leur intelligence, leur bon sens, transmettent le courage,
l'espoir, l'élan. Défenseuses irréductibles de la vie sous toutes ses
formes, plantes, oiseaux, nature, enfants, elles font échec au désarroi
et au pessimisme morbide des personnages masculins, placés en pa-
rallèle et en contraste, et sont garantes de l'avenir possible de la
femme et de l'humanité.

TRACY C. DAVIS

A Doll's House *and the Evolving Feminist Agenda*

When Nora (the heroine of Ibsen's *A Doll's House*) left her home and family "to think things out" for herself and "get things clear," the noise of the door slamming behind her is said to have reverberated throughout Europe. Since 1879, hundreds of thousands of women have been moved by Nora's plight and inspired by her resolve to understand what made her as she was, to seek a self-defined truth, and to win independence from her male masters. Through an examination of selected productions, adaptations, and sequels of *A Doll's House* written over the course of a century, the priorities and perceptions of the evolving feminist movement can be traced in representations of Ibsen's characters and situations.

La Maison de poupée *et le développement de l'ordre du jour féministe*

On dit que lorsque Nora, (l'héroïne de la *Maison de poupée* d'Ibsen) quitta son foyer et sa famille « pour réfléchir » et « essayer d'y voir clair, » l'écho de la porte qu'elle claqua derrière elle retentit à travers l'Europe. Depuis 1879, des centaines de milliers de femmes ont été touchées par la situation de Nora et inspirées par sa détermination de comprendre ce qui l'avait amenée à être ce qu'elle était, à trouver sa propre définition de la vérité et à s'émanciper de ses maîtres masculins. En étudiant une sélection de productions, d'adaptations et de suites de la *Maison de poupée* écrites dans l'espace d'un siècle, on peut retracer les priorités et les perceptions du mouvement féministe dans son évolution, à travers les représentations des personnages et des situations créés par Ibsen.

When Nora and Torvald Helmer sit down opposite each other in Ibsen's play *A Doll's House* and hold their first serious discussion in an eight-year marriage, something surprising happens. At the beginning of the play, Nora is a promising heroic figure – an erotically alive wife, a cheerful companion to her husband's friends, an attentive mother, socially popular, and extremely decorative – but she has a secret that no conventional heroine is allowed to possess. When Torvald learns that Nora illegally borrowed money (independent of masculine counsel) to save his life, and that through this act she became a forger, a dissembler, an associate of usurers, and a threat to the family's bourgeois equilibrium, his true colours are revealed and he bars her from their children and from their marital bed. At this point, Nora begins to seriously question the authority and values of those who control women's lot. She had wrongly assumed that if the circumstances had been reversed, her husband would have done whatever was necessary to save her life, though of course his sex would not have been an impediment to straightforward legal dealings. She sees the hypocrisy, injustice, and cruelty of the law and the double-standard of society; once she is marked indelibly by the taint of female independence, she also sees the meagre, shallow righteousness of patriarchal scions like her husband. Although Torvald is "a good match" by nineteenth-century standards (a devoted husband, an excellent father, and a proficient earner) Nora rejects him, his concept of marriage, and his children. If she were to continue to cooperate with him and others like him, she sees she would be abetting the established order, which would be a grievous crime against herself. The system is so awry that only a "miracle of miracles" can sufficiently change relations between the sexes to allow for real marriage. Her only practical option is to leave her home, husband, and three young children and go in search of herself. She packs a valise, goes into the hall, descends a set of stairs, and exits onto the street, slamming the door behind her.

This combined visual and sonic metaphor was the talk of Europe in the winter of 1879–80, and continued to inspire controversy for years afterward. This discomfiting, accusing, and crashingly dramatic exit, which is so metaphorically and theatrically simple, succinctly represents the sexual debate of the era and epitomizes the fears and hopes of women and men about the outcome of the debate. It is a revolutionary and thus a dangerous example: if Nora's selfish logic caught on, excellent husbands everywhere could be left alone to ponder why their wives criticize patriarchy and what they mean by "the miracle of miracles" leading to true marriage.

Countless women were moved by Nora's discoveries and inspired by her resolve to understand what made her as she was and to seek a self-defined truth independent of male masters.[1] Since 1879, A

Doll's House has appeared in hundreds of editions and a babel of languages. It has been regarded as a masterpiece of the modern theatre, a gospel of family reform, and a historic turning point in the expression of late nineteenth-century women's struggles. And it is still cogent: if Nora's speech "I believe that first and foremost, I am an individual, just as much as you are – or at least I'm going to try to be" is familiar today, it is partly because the National Organization of Women (NOW) knitted a paraphrase of it into its manifesto (1966). But NOW's manifesto is neither the first nor the only appropriation from *A Doll's House*. Through an examination of selected productions and adaptations of the play, the evolving feminist and antifeminist agendas can be traced over the course of a century.

The first English stage treatment of the play was an adaptation called *Breaking a Butterfly* (Jones and Herman 1884), which emphasized Nora's rite of passage into mature, responsible, home-centred womanhood. In conformity with audience taste, Henry Arthur Jones and Henry Herman, the adaptors, excised the confrontational discussion scene and whittled the character of Nora down to little more than a *Frou-Frou*. The marriage undergoes a test, but it is Torvald's latent heroism that is revealed, while Nora learns the nasty lesson that she should trust her husband's innate superiority.

Some responses to the play allowed Nora's argument to be put forward while adamantly denying the logic of her reasoning. In a short story, "A Doll's House," August Strindberg (1884) recast Nora's confidante Christine as Ottila, a sexually repressed religious spinster who befriends Gurli, a naval captain's wife. Gurli's happy, passionate marriage is spoiled when Ottila introduces her to the nefarious play by Henrik Ibsen, which turns her attention from her home, husband, and children and toward social work, fallen women, and infectious diseases. Strindberg makes the captain his *raisonneur*, against whom the arguments about female chattels, sensual excesses, play acting, and lack of education fall easy prey. When the captain philanders with Ottila and rekindles Gurli's jealous spirit, his marriage is saved and his supremacy is restored. "Miracles," he declares, "only happen in story books." His home is once again "a real doll's house" which, according to Strindberg, is the most desirable thing it can possibly be (184).

The first faithful, unadapted English treatment of the play was a production mounted in 1889 by the socialists Charles Charrington and Janet Achurch. This production attracted between eleven thousand and fifteen thousand spectators of all classes and ideologies (Davis 1985). Controversy about the production focussed on Nora's family and social roles. Most critics harped on the play's inappropriateness for theatrical depiction, its sham morality and false doctrine, seeing the dénouement either as a stale and passé twist of the plot, or an utterly implausible outcome. In its unadapted form, however, feminists saw a blueprint for female emancipation and rallied outside the aptly named Novelty Theatre to take Ibsen's resolution for debate into their drawing rooms, clubs, reform societies, and theatres. As Elizabeth Robins noted, "to eyes that first saw it in '89, [it was] less like a play than like a personal meeting – with people and issues that seized us and held us, and wouldn't let us go" (Robins 1928, 11). Like Emma Goldman, feminists saw that: "When Nora closes behind her the door of her doll's house, she opens wide the gate of life for woman, and proclaims the revolutionary message that only perfect freedom and communion make a true bond between man and woman, meeting in the open, without lies, without shame, free from the bondage of duty" (Goldman 1914, 25). Between 1889 and the next production in January 1891, *A Doll's House* was so widely and thoroughly discussed that sceptics no longer bothered to disclaim Nora's wayward follies; Ibsen was still called a writer of "morbid studies of hysterical feminine disease," but his arguments about women's economic and social self-sufficiency, home and family life, and the necessity of widespread educational and legal reform were recognized. In keeping with the discourse of the first feminist wave, Nora's subjugation was attributed to legal inequalities, and her opposition to marriage was tied to issues of child custody, control of property, and suffrage.

The perception of Nora as an animated version of a propagandistic feminist tract was partly due to the political concerns of Ibsen's supporters, and partly to Achurch's performance. When Eleanora Duse performed the role in London in 1893, discussion about acting took precedence over polemics for the first time. Whereas Achurch based her interpretation on a series of tricks and points that signposted the way for Nora's transformation from a dependent innocent to a door-slamming crusader, Duse's Nora had, from the outset, an inkling of dissatisfaction; it was the undesirability of her melodramatic options (infidelity, suicide, and sexual compromise) that led her to imagine what might possibly lie beyond her experience. Duse convinced her English audiences that Nora could be perceived in socio-psychological terms; Duse's Nora rejoiced in her emerging consciousness, for it was her personal growth that mattered, and not a political critique. This left the impression that Nora's enlightenment would continue and that she would eventually, through considerable struggle, attain a strong sense of integrity and self-worth. By playing for psychological truth, Duse embodied a woman in crisis:

struggling when Achurch was resolute, and assertive when Achurch was merely argumentative. Although Duse's interpretation posed no immediately apparent threat to the established order, it presaged an all-inclusive feminist critique that more closely resembles the agenda of the 1980s than the 1890s. By closing one door on her husband and children, Duse's Nora opened another in order to address the modern agenda that endures, never-ending, within each feminist and her family. The slam resonated with possibility rather than finality.

It is ironic that Ibsen's famous alternative ending – which was written in 1880 as a compromise to audience taste and to the German actress Hedwig Niemann-Raabe (who refused to appear in an unsympathetic role) – actually has an effect which is somewhat similar to Duse's performance. In this version, before Nora leaves forever, Torvald forces her to look in on the children. She cannot bear the thought that they will grow up motherless, as she herself did, and in a state of physical collapse says: "Oh, this is a sin against myself, but I cannot leave them" (Ibsen 1961, 5:288). With these words, Nora's need to explore her individuality is retained, though her attachment to the nursery is preeminent. The profound and deep-seated fears of male spectators are not ruffled by this ending, but female spectators are still invited to empathize with Nora's dilemma; the onus is passed to them to resist, when their time comes, the physical and emotional manipulation that defeats Nora. Although this resolution excuses Torvald from immediately tackling the "woman question," his responsibilities in child care, sexual double standards, and gender role-conditioning, it is implied that Nora will probably continue to struggle with these issues from inside her home. She is duty-bound, but her consciousness is enlightened.

Modern reworkings of the theme of *A Doll's House* illustrate recent feminist ideas on marriage and women's independence, and also the universality of Nora's dilemma. Clare Booth Luce's *Slam the Door Softly* (1979) transports the Helmers to the year 1970. Ninety years after her inception, Nora is still within "the cosy walls of home," and once again she asserts that she wants to break out of the doll's house to be something other than a wife and a mother. As Luce's play begins, Thaw is watching a televised debate on women's lib and is too preoccupied to notice that his wife is about to leave him. She goes, quietly closing the door behind her. Thaw yells, with the resonance of Stanley Kowalski, "Nora? Nora? *Nor-ra!*" and literally drags her back into the house. Like Strindberg's captain, he cannot comprehend his wife's complaint. Is she seeing another man? Is it her period? Is she getting an abortion? Does she want another baby?

She explains that she is already pregnant, but with ideas: "For me there are no more splendid, new truths to be learned from scanning the contents of babies' diapers." Nora rejects the mystique. Like Gurli, she has been reading feminist propaganda, though her titles are chosen from the literature of the second wave and her Wellesley education enables her to draw up the bibliography herself: Mary Ellman, Kate Millett, Betty Friedan, Simone de Beauvoir, and Cynthia Fuchs Epstein. Unlike Gurli, she is able to label all her husband's arguments, recognize each of his masculine wiles, and make her conditions very clear: she wants $53,000 severance pay, and a job. "I want to do some share, however small, of the world's work and be paid for it ... I don't have the physical or moral strength to swing two jobs. So I've got to choose the one, before it's too late, that's most important for me – oh, not for me just now, but for when *I'm fifty*" (Luce 1970, 193). She needs to regain her self-esteem to make the most of her life – for her own sake and that of her family: "A [man needs] a sleep-in, sleep-with body servant of his very own. Well, that's your problem. Just now, I have to wrestle with my problem ... I'm not bursting with self-confidence, Thaw. I do love you. And I also need ... a man. So I'm not slamming the door. I'm closing it ... very softly." (She leaves) (194). She takes up Alice S. Rossi's suggestion, recentering herself from suburban isolation to an urban existence by catching the commuter train into town (Rossi 1964, 624–5). The "New Genesis" of 1879 is a commonplace household pattern in 1970.

In addition to the final confrontation scene provided by Ibsen, conjecture about Nora's life after the doll's house has also preoccupied every generation that has known the play. Early sequels depict Nora as a career nurse, a famous "emancipated" novelist, a women's rights activist, and a sexless malefactor.[2] In Erika Ritter's "A Renovated Doll's House," a Virginia Slimsmoking Nora, "jauntily jumpsuited with a smart little haircut," is on television, conversing with Phil Donnybrook about her life since 1879. Despite her flippancy, Ritter makes a serious and successful attempt to channel Nora through the likely exhilarations and disappointments of the 1970s and 80s. "I took the only work I could find that seemed commensurate with my skills: I danced in a cheap club until the sexual harassment drove me out. Then I got a job in a chocolate macaroon factory." Through work, she became politically awakened: "I found that the guy packing chocolates next to me was earning 20 kroner a week more. By the next week, I'd become one of a group of women who met regularly over cheap red wine and cheez-twists to discuss subsidized day care, male domination and whatever else came up."

Her consciousness-raising group produces a magazine and pickets beauty pageants. Her career blossoms: she becomes a vicepresident and invents a new sugar-free macaroon. "Oh sure, my love life was the pits, thanks to IF – that's career-lady talk for Intimidation Factor. But I'd forged some real bonds with other women and had my priorities straight." Feminists' inadvertent alignment with the Right over pornography, and the replication of male power structures in groups of prosperous liberated women, cause Nora to reflect on just how far her sex has come. In the meantime, while she forges a women's community, tackles labour inequalities, copes with the repercussions of a severe ideological challenge to the movement, and fights a court battle for wrongful dismissal after it is alleged that her promotions were due to an affair with her boss, her ex-husband has not been idle. "Torvald's been through some changes too, in the past 100 years. After he ran through a succession of young bimbos, there was a brief flirtation with homosexuality ... then there was a long period of complete sexual uninterest. But now I think Torvald's really learning how to relate to women in an open, noncompetitive way ... " (Ritter 1984, 14). Significantly, her explanation is cut off. Ritter implies that men are not regarded as mediaworthy, and that after a hundred years of seeking a successful formula for what Ibsen enigmatically called the "miracle of miracles" (evidently the goal of feminist heterosexuality), there is no equal time or equal interest in discussing men's readiness for reconciliation. After all, the struggle (not the outcome) makes the drama, and Ritter astutely hints that men's responsibility in engineering the "miracle of miracles" and preparedness for a new era have not been given due emphasis. According to this sequel, the media slams the door on Torvald and leaves him so utterly alone that he exerts no presence and attracts no audience. Time after time, spectators have also turned their backs on him and followed Nora out the door and into the street.

Although interest in Nora is perennial, *A Doll's House* is about the family, and the parental responsibilities of both sexes. Ibsen implies that a social reformation requires men as well as women to reexamine their roles, conditioning, and behavioural parameters, but early writing on the doll's house theme soon established that mere gender reversals would be unsatisfactory.[3] With the gains made by the women's movement since the 1960s, recent productions have interpreted the challenge to heterosexual marriage in completely new ways, but ways that are perfectly synchronous with contemporary social trends, and with the play as Ibsen originally wrote it. In a 1981 Royal Shakespeare Company (RSC) production, Nora's exit was followed by several startling minutes during which Torvald – left alone on stage and alone in a household of children and female servants – gradually recognized his own part in the feminist agenda. Torvald's mime is described in the stage directions of the published script, and yet the emphasis given to this moment by playing it through to a logical crisis allowed the RSC production, without interpolated prolongation, to show a Torvald whose grief and emotional awakening are synonymous with postliberation manhood. In a 1987 Stratford Festival production (based on Ingmar Bergman's adaptation of the text), this moment was not as effective; nevertheless, by setting the final scene in the boudoir rather than the parlour, and staging the discussion over the marital bed rather than the dining-room table, it placed procreative and sexual issues in the foreground along with the social (gender) issues expounded in the text. In the Stratford Festival production, Torvald was left alone in the space where he thought his marriage was most perfectly constituted. If the Royal Shakespeare Company interpreted the play in the light of *Kramer vs Kramer*, the Stratford Festival presented it as a practical working-out of the latest Hite Report. Having been educated by the old order, Torvald must undergo reeducation – but not on women's time.

Elenore Lester (1978) observes that Ibsen's women live (if at all) through men, which is hardly politically correct. It is arguable that although Nora learns to see her husband's flaws, she leaves the house with her romantic ideals more or less intact, in which case the patriarchal order is not doomed (as Elaine Hoffman Baruch asserts, [1980]) and woman is not on the verge of establishing a new order in history. Ibsen's professed concern was always with humanity, not feminism. The problem that *A Doll's House* and its reworkings and sequels raise is not one of gender supremacy or gender succession, but of gender balance. To imagine Nora's life after she leaves her home is fascinating, but conjectural. It is Torvald, not Nora, whom Ibsen leaves on stage. It is Torvald whom we *see* coping with the aftermath, and contemplating the agenda.

Neither *A Doll's House* nor its sequels contain a radical call for a feminist world without men. One would hardly expect Ibsen to have launched his *raisonneur*, Nora, into a world that excludes her creator, but it is curious that recent producers have returned to the text and found ways to ensure that both the sexes can be held in focus. This may be because the righteous response Torvald often invoked in the 1880s has finally changed to reveal him as an individual, as much as Nora, or at any rate someone who is trying to become one. While Torvald is left in the home to discover the domestic issues that women confront daily, Nora embarks on a new series of discoveries in the masculine world beyond. For over a hundred years, *A Doll's House* has been used to stimulate controversy on various aspects of the feminist debate. As the issues change, so do treatments of the play.

Time and again, Nora's questioning of male authority and male-created institutions has led to two great questions that require both partners to resolve fully. Reworkings of the final scene consider why or if Nora will leave, or stay in, her doll's house. Sequels consider whether Torvald will remain content in the doll's house or whether dire measures will enable him to see its limitations and also desire change. The terms of the questions are embodied in the dominant metaphors: the crash of the street door, the sudden enlightenment of a feather-brained *Hausfrau*, the emergent consciousness of a deep-feeling family woman, a departure that frequent repetition renders into a cliché, society's single-minded preoccupation with the icono-clasm of only one of the sexes, the emotional implications of a re-versal of domestic responsibilities, and the marital bed as a zone where patriarchy and feminism square off. No one has yet resolved the sexual and gender differences entirely, discovered the "miracle of miracles," made a motion for adoption of a final agenda, or moved for closure of the debate. Clearly, the questions and the discussion that *A Doll's House* can reflect are still evolving.

NOTES

1 For further elaboration, see my doctoral thesis, "Critical and Popular Re-action to Ibsen in England: 1872–1906" (University of Warwick, 1984).

2 For more on the sequels, see my article "Spoofing 'the Master': Parodies and Burlesques of Ibsen on the English Stage and in the Popular Press" (*Nineteenth Century Theatre Research* 13, no. 2 [Winter 1985]: 87–102).

3 A good example of a comic parody on this theme is "After the Novelty. A Drama of To-Night" (*St. James Gazette*, 13 June 1889, 6).

Power and Political Strategies
Le pouvoir et les stratégies politiques

MICHELINE DE SÈVE

Les femmes et le pouvoir: faire face à la musique

L'accès à des positions de pouvoir rebute nombre de femmes malgré la volonté qui est la leur de lutter contre la hiérarchie et les inéquités sociales. Refuser le caractère oppressif de la domination est certes légitime. Cependant il convient de reconnaître d'autres mobiles à ce rejet du pouvoir-mobiles liés à la crainte de conflits vécus comme une rupture des communications et un déni d'amour. L'emprise des liens affectifs peut faire qu'on s'abandonne au désir de l'autre, reproduisant ainsi la domination des hommes sur les femmes. La relation mère-fils est donnée en exemple pour inviter les féministes à s'interroger davantage sur l'ambiguïté de leur rapport au pouvoir.

Women and Power: Facing the Music

Many women are reluctant to assume positions of power in spite of their wish to struggle against hierarchy and social inequities. To oppose the oppressive nature of domination is certainly legitimate. However, it is useful to recognize other motives women may have for rejecting power, motives which are linked to a fear of conflict which is experienced as the breakdown of communication and the denial of love. The strength of emotional ties can impose a type of overwhelming desire for human warmth, which is particularly likely to reproduce the domination of women by men. The mother-son relationship is given as an example of this in order to invite feminists to pose additional questions about their ambiguity toward power relationships.

Ce titre m'a été soufflé par la remarque d'une syndicaliste juste avant son élection à la cinquième vice-présidence de la Centrale de l'enseignement du Québec, en juin 1986. Secrétaire de son métier, étu-

diante inscrite au certificat en droit social et du travail à l'Université
du Québec à Montréal, présidente de la Fédération des employé-es
de soutien, Solange Pronovost allait se retrouver à la même table de
direction que de savants-tes professeurs-es et des politiciens ou poli-
ticiennes chevronnés-es comme Yvon Charbonneau ou Rosette Côté.
Cette perspective la terrifiait mais, forte de la confiance de sa fédération, sûre de ses motivations et consciente du travail à accomplir,
elle s'était dit à elle-même au beau milieu d'une crise de larmes:
« Sainte Misère! ma fille, c'est le temps de faire face à la musique. »
Intervenant lors d'un débat-midi organisé par le Comité des femmes
de la CEQ deux jours avant d'être élue par acclamation, Solange
ajoutait qu'elle « rêvait de voir un jour où elle [serait] partout aussi
à l'aise de s'exprimer qu'elle l'était au réseau des femmes » et qu'il
fallait « trouver ensemble » les solutions pour lever l'obstacle de la
hiérarchie sociale, partout présente dans les instances de pouvoir
des syndicats comme de tout autre appareil politique.

Le pouvoir, qu'il s'agisse d'obtenir un temps de parole ou d'accéder
à un poste clé, comporte un élément de visibilité. Nous en reven-
diquons l'accès comme féministes mais comme femmes, il continue
de nous embarrasser. Et d'abord, comment le caractériser? J'en re-
tiendrai la définition suivante: le pouvoir, c'est la capacité d'agir ou
de ne pas agir sans crainte des conséquences, quelle que soit la
solution retenue. Historiquement, les femmes ont été privées de la
deuxième possibilité, d'abord parce que leur pouvoir spécifique d'en-
fanter était régi par la nature ou par la volonté des hommes plutôt
qu'objet de leur libre arbitre; ensuite, parce qu'elles étaient exclues
des champs de bataille, lieux où se réglaient plus souvent qu'autrement les affaires de la cité.

La séparation du privé et du public, qui nous maintient à l'écart
sous prétexte de nous protéger, entraîne une perception du pouvoir
radicalement distincte selon qu'il est envisagé du point de vue des
activités liées à la reproduction de la vie humaine ou du point de
vue des activités liées à la production et à la répartition des ressources
dans la communauté. En effet, pour les femmes qui oeuvrent dans
la sphère de la reproduction, le pouvoir n'est pas lié à la capacité
d'imposer une orientation de préférence à une autre mais à la relation d'aide qui marque leur participation à l'entretien et au développement de personnes dépendantes. Dans l'univers des rapports
privés où les femmes évoluent depuis des siècles, le refus d'agir dit
moins le pouvoir sur l'autre que l'incapacité de faire plus. Dire non
à l'enfant à naître (pour prendre l'exemple de l'avortement) est toujours douloureux. Refuser son aide à l'être aimé parce qu'on est
recluse de fatigue ou que l'on ne peut tout simplement satisfaire une

demande déraisonnable n'est pas un acte de pouvoir exaltant. Le refus d'agir peut aussi manifester une intention pédagogique. Témoin, la mère qui surveille les premiers pas de son enfant en se gardant d'intervenir. Sa joie se mêle d'inquiétude; mais c'est l'enfant qui développe son autonomie, son pouvoir d'action personnel grâce à sa capacité à elle de consentir à ce que son fils ou sa fille échappe progressivement à son contrôle. Cela s'appelle couper le cordon ombilical.

Dans ce domaine, le non n'est pas porteur de domination comme tel. Il peut cependant marquer un point limite, se traduire par une rupture des communications, le déni d'amour entre des êtres jusque là très proches. C'est bien pourquoi, même si la fatigue nous empêche parfois de poursuivre plus avant la relation d'aide, nous aurons tendance à abuser de nos forces de peur de voir notre refus interprété comme un manque d'amour. Qui de nous n'a pas eu le coeur fendu par la colère de l'enfant qui nous crie: « Si c'est comme ça, t'es pas fine, je ne t'aime plus » À d'autres moments, un retrait prématuré d'appui de notre part se renversera en culpabilité face à l'échec de l'enfant mal préparé à assumer sa liberté. Pas étonnant dans ces conditions que la définition du pouvoir comme capacité de refuser son concours à une action quelconque soit pour nous lourde de connotations négatives. Attentives à préserver l'harmonie dans nos rapports avec nos intimes, nous avons aiguisé notre sensibilité dans le but d'éviter le plus possible le genre de rupture des liens affectifs qu'entraîne un non brutal. En psychanalyse, Jacques Lacan définissait précisément la femme comme « un oui béant. » La formule peut choquer mais là même où nous disons non à l'intérieur d'un rapport pédagogique, n'est-ce pas le oui au développement de la personnalité, de la vie de nos proches, qui dit la spécificité de notre rapport au pouvoir?

Mais il est important de noter les retombées négatives de notre trop grande tolérance à certaines occasions. Par exemple, dans la mesure où nous n'exigeons pas de réciprocité de nos enfants dans leurs échanges avec nous, nous les habituons à penser leurs propres désirs sans considération de nos propres besoins, à moins d'y être absolument forcés-es. Cela est encore plus vrai dans le cas de mères non féministes qui traitent leurs fils en véritables roitelets. Le traitement différencié des enfants selon leur sexe accentue ici le problème posé par l'acceptation passive de la vocation de service inconditionnelle des mères traditionnelles. Alors que nous demandons aux petites filles, appelées à nous succéder, de partager avec nous, ne serait-ce que symboliquement, la responsabilité des tâches domestiques, nous reproduisons l'indifférence et le pouvoir des petits mâles qui commandent nos soins ou ceux de leurs soeurs sans avoir à donner quoi que ce soit d'autre en échange qu'un merci occasionnel.

Sommes-nous assez conscientes de notre rôle clé de reproductrices non seulement de la vie mais de l'attitude des enfants face à une quelconque obligation de solidarité avec leur entourage? Car, loin d'exercer du pouvoir sur les autres, ce que nous faisons comme éducatrices, c'est d'habiliter ceux ou celles que nous socialisons à développer leur propre identité, leur propre pouvoir personnel. En pareil cas, notre effacement risque de se traduire par l'apprentissage, par les garçons en particulier, de l'indifférence à nos propres besoins d'affirmation personnelle. Nous exerçons là une fonction éminemment politique puisqu'à travers nous, nos enfants apprennent à se poser comme des êtres autonomes et indépendants-tes, au besoin en nous tyrannisant. Nous aurions intérêt à considérer que ce faisant, notre « politique reproductive » (O'Brien 1981, 87) établit un modèle général de comportement dont nous sommes les premières à subir les conséquences.

Il sera donc plus qu'intéressant d'étudier en quoi l'adoption de valeurs féministes par les mères transformera le mode d'apprentissage des attributs machistes du rôle masculin. Jusqu'ici, le rapport mère-fils s'est fondé sur une relation foncièrement tyrannique entre une servante et son petit roi adoré. Il faudra voir comment l'exigence de respect mutuel et l'imposition, aux fils comme aux filles, du partage des tâches domestiques introduira une nouvelle dimension dans la construction de la masculinité. C'en sera fini de l'insouciance des petits mâles, qui ne pourront plus compter sur l'accessibilité en permanence des soins maternels – accessibilité telle qu'ils oublient qu'elle puisse ne pas aller de soi. Jusqu'à présent, le garçon n'avait pas à refuser sa quote part des tâches domestiques; au contraire, il s'attendait très vite à en bénéficier comme son dû. Il apprenait ainsi très jeune – et malheureusement beaucoup l'apprennent toujours – à se servir des autres et a fortiori des femmes, sans avoir à penser donner quelque chose en retour. Ce n'est que confronté à « l'égoïsme » comparable de ses aînés que le jeune tyran découvrait la nécessité de négocier avec d'autres un accord de réciprocité lorsque les ressources étaient rares. Cependant que les filles apprenaient à ne penser de leurs besoins qu'en fonction de leur insertion dans un tissu d'échanges de services avec leurs semblables, les garçons imposaient leur volonté sans rencontres d'autres limites que la capacité de résistance à l'énervement et à la fatigue des femmes de service.

C'est bien ici que s'est forgé l'aveuglement des hommes à une existence des femmes comme animaux politiques, au même titre qu'eux. Ils n'avaient pas à faire face aux exigences des femmes puisque celles-ci n'étaient pas avec eux dans un rapport de réciprocité mais dans un rapport de service. L'homme pouvait remercier la femme, mais il ne se sentait pas redevable d'agir envers elle comme elle le faisait envers lui. La femme travaillait pour l'homme qui lui, partait ensuite ailleurs, dans un autre espace, pour travailler pour ou avec d'autres hommes.

Le terrain de l'action s'est ainsi fractionné selon les sexes. D'un côté, les femmes, éduquées à anticiper les désirs et les besoins de leur entourage; de l'autre, les hommes, habitués à considérer comme allant de soi que les femmes mettent leurs énergies à les servir. D'où leur choc quand l'arrivée d'autres hommes, capables de leur disputer avec succès l'attention de leur mère ou de leurs soeurs, leur fait découvrir les limites de leur souveraineté.

Les femmes en sont venues à considérer le pouvoir de l'extérieur, à craindre ses remous-spectatrices ou objet des luttes des hommes pour s'approprier les ressources disponibles, à commencer par elles. Les hommes ont, eux, appris à rechercher le pouvoir, garant de l'accès aux biens terrestres y compris les services et la considération des femmes. Ils ont appris aussi que le pouvoir signifiait, pour eux, de commander tranquillement aux femmes tout en se reposant sur elles de leurs activités guerrières, tandis que pour elles le pouvoir demeurait celui des autres, non le leur propre. Nous sommes maintenant en mesure de transformer cette situation. A condition bien sûr de changer d'approche et dans le domaine du privé et dans le domaine du public.

J'ai d'abord cru comme la plupart des théoriciennes féministes (cf. Hartsock 1983, 210), que notre réticence devant le pouvoir tenait tout entière à notre rejet de la domination comme telle: que nous n'avions d'autre choix que de déserter les institutions en place et de construire notre propre réseau de structures alternatives en faisant table rase de tout ce qui nous a précédées. C'est entre autres, la proposition avancée par l'anarchoféminisme de Carol Ehrlich. Elle souhaite « creuser la vieille société de l'intérieur comme un vieil arbre pourri, jusqu'à ce qu'elle devienne faible et prête à tomber » (1965, 78). Comme choix stratégique, j'en suis; c'est certes une étape nécessaire pour construire nos propres bases, accumuler de l'énergie, affirmer notre identité, mais cela ne nous offrira jamais qu'un espace de manoeuvre restreint sinon carrément marginal. Carol Ehrlich elle-même reconnaît que le succès du projet de radio communautaire auquel elle participait reposait sur un filtrage soigneux des personnes admises à faire partie de l'équipe. Mais la société, dans son ensemble, ne nous offre pas de telles possibilités d'exclure quiconque ne partage pas nos convictions ou nos objectifs. Se confronter au pouvoir, n'est-ce pas d'abord et avant tout apprendre à dire ses besoins, et si nécessaire, à imposer nos priorités à l'attention des autres avec qui nous avons à négocier notre part des ressources disponibles? Derrière nos réticences à assumer certaines responsabilités, n'y a-t-il pas plus que le refus légitime de dominer nos semblables? N'y a-t-il pas, entre autres, une certaine complaisance à accepter notre position traditionnelle d'observatrices sinon de victimes? Quelque part en nous, ne subsisterait-il pas une crainte inavouée d'assumer la responsabilité des tâches que nous exécutons sans avoir à en décider?

Notre critique du pouvoir n'est pas en cause. C'est bien parce qu'il importe de renverser le mode de domination patriarcal que nous ne pouvons nous contenter de rester en marge et d'attendre que l'État et ses appareils pourrissent sur pied. Parce que nous vivons aujourd'hui, maintenant, des situations d'injustice liées à notre marginalisation des circuits de décision à tous les niveaux de la société, c'est aujourd'hui, maintenant, qu'il importe d'intervenir pour casser une bonne fois un rapport de forces construit sur notre exclusion systématique. Comme le rappelait Françoise Collin:

les femmes, reconnues comme *animal laborans*, ... restent encore exclues de l'*activité* constitutive de la *polis* (même si quelques-unes d'entre elles se célèbrent dans la vie des partis). Elles n'ont pu accéder à ce type d'existence qu'en constituant leur propre *polis*, leur vie politique, entre elles: position importante mais qui reste, me semble-t-il, insuffisante, sauf à s'installer dans un séparatisme définitif, et d'ailleurs illusoire ou à escompter un miraculeux effet de contamination spontanée. (1985, 82)

Toute la question est là. Indépendamment du type de pouvoir proposé, ce qui fait problème, c'est notre peur de transgresser les limites historiques qui ont été posées à notre action, de déborder du privé dans le public. Dans un texte remarquable intitulé « Plus femmes qu'hommes, » un collectif de féministes italiennes expliquaient se sentir « étrangères » sur la scène des affaires publiques: « L'échec dont nous faisons l'expérience en essayant d'avoir une existence sociale révèle, en même temps qu'une tenace envie de vaincre, une résistance ou une extranéité: quelque chose en nous résiste à entrer dans les jeux sociaux, ne veut pas jouer, ne joue pas » (*Change international* 1983, 75). Ce « quelque chose en nous » qui résiste me semble lié à notre mode historique de rapport au pouvoir. Carrément extérieures, nous n'avons été admises à siéger dans les assemblées des hommes qu'à la condition expresse de singer leurs pires comportements (telle la dame de fer en Grande-Bretagne ou les grandes reines de l'histoire). Dans ces conditions, nous avons raison de rejeter l'intervention sur un terrain qui n'est pas le nôtre et qui ignore totalement ce que nous sommes.

Par contre, la société ouverte dont nous rêvons (De Sève 1985; Miles 1981), demeurera une utopie si nous ne prenons pas les moyens pour gagner l'espace qui nous manque et affirmer nos propres valeurs. Les féministes ne peuvent se passer de l'action politique parce que leur émancipation des liens du quotidien dépend de l'existence de services collectifs adéquats. Parce que nous continuons de nous choisir solidaires des personnes qui dépendent de nous, enfants, personnes âgées, malades ou provisoirement hors circuit, notre liberté ne saurait trouver à se réaliser s'il n'existe pas de services de qualité capables de nous relayer régulièrement. Nous ne pouvons nous réfugier dans le privé à moins de consentir à vivre dans un isolement fatalement réducteur. Élargir notre rayon d'action suppose donc forcément que nous soyons en mesure d'imposer nos priorités à l'attention générale de la communauté, trouvant par là l'appui qui nous fait trop souvent défaut. Or cet objectif, s'il doit devenir autre chose qu'un voeu pieux, suppose notre présence dans l'arène publique pour dire et revendiquer les moyens de notre liberté personnelle.

Par conséquent, nous nous devons d'intervenir assez nombreuses pour en finir avec notre situation de majorité invisible parce que non seulement silencieuse mais éternellement absente. Nous ne serons pas du jour au lendemain en mesure de renverser un pattern politique séculaire mais déjà notre ombre se profile sur la scène publique et nos valeurs commencent à percer dans plusieurs domaines, au niveau de la politique municipale par exemple ou à l'intérieur d'une multitude d'organisations populaires et communautaires dont les comités pour la paix ou la sauvegarde de l'environnement et les comités de condition féminine des centrales syndicales et des partis politiques.

Il serait présomptueux de penser forcer en masse l'entrée des lieux de pouvoir du jour au lendemain. Tout un ensemble de décisions continueront de se prendre avec ou sans notre accord. À nous d'évaluer chaque fois notre poids relatif et nos chances de succès face aux potentialités d'action offertes dans des contextes infiniment variables. L'important sur ce plan, c'est d'intervenir sur la base de nos valeurs propres en tant que féministes et en nous appuyant sur des solidarités réelles forgées dans la chaleur des échanges d'information et de ressources avec des personnes ou des groupes désireux, comme nous, de promouvoir un projet de société enfin ouvert à l'expression de toutes et chacune des personnes composant la communauté humaine. « Le pouvoir n'est jamais une propriété individuelle; il appartient à un groupe et continue à lui appartenir aussi longtemps que ce groupe n'est pas divisé » (Arendt 1972, 153).

Ce pouvoir lié à l'expression d'une volonté collective, nous l'avons souvent rejeté parce que nous l'identifiions à la forme dominatrice qu'il a adoptée dans les sociétés androcentriques. Nous avons parfois tenté d'échapper à la difficile recherche de formes de médiation entre des groupes rassemblés autour d'objectifs distincts et divisés par leurs différences. N'a-t-il pas fallu que la planète elle-même soit menacée pour que nombre de nous se mobilisent enfin et fassent valoir la nécessité d'inventer des modalités de rapport non-violentes pour résoudre les conflits entre grandes puissances? Reste que dans l'ensemble, nous n'intervenons encore qu'en cas d'extrême urgence; ce n'est qu'à notre corps défendant que nous acceptons d'affronter des situations de crise, quel qu'en soit le cadre, et même si la qualité de notre existence quotidienne en dépend. Et pourtant, que de raisons de protester, que de choses à changer!

Je sais bien que la surcharge de travail liée à nos responsabilités domestiques explique largement notre manque de disponibilité politique. Diverses enquêtes sur le militantisme dans les centrales syndicales au Québec, par exemple, ont confirmé la quasi-impossibilité de concilier vie familiale et participation active à la vie syndicale (Tremblay 1985). Mais même là où des femmes célibataires ou assez riches pour s'offrir des services d'aide familiale pourraient se lancer en politique, elles sont très peu nombreuses. Pour une Claire Bonenfant, mère de cinq enfants et qui fut présidente du Conseil du statut de la femme au Québec entre autres responsabilités politiques actives, combien de féministes exclusivement préoccupées de leur vie intérieure ou de leur entourage immédiat? Personnellement, si je me réfère à ma propre expérience et à ce que je connais des femmes de mon milieu, je pense que nous avons du mal à assumer la visibilité associée à notre accès à des positions de pouvoir, que l'exercice en soit répressif ou pas.

Encore une fois, je ne nie pas la nécessité de transformer les structures de domination qui régissent présentement les rapports politiques, de contester la hiérarchisation qui fige les différences de rôles en inégalités sociales permanentes – de briser la mécanique patriarcale du pouvoir. Il m'apparaît simplement qu'à côté des mobiles légitimes de notre refus de joindre les rangs des oppresseurs, nous devons prendre garde à l'existence d'autres mobiles de notre abstention politique, dictés par tout autre chose que notre refus de dominer nos semblables.

Dans notre vie privée, notre pouvoir ne relève pas de l'imposition de notre volonté mais plutôt de ce que Hannah Arendt nomme « puissance, » à la reconnaissance de nos qualités personnelles, aux liens d'amour forgés entre nous et nos proches. Dans ce contexte, ce qui prime, c'est l'affection, l'empathie créée par une communication patiemment entretenue, une attention à l'autre de tous les instants. Or rien n'est plus nocif dans ce contexte que ces affrontements qui dressent soudain les uns contre les autres les membres d'une même unité de vie. Pas étonnant que soucieuses d'harmonie familiale et de paix intime, nous en soyons venues à craindre presque instinctivement tout conflit susceptible de dégénérer en antagonisme. Notre spécialité c'est l'amour, pas le pouvoir et nous craignons parfois tellement de provoquer le rejet de notre entourage que nous préférons supporter les conséquences de notre faiblesse plutôt que de soulever des oppositions que nous ressentons comme autant de ruptures affectives entre nous et les autres.

Quand nous disons favoriser le pouvoir de et non le pouvoir sur, nous avons raison de désigner par là notre refus d'opprimer nos semblables. Néanmoins, le pouvoir « de » passe aussi par ces lieux où nous refusons trop souvent d'intervenir. Pour y accéder, il nous faut faire face au pouvoir en place – le pouvoir « sur » – dans le but de promouvoir le projet de société alternatif qui nous tient à coeur. Rien ne changera si nous refusons d'assumer, dans le domaine public comme auprès de nos proches, ce rôle de médiatrices qui caractérise notre approche du pouvoir dans l'espace privé de nos vies intimes. Nous devons prendre garde d'entériner une fois de plus la séparation privé-public alors même que nos talents d'ouverture à l'autre, de conciliatrices, d'expertes de la communication entre les personnes et du développement des relations humaines sont plus que jamais nécessaires pour substituer le dialogue et la négociation à la violence et aux rapports de force comme mode d'échange privilégié dans le domaine des affaires publiques. Notre refus légitime d'établir notre rapport au pouvoir sur le mode de la domination ne saurait servir d'échappatoire à la lutte nécessaire pour promouvoir notre vision d'une société libertaire, instrument de notre autonomie. Et d'abord, parlant de nous, femmes de savoir, savons-nous seulement assumer notre statut de femmes de pouvoir? Le savoir, dit-on, est un pouvoir (Morgan 1984, 268). Serait-ce le cas s'il se bornait à n'être qu'un refuge, celui de la tour d'ivoire de nos cabinets d'études ou de recherche?

Il est parfois tentant de nous entourer d'un cocon protecteur, en évoluant à l'intérieur d'un cercle connu où l'on nous comprenne à demi-mot, de façon à éviter la dureté des confrontations indissociables du choix de diffuser ou d'élargir notre rayon d'action. Et pourtant, les diverses pratiques de luttes du mouvement des femmes sont là pour nous interpeller: nos étudiantes et nos collègues en usent de même à notre égard. Là comme ailleurs, là plus qu'ailleurs, nous pouvons fourbir nos outils pour trouver leur utilité comme instruments de maîtrise du réel. Mais cela implique des choix, l'exercice du pouvoir dans ce qu'il a pour nous de plus repoussant: la nécessité de trancher non seulement entre des idées mais entre des personnes.

Nous aurons beau prétendre transformer le pouvoir sur en pouvoir de, à moins de rêver une société d'abondance impossible, les situations pénibles par certains côtés sont inévitables. Il va de soi que conscientes des limites de nos interventions, nous ayons à coeur de multiplier les ressources de façon à minimiser les déchirements entraînés par des décisions d'autant plus angoissantes à prendre que nos moyens sont plus limités et les « victimes » de nos choix plus démunies. Ne serait-ce que pour cela, nous aurions intérêt à ne pas bouder les conseils d'administration, les jurys et les comités consultatifs où se décident les modalités de répartition et d'affectation de ressources à juste titre convoitées. Femmes de savoir, sachons étudier nos motivations et nous critiquer nous-mêmes jusque, et y compris dans ce que nous croyons le plus juste: la recherche d'un consensus qui n'est peut-être, par moments, que le nouveau visage d'une peur toute féminine de prendre parti, de franchir les frontières du cercle protégé de notre univers intime. Sachant qui nous sommes, ce que nous sommes et ce que nous voulons, apprenons à faire face au monde politique qui est à notre portée, dans nos propres institutions d'enseignement ou dans nos divers groupes de référence.

L'expérience acquise dans la sphère des rapports privés entre intimes peut nous amener à développer notre aptitude à nous solidariser dans un espace plus large. Mais ne nous laissons pas brouiller la vue par le mythe de l'harmonie universelle. Entre adultes, dans le contexte d'institutions politiques démocratiques, les débats sont prévisibles et les choix très souvent douloureux mais nécessaires. Le pouvoir n'est pas aimable mais il est essentiel. Décidées à exiger pour nous comme pour toute personne des conditions d'existence optimales, compte tenu de l'ensemble des ressources et des tâches à partager, il nous reste à sortir définitivement de l'ombre pour négocier sans crainte avec nos concitoyens-nes les moyens de rencontrer nos objectifs politiques respectifs.

MARIE-ANDRÉE BERTRAND

La Femme et la loi: réflexions à partir d'une étude féministe du droit pénal

On a souvent cru que les différents systèmes normatifs, comme les lois criminelles par exemple, visaient « le bien commun. » Tel est loin d'être le cas, comme le montre une étude récente entreprise par quatre Canadiennes sous l'égide de Condition féminine Canada, et visant à produire une analyse féministe du droit criminel. Non seulement le droit substantif, la lettre de la loi, exclut souvent les aspirations des femmes et leurs revendications les plus légitimes, mais l'application même de ces lois, sujette aux jugements d'hommes, est souvent discriminatoire pour les femmes et les jeunes filles. L'auteure résume les principales conclusions du rapport et conclut en faisant la critique de l'expérience d'une recherche « plurielle » dans sa réalisation mais malheureusement trop peu « collective » dans sa conception.

Reflections on A Feminist Review of the Criminal Code

One would like to believe that our different normative systems, such as criminal law, aim at promoting the "common good." That is far from being the case as shown by a recent study done by four Canadian women under the auspices of Status of Women Canada. In *A Feminist Review of the Criminal Code*, the authors demonstrate that not only does substantive law often exclude the most fundamental aspirations of women but that the application of the law is also discriminatory, being in fact in the hands of men in the great majority of cases. The author sums up the conclusions of the study and goes on to critically examine the experience of a "pluralistic" research project, conducted by four persons, but not really collectively.

Pour aborder un sujet qui m'apparaît extrêmement important, les femmes et la loi, je voudrais m'inspirer d'un texte de Platon. Il s'agit de l'un de ses tous derniers dialogues, écrit vraisemblablement durant les trois ou quatre dernières années de sa vie. L'Athénien est en conversation avec Cleinias et lui expose dans quel sens les hommes au pouvoir sont amenés à légiférer.

L'Athénien est en conversation avec Cleinias et lui expose dans quel sens les hommes au pouvoir sont amenés à légiférer.

L'Athénien: Ainsi, disent-ils, vous vous imaginez bien que quand une démocratie a réussi à prendre le pouvoir ou quelqu'autre forme constitutionnelle, y compris une dictature, ce type de gouvernement ne va jamais légiférer, sauf sous une pression considérable, sinon dans le sens qui va favoriser ses intérêts et lui permettre de demeurer toujours au pouvoir. Cela sera sa grande préoccupation, n'est-ce pas? ... Et voici ce qui est en cause: les gens qui ont le contrôle à quelque moment que ce soit prétendent qu'il leur revient entièrement de faire la loi dans un pays, ... alors, bien sûr, notre position c'est que ce genre d'arrangement est loin de constituer un véritable système politique; nous soutenons que les lois qui ne sont pas faites pour le bien de tout le groupe social sont des semblants de lois. Et quand elles privilégient une faction particulière de la communauté, leurs auteurs montrent bien qu'ils ne sont pas des vrais citoyens, mais des hommes de parti, et les gens qui prétendent que ces lois appellent l'obéissance perdent leur temps. Nous disons cela parce que dans notre nouvel État, nous n'allons pas nommer au poste de législateur quelqu'un à cause de sa richesse ou à cause d'autres attributs de ce genre soit, par exemple, la force ou la taille ou la naissance. Nous allons exiger que celui qui sera nommé au poste le plus haut soit celui qui se montre le plus capable d'obéir à la loi.[1]

Ce passage de *Les Lois* de Platon nous perment de mieux comprendre quelques-uns des aphorismes de Nietzsche dans *La généalogie de la morale* (1887) par exemple, quand cet auteur rappelle que « les bons » sont ceux qui se sont eux-mêmes déclarés bons et que la bonté n'est pas un attribut de la personne, mais une qualité que se décerne celui qui est au pouvoir, et de même la justice.

Le pouvoir de faire des lois, c'est celui de faire la norme, les règles. C'est un pouvoir considérable. Le législateur, en effet, décide non seulement de ce qui est permis et défendu, départageant ainsi les conformes et les marginaux, mais statue sur les principes au nom desquels on fait cette répartition, sur les valeurs à privilégier dans la codification des lois civiles, pénales, administratives, etc.

Historiquement, les femmes n'ont jamais été présentes à cette fonction. S'il est vrai qu'au cours du siècle dernier, des groupes de femmes ont été à l'origine d'amendements importants aux lois civiles et pénales, il faut bien avouer que leur influence sur l'esprit des lois est marginale ou inexistante; leur capacité d'en modifier l'application peu importante. Aussi sommes-nous amenée, dans le cadre particulier de cet essai sur les femmes et la loi, à parler de l'un des aspects les plus frappants et les plus lourds de conséquence de notre absence et de notre impuissance. Mais comment les femmes pourraient-elles transformer leur rapport au pouvoir normatif? Comment peuvent-elles s'inscrire, imprimer leur ordre de valeurs dans la définition de l'ordre?

L'oeuvre récente d'un groupe de femmes qui se sont penchées sur le droit criminel canadien m'apparaît comme un pas dans cette direction, un pas parmi d'autres, et venant après les efforts de nombreux groupes féministes, d'ailleurs, qui ont contribué à modifier les lois sur le mariage et la société familiale. Comme il s'agit, dans le cas du droit criminel, d'un exemple récent et d'une analyse qui porte sur toutes les lois, il m'est apparu utile d'en faire l'étude critique pour ensuite poser les jalons de recherches-actions susceptibles de modifier nos rapports à l'univers des normes ...

UN EXAMEN FÉMINISTE DU DROIT CRIMINEL AU CANADA

En 1984, Condition féminine Canada proposait à quatre femmes de travailler ensemble à une analyse de la loi criminelle au Canada, sous tous ses aspects. Les personnes recrutées étaient trois juristes et une criminologue. Je décrirai, dans un premier temps, les aspects de cette entreprise qui me semblent avoir concouru à ce que le travail soit achevé dans des délais raisonnables, à ce qu'il soit d'orientation résolument féministe et renferme des propositions originales. Ensuite, je m'attarderai à quelques critiques sur la commande et la méthode de travail. Cela m'amènera à poser des jalons pour des recherches ultérieures.

Concernant les aspects positifs, notons deux choses. Premièrement, le « patron », le commanditaire de cette étude, était particulièrement approprié: non seulement l'organisme lui-même, Condition féminine Canada, mais la personne responsable de ce travail à Condition féminine Canada. L'animation de notre petit groupe d'auteurs se faisait sous un angle propice à une véritable étude de la condition des femmes à travers une critique du droit pénal, et à la formulation de réformes radicales lorsque l'analyse des lois existantes le justifiait.

Deuxièmement, les personnes recrutées participaient de la même volonté de démystifier le caractère prétendument neutre des lois elles-mêmes, de la procédure et de l'application des lois.

Du côté des aspects moins positifs, parlons de la méthode de travail. Le commanditaire avait approché les auteures sur la foi de leurs publications et leur avait proposé individuellement de travailler à un ou plusieurs chapitres d'un ensemble dont la structure était en définitive déterminée par la baîlleur de fonds. Les chercheures devaient soumettre un plan à Condition féminine Canada, ce plan pouvant être révisé par le commanditaire et devant être agréé par celui-ci. Puis, on réunissait les coauteures qui, au cours de deux journées de discussion, avaient à coordonner leurs projets, identifier les recoupements possibles et les lacunes. Suite à cette réunion, les auteures partaient rédiger en solitaires leurs chapitres respectifs. Elles ne pouvaient, au terme de leurs travaux, se revoir pour en discuter l'articulation et la cohérence théorique. L'oeuvre produite dans ces conditions risquait fort de s'apparenter à un collage, et c'est finalement l'apparence qu'elle présente en plusieurs de ses parties, à mon avis.

Conséquence, donc, des échéances trop courtes et de l'origine hiérarchique de la commande: l'absence de perspective commune, tant scientifique qu'idéologique. Certes, il n'est pas facile de faire concourir à un travail de réforme législative des chercheures de disciplines différentes, à moins de s'assurer au départ qu'elles partagent au moins une définition commune des principales voies d'analyse, ou qu'à défaut d'en adopter une, elles acceptent de se situer les unes par rapport aux autres. À mon avis, une oeuvre écrite en collaboration ne doit pas *nécessairement* refléter une grande *unité* idéologique (encore que dans le cas présent il était normal d'exiger au moins que les auteures soient féministes ...), encore faut-il que les référents, c'est-à-dire les cadres théoriques et idéologiques de chacun-e soient connus des autres.

Venons-en maintenant à ce que cette expérience m'inspire du point de vue de la recherche future touchant la femme et la loi. Parmi les points chauds que notre rapport a touchés, il s'en trouve quatre principaux:

1   Les quatre auteures constatent et dénoncent le caractère illégitime de législations formulées sans que les valeurs et les aspirations de plus de 50 pour cent du groupe social, c'est-à-dire des femmes, aient pu s'exprimer, si bien que plus de la moitié de la population ne trouve pas son compte dans les lois en question ou dans la façon dont elles sont appliquées;

2   Les auteures montrent le caractère immoral des lois sexistes ou de l'application discriminatoire des lois pénales (suite à l'inégalité des ressources, par exemple) ainsi que le caractère illégitime et immoral des procédures qui défavorisent et handicapent un groupe sexuel face aux instances judiciaires;

3   En même temps, le groupe de chercheures reconnaissait bien volontiers que pour traiter les femmes de façon juste, il n'est pas toujours recommandable de les traiter de façon identique aux hommes. Un traitement identique pouvait même constituer une injustice. C'est le cas, par exemple, lorsqu'on ne prend pas en considération le statut de mère d'un-e jeune enfant, dans le cas d'une peine d'emprisonnement: la peine imposée est alors plus grave, beaucoup plus sévère qu'elle ne le serait, par exemple, à l'endroit d'une femme ou d'un homme sans enfant, ou d'un père qui n'a pas d'attachement particulier pour son enfant. Par exemple aussi (ce qui nous fait plus entrer dans le coeur du sujet), la situation de pauvreté dans laquelle se trouvent au Canada bien plus de femmes que d'hommes peut être admise comme excuse, pour ce groupe défavorisé, au fait de commettre des infractions sans violence contre la propriété privée;

4   D'autre part, l'absence remarquée de femmes parmi les juges, les agents de police, voire les procureurs, constitue une source structurelle de méconnaissance de leurs besoins particuliers, non seulement devant le système de justice pénale, mais aussi devant la justice civile, par exemple: les cours, les tribunaux de la famille et du divorce.

Les auteures sont donc amenées à des conclusions apparemment contradictoires mais sans doute aussi complémentaires, selon qu'elles s'inspirent d'une perspective historico-critique qui dénonce l'illégitimité du système pénal; ou d'une perspective socialiste, qui analyse correctement la situation de pauvreté économique des femmes et réclame que cette condition soit invoquée comme excuse dans les cas de délits contre la propriété non accompagnés de violence; ou d'un modèle égalitaire au nom duquel elles réclament une présence plus grande des femmes dans l'appareil pénal, afin de favoriser une application équitable des lois.

À mon avis, il est tout à fait justifié d'utiliser l'un ou l'autre modèle féministe et critique selon qu'on traite, par exemple, des fondements du droit pénal ou de son application. Il est tout à fait correct de réclamer à la fois des lois équitables et justes, non discriminatoires, non paternalistes, non infériorisantes, et de reconnaître en même temps que la condition économique réelle des femmes *exige* une application *différentielle* des sanctions, ou que l'état même des services pénaux commande une application différente. Il est tout aussi correct, dans un même temps de s'activer pour que les femmes soient présentes à tous les échelons du système pénal, de dénoncer les lois qui reflètent une vision exclusivement masculine de l'ordre socioéconomique et de faire en sorte que les femmes parvenues dans les appareils de pouvoir accélèrent les changements législatifs.

Pourtant la recherche féministe, lorsqu'elle doit déboucher sur des stratégies de changement, doit éviter de se faire prendre en flagrant délit de contradiction même apparente. Autrement, trop d'énergies sont dépensées sur les marges, c'est-à-dire à défendre une cohérence interne fragile et non évidente aux yeux des journalistes et des hommes d'État. C'est entre nous d'abord qu'il faut établir les ponts entre nos perspectives.

QUELQUES PISTES POUR ACCROÎTRE NOTRE INFLUENCE SUR LES RÉFORMES LÉGISLATIVES

Au plan intellectuel et en ce qui a trait aux orientations scientifiques qui me sont apparues fécondes dans l'analyse du droit criminel, j'identifie les perspectives féministes matérialiste d'une part et socialiste de l'autre, comme des instruments critiques tout à fait utiles et décapants. Le féminisme « de la différence » a toute son efficacité et sa portée dans l'analyse des traitements qu'il faut réclamer pour les femmes et d'ailleurs dans l'exigence d'une place réelle, importante, de personnes de sexe féminin à tous les niveaux de l'appareil pénal: législatif, des tribunaux, des appareils correctionnels, etc. Toutes ces approches ont été mises à contribution dans *Un examen féministe du droit criminel au Canada* (Boyle et al 1985) à des niveaux d'explicitation différents mais réels. Une analyse plus radicale de type sémantique à la Mary Daly (voir, par exemple, la déconstruction du langage dans *Gyn/ecology* [1976]) aurait à mon avis, de par son caractère littéral, un effet important sur le droit. On aurait pu, donc (et il est facile d'en parler a posteriori), compléter les approches privilégiées par les auteures.

Mais c'est surtout de la méthode de travail et des faiblesses relatives de l'étude réalisée qu'il convient de tirer parti. Le travail en petits groupes, si cher aux féministes, est particulièrement nécessaire dans ces entreprises que je qualifierai de recherches-actions, ou d'études appelées à déboucher sur la recommandation de réformes capitales. Ces groupes de travail doivent devenir des groupes d'interconscientisation des chercheures, où le partage des perspectives idéologiques et la reconnaissance de la fécondité des orientations des co-auteures président à la cohérence du tout. Quand des femmes chercheures, auteures de recommandations dans le sens de réformes fondamentales du droit ou de ses applications, s'attaquent à des appareils aussi puissamment définisseurs de valeurs que le droit pénal et d'une conception aussi exclusivement masculine, il est particulièrement important qu'elles le fassent à partir de travaux dont la convergence théorique et politique soit inattaquable. Il n'est pas indispensable que la grille d'analyse soit unique ni la vision uniforme, mais il est au plus haut point important que les objectifs visés soient identiques, les recommandations interreliées, les stratégies de combat bien débattues et partagées.

C'est donc dire qu'un groupe de chercheures appelées à faire, au terme de son analyse, des recommandations qui s'attaquent à un objet puissant, la loi, dont le retentissement sur le sort des femmes est déterminant, doit réclamer de ses commanditaires les moyens et donc le temps de faire véritablement oeuvre commune: c'est-à-dire faire sienne une commande extérieure et veiller à ce que soient bien articulées les perspectives et les réformes qui en découlent, car les sources de notre aliénation se trouvent jusque dans la façon de recevoir les commandes et de les réaliser. Nous approprier réellement les instruments, la méthode de nos travaux, et les conséquences de leur énonciation sur la place publique, voilà le premier pas, la première étape dans notre lutte contre l'hégémonie normative du droit – des différents droits, lesquels nous sont étrangers à bien des égards.

NOTES

1 Platon, *The Laws*, dans la version de T.J. Saunders, livre 4, section intitulée: la suprématie des lois, 172–3, ma traduction. Voir la référence complète à l'oeuvre de Saunders (1975). Le passage cité dans l'article est notre traduction.

Tokenism

It is argued here that tokenism is negatively evaluated by feminists because of its persistent association with individualistic conceptions of subjectivity. As long as token women are expected to merge into existing
social structures as one individual among many, the political potential of
tokenism will not be realized. But token women who act in awareness of
their part in a collective movement, who practice "identity politics," may
be better able to realize some of that potential.

Les femmes symboliques

On soutient que les nominations de pure forme sont mal vues par les féministes parce qu'on les associe toujours à une conception individualiste
de la subjectivité. Tant qu'on s'attendra à ce que les femmes symboliques
se perdent dans les structures sociales déjà en place, comme un individu
parmi tant d'autres, le but politique de la nomination symbolique ne
pourra être atteint. Mais les femmes qui, conscientes de leur rôle au sein
d'un mouvement collectif, pratiquent et agissent en fonction d'« une politique d'identification » sont mieux à même d'en réaliser de potentiel.

A plausible explanation for the persistence in feminist thought of
negative evaluations of tokenism may well lie in an implicit alignment
of tokenism with individualistic conceptions of subjectivity. That such
an alignment should be assumed is not surprising, given that tokenism has been used by dominant social and political groups to rein-
force individualistic interpretations of its significance. But the mere
fact that it *has* been used in this way is no reason to close off the
possibility of developing different interpretations – interpretations
which can be enlisted in the service of feminist political ends.

As it is commonly encountered, tokenism can be described as the practice of hiring, or admitting into hitherto exclusive organizations, a limited number of women, blacks, or other standardly oppressed and excluded groups, ostensibly as evidence of sympathy with egalitarian public opinion and/or legislation. The description is a little too crude in that it gives the impression that tokenism is uniformly perceived in this way. One cannot assume that all persons regarded as tokens, either by their employers or by other members of a community, would perceive themselves as such; or that employers would describe their own practices as tokenism. Isolation as the only "different" employee, or member in a group, does not automatically count as tokenism; and the phenomenon itself looks different from different places in the social structure. But the description pinpoints the core of the practice, leaving open possibilities for refinement and elaboration.

Token members are generally expected to make themselves "fit in," to conduct themselves according to the standards of the dominant group, and to avoid calling attention to their "difference". This difference should not be allowed to upset other members of the group or to intrude upon their normal patterns of action. Token members are supposed, in effect, to become indistinguishable from the others and, in so doing, to attribute the achievement of their position to their own merits, rather than to their difference. Yet, paradoxically, they are expected to continue to act and be judged according to the stereotype in which they have long been cast: as servile, obsequious, or alluring, for example. This indicates something of the anomaly of a token person's situation.

Where token women are concerned, it is clear that there is a crucial gap between their actual position, and the full realization of the enlightened political stance their presence is supposed to represent. What poses as an indicator that women as such are welcome, often amounts to nothing more than the fact that this particular woman has "made it," more likely on terms acceptable to those in positions of power than on her own terms. A contrast with the significance of other kinds of tokens shows what is amiss here. If I offer you a token of my friendship, it stands as a sort of promissory note, an indication that my friendship is there for you to draw upon. One might expect token appointments of women to work, analogously, to show that the appointment of this woman is a promissory note to other women seeking similar treatment. But, in fact, one woman's token presence is more often presented as proof that the hiring or admission practices of a particular firm or institution are in order, that the "woman question" has been settled, and that no more women will be admitted.

Gayatri Spivak observes: "The putative center welcomes selective inhabitants of the margin in order better to exclude the margin. And it is the center that offers the official explanation; or the center that is defined and reproduced by the explanation that it can express ... " (Spivak qtd. in Gunew 1985, 142). Tokenism generally amounts neither to a refusal of marginal status on the part of a woman, nor to an end of marginalizing practices on the part of those who designate her status. It does not betoken the end of oppressive social and political structures; rather, it attests to their persistence. These facts create a strong presumption against according it any particular worth.

Feminist criticism of tokenism tends to focus upon the amenability of individual token women to being used to fulfill the purposes of dominant groups. Thus Carolyn Heilbrun writes of the "distressing attitude of token women ... [who] refuse to see that their single presence, far from proving that anyone can make it, determines, under the present system, that no one else will" (1979, 42). Men, she observes, readily discover that "they can count on token women of achievement to isolate themselves from other women, from the causes of women, and from identification with women" (24). The implication is that a token woman occupies a self-deceptive, morally ambiguous position, that she is blind to the truth of her situation. Hence, Golda Meir "misses the entire significance of the tokenism she represents; the occasional woman will be accepted as a man, indeed, if capable, as the best of men" (Heilbrun 1979, 112). If Meir is typical, then token women are not the self-determining, autonomous women they might claim to be. They are constrained by *masculine* stereotypes. The tone of Heilbrun's discussion suggests that they are blameworthy on this account.

Mary Daly's condemnation of token women rests on similar grounds. She describes token women as "women with anatomically female bodies but totally male-identified, male possessed brains/ spirits" (1978, 57). To fulfill her designated role, Daly maintains, a token woman must develop a selective blindness so that she can be absorbed well into masculine social norms; she must learn to think like a man, yet behave according to a narrow interpretation of the feminine stereotype. Her primary mode of existence is an anesthetized "unselfconscious inclusion" (375). Such victories as token women seem to achieve are merely victories in the vacuum of a persistently oppressive social order, yet these victories mask both the fact of that oppression, and any possibilities for the realization of more radical freedom.

Now both of these critiques clearly articulate the negative implications of tokenism as they are manifested in patriarchal institutions and experienced in the lives of token women. Yet both are flawed, I think, by the implicit theory of human subjectivity that informs them. Indeed, for both of them, the scope of tokenism is no broader than the scope of abstract liberal individualism. It may be this narrow view of the drawbacks of tokenism that limits their vision of the possibilities of exploiting it for feminist advantage.

Consider the examples Heilbrun selects to illustrate what she finds wrong with tokenism, and her attributions of blame to women in token positions. Blaming the women themselves is a particularly stark manifestation of individualistic assumptions at work, for it suggests that these women should have been selfdefining to the point of transcending the situation through their own, autonomous efforts. In so doing it glosses over the extent to which people are created and constrained by social forces and material circumstances (which include class and race as well as gender). Singling out such extraordinary examples as Thatcher and Meir (by implication, the ultimate self-made women!) – women who have "made it" more significantly than most men do, and in a strikingly masculine way – distorts the issue by implying that these are typical women who set the standards by which tokenism is to be judged. Yet the figures selected for criticism are not women many feminists would be inclined to regard as exemplars of female potential.

Daly's criticisms are even more strongly marked by individualistic assumptions. Despite her view that tokenism is a patriarchal plot to suppress sisterhood, a view which appears to betoken a different theory of subjectivity, it is clear both from the tone of her discussion and from the kinds of emancipatory practice she champions, that sisterhood as she understands it falls far short of the solidarity of true collectivity. Indeed, the central thrust of her celebration of femininity, as it emerges in the pages of *Gyn/Ecology* (1978) is most strongly reminiscent not just of individualism in the abstract, liberal sense, but rather in a Nietzschean sense of self-aggrandizement. She would have women become Amazons, super-women, who might differ from the Margaret Thatchers of the world in proclaiming their feminine identity, but in such a way that they could hardly be said to be woman-identified. The form of self-actualization and self-affirmation she ostensibly advocates is, as Jean Grimshaw aptly puts it, "*totally* inconsistent with things like pity or concern for others; it [is] a form of total individualism and egoism" (1986, 156). While condemning all participation in patriarchal institutions as tokenism, Daly in fact advocates a mirror image of these same institutions – social structures where women are self-affirming according to a particular, heroic construct of masculine standards, and men are simply ignored. How such a reversal could produce a more just and harmonious social order than the one feminists are concerned to eradicate is not at all clear.

It would be as naïve as it would be depressing to think that tokenism is the best that women can hope for in moving toward a realization of feminist ideals. Yet it is one of the few avenues open to women; feminists would surely be reluctant to argue *against* hiring token women in favour of hiring men instead, and to urge an end to affirmative action programs, under whose aegis token women are often hired. Reasons for this reluctance seem to attach to a persistent belief, which the Margaret Thatchers of the world have not managed wholly to destroy, that token women have within their reach the capacity to make significant, and even occasionally radical, changes in patriarchal structures.

It is true, then, that the very concept of tokenism is created out of structures of domination; hence there is reason to be wary of it. But it has the potential to turn the dominant discourse against itself and to disrupt deep-seated expectations; hence there is reason for (cautious) endorsement of it.

What, then, can be said to make the political potential of tokenism visible? In the space that remains I shall attempt to answer this question briefly by giving some sense of the conceptual and moral problems that might follow rejection of individualistic perspectives on this complex phenomenon. There are no easy solutions to these problems. On the conceptual level, given the nature of tokenism, it is not possible simply to reconceptualize it in collective terms, and on the moral level, it is not easy to see how one could reasonably argue that every woman (and hence every token woman) has an outright obligation to support feminist causes.

Token women are, by definition, isolated women in predominantly male groups. Hence, to recast their situation in collectivist terms invites conceptual confusion. Should large groups of women be admitted into organizations where there are now only token women, members of such groups would not count as tokens. So collectivist principles cannot be straightforwardly enlisted to describe the political potential of tokenism as it is currently practised.

The shift from individualist to collectivist thinking in this context, then, must pivot around a token woman's preparedness to think and act *as a woman*, as part of a network of women, and to acknowledge the strengths as well as the risks inherent in that stance. This would involve rejecting conceptions of oneself as an autonomous (and indeed atomistic) individual, in favour of working to understand the role of worthwhile, supportive relationships in creating and sustain-

ing one's possiblilities. Publicly, and to the extent that this is possible
without jeopardizing one's position, it would involve practising "identity politics":[1] rejecting the liberal feminist practice of trying to fit
in without a ripple, as "one of the boys," in favour of an active (if,
of necessity, subtle) assertion of one's female identity, with the conviction that the identity is a worthy one that needs neither to be
masked nor denied. I am not suggesting that this would be an easy,
straightforward substitution of identity politics for liberal individualism. Identity politics is fraught with difficulties, as other oppressed groups have found. It often seems to invite expressions of
racism and anti-Semitism; in its feminist mode, it might invite expressions of sexism. Furthermore, those who practise it would need to
avoid asserting an *essential* identity of Woman which would play
directly back into the old stereotypes. But the risks involved are worth
taking.

In effect, what is at issue here is a reworking of the interplay of
sameness-and-difference.[2] An "outsider" in any situation needs to
locate her/himself somewhere along a continuum whose poles are
marked by sameness and difference. In the individualistic, liberal
practice of tokenism, a token woman moves as closely as possible
toward the "sameness" pole, downplaying her differences, emphasizing her similarities, and posing no challenge to prevalent norms.
A woman practising identity politics might move further along the
continuum toward the difference pole, attempting to bring members
of the group to understand that, if she is different from them, then
they are different from her. The best outcome of such a situation
would be the sowing of seeds of doubt in receptive minds within the
dominant group about whether the norms they have been taking
for granted really deserve their normative status. (The situation is
analogous to that of a group of "normal" Boston schoolchildren who
were taught sign language so that they could talk to a hearing-
impaired child who joined their class. The point was to demonstrate
the symmetry of difference: to help them realize that his difference
from them had its counterpart in their difference from him.)

Collectivity is not *directly* at work in this situation. But an extension
of principles of collectivity into a woman's life apart from other
women, drawing upon the strength that network solidarity provides,
may enable a token woman to carry out such a strategy. By contrast
with individualism, her actions would be informed by the recognition
that what one is and does, is, in large measure, shaped by human
commonality; one need not act only as part of a *visible* collective to
realize the force of collectivity. To appreciate the strength of such
a position requires serious thought about spheres of influence, and

about the kinds of influence that count as politically worthy. We commonly think of political activity on a macro, global scale; hence its particular, micro effects are accorded less credit than they deserve. To perceive the worth of these micro effects, one must learn to see beyond the oppressive political structures that are imposed from above – by legislation and large-scale institutional machinery – to recognize the political force of those minuscule manifestations of power that well up out of institutional and cultural practices. The latter are only dimly visible, in the absence of knowledgeable critics. They appear, for example, in language and in the media, and in the provision of inadequate facilities and minimal respect for women and their activities. The point is that micro-practices spread through the production of discourse, knowledge, and power, and serve to *create* certain kinds of people: people who are marginalized, oppressed, and powerless.[3]

A valuable resource for feminist reflection upon the structure of power-knowledge is to be found, according to Jana Sawicki, in Foucault's *expansion* of the domain of the political "to include a heterogeneous ensemble of power relations operating at the micro-level of society." This expansion enables us to see that resistance "must be carried out in *local* struggles against the many forms of power exercised at the everyday level of social relations" (Sawicki 1986, 28). Power can be subverted bit by bit, in its myriad, discontinuous manifestations, without taking on the entire structure. And token women have gained entry into institutions where it may be possible for them to upset the prevailing order in a way that no outsider could.

The issue of spheres of influence is pertinent here. It may be that a token woman, even during a long period of membership in a group, will influence only a few of its members, bringing them to reconsider long-held assumptions, and abandon certain small discriminatory practices. But it would be foolish to minimize the importance of this achievement. Since each of the people she influences is part of a complex network of other lives and influences, it is not inconceivable that changes in his or her attitudes and practices will be felt in those lives which, in their turn, touch other lives. Even if a token woman is instrumental in opening opportunities to one or two other women, in influencing their thinking or in supporting their employment efforts, this is no mean achievement.

Truly effective, macro-political subversion tends (both in Foucault's and in feminist terms) to manifest itself in more global collective struggle. Our impatience to effect the sweeping changes that a thorough undermining of patriarchal structures requires may blind us to smaller changes that serve, often systematically but sometimes only piecemeal, to chip away at those structures and genuinely to change their shape.

A self-conscious, politically aware willingness to be appointed as a token woman, with the conviction that it is necessary to be on the scene in order to make a difference, is laudable in principle. My point is that it can also be effective in practice. Yet the requirements of self-consciousness and political awareness cannot be over-stated: they are surely the preconditions *sine qua non* of effective action. Both Heilbrun and Daly rightly criticize certain token women for their failure in these respects. Heilbrun's references to their refusal to see the significance of their situation, and Daly's comments on selective blindness and unself-conscious inclusion, are the salient points here. Both analyses suggest that the real risk in becoming a token woman is that of violating a fundamental epistemic requirement, namely to know oneself and one's situation responsibly and well.

I am suggesting that, if token women are to be politically effective, they must attempt to fulfill this requirement with a particular scrupulousness and sensitivity.[4] Indeed, the effectiveness of tokenism, in feminist terms, appears to be dependent not only upon a token woman's willingness to understand her situation as clearly as possible, but also on her readiness to allow that she is where she is *because* of, not in spite of, her gender. Such a realization, in fact, creates the freedom for her to interpret and live the situation according to her own best abilities.

Now this leads directly into the question of whether token women can be declared to have a moral obligation to live that situation according to feminist principles. I think the answer must clearly be no. A token woman might counter the charge of moral ambiguity implicit in Heilbrun's criticisms with the claim that she has chosen allegiance to her discipline, her party, or her company over any primary allegiance to other women. It is not easy to find valid moral reasons for overriding this claim with a counterclaim that she does, in fact, owe her first allegiance to other women. Feminists rightly deplore the stance such women adopt, and the fact that the positions they occupy are lost to feminist purposes. But it seems that their energies would be better directed toward ensuring that feminist women come to occupy places in the patriarchy where they can make a difference, rather than in attempting to impose an indefensible moral requirement on women who are already there.

Nonetheless, if the epistemic imperative I have mentioned is recognized as a directive for living well, it is important to note that it has both epistemic *and* moral relevance. Part of what is involved is learning to see oneself and one's situation clearly and well: knowing oneself to the fullest extent possible. Yet many token women, as Daly and Heilbrun indicate, can be faulted on this score. It is at least possible that they might, were they to come to respect this epistemic imperative, recognize either that the women's movement has indeed had a role to play in making their success possible, *or* that their hitherto unperceived lack of success (failure, for example, to be promoted, or to receive adequate remuneration) can be linked to their femaleness. It is necessary to understand the subtleties of the structures that sustain subjugation, if one is either to defend them or to counter them. In either case, one must first make the effort to *see* them for what they are.

Once an appropriate understanding is achieved, one may realize that for the oppressed, too, the equation between knowledge and power can be made to hold: that knowledge is empowering. Whether that realization entails a moral injunction to the effect that the power thus recognized must be used for feminist ends must, I think, remain an open question.[5]

NOTES

1 See Alcoff's interesting discussion of identity politics as a strategy for oppressed groups (1986); and Theresa de Laurentis' discussion of some of the hazards of identity politics (1986, 5–7).

2 I am indebted for my thinking about sameness and difference, and for the example cited here, to Clare Dalton (1985).

3 The effects of such practices are brilliantly detailed in Michel Foucault's analyses of cultural phenomena (see especially 1965, 1972, 1980).

4 For a fuller discussion of this epistemic requirement, see Code (1987).

5 Work on this paper was made possible by a Strategic Grant from the Social Sciences and Humanities Research Council of Canada. The paper is reprinted here, with permission, from *Resources for Feminist Research* (16, no. 3 [September 1987]: 46–8); a preliminary version was presented at the 1986 CRIAW conference.

DOROTHY ZABORSZKY

Feminist Politics: The Feminist Party of Canada [1]

The Feminist Party of Canada (FPC) was founded in 1979. This discussion is based on my own and others' personal experiences as founding members. The FPC's aim was to introduce feminist politics into the public arena; it arose out of a shared perception that the three main political parties in Canada did not adequately reflect women's concerns, therefore creating a need for such a party. Although the FPC is at present on hold, the time has come to assess this experience. It is, first, important to record this development, in order that it may not be lost from our collective memories. Second, it is useful to explore what can be learnt and what conclusions drawn from this event and the related issue of women and party politics.

La politique féministe: Le parti féministe du Canada

Le parti féministe du Canada (PFC) a été fondé en 1979. Cet exposé relate mon expérience personnelle et celle des autres membres fondatrices du parti. Le but du PFC était d'attirer l'attention du public sur une politique féministe; le PFC est né de la conviction que les trois partis politiques du Canada ne reflétant pas de façon adéquate les préoccupations des femmes, il existait un besoin pour un parti tel que celui-ci. Bien que les activités du PFC aient été suspendues, le temps est venu de faire le bilan de cette expérience. Premièrement, il est important de prendre acte de cet épisode et de faire en sorte qu'il ne soit pas effacé de notre mémoire collective. Deuxièmement, il peut être utile d'essayer de voir les leçons et les conclusions que l'on peut en tirer sans compter les indications qu'il peut nous fournir sur la question connexe de la représentativité des femmes au sein des partis politiques.

My purpose in this paper is twofold: first, to record the facts connected with the formation of the Feminist Party of Canada in 1979,
and second, to analyze the significance of this event and to evaluate
its implications. The first aim is to a large extent linked to a feminist
desire to prevent its erasure. I will therefore provide a brief overview
of the sequence of events, as well as attempt an analysis.

On 11 February, 1979 a group of women met at Hart House,
University of Toronto, "for the purpose of founding a women's
political party." This aim was the result of a growing dissatisfaction
with the lack of impact women had made within and outside formal
structures, the scant attention paid by politicians to women's concerns, and the very small number of women in elected office. Furthermore, there was a shared perception, from an analysis of the
record of the few women in office that, "most female politicians,
regardless of background or party affiliation, reduced their connections with women's organizations to a minimum, when they obtained office." Therefore, the problem was and is that: "no matter
how many women are elected, ... they do not, on the whole, address
themselves to those issues of concern to women, that have been
continually neglected by everyone else." Although some of the Hart
House group were resistant to the formation of an actual political
party, there was a realization that a feminist caucus would be inef-
fective. Consequently, the interim committee recognized the necessity of a women's political party,[2] because only "when the potential
candidate has a context within the party and is shielded by the party
structure, would she be able to maintain feminist beliefs while in
office" (Feminist Party of Canada, 1979). It remained to be seen
whether it would be possible to draw together women from a large
variety of backgrounds and political persuasions, and whether the
common denominators of gender and a concern for improving the
status of women would be unifying factors.

Undoubtedly, there was a very strong need for such action. Laura
Sabia said, in 1975, that: "Not until women are thoroughly involved
in the political system, not until fifty per cent of our federal, provincial, and municipal politicians are women, will women change the
laws that keep them from the elusive equality they all seek" (1978,
33). The basic points of this statement are as relevant today as they
were eleven years ago. M. Janine Brodie and Jill McCalla Vickers,
speaking about the 1979 federal election, concluded:

Most women candidates in 1979 had little chance of being elected, and the
most visible and established elements of the women's movement did not
attempt to politicize and mobilize their substantial membership to force the

major political parties either to recruit women in winnable constituencies, or to make the status of women a central issue in the campaign. Thus, most Canadian women chose between the parties without reference to their status as women or a clear estimation of the partisan options available to them. (1982, 46)

It is precisely because the women who were behind the founding of the Feminist Party perceived the situation rather as Brodie and Vickers did, that they felt a need to start a specifically feminist party.

Olive Banks wrote that: "The failure, for most of its history, to secure mass support for its policies has meant that the feminist movement has relied to a large extent on pressure group politics ... Feminism has always needed the support of a mass movement, and when there is general apathy about feminist goals the movement languishes" (1981, 248). The question that arises from this not inaccurate analysis is *why* such pressure group politics are necessary for the most elementary ameliorative measures for women? It is difficult to escape the conclusion that this immense expenditure of time and energy has been necessary because women were stuck with a political structure which historically they did not create, to which they were unable to contribute for a long time, and which, consequently, did not reflect their needs and concerns.

The interim committee of the Feminist Party met every Sunday after 11 February, 1979, as well as once a week as members of various subcommittees. Once a decision was made to work on a feminist political party, the women were faced with the "formidable task of turning vision into policy and policy into strategy" (Feminist Party of Canada, 1979). The procedure for registering as a political party, and the constitutions of established parties were studied. All this difficult and detailed work was followed by the first public meeting at OISE in Toronto on Sunday, 10 June, 1979. There were readings and music, an introduction by Margaret Evans, and speeches by Laura Sabia, Angela Miles, Mary O'Brien, and Maryan Kantaroff. Party memberships were sold before the meeting and the press was present to cover the event. There was open discussion from the floor, and the participants sang "Bread and Roses." For everyone present, whatever their reservations, it was a heady, exciting, moving occasion. I was not only extremely moved, but also very conscious that I was participating in an historic and unique event.

Certainly there were reservations. Laura Sabia wondered if we could avoid becoming divided, and if we could manage to obtain enough money to function properly. However, in my opinion, Mary O'Brien provided the most thoughtful and impressive speech, in which she said: "Feminism is growing, not because it is a good theory, but because if we don't do it we won't be around. We aren't going to build a new world on vision alone – but we're not going to build one without it" (qtd. in *Broadside* 1, no. 1 [1979]: 8). This expressed the aims of the founders far more accurately than the malestream press coverage, which was mostly trivial and irrelevant.

It needs to be stressed that the aim was not to replace any existing women's groups, but to continue to cooperate with them. There was already a varied and broadly based women's movement, from which the Feminist Party emerged as a putative political party. From the start, the educational aspect was held to be important, and plans were made for study groups, consciousness raising groups and issues discussion groups. It was recognized that although there were numerous women who were already committed, there were also many who had to be convinced of the need for such a party. The serious problem confronting the founders was how to convince women, many of whom had in the past supported the established political parties, to switch their allegiance to the FPC; consequently, education was seen to be crucial. The task was to convince potential members of the validity and significance of the FPC's aims; to this end it was necessary to create a woman-centred party. The need for this is reinforced by electoral patterns; for instance, the number of women seeking federal office rose from 4 in 1921 to 137 in 1974. But the number of women who won seats in those 53 years rose only from 1 to 9. At this rate, women would need another 842 years to achieve equal representation at the federal level. In 1986, the situation has slightly improved, but not to the extent of invalidating the basic premise.

As Mary O'Brien has said, "Feminism is the political expression of the gestation of a politics of care and community which will replace the politics of conquest and chaos" (1979, 4). It was this mode of thinking which informed and guided the members of the FPC and which they endeavoured to share with prospective members. But it can be seen that this is not the language of ordinary party manifestos, nor of the usual *modus operandi* of political parties. What the FPC attempted was to offer not only new ideas, but also a different mode of practising them: their very uniqueness mandated an innovative praxis. And because feminism also "rejects the symbolism of the patriarch, the prostration before power, the solutions of violence to private and public problems" (O'Brien 1979, 5), it follows that the FPC did not have a hierarchical structure or a "leader," but rather, functioned on the basis of a loosely organized and voluntary committee system. This is an important point to which I will return later.

The party held regular weekly committee meetings, all-day educational meetings (usually monthly), and prepared policy statements. There were also smaller study groups and strategy meetings. Eventually, chapters were formed outside Toronto, for example in Peterborough and Peel/Halton; there was great interest in the party from a variety of places and provinces across Canada. A *Newsletter* was founded, whose first editor (until December 1981) was Mary O'Brien. The *Newsletter* was sent to all members and was an invaluable way of keeping in touch; it also contained notices of meetings organized by various women's groups. From time to time half of it appeared in French, highlighting a desire to be truly a national party. One of the issues of the *Newsletter* reprinted excerpts from the constitution of the Partis Féministes Unifiés of France and Belgium (founded 1975) as a way of studying a party "under the rubric of feminism" and "constituted on the strength of a definitive written platform" (1: 3, 1) An office was rented, a postal box secured, and stationery was ordered, although of course finances were always something of a problem. By June 1981, the party had 700 members, which was quite an impressive number, albeit short of our best hopes.

At a general meeting in 1981, the decision was made to pursue the possibility of becoming an official political party in the Province of Ontario. For this, it was necessary to collect ten thousand signatures which endorsed the fact that the FPC had a right to exist. The editorial in the *Newsletter* of June 1981 stated, "The notion of becoming an official party isn't without its dangers, of course. There are no safe strategies for progressive political movements like ours. Some members feel that to be 'official' is in some sense to be coopted by the patriarchal establishment. Others – and this includes me- feel that we are strong and confident enough to take what we need and keep our feminist integrity" (3: 3). Here we have the classic problem of integrity versus cooptation; this was one of the factors which was to have a negative effect on the party's future. While it is possible to preserve integrity, certain compromises are necessary if one wants to move from marginality and powerlessness to the centre of a political structure.

Another problem which continued within the FPC was the question of men as members and the related issue of whether men in fact could be feminists. From the beginning there had been a few male members in the party, but their numbers were never significant enough to create any serious structural problems. As it turned out, this was to become another divisive issue. This experience is a classic one – like the question of cooptation – and is related to the ideas of separatist or integrationist feminism. I should add that for many of us at the time this was not a substantive problem.

In early 1981 there were also the issues of the patriation of the constitution, and the need to change the Charter to reflect women's interests. While several FPC members were active in the Ad Hoc Constitutional Committee, the constitutional issue was not developed politically by the FPC, and the party as such was not invited to the original Ad Hoc deliberations. In the opinion of Mary O'Brien (with which I agree), the reason for this was the FPC's "continued failure to get our party organized to make decisions rather than respond to events. Our membership continues to expand while our profile is not only low but close to disappearing altogether" (*Newsletter*, April 1981, 1). The point made here, I think, is that there is a difference between an actual political party, such as some members were striving to create, and a lobby group or caucus, such as, for instance, the National Action Committee for the Status of Women.

The 17 May 1981 general meeting tackled this issue and decided to pursue the matter of becoming an official political party. As Mary O'Brien put it at the time, "It is very urgent that we face up to our feminist distaste for structure and leadership and ask how we can actually propose to do political things" (*Newsletter*, April 1981, 1). There was a need for a definite structure and even some leadership, to enable the party to act efficiently, indeed, to act at all. While there was an understandable reluctance to imitate patriarchal structures, there was nevertheless a need for *some* structure if the FPC was to function at all, especially if it was to become a political party.

The last *Newsletter*, no longer edited by Mary O'Brien, posed several questions related to these problems. Some were those pertaining to sexual orientation, class, separation versus integration, and how these affect one's feminism. The writer of this *Newsletter* editorial stated that "we cannot afford this division within the ranks when our common enemy, the patriarchal system, is so strong." Significantly, the editorial ended with the introduction of an oversized red herring, namely the question, "now what does it mean for a man to claim to be a feminist?" (*Newsletter*, March 1982). While some of us imagined that we were working for a nascent political party which would at last make a serious feminist, political impact on the existing structure, others were not interested in such an endeavour. Some members wished to pursue the overtly political direction which had in fact been implicit since the beginning, while others, an active and vocal minority, did not share this approach. It is the latter group which in the end was more dominant, and this in effect meant the cessation of the FPC as it had been planned since the beginning. The outward sign of this was to be seen in the vanishing of the *Newsletter*, the last number of which was the March, 1982 issue referred to earlier. However, many of us consider that the FPC is not really dead, but merely on hold.

If we look at history, malestream though much of it may be, we find that most of the feminist political groups which made a political impact did have men as members. What is also noticeable is that in none of these groups, for example, the Women's Social and Political Union (WSPU), did men have any decisive influence in terms of policy decisions, nor were they members of executive committees. They functioned in a generally supportive but ancillary manner, rather as women did in male parties.

What needs to be emphasized is that, in my opinion, the issue of male members was not the cause of the FPC's demise; rather, it became in a way the catalyst for bringing various differences to the fore. Essentially, the whole experience seems to have accentuated and sharpened the distinction between the separatist and the integrationist types of feminism, with, in this instance, the former predominating. In the case of the FPC, the separatist approach resulted in the abandonment of the pursuit of a political presence, the inward-turning of the party's direction and, therefore, the marginalization of what had been a potentially vibrant organization. Since marginalization is a crucial concern for feminism, this development did nothing to ameliorate the issue, but, on the contrary, merely aggravated it. Many of us who favoured a more public political presence felt unable to continue to identify and work with the FPC, especially because this latest development ran counter to the original aims of the party.

In her essay "Fighting the Good Fight: Separation or Integration?" Patricia Hughes has ably analyzed this question. She remarks that

since a feminist society could not tolerate any form of oppression, it would be incompatible with feminist theory not to accept that all people are at least implicitly affected by that transformation. It is not realistic to believe that the world of women will be dramatically transformed without its having repercussions for men ... while feminist practice does not *require* men, it must recognize their existence and determine their place in the theory and practice because they, too, will be part of feminist society. (1982, 286)

Since men are also part of the human race, it is neither practical nor realistic to exclude them entirely from one's calculations for the future, let alone the present. Therefore, Hughes continues, "a political party dedicated to the objectives of a feminist political party ... cannot be exclusionary ... The reasons for not excluding men are pragmatic, theoretical and ethical" (Hughes 1982, 293–4). The events of early 1982 were especially puzzling in that, as I pointed out earlier, the number of male members in the FPC was always minuscule and never presented a practical problem: one might say therefore that these events were the result of a purely theoretical but not a practical situation.

Dale Spender, in her insightful *Women of Ideas* (1982), repeatedly stresses the importance of knowing our collective history, in order not only to avoid erasure, but also to obviate the need to reinvent the feminist wheel every fifty years or so. It is in this spirit that I wanted to record the existence of the Feminist Party. At the same time, I take seriously Spender's injunction that we need to be able to learn from each other's ideas and actions. And this is only possible if we are fully informed about each other's ideas and actions. It is also crucial to try to work out what we learn from our past, and specifically, from the relative failure of the Feminist Party.

I have pointed out that there was no leader in the FPC. Indeed, the very idea of leaders is one which runs counter to the collectivist, cooperative nature of feminist thinking. Therefore, the party functioned with a loosely based committee structure, which was fairly efficient for a time. There was much discussion on the issue of our name; while many of us realized that the name itself might result in a certain amount of adverse publicity, we nonetheless believed that it was very important to call ourselves what we really believed we were. In effect, it was decided that on this issue we must not make any compromises.

The FPC did not have a constitution, nor did it have an executive in a formal sense. With the easy benefit of hindsight, I think that this was a mistake. A formal structure, including a constitution, by-laws, and an executive, would have been better for the smooth functioning of the party. In addition, it would have provided a more neutral way of handling dissension and disagreement, and thus perhaps we could have avoided the more hurtful and subjective situations which were inevitable as a result of the lack of structure. A structure also means that an organization will be less dependent on more or less powerful personalities to transact business. It would also mean that the feminist goals of co-operative endeavours could be better realized.

Examples of similar situations in history can be seen in two events in the history of the WSPU. The first occurred in 1907,[3] when Charlotte Despard, the Secretary, left because she disagreed with Emmeline Pankhurst's handling of the WSPU constitution and formed the Women's Freedom League. The WSPU had a draft constitution, but the real decisions were made by the Emergency Committee, largely controlled by Mrs Pankhurst and her supporters. Subsequently, both sides behaved with great generosity and worked for the same ends. The second event occurred in 1912, when Mrs Pankhurst severed her connection with Emmeline and Frederick Pethick-Lawrence in a disagreement over militancy. The Pethick-Lawrences joined the Women's Freedom League. Again, the behaviour of the Pethick-Lawrences was singularly generous and lacking in rancour. The lesson which can be drawn from these events seems to be the fact that in both cases the constitutions of the organizations had been violated, thus precluding a more consensual solution. Mrs Pankhurst's *modus operandi* was not consensual, even though it was immensely effective. So the importance of the mediating influence of a structure becomes greater, as does the need to respect and abide by it.

Connected with the importance of some type of structure is the issue of goals. It is obvious that an organization needs to have broad agreement on its goals from the outset. This means the formulation of policies and what might be called a party platform. Certainly this was not lacking in the Feminist Party, which from the beginning worked very hard to formulate its aims, position papers, and policies. The early press releases were in effect position papers. And while these were being produced, the educational activity of the FPC also continued, for the practical reason that the members' knowledge of feminism and current issues was varied, and there was a need to make ourselves knowledgeable enough to cope with our work, with the media, and with the public. So the educational and policy-formulating activities took place simultaneously, resulting in a new type of endeavour. The emergence of the FPC as a political presence, and the grassroots organizing coincided, thus making for a complex experience. This in turn was rendered more difficult by the absence of a constitution.

It was this absence which hampered the FPC in dealing constructively with what Hughes has called "the Man Question." I said earlier that this issue, which surfaced in early 1982, was one of the most divisive. As Hughes and others have demonstrated, the requirements and conditions of a political party are quite different from those of other groups, be they consciousness-raising or lobby groups. It is, of course, because a political party aims to make an electoral impact that certain pragmatic realities cannot be ignored. In Hughes' words:

It makes sense when forming a political party to think of it as trying to appeal to as many people as possible within the confines of its ideological base. A party cannot expect support if it deliberately excludes half the electorate (that traditional parties have effectively done so is no reason to continue the practice); blatant sexism, even if by the subordinate group, does not lie well beside a platform against exclusion (1982, 294).

It can be seen, then, that an integrationist kind of feminism is a necessary condition for the functioning of a feminist political party. This need not result in "selling out" or co-optation, as long as it is women who define the parameters, set the terms and devise the rules. Women should be the subjects rather than the objects of political processes, and in this way acquire control over their activities. So long as such control is maintained, there need be no difficulty with "the Man Question."

The greatest problem for the FPC was that of "selling" our visions for a just society to potential members. And here we had to confront the problem of trying to fight against long-established political allegiances. The task was to persuade women who had worked or voted for, for instance, the Conservatives, to switch allegiances. Our educational sessions were particularly important here. Canada, unlike the US, seems not yet to have a women's vote, although some indication of its existence was shown in the 1984 federal elections. It is important to note that the initiative for the historic debate on women's issues in August 1984 came from a feminist organization, the National Action Committee on the Status of Women, and not from one of the established parties. Although in the 1984 elections more women MPs were elected than previously (largely in Québec, and probably as a result of an anti-Liberal backlash), the number (twenty-five) is still pathetic in relation to the percentage of women voters (fifty-two percent) in the electorate. My opinion is that women still vote for reasons which have little if anything to do with their interests as women. And while some of the established parties have better platforms with regard to women's issues than others, none give priority to them. The very fact that they are called "women's issues" denotes ghettoization of interest, as if, on the one hand, there were women's issues, and on the other, there were human ones.

By contrast, Hughes states "the political party is our [women's] most public vehicle of our values and our vision; it seeks to advance our cause and our demands for justice throughout the entire society" (1982, 297). The founders of the FPC believed that our values and vision could not satisfactorily be advanced through the existing political parties, which is why they founded the party. Whether reform from within existing structures is possible, or efforts to do so are futile, is a matter of judgement. Traditionally, left-leaning parties have been more receptive to women's concerns, but even in these, women have had to fight every inch of the way, and they have not set the terms of discourse but have had to respond to existing ones.

Dale Spender has said that "in a society in which there is widespread acceptance that 'normal' means women in the kitchen and men in the corridors of power, we are likely to see our protest against these conditions as *abnormal*, as requiring explanation, demanding defence" (1984, 2). As we discover from our history, women have always engaged in protest one way or another; this knowledge reinforces our sense of the justness and rightness of our activities. This is one of the main reasons why I wanted to record, however inadequately, one episode from our collective past, and to illustrate that it was far from an unusual or unique occurrence, although it *was* precedent-setting in this country.

In conclusion, I believe that even though the FPC is at present on hold, the possibility of a feminist political party remains a realizable goal. If we take the long-range historical view, we have to recognize that feminism is relatively new. O'Brien says that "like all new political forms, it is in an early and unclear stage, just as Liberalism was in 1640, or democracy in 1790 or socialism in 1870" (1979, 5). All new political forms go through a period of trial and error. For those of us involved with the FPC, our collective effort remains a noble and worthwhile experience, albeit one which seems at present to be an exciting experiment. This is especially so because, as Mary O'Brien has said, feminism "struggles for rational political expression of an ethical polity and a just economy. It has no illusions about its difficulties, no doubt about its coming triumphs and a firm confidence in its historical necessity" (1979, 5).

NOTES

1 An earlier version of this paper was published in *Women's Studies International Forum* (10: 6 [1987], 613–21), following initial presentation at the 1986 CRIAW conference.

2 It is worth noting that American feminists, largely inspired by Alice Paul, formed the National Woman's Party in 1916, as part of the struggle for the vote. It lasted into the early 1970s. See Dale Spender (1982, 387ff), and Doris Stevens (1920). See also Joanne Edgar (1987, 30) for recent developments in Iceland.

3 The WSPU was formed in 1903.

LORNA ERWIN

What Feminists Should Know About the Pro-Family Movement in Canada: A Report on a Recent Survey of Rank-and-File Members

This article reports on the preliminary findings of a 1986 survey on the rank-and-file members of organized antifeminist groups in anglophone Canada – the pro-family movement. Data on the social composition, religiosity, ideological perceptions, and political activities of these members are presented. Where applicable, the pro-family data are compared with similar findings on Canadians generally with an eye to the representativeness of the movement's concerns. The study concludes that the members' social isolation, religiosity, and disaffection with the media and politics are likely to frustrate the leadership's hopes to impose their agenda on mainstream institutions.

Ce que les féministes devraient connaître du mouvement pro-famille au Canada; rapport d'un sondage récent

Dans cet article, nous faisons état des données préliminaires d'un sondage effectué en 1986 sur les membres des groupes organisés anti-féministes au Canada anglophone, notamment le mouvement « pro-famille ». Nos données portent sur la constitution sociale, le sentiment religieux, les perceptions idéologiques et les activités politiques de ses membres. Lorsque pertinent, les données des groupes pro-famille sont comparées à celles de la population canadienne en général, en tenant compte de la représentativité des préoccupations de ce mouvement. Notre conclusion est que l'isolement social des membres, leurs sentiments religieux et leur mécontentement face aux médias et à la politique rendent vains les espoirs qu'ont leurs dirigeants d'imposer leur programme aux institutions dominantes.

An anti-feminist backlash, arising out of the politics of abortion and related campaigns against sex education in the schools, pornography, and gay rights, has recently emerged in Canada.[1] Calling itself the "pro-family" movement, its press resounds with such slogans as "Strong families make strong nations" and "Women's rights but not at the expense of human rights." The leading organizations have contested government funding of feminist umbrella organizations like the National Action Committee (NAC) and in the process have won funding for themselves. Above all, this movement represents an attempt to challenge – in the media, the schools, the courts, the welfare agencies, and in other public settings – the hard-won and fragile legitimacy of feminist ideas, most obviously by appealing to women who have come to feel anxious, vulnerable, and even slighted by feminist demands and symbols.

While a growing and impressive literature exists on the antifeminist backlash in the United States,[2] very little research has been done in Canada.[3] Given that the pro-family phenomenon has captured the attention of the media and of government officials in this country, feminists need to know more about its strengths and future prospects if we are to respond effectively to its challenges.

In this article, I report on a Canada-wide 1986 survey of some 1,200 rank-and-file members of the pro-family movement. A key feature of the pro-family survey, which had a response rate of 75%, was the incorporation of a number of questions from the recent Gallup polls, the General Election Survey (1984), and the Quality of Life (QOL) survey, in order to facilitate comparisons with Canadians generally. (For details on how the survey was carried out, see the appendix.) Studies undertaken by myself on the press, and the leadership of the movement, also figure in the discussion. The focus is on both the organizational ties and political views and activities of these rank-and-file adherents, and on the life experiences and moral-religious concerns that underlie their involvement. Do the pro-family forces indeed speak for the silent majority of Canadians as they claim to? Will they be able to capitalize on the presumed representativeness of their concerns? These are the key questions.

ORGANIZATION OF THE MOVEMENT

That the pro-family phenomenon has its origins in the success of various umbrella groups of feminists in obtaining public funds testifies to the power of governments to legitimize the activities of movements in general. The first pro-family group to emerge in Canada, the Alberta Federation of Women United for Families (AF-WUF), was founded in 1981 to oppose the policies and influence of the Alberta Status of Women Committee (ASWAC). It now boasts a membership in excess of 10,000, and has received several government grants. REAL Women of Canada (an acronym which stands for *R*ealistic, *A*ctive, for *L*ife) was founded in Toronto in 1983 and has affiliates in each province and a selfreported membership of 45,000. (It is impossible to determine the precise number of supporters because these groups refuse to make their membership lists public.)

While AFWUF and REAL Women are the largest and best-known pro-family organizations in Canada, there are others, including Women for Life, Faith and Family, a group which subscribes to Catholic dictates and makes a special point of opposing the ordination of women, and the Canadian Society for the Defense of Tradition, Family, and Property, a world wide association of Catholic men which plays up the "evils of communism and socialism" in its literature. Also worth mentioning in this connection is the National Citizen's Coalition (NCC), the rightwing big business lobby, which has recently been taking an interest in family-related social policy issues and – according to some reports – helping to fund pro-family activities. Finally, there are two pro-family political parties in Canada: the Christian Heritage Party (CHP), which operates at the federal level and, in Ontario, the Family Coalition Party (FCP). In the 1987 provincial election in Ontario, which saw the Conservatives decline drastically, the FCP obtained four percent of the overall vote – a result that disappointed party leaders.

The pro-family phenomenon is clearly an outgrowth of the anti-abortion movement. While there are some anti-abortion groups that do not support the larger cause (e.g., Feminists for Life), the pro-life press has been increasingly appropriating pro-family themes in its literature. By the same token, abortion is a central concern of all the pro-family groups; 99.5% of the respondents surveyed indicated that it was an important reason for their involvement. Of special interest is the percentage of respondents (p $\langle$ .01) holding memberships in both pro-family and anti-abortion groups. For example, 96% of the respondents holding memberships in the AFWUF and 85% of those involved in REAL Women also belong to "right-to-life" groups. Furthermore, all of the leaders of the pro-family movement that I interviewed had been activists in the anti-abortion movement. Such overlaps suggest the high compatibility of groups that are specifically anti-abortion with groups that label themselves pro-family.

PRO-FAMILY ADHERENTS

Women constitued 57% of the survey respondents, and the average

age of both women and men was a surprisingly high 49. Otherwise the pro-family supporters are close to the Canadian norm. Seventy-one percent were born in Canada, and slightly over half (54%) of this mostly English-speaking group are of British Isles descent. They grew up on farms, in small towns, or in medium-sized villages; only 33% were raised in metropolitan centres. Their parents were people of average or somewhat below average education and income. A large majority reported that their parents did not finish high school (not surprising, perhaps, for people who were of school age prior to World War II), while only 27% reported that their fathers held professional or even semiprofessional jobs. Asked how well off they were when growing up, only 14% reported their childhood circumstances "above average"; 29% said that their families were "poor."

Not surprisingly for a group with an average age of almost fifty, there are obvious gender differences in occupation, income, and education. Of those men that are in the paid labour force (72% of all men in the sample), an impressive 50% have professional status (16% are semi-professionals; 7% are in clerical positions; 22% are skilled or semi-skilled workers; and 5% are unskilled). In terms of income, 41% of the men earn $49,000 or more per annum, and only 20% earn less than $20,000. Regarding education, some 28% have MA, Ph.D., or professional degrees, while another 18% have BAS Only 18% did not finish high school. Pro-family men, it seems, are upwardly mobile to a remarkable degree – an experience that is likely to colour their views on many political matters.

Among women, this accent on upward ascent, career achievement, and economic privilege is not nearly so pronounced. Only 34% of female respondents are in the paid labour force, and among this minority, 27% are professionals – a not inconsiderable number, but not nearly as high as among their male counterparts. Even more indicative is the fact that only 15% of these jobholding women have advanced academic or professional degrees; and by the same token only 9% reported personal incomes of $49,000 or more per annum.

But if these women had fewer career and educational achievements to their credit (which is only what we might expect), they were not necessarily less satisfied with their lives. Among the 51% who were homemakers, very few indicated any desire to work outside the home (25% reported that they were "satisfied" and an extraordinary 75% "very satisfied" in this role). And even among the few who reported that they would like to be employed, virtually all (99%) said that they were thinking of part-time, not full-time work.

Adding to this general picture of achievement and satisfaction is the fact that a full 39% of respondents had a total family income of

$49,000 or more, while 79% owned their homes. Some 79% also were married (for an average of 22 years) or widowed, while only 3% were divorced or separated. Respondents tended to have large families, 69% had more than three children.

All told, then, we are dealing with people who not only have made a success of their marriages and careers, but have done so by playing by the rules. Their lives, in effect, are an affirmation of the traditional marital and gender values of the pre-pill era. That a solid majority of these mostly middle-aged and middle-class individuals had the advantage of beginning their marriages and careers in the forties, fifties, and sixties – before the contractions of the Canadian economy and the increased competition for middle-class jobs and status of the past fifteen years – is not something that impinges a lot on their political consciousness. But it does much, I feel, to explain their high idealism and their fierce commitment to their cause.

RELIGIOUS INTERESTS

Seventy-eight percent of the sample were Roman Catholics and 17% Protestant fundamentalists, with only a scattering (less than 5%) from the United and Anglican churches and other faiths. But this distribution – which may overstate the preponderance of Catholics[4] – is less important than what respondents report about the place of religion in their lives. Here they differ sharply from average Canadians.

Ninety-three percent of the respondents said religion was "very important" to them, while 65% said it had been "very important" in the families they grew up in. More than threequarters (78%) sent their children to religious schools. Even more revealing, a full 63% attend church twice or more a week. That this indicates an unusual degree of religiosity is evident when we make some comparison with the 1981 Quality of Life (QOL) survey of adult Canadians. For example, some 96% of pro-family supporters attend church at least once a week, compared to only 30% of QOL respondents. When we recall that fewer than 5% of pro-family supporters belong to the United, Anglican, and other mainstream Protestant churches, it is difficult not to conclude that the movement has thus far had little success in breaking out of an atypical constituency of devout Canadians.

Religion also plays a key role in the mobilization of the pro-family forces; their recruitment network is located in the fundamentalist and Catholic churches. This type of networking provides the tremendous advantage of a large potential base of sympathetic, like-minded people who are not only susceptible to pro-family appeals, but also accessible, since the church encourages members to support the movement and to promote its causes.[5] The church provides financial support, office space, equipment, and free advertising in religious publications. In sum, the movement's support base is located in established, sympathetic groups, which largely accounts for their capacity to mobilize such large numbers of supporters on any given occasion. (REAL Women claimed a membership of 10,000 at their first press conference, before they had published their first newsletter.) There has been little attempt to recruit outside existing networks.

IDEOLOGY

The degree of seriousness with which different "threats to the family" are perceived indicates the siege-like mentality that characterizes the movement. Table 1 shows that the declining influence of religion, the undermining of traditional values in the media, pornography, and the spread of secular humanism represent "very serious" threats to 69% or more of pro-family supporters (loss of parental control over children, gay rights, and feminism are seen as only slightly less menacing by 63%, 57% and 54% respectively).

By contrast, the least serious threat is the economic hardships that families face today – a not unexpected finding among people whose own lives tend to exemplify the success ethic of the forties and the fifties.

When we look more closely at attitudes toward the women's movement, divorce, day care, mothers working outside the home, and other matters impinging on the family (these data are not included in this article), there are few inconsistencies in the pro-family outlook. Eighty-nine percent agree that feminism has devalued motherhood; 86% feel that it has undermined the traditional family; and almost as many (74%) believe that most Canadians do not support the goals of the women's movement. On the other hand, 63% allow that feminism has helped women in the work force, which suggests some acceptance of feminist efforts in this area.

In the pro-family world view, women and men are seen as occupying complementary but different spheres; as the REAL Women motto states "men and women are equal but different." "Different spheres" translates into women as mothers, in the home, caring for their families, and men as the breadwinners. A woman's very essence is defined by her childbearing capabilities and responsibilities. Not only is mothering and homemaking the most important role in so-

Table 1
Threats to Family as Perceived by Pro-Family Supporters

Threat	Seriousness of Threat					
	Very Serious		Somewhat Serious		Not Serious	
	%	No.	%	No.	%	No.
Declining influence of religion	83	677	15	120	2	15
Undermining of traditional values	81	654	18	143	1	10
Pornography	73	592	23	185	4	32
Spread of secular humanism	68	544	27	212	5	40
Loss of parental control over children	63	511	31	252	6	48
Influences of the gay rights movements	57	462	31	253	12	93
Influences of the feminist movement	54	437	36	289	10	83
Sex education in the schools	43	338	36	284	21	172
Economic hardships facing families today	26	210	44	358	30	243

ciety, but it is both naturally given and divinely sanctioned. Hence the frequent references in pro-family rhetoric to the sanctity of the family (read: the continuation of the public/private division). As we see in table 2, fewer than 15% of respondents approved of women with children under thirteen years working outside the home.

Pro-family supporters do not see a need for daycare reforms or affirmative action programs. Needless to say, the actual stresses and strains that beset families today and the concrete measures that might alleviate them are not a concern of the movement. For example, as indicated in table 3, only one person in the sample was prepared to say that daycare funding should be entirely the government's responsibility. More revealing is the finding that only 6% of respondents wanted daycare costs shared between government and parents, compared with 41% of Canadians generally (QOL 1981). The irony is, of course, that today the majority of women are in the paid labour force where they are unlikely to receive equal treatment, and are further disadvantaged by lack of daycare.

The pro-family view that women should stick to traditional roles is further reflected in the finding that those approving of the ordination of women as Catholic priests or Protestant ministers were only 12% and 19% respectively. This is compared with 76% approval found for women as Protestant ministers in a 1976 Gallup poll. Seventy-three percent of pro-family respondents said that husbands

Table 2
Opinions on Married Women Taking Full-Time Jobs Outside the Home
(in Percentages)

	Pro-Family Survey			1982 Gallup Poll		
	Approve	Disapprove	Depends*	Approve	Disapprove	Don't Know
Family Circumstances						
With pre-schoolers	3	62	35	38	54	8
With children 6–12 years old	11	38	51	NA	NA	NA
With teenagers	26	22	52	NA	NA	NA
With no children	77	4	19	87	8	5
With elderly parents that need care	16	28	56	NA	NA	NA
With child with handicap that needs care	8	53	39	NA	NA	NA

* Depends on financial need.

Table 3
Attitudes Towards Day Care Funding

Source of daycare funding	Pro-Family Respondents		1982 Gallup Poll	
	%	No.	%	No.
Entirely from government taxes	0.1	1	NA	NA
Entirely from parents' incomes	42.0	340	49.0	514
Partly from taxes and partly From parents' incomes	6.0	50	41.0	431
Depends on parents' income*	51.0	415	5.0	52
Don't know**	NA	NA	5.0	52

Source: Ginette Lafleur, "L'industrialisation et le travail rémunéré des femmes, Moncton, 1881–91"

* This response was worded "qualified" in the Gallup Poll.
** This response was *not* included in the pro-family survey.

should take more responsibility for childcare, while 68% felt that husbands should share in housework while still remaining head of the family. That more men (77%) than women (61%) (p ⟨ .05) approved of such sharing is especially interesting. It is consistent with a similar finding that 35% of pro-family women but only 19% of men felt help should be provided only when the wife works outside the home. While the difference may simply reflect a kind of surface worldliness among male respondents, it may well be linked to the status of women supporters as homemakers. In their zeal to protect what little power they may have in this domain, they may have become even more conservative than their male counterparts.

Pro-family supporters are also alarmed by a loss of control over their children, especially where sexual attitudes are concerned; they oppose sex education and feel that the schools and the media are transmitting amoral, anti-family values. Since respondents believe that sex should be bound to procreation, homosexuality is frowned upon. While they have secular reasons for this antipathy, the core of pro-family opposition to gay rights is religious. Homosexuality is not only anti-family, it is obscene and blasphemous.

POLITICAL ATTITUDES AND AFFILIATIONS

Not only are pro-family supporters more interested in politics than the average Canadian professes to be (84% versus an interest level of 60% found in a 1981 QOL survey), they are also a good deal more politically active. Thus 29% had volunteered during a political campaign (compared with a QOL finding of 16%); 57% had worked with others to solve community problems (compared with a QOL finding of 33%); 83% had signed petitions directed at government agencies (compared with a QOL finding of 41%); and 57% had attended demonstrations or rallies (compared with a QOL finding of 18%).

Conclusions about whether this high degree of political interest and activity accounts for respondents' involvement in the pro-family movement or whether it is a consequence of their involvement cannot be drawn from the data collected in this survey. However, the finding that 72% of respondents had *never* been active in a political group prior to joining a pro-family organization, suggests that it is their experience in the movement that "politicized" them.

Evidence of extensive alienation from the political process shows up in the survey findings. Eighty-six percent of respondents felt that the Progressive Conservative sweep in the 1984 federal election has done little or nothing to promote profamily causes. Furthermore, responses to the question: "If a federal election were held today who would you vote for?" show that respondents were dissatisfied with *all* three political parties: 10% would vote for the Liberals, 11% for the Progressive Conservatives, and only 2% for the New Democrats; by contrast, 55% would vote for the strongest pro-life candidate regardless of party affiliation. (Many respondents, however, indicated in the margin of the questionnaire that they would not vote for the NDP under any circumstances.)

Significantly, 32% of the sample saw themselves as single-issue voters, that is, "supporters of the strongest pro-life/profamily candidate," which compares with the 25% who saw themselves as Conservatives, 22% as Liberals, or 2% as New Democrats. By the same token, some 40% said they supported the formation of a pro-family political party, while another 23% are undecided on this matter.[6]

And if disaffection with the political parties was pronounced, disaffection with the media was even more so. Not only do pro-family adherents see the media as a major threat to the family, some 81% also believe that it has too much power. A remarkable 83% felt that media coverage of their own activities is "poor," compared with only 5% who saw it as "good." Interestingly enough, there were no significant differences in attitudes toward different types of media, though local press coverage was rated slightly more favourably.

There were no significant (p $<$ .05) gender or occupational differences for any of the variables measuring political activity or attitudes. This is an especially interesting finding inasmuch as it suggests that the pro-family movement has been successful in getting homemakers, who comprise over 30% of the respondents, to participate in the political arena. Homemakers are a constituency which, despite the influences of the feminist movement and the increasing number of women entering the paid labour force in the past two decades, has tended to remain politically isolated because of their immersion in the family. Because the movement's recruitment network is largely located in the conservative churches, it has succeeded in mobilizing a specific type of homemaker – the deeply religious one.

Among the most noteworthy findings of this research are the homogeneity of pro-family opinions across gender, class, and religious boundaries; the intensity with which these opinions are held; and the evidence that the movement has mobilized people who have not previously participated in politics. Can we also conclude that the movement speaks for a "silent" majority of Canadians? Certainly pro-family supporters are much like average Canadians in many of their social-demographic characteristics. By the same token, however, their extraordinary religiosity and moral absolutism – that fewer than 5% belong to the mainstream Protestant churches is especially telling in this regard – and their marked disaffection with the parties and the media – all suggest a high degree of social isolation.

Sometimes, of course, such isolated and dedicated types do succeed in putting their stamp on society, but rarely when they constitute a backlash phenomenon. Here it is well to recall the relatively ad-

vanced years of these ardent antifeminists. To repeat a point made
earlier, we see among their ranks a relatively affluent, largely middle-
class, and, with an average age of forty-nine, a decidedly middle-
aged contingent – people whose lives exemplify the conservative
values of the post-World War II period. That those values have been
eroded sharply since the sixties has a lot to do with economic factors
that have not, for the most part, impinged on this upwardly mobile
group. Should we see a severe worsening of economic conditions
and living standards (not a remote possibility, by any means) then
the latent message of the pro-family movement – that it makes sense
to swing the pendulum back to traditional lifestyles – may well appeal
to a much wider constituency. Otherwise, the ambivalence that most
Canadians feel towards abortion, mothers working outside the home,
and other matters touching on gender roles is likely to remain a
barrier to the movement's advance.

Perhaps the most important lesson feminists can draw from the
recent appearance of the pro-family phenomenon is that a significant
number of Canadian women feel slighted or threatened by the feminist agenda, and that it behooves us, as feminists, to try to understand their outlook. Rather than simply dismissing their politics as
irrational, we need to look closely at both the status and material
benefits such women have derived from their positions as traditional
wives and mothers. And perhaps, most significantly, we need to
address ourselves to why these women choose antifeminism over
feminism. Only by looking at these kinds of issues will we begin to
find effective ways of responding to pro-family appeals.

APPENDIX

Survey Design and Data

The sample used in the pro-family survey was drawn from the subscription lists of *The Interim*, a movement publication edited in Toronto, which calls itself "Canada's pro-life, pro-family newspaper."
Its readership numbers in the tens of thousands, it circulates in all
parts of Canada, and it is not officially tied to any particular organization or subsection of the pro-family universe. In other words,
its claim to being the national voice of the movement is a reasonable
one. One would assume that its subscribers, almost all of whom had
paid the subscription fee when the questionnaires were mailed, were
relatively, though not necessarily inordinately, committed to the
cause it served.

Accordingly, standard probability methods were used to select a random sample of subscriber names and addresses from the *The Interim*'s list (N = 46, 677). A total of 1,200 names and addresses were selected to receive the survey questionnaire. At selected addresses where two or more names were listed, one respondent was chosen (N = 160, thus reducing the sample by 80 to 1,120). Incorrect addresses or vacant dwellings accounted for 41 of these addresses, further reducing the base to 1,079. From this base, some 812 questionnaires were returned, a completion rate of 75%. The tasks of drafting the questionnaire, collecting and analyzing the data were my responsibility. The data processing was handled by York University's Institute for Social Research.

The questionnaire took about twenty-five minutes to fill out. The first of its four sections dealt with the various ways in which respondents were involved in the movement, the intensity of that involvement, and how the respondents themselves interpreted their activities. The second section elicited attitudinal data on the family and the forces perceived to be threatening it, as well as on a number of related social and moral issues. The third section included measures of attitudes and behaviour concerning more general political matters such as political efficacy, support for political parties, and support for government spending in various areas. The final section elicited standard "demographic" information on each respondent, including extensive measures of religious interests and behaviour.

NOTES

1 Chafetz and Dworkin, in their historical and crosscultural analysis of antifeminist movements, point out that women's movements have frequently given rise to backlash movements. Arguing that the changes women's movements have called for have "inevitably threatened vested interests," they suggest that "when their threat is perceived as major, backlash movements have arisen" (1987, 33–5).

2 See, for example, Eisenstein (1982, 77–98); Gordon and Hunter (1977–78, 9–25); Davis (1981, 28–49); Dworkin (1983); Pohli (1983, 529–58); Frenier (1984, 455–65); Mueller (1983, 213–29); Conover and Gray (1983); Crawford (1980); Chafetz and Dworkin (1987, 33–60); Marshall (1985, 348–62); and Luker (1984); and for the most comprehensive and insightful discussion of antifeminism and New Right politics, see Petchesky (1981, 206–46).

3 See Eichler (1985), and Dubinsky (1985).

4 While *The Interim* has an ecumenical appeal to all sections of the movement, it does have informal ties with Campaign Life, which has a large number

of Catholic supporters.

5 Pohli (1983) makes the point that Protestant evangelical women are not a monolith; while some of these women are susceptible to "pro-family" appeals, others may be equally susceptible to feminist agendas.

6 While the temptations of electoral office for movements seeking a platform for their views are always large, operating outside the existing parties is likely to pose grave risks for the movement's leadership. Not only will they risk losing some religious backing, but the movement may well appear to be even more marginalized than it already does to the Canadian public. Yet operating within the existing parties also poses its problems, inasmuch as it entails compromising and muting the message – no easy feat for those with idealistic and absolutist views. So far, in any case, the anti-abortion groups have largely confined their efforts to attempting to defeat pro-choice candidates. I know of no pro-family attempts to capture Conservative riding associations (so as to ensure candidates whose first loyalty is to the cause, not to the party). And unlike their feminist rivals, they have yet to exploit the electoral process to get their message across.

Bibliography
Bibliographie

Acton, Janice et al., eds. 1974. *Women at Work: Ontario, 1850–1930.* Toronto: Canadian Women's Educational Press.

Alcoff, Linda 1986. "Cultural Feminism Versus Post-Structuralism: The Identity Crisis in Feminist Theory." Paper presented to the Society for Women in Philosophy at the American Philosophical Association, Boston.

Al-Issa, I., ed. 1982. *Gender and Psychopathology.* New York: Academic Press.

Alpine's St. John's Business Directory. 1907–1908.

Amenson, C.S. and P.M. Lewinsohn 1981. "An Investigation into the Observed Sex Difference in Prevalence of Unipolar Depression." *Journal of Abnormal Psychology* 90: 1–13.

American College of Obstetricians and Gynecologists 1983. *Ethical Issues in Surrogate Motherhood.* ACOG Statement of Policy.

The American Fertility Society (Ethics Committee) 1986. "Ethical Considerations of the New Reproductive Technologies." *Fertility and Sterility* 46 (3), supplement 1.

Andersen, Marguerite 1983–4. « Le Québec: féminisme contemporain et écrits de femmes (1970-83). » *Documentation sur la recherche féministe* 12 (4): 18–28.

American Psychiatric Association 1980. *Diagnostic and Statistical Manual of Mental Disorders.* 3rd ed. Washington, D.C.

Anderson, John E. 1976. "Planning Status of Marital Births, 1975–76." *Family Planning Perspectives* 13 (2): 62–70.

Angst, J., and A. Dobler-Mikola 1984. "Do Diagnostic Criteria Determine the Sex Ratio in Depression?" *Journal of Affective Disorders* 7: 189–98.

Antler, Ellen 1983. "Fisherman, Fisherwoman, Rural Proletariat: Capitalists' Commodity Production in the Newfoundland Fishery." Ph.D. diss., University of Connecticut.

Arditti, Rita, Renate Julie Klein and Shelley Minden, eds. 1984. *Test-Tube Women: What Future for Motherhood.* London: Pandora Press.

Arendt, Hannah 1972 [1969]. *Du mensonge à la violence: Essais de politique contemporaine.* Paris: Calmann-Lévy.

Arms, Suzanne 1975. *Immaculate Deception: A New Look at Women and Childbirth in America.* Boston: Houghton Mifflin.

Armstrong, Pat and Hugh Armstrong 1984. *The Double Ghetto.* Toronto: McClelland and Stewart.

Atwood, Margaret 1985. *The Handmaid's Tale.* Toronto: McClelland and Stewart.

Banks, Olive 1981. *Faces of Feminism.* Oxford: Oxford University Press.

Barber, M. 1985. "The Women Ontario Welcomed: Immigrant Domestics for Ontario Homes 1870–1930." In *The Neglected Majority,* vol 2. See Prentice and Trofimenkoff 1985.

Barel, Yves 1982. *La Marginalité sociale.* Paris: Presses Universitaires de France.

Barker-Benfield, G.J. 1976. *The Horrors of the Half-Known Life.* New York: Harper and Row.

Barrett, Michelle 1985. *Women's Oppression Today.* Thetford, England: Thetford Press.

Barrett, M. and Mary McIntosh 1980. "The 'Family Wage': Some Problems for Socialists and Feminists." *Capital and Class* 2 (Summer): 51–72.

Barthez, A. 1983. « Le travail familial et les rapports de domination dans l'agriculture. » *Nouvelles questions féministes.* Labourage et pâturage: le patriarcat en campagne. 5 (printemps): 19–46.

Baruch, Elaine Hoffman 1980. "Ibsen's *Doll's House*: A Myth for Our Time." *Yale Review* (Spring): 374–87.

Beaulieu, Carole 1985. "Droits de la reproduction: serons-nous des incubateurs ambulants?" *La vie en rose* (avril): 14–15.

Bebbington, P., J. Hurry, C. Tennant, E. Sturt, and J.K. Wing 1981. "Epidemiology of Mental Disorders in Camberwell." *Psychological Medicine* 11: 561–79.

Bebbington, P., E. Sturt, C. Tennant, and J. Hurry 1984. "Misfortune and Resilience: A Community Study of Women." *Psychological Medicine* 14: 347–63.

Beck, A.T., A.J. Rush, B.F. Shaw, and G. Emery 1979. *Cognitive Therapy of Depression.* New York: Guilford Press.

Beckman, L.J. 1984. "Treatment Needs of Women Alcoholics." *Alcoholism Treatment Quarterly* 1 (2): 101–13.

Beechey, Veronica 1981. "Women and Production: A Critical Analysis of Some Sociological Theories of Women's Work.'. In *Education and the State,* vol. 2 of *Politics, Patriarchy and Practice.* Lewes: Falmer Press, 115–40.

– 1982. "Algunas Notas sobre el trabajo asalariado femenino en la producción capitalista." In Secretaria de Programación y Presupuesto. *Estudios sobre la Mujer.* Tomo I. Mexico. 377–99.

Belenky, M.F., B.M. Clinchy, N.R. Goldberger, and J.M. Tarule 1986. *Women's Ways of Knowing: The Development of Self, Voice and Mind*. New York: Basic Books.

Benbow, Camilla P., and Julian C. Stanley 1980. "Sex Differences in Mathematical Ability: Fact or Artifact?" *Science* 210: 1262–4.

Bernard J. 1973. "My Four Revolutions: An Autobiographical History of the American Sociological Association." *American Journal of Sociology* 78 (4): 773–91.

– 1981. *The Female World*. New York: Free Press.

Black. N., and A.B. Cottrell, eds. 1981. *Women and World Change*. London: Sage.

Bordo, Susan 1986. "The Cartesian Masculinization of Thought." *Signs: Journal of Women in Culture and Society* 11 (3): 439–56.

Bowker, L.H. 1983. *Beating Wife Beating*. Toronto: Lexington.

Bowles, Gloria and Renate Julie Klein, eds. 1983. *Theories of Women's Studies*. Boston: Routledge and Kegan Paul.

Boyle, Christine, Marie Andrée Bertrand, Céline Lacerte-Lamontagne, et Rebecca Shamai 1985. *Un examen féministe du droit criminel au Canada*. Ottawa: Ministre des approvisionnements et services, et Condition féminine Canada.

Bradbury, Bettina 1983. « L'économie familiale et le travail dans une ville en voie d'industrialisation: Montréal dans les années 1870. » Dans *Maîtresses de maison et maîtresses d'école*. Voir Fahmy-Eid et Dumont 1983, 287–318.

Brandt, G.C. 1981. "Weaving It Together: Life Cycle and the Industrial Experience of Female Cotton Workers in Quebec, 1910–1950." *Labour/Le Travailleur* 7 (Spring): 113–26.

Breton, Y. 1977. "The Influence of Modernization on the Modes of Production in Coastal Fishing: An Example from Venezuela." In *Those Who Live from the Sea*. See Smith 1977, 125–37.

Broadside 1 (1).

Brodie, M. Janine, and Jill McCalla-Vickers 1982. *Canadian Women in Politics: An Overview*. The CRIAW Papers 2. Ottawa: CRIAW.

Brossard, Nicole 1982. *Picture Theory*. Montreal: Nouvelle Optique.

Buerk, Dorothy 1986. "Sharing Meanings in Mathematics." *Radical Teacher* 30: 26–29.

Bureau international du travail (BIT) 1982. *Women and Development: The Sexual Division of Labour in Rural Societies: A Study*.

Burton, Leone, ed. 1986. *Girls into Math Can Go*. London: Holt, Rinehart and Winston.

Buvinic, Mayra, Margaret Lycette, and W.P. McGreevey 1983. *Women and Poverty in the Third World*. London: Johns Hopkins University Press.

Campbell, J. 1984. "Nursing Care of Abused Women." In *Nursing Care of*

Victims of Family Violence, edited by J. Campbell and J. Humphreys. Reston: Reston. 246–80.

Canada 1929. *Sixth Census of Canada. 1921*. Ottawa: The King's Printer.

– 1986. *Rapport de la Commission d'enquête sur l'assurance chômage (Commission Forget)*. Approvisionnement et Services. 259–65, 517–20.

– 1975–84. *Revue statistique annuelle des pêches canadiennes*. Pêches et Océans Canada no. 9–17.

– 1985. *Commission royale sur l'Union économique et les perspectives de développement du Canada (Rapport MacDonald)*. Approvisionnement et Services. Tome 2. 647–76.

"Can You Choose Your Child's Sex? Maybe." *Verve*, (Aug./Sept. 1986): 71.

Cartwright, Ann 1979. *The Dignity of Labour: A Study of Childbearing and Induction*. London: Tavistock.

Castel, Robert 1983. « De la dangerosité au risque. » *Actes de la recherche en sciences sociales* 47–8: 119–27.

Chafetz, Janet Saltzman, and Anthony Gary Dworkin 1987. "In the Face of Threat: Organized Antifeminism in Comparative Perspective." *Gender and Society* 1 (1): 33–60.

Chegwidden, P., L.F. Felt, and A. Miller 1981. "Battered Women: Myths, Realities and New Directions for Future Research." *Atlantis* 6: 186–93.

Chickering, A., ed. 1981. *The Modern American College*. CA: Jossey Bass.

Chipman, Susan F., R. Lorelei Brush, and Donna M. Wilson, eds. 1985. *Women and Mathematics: Balancing the Equation*. Hillsdale, New Jersey: Lawrence Erlbaum.

Chisholm, Jessie 1986. "Working-Class Women as Wage Earners, St. John's 1890–1914." Unpublished paper, Memorial University of Newfoundland.

Code, Lorraine 1987. *Epistemic Responsibility*. Hanover: University Press of New England.

– 1987. "Tokenism." *Resources for Feminist Research* 16 (3): 46–8.

Colby, Marion. "Women's Studies: An Inclusive Concept for an Inclusive Concept." *Canadian Women's Studies* 1 (1): 4–6.

Collectif Clio 1982. *L'histoire des femmes au Québec depuis quatre siècles*. Montréal: Quinze.

Collectif italien 1983. « Plus femmes qu'hommes. » *Change international* 1: 74–9.

Collin, Françoise 1985. « Le temps natal. » *Cahiers du GRIF* 30: 63–83.

Comparat, Françoise 1981. « Stéréotypes, métier scientifique et féminisme. » *Pénélope* 4: 28–31.

Conover, Pamela Johnston, and Virginia Gray 1983. *Feminism and the New Right: Conflict over the American Family*. New York: Praeger.

Conrad, Peter, and Rochelle Kearn, eds. 1967. *The Sociology of Health and Ilness: Critical Perspectives*. New York: St, Martin's Press.

Conseil de la science et de la technologie 1986. *La participation des femmes en science et technologie au Québec. Avis au ministre de l'enseignement supérieur et de la science.* Document no 86.06. Québec: Gouvernement du Québec.

Copeland, Jeff, and Mary Hagar 1986. "Couples Playing Doctor and God." *Newsweek* Oct. 6.

Corea, Gena 1985. *The Mother Machine: Reproductive Technologies from Artificial Insemination to Artificial Wombs.* New York: Harper and Row.

– 1984. "Egg Snatchers." In *Test-Tube Women.* See Arditti et al. 1984, 37–51.

– 1977. *The Hidden Malpractice: How American Medicine Mistreats Women.* New York: Jove Publications.

Countryman, Joan 1986. "Gender and Mathematics." *Radical Teacher* (30): 23–5.

Cournoyer, Monique 1987. « L'accouchement, d'hier à aujourd'hui: les femmes crient de la Baie-James. » Dans *Accoucher autrement.* Voir Saillant et O'Neill 1987, 99–122.

Covington, S.S., and J. Kohen 1984. "Women, Alcohol and Sexuality." *Advances in Alcohol and Substance Abuse* (41): 41–56.

Crawford, Alan 1980. *Thunder on the Right: The "New Right" and the Politics of Resentment.* New York: Pantheon Books.

Cross, D. Suzanne 1977. « La majorité oubliée: le rôle des femmes à Montréal au 19e siècle. » Dans *Les femmes dans la société québécoise: aspects historiques.* Montréal: Boréal Express. 33–59.

Culley, Margaret 1985. "Anger and Authority in the Introductory Women's Studies Classroom." In *Gendered Subjects.* See Culley and Portuges 1985, 209–17.

Culley, Margaret, and Catherine Portuges, eds. 1985. *Gendered Subjects.* Boston: Routledge and Kegan Paul.

Cyr, Jean-Roch 1982. « Les Acadiens de Moncton: aspects d'histoire sociale, 1698–1881. » Master's thesis, University of Moncton.

D'Entremont, Henri L. 1888. « À nos filles acadiennes. » *L'Evangéline* (Digby N.-E.) 28 mars.

Dalton, Clare 1985. "Remarks on Personhood." Paper presented to the Faculty of Law, Queen's University, Kingston.

Daly, Mary 1978. *Gyn/Ecology: The Metaethics of Radical Feminism.* Boston: Beacon Press.

Dassylva, Martial 1972. « Évangéline est morte; vive la Sagouine. » *La Presse* (Montréal), 14 oct.

Davis, Tracy C. 1985. "Ibsen's Victorian Audience." *Essays in Theatre* 4 (1): 21–38.

Davis, Mike 1981. "The Rise of the New Right." *New Left Review* 128 (July-Aug.): 28–49.

Davis, Barbara Hillyer 1985. "Teaching the Feminist Minority." In *Gendered Subjects.* See Cully and Portuges 1985, 245–52.

Davis, N. 1981. "Women's Work and Worth in Acadian Maritime Villages." In *Women and World Change*. See Black and Cottrell 1981.

Dawkins, R. 1976. *The Selfish Gene*. London: Oxford University Press.

Deere, Carmen Diana 1982. « La producción de subsistancia de la mujer rural en la periferia capitalista." In Secretaría de Programación y Presupuesto. *Estudios sobre la Mujer*. Tomo I. Mexico. 123–217.

De Koninck, Maria 1987. « Multiplication des césariennes: phénomène chirugical ou ... officine de laboratoire. » Dans *Accoucher autrement*. Voir Saillant et O'Neill 1987, 239–59.

de Laurentis, Theresa 1986. "Feminist Studies/Critical Studies: Issues, Terms and Contexts." In *Feminist Studies/Critical Studies*, edited by Theresa de Laurentis. Bloomington: Indiana University Press.

Delphy, Christine 1984. *Close to Home*. London: Hutchinson.

– 1983. « Agriculture et travail domestique: la réponse de la bergère à Engels. » *Nouvelles questions féministes*. Labourage et pâturage: le patriarcat en campagne 5 (printemps): 3–17.

Descarries-Bélanger, Francine, and Micheline de Sève 1985. « Bilans et enjeux des études féministes au Québec. » *Perspectives féministes 3*.

de Sève, Micheline 1985. *Pour un féminisme libertaire*. Montréal: Boréal Express.

DeVries, Raymond G. 1985. *Regulating Birth: Midwives, Medicine and the Law*. Philadelphia: Temple University Press.

Dewey J. 1938. *Experience and Education*. Kappa Delta Pi.

Dickson, David 1986. "Britain's Royal Society Condemns Sex Bias in Math Teaching." *Science* 233: 618–19.

Dinitz, S., R.R. Dynes, and A.C. Clarke 1954. "Preferences for Male or Female Children: Traditional or Affectional?" *Marriage and Family Living* 16: 128–30.

Dixon, Richard D., and Diane Levy 1985. "Sex of Children: A Community Analysis of Preferences and Predetermination Attitudes." *Sociological Quarterly* 26 (2): 251–71.

Dobash, R.E., and R.P. Dobash 1979. *Violence Against Wives: A Case Against the Patriarchy*. New York: Free Press.

Dohrenwend, B.P., B.S. Dohrenwend, M.S. Gould, B. Link, R. Neugebauer, and R. Wunsch-Hitzig, eds. 1980. *Mental Illness in the United States: Epidemiological Estimates*. New York: Praeger.

Donegan, Jane 1978. *Women and Men Midwives: Medicine, Morality and Misogyny in Early America*. Westport, Conn.: Greenwood Press.

Donnison J. 1977. *Midwives and Medical Man*. London: Heineman.

Dubinsky, Karen 1985. "Lament for a 'Patriarchy Lost'? AntiFeminism, Anti-Abortion and R.E.A.L. Women in Canada." Ottawa: CRIAW.

Dubois, Barbara 1983. "Passionate Scholarship." In *Theories of Women's Studies*. See Bowles and Klein 1983.

Dumais, Hélène 1987. « Du côté des personnes du sexe ... » *Québec français* 66: 22–3.

Dumont, Micheline 1983. « Des garderies au 19e siècle: les salles d'asile des Soeurs Grises à Montréal. » Dans *Maîtresses de maison et maîtresses d'école.* Voir Fahmy-Eid and Dumont 1983, 261–85.

Dworkin, Andrea 1983. *Right Wing Women.* New York: Putman's Sons.

Edgar, Joanne 1981. "Iceland's Feminists: Power at the Top of the World." *MS* 16 (6): 30–7.

Ehrenreich, Barbara, and Deidre English 1973. *Witches, Midwives and Nurses: A History of Women Healers.* Old Westbury, N.Y.: Feminist Press.

Ehrlich, Carol 1965. "An Anarchofeminist Looks at Power Relationships." *Quest, A Feminist Quarterly* 5 (4): 76–83.

Eichler, Margaret 1986. "The Pro-Family Movement: Are They For or Against Families?" Ottawa: CRIAW.

Eisenstein, Zillah 1982. "The Sexual Politics of the New Right: In Understanding the 'Crisis of Liberalism' for the 1980's." In *Feminist Theory: A Critique of Ideology.* See Keohane, 1982. 77–98.

Elgin, Suzette Haden 1984. *Native Tongue.* New York: Daw Books.

England 1898. *Evidence as to a Revision of the Tariff Taken Before the Receiver-General.* St. John's.

– 1915. *Royal Commion on the Natural Resources, Trade and Legislation of Certain Parts of His Majesty's Dominions.* The Dominions Royal Commission. London: Eyre and Spattiswade.

– 1923. *Census of Newfoundland and Labrador, 1921.* St. John's: Colonial Secretary's Office.

Ericsson, R.J., C.N. Langevin, and M. Nishino 1973. "Isolations of Fractions Rich in Human Y Sperm." *Nature* 246: 421–4.

Etzioni, Amitai 1968. "Sex Control, Science and Society." *Science* 161: 1107–12.

Evans, Marg 1979. "Feminist Party of Canada." *Broadside* 1(1).

Fahmy-Eid, Nadia, et Micheline Dumont, eds. 1983. *Maîtresses de maison et maitresses d'école.* Montreal: Boréal.

Feminist Party of Canada 1979–82. *Newsletter.*

– 1979. "The Beginnings of the Feminist Party of Canada" (broadsheet).

Femmes et formalisme 1985. Séminaire limites-frontières. Paris: Association LMF.

Fennema, Elizabeth 1979. "Women and Girls in Mathematics: Equity in Mathematics Education." *Educational Studies in Mathematics* 10: 389–401.

Ferland, Jacques 1982. « Le rôle des déterminismes sociaux dans le développement des forces productives de l'industrie textile du Canada – 1870 à 1910. » Master's thesis, McGill University.

Ferraro, K.J. 1983. "Rationalizing Violence: How Battered Women Stay." *Victimology* 8 (3–4): 203–12.

Ferraro, K.J. and J.M. Johnson 1983. "How Women Experience Battering: The Process of Victimization." *Social Problems* 30 (3): 325–39.

Finkelhor, D. 1979. *Sexually Victimized Children*. New York: Free Press.

Finkelhor, D. and K. Yllo 1982. "Forced Sex in Marriage: A Preliminary Research Report." *Crime and Delinquency* 28: 459–78.

Flitcraft, A. 1977. "Battered Women: An Emergency Room Epidemiology with a Description of a Clinical Syndrome and Critique of Present Therapeutics." Master's thesis, Yale Medical School.

Flynn, J.B., and J.C. Whitcomb 1981. "Unresolved Grief in Battered Women." *Journal of Emergency Nursing* 7: 250–4.

Forestell, Nancy 1987. "Women's Paid Labour in St. John's between the Two World Wars." Master's thesis, Memorial University of Newfoundland.

Foucault, Michel 1980. *Power/Knowledge*, edited by Colin Gordon. Translated by Colin Gordon, L. Marshall, J. Mepham, and K. Soper. New York: Pantheon.

– 1972. "The Discourse on Language." Translated by R. Swyer. In *The Archaeology of Knowledge*. Translated by Alan Sheridan. New York: Pantheon.

– 1965. *Madness and Civilization*. Translated by R. Howard. New York: Pantheon.

Franklin, U. 1984. " Will Women Change Technology or Will Technology Change Women?" In *Knowledge Reconsidered: A Feminist Overview*. Ottawa: CRIAW.

Freire, Paulo 1985. *The Politics of Education, Culture, Power and Liberation*. South Hadley: Bergin and Garvey.

– 1970. *Pedagogy of the Oppressed*. New York: Seabury Press.

Frenier, Mariam Darce 1984. "American Anti-Feminist Women: Comparing the Rhetoric of Opponents of the Equal Right's Amendment with that of Opponents of Women's Suffrage." *Women's Studies International Forum* 7 (6): 455–65.

Frerichs, R.R., C.S. Aneshensel, and V.A. Clark 1981. "Prevalence of Depression in Los Angeles County." *American Journal of Epidemiology* 113: 691–9.

Friedman, Susan Stanford 1985. "Authority in the Feminist Classroom: A Contradiction in Terms." In *Gendered Subjects*. See Culley and Portuges 1985, 203–8.

Frougny, Christiane, et Jeanne Peiffer 1984. *Formes et normes: Critiques du formalisme en mathématiques*. Séminaire limites-frontières, Bulletin 36.

Gilligan, C. 1982. *In a Different Voice*. Cambridge: Harvard University Press.

– 1979. "Women's Place in Man's Life Cycle." *Harvard Educational Review* 49: 431–46.

Gilroy, F., and R. Steinbacher 1983. "Preselection of Child's Sex: Technological Utilization and Feminism." *Psychological Reports* 53: 671–6.

Goldman, Emma 1914. *The Social Significance of Modern Drama*. Boston: Richard G. Badger.

Gordon, Linda, and Allen Hunter 1977–8. "Sex, Family, and the New Right: Anti-Feminism as a Political Force." *Radical America* 11–12 (Nov.-Feb.): 9–25.

Gore, S., and T.W. Mangione 1983. "Social Roles, Sex Roles and Psychological Distress: Additive and Interactive Models of Sex Differences." *Journal of Health and Social Behaviour* 24: 300–12.

Grace Maternity Hospital (Halifax, N.S.) 1983. *Role Study*.

Grimshaw, Jean 1986. *Philosophy and Feminist Thinking*. Minneapolis: University of Minnesota Press.

Guilbert, Louise 1985. « L'entrée des femmes dans les sciences, le génie et la technologie : dv/dt⩾0? » *Spectre* oct.

Guilbert, Madeleine 1966. *Les fonctions des femmes dans l'industrie*. Paris: Mouton.

Guillaumin, Colette 1978a. « Pratique du pouvoir et idée de Nature, (I) l'appropriation des femmes. » *Questions féministes* 2: 5–30.

– 1978b. « Pratique du pouvoir et idée de Nature, (II) le discours de la nature. » *Questions féministes* 3: 5–28.

Gunew, Sneja 1985. "Framing Marginality: Distinguishing the Textual Politics of the Marginal Voice." *Southern Review* 18.

Guttentag, M., S. Salasin, and D. Belle, eds. 1980. *The Mental Health of Women*. New York: Academic Press.

Hacker, Sally L. 1983. "Mathematization of Engineering: Limits on Women in the Field." In *Machina Ex Dea*. See Rothschild 1983, 38–58.

Hall, R.M., and B.R. Sandler 1982. *The Classroom Climate: A Chilly One for Women?* Washington D.C.: Project on the Status and Education of Women.

Hammen, C.L. 1982. "Gender and Depression." In *Gender and Psychopathology*. See Al-Issa 1982,133–52.

Hammen, C.L., and S.D. Peters 1977. "Differential Responses to Male and Female Depressive Reactions." *Journal of Consulting and Clinical Psychology* 45: 994–1001.

Hartsock, Nancy C.M. 1983. *Money, Sex and Power: Toward a Feminist Historical Materialism*. New York: Longman.

Harvey, Fernand 1978. *Révolution industrielle et travailleurs: une enquête sur les rapports entre le capital et le travail au Québec à la fin du 19e siècle*. Montréal: Boréal Express.

Hébert, Anne 1982. *Les fous de Bassan*. Paris: Editions du Seuil.

Heilbrun, Carolyn 1979. *Reinventing Womanhood*. New York: W.W. Norton 1979.

Henderson, S., P. Duncan-Jones, D.G. Byrne, R. Scott, and S. Adcock 1979. "Psychiatric Disorder in Canberra: A Standardised Study of Prevalence." *Acta Psychiatrica Scandinavica* 60: 355–74.

Hickey, Daniel 1986. "Moncton, 1871–1913: Commerce and Industry in a Railtown." Paper presented at the Atlantic Canada Workshop.

Holcombe, Lee 1973. *Victorian Ladies at Work*. Hamden.

Hughes, Patricia 1982. "Fighting the Good Fight: Separation or Integration?" In *Feminism in Canada*. See Miles and Finn 1982, 283–97.

Ibsen, Henrik 1961. *The Oxford Ibsen*. Vol. 5. Translated by James Walter McFarlane. London: Oxford.

Ilcan, Susan 1986. "Independent Commodity Production in the Nova Scotia Fishery." Gorse Brook Research Institute for Atlantic Canada Studies. Halifax, Nova Scotia: Saint Mary's University.

Isaacson, Zelda 1982. "Gender and mathematics in England and Wales." In *An International Review of Gender and Mathematics*. See Schildkamp-Kündiger 1982, 57–65.

Jacobs, Janis E., and Jacquelynne S. Eccles 1985. "Gender Differences in Math Ability: The Impact of Media Reports on Parents." *Educational Researcher* (March): 20–5.

Jenkins, R. 1985. "Sex Differences in Minor Psychiatric Morbidity." *Psychological Medicine*. Monograph Supplement 7.

Johnson, Leo 1974. "The Political Economy of Ontario Women in the Nineteenth Century." In *Women at Work*. See Acton et al. 1974, 12–31.

Johnston, P. 1984. "Abused Wives: Their Perception of the Help Offered by Mental Health Professionals." Unpublished independent inquiry project, Carleton University.

Jones, A. 1980. *Women Who Kill*. New York: Fawcett Columbine.

Jones, Henry Arthur, and Henry Herman 1884. *Breaking a Butterfly*. Produced at the Prince's Theatre and privately printed.

Jordan, Brigitte 1983. *Birth in Four Cultures*. Montreal: Eden Press.

Joy, John 1977. "The Growth and Development of Trades and Manufacturing in St. John's." Master's thesis, Memorial University of Newfoundland.

Kaplan, A. 1986. "The 'Self-in-Relation': Implications for Depression in Women." *Psychotherapy* 23: 234–42.

Katz Rothman, Barbara 1984. "The Meaning of Choice in Reproductive Technology." In *Test-Tube Women*. See Arditti et al. 1984, 23–33.

Katzman, D. 1978. *Seven Days a Week: Domestic Service in Industrializing America*. New York: Oxford University Press.

Kealy, Linda ed., 1979. *A Not Unreasonable Claim: Women and Reform in Canada, 1880's–1920's*. Toronto: The Women's Press.

Kelpin, Vangie, and Angéline Martel 1984. "The Language of Obstetrics from the Experience of Birthing." *Women: Images, Role Models*. Proceedings of the CRIAW Conference.

Keohane, Nannerl O., Michelle Z. Rosaldo, and Barbara C. Gelpi, eds. 1982. *Feminist Theory: A Critique of Ideology*. Chicago: University of Chicago Press.

Kieffer, Charles 1981. "The Emergence of Empowerment: The Development of Participatory Competence Among Individuals in Citizen Organizations." Ph.D. diss., University of Michigan.

Kimball, Meredith 1987. "A New Perspective on Women's Math Achievement." Unpublished manuscript, Department of Psychology, Simon Fraser University.

Kirkpatrick, Jean 1978. *Turnabout: Help for a New Life*. Garden City: Doubleday.

Klerman, G.L., and M.M. Weissman 1980. "Depressions Among Women: Their Nature and Causes." In *The Mental Health of Women*. See Gutentag et al. 1980, 57–92.

Knoppers, Bartha, and Elizabeth Sloss 1986. "Legislative Reforms in Reproductive Technology." Mimeographed.

Koblitz, Ann H. 1983. *A Convergence of Lives: Sofia Kovalevskaia, Scientist, Writer, Revolutionary*. Boston: Holt-Birkâuser.

Kolb, D. 1985. *Bibliography of Research on Experiential Learning Theory and the Learning Style Inventory*. Mimeograph.

– 1985 [1976]. *The Learning Style Inventory: Technical Manual*. Rev. ed. Boston: McBer.

– 1984. *Experiential Learning: Experience as the Source of Learning and Development*. Englewood Cliffs, N.J.: Prentice Hall.

– 1973. "On Management and the Learning Process." Sloan School Working Paper. Cambridge: MIT. 652–73.

Kubler-Ross, E. 1969. *On Death and Dying*. New York: Macmillan.

Labrecque, Marie F. 1986. « Femmes, travail et domination masculine au Mexique. » In *Anthropologie et Sociétés*. 10(1): 199–217.

Lacelle, Claudette 1982. « Les domestiques dans les villes canadiennes au XIXe siècle: effectifs et conditions de vie. » *Histoire Sociale/Social History* 15 (29): 181–207.

Lafortune, Louise, ed. 1986. *Femmes et mathématique*. Montréal: Les éditions du remue-ménage.

Landsberg, Michele 1986. "Norway's 40 per cent law: making equality second nature." *Globe and Mail* 7 June.

Langley, R., and R. Levy 1977. *Wife Beating: The Silent Crisis*. New York: Pocket.

Largey, Gale 1972. "Sex Control, Preferences, and the Future of the Family." *Social Biology* 19: 379–92.

Laurendeau, France 1983. « La médicalisation de l'accouchement. » *Recherches sociographiques* 24 (2): 203–34.

Lavigne, Marie, et Yolande Pinard 1983. *Travailleuses et féministes: les femmes dans la société québécoise*. Montréal: Boréal Express, 7–60.

Leacock, Eleanor, Helen I. Safa, and contributors 1986. *Women's Work: Development and the Division of Labor by Gender*. Massachussetts: Bergin and Garvey.

Leifer, Myra 1980. *Psychological Effects of Motherhood: A Study of the First Pregnancy*. New York: Praeger.

Leslie, Genvieve 1974. "Domestic Service in Canada, 1880–1920." In *Women at Work*. See Acton et al. 1974, 71–125.

Lester, Elenore 1978. "Ibsen's Unliberated Heroines." *Scandanavian Review* 66 (4): 58–66.

Lewin, K. 1951. *Field Theory in Social Sciences*. New York: Harper and Row.

Link, B., and B.P. Dohrenwend 1980. "Formulation of Hypotheses About the True Prevalence of Demoralization in the United States." In *Mental Illness in the United States*. See B.P. Dohrenwend et al. 1980, 114–32.

Longfellow, Henry W. 1912. *Évangéline et autres poèmes de Longfellow*. 3e éd. Montréal: J.-Alfred Guay.

Loseke, D.R., and S.E. Cahill 1984. "The Social Construction of Deviance: Experts on Battered Women." *Social Problems* 31 (3): 296–310.

Loseke, D.R. and S.F. Berk. 1982. "The Work of Shelters: Battered Women and Initial Calls for Help." *Victimology* 7 (1–4): 35–48.

Luce, Clare Booth 1979. *Slam the Door Softly*. In *A Century of Plays by American Women*, edited by Rachel France. New York: Richards Rosen Press, 185–94.

Luker, Kristin 1984. *Abortion and the Politics of Motherhood*. Berkeley: University of California Press.

Lundy C. 1987. "Sex-Role Conflict in Female Alcoholics: A Critical Review of the Literature." *Alcoholism Treatment Quarterly* 4 (1): 69–78.

Lyons, N.P. 1983. "Two Perspectives: On Self, Relationships and Morality." *Harvard Educational Review* 53 (2).

Maher, Frances 1985. "Classroom Pedagogy and the New Scholarship of Women." In *Gendered Subjects*. See Culley and Portuges 1985. 29–48.

Maillet, Antonine 1975. *Évangéline deusse*. Ottawa: Leméac.

– 1971. *La Sagouine*. Ottawa: Leméac.

Marcuse, Herbert 1968. *L'homme unidimensionnel*. Paris: Minuit.

Markle, Gerald E., and C.B. Nam 1971. "Sex Predetermination: Its Impact on Fertility." *Social Biology* 18 (1): 73–83.

– 1974. "Sex Ratio at Birth: Value, Variance, and Some Determinants." *Demography* 11 (1): 131–42.

Marshall, Susan 1985. "Ladies Against Women: Mobilization Dilemmas of Antifeminist Movements." *Social Problems* 32: 348–62.

Martel, Angéline 1986. « La notion d'authenticité en didactique des langues secondes. » *Bulletin de l'AQEFLS* 8 (1–2): 21–7.

Martel, Angéline and Linda Peterat 1988. "From Hopelessness to Hope: Womanness at the Margin of Schooling." *Journal of Curriculum Theorizing* (forthcoming).

Martin, Jane Roland 1986. "Redefining the Educated Person: Rethinking the Significance of Gender." *Educational Researcher* 15 (6): 6–10.

– 1985. *Reclaiming a Conversation: The Ideal of the Educated Woman*. New Haven: Yale University Press.

Mathieu, Nicole-Claude 1985. « Femmes, matière à penser ... et à reproduire. » Dans *L'arraisonnement des femmes*. Voir Mathieu et. al 1985, 5–16.

Mathieu, Nicole-Claude et al. eds., 1985. *L'arraisonnement des femmes: essais en anthropologie des sexes*. Paris: Ecole des haute études en science sociales.

Maxmen, J.S. 1986. *The New Psychiatry*. New York: Mentor.

Mazur, Carol, and Sheila Pepper 1984. *Women in Canada: A Bibliography 1965 to 1982*. Toronto: OISE Press.

McInnis, Peter 1987. "Newfoundland Labour and World War I: The Emergence of the Newfoundland Industrial Workers Association." Master's thesis, Memorial University of Newfoundland.

McMillan C. 1982. *Women, Reason and Nature*. Princeton: Princeton University Press.

Meillassoux, C. 1975. *Femmes, greniers et capitaux*. Paris: Maspero.

Merikangas, K.R., J.F. Leckman, B.A. Prusoff, D.L. Pauls, and M.M. Weissman 1985. "Familial Transmission of Depression and Alcoholism." *Archives of General Psychiatry* 42: 367–72.

Michel, A. 1983. « Inégalité des classes et de sexe et système agro-alimentaire en milieu rural en Amérique latine. » *Nouvelles questions féministes*. Labourage et pâturage: le patriarcat en campagne 5 (printemps): 59–76.

Mignot-Lefebvre, Yvonne 1985. « Les femmes dans l'économie, de l'invisibilité à de nouveaux modes d'organisation. » *Revue Tiers-Monde* 26 (102): 247–60.

Miles, A., and G. Finn, eds. 1982. *Feminism in Canada: From Pressure to Politics*. Montreal: Black Rose Books.

Miles, Angela 1981. "The Integrative Feminine Principle in North American Feminist Radicalism: Value Basis of a New Feminism." *Women's Studies International Quarterly* 4 (4): 481–95.

Mitchell, Juliet, and Ann Oakley, eds. 1976. *The Rights and Wrongs of Women*. Harmondsworth, UK: Penguin.

Mollard, A. 1978. *Paysans exploités*. Presses universitaires de Grenoble.

Moncomble, Françoise 1985. « De l'insécurité au politique. » *Actions et recherches sociales* 4: 45–57.

Morgan, Robin 1984. *The Anatomy of Freedom: Feminism, Physics and Global Politics*. New York: Anchor Books.

Morris, William, ed. 1980. *The Houghton Mifflin Canadian Dictionary of the English Language*. Markham, Ont.: Houghton Mifflin.

Mottini-Coulon, Edmée 1978. *Essai d'ontologie spécifiquement féminine: vers une philosophie différentielle*. Paris: Edition Jean Vrin.

Mueller, Caroll 1983. "In Search of a Constituency for the 'New Religious Right'." *Public Opinion Quarterly* 47: 213–29.

Mura, Roberta 1986. « Regards féministes sur la mathématique. » Dans *Femmes et mathématique*. Voir Lafortune 1986, 201–15.

Murphy, Julie 1984. "Egg Farming and Women's Future." In *Test-Tube Women*. See Arditti et al 1984, 76–91.

Myers, J.K., M.M. Weissman, G.L. Tischler, C.E. Holzer, P.J. Leaf, H. Orvaschel, J.C. Anthony, J.J.H. Boyd, J.D. Burke, M. Kramer, and R. Stoltzman 1984. "Six-Month Prevalence of Psychiatric Disorders in Three Communities: 1980–82." *Archives of General Psychiatry* 42: 959–67.

Nadeau, Lucie 1985. « À quand les mères-machines. » Entrevue avec Louise Vandelac. *Pour le socialisme* (automne): 3–10.

Nash, June, and Helen Safa, eds. 1986. *Women and Change in Latin America*. Massachusetts: Bergin and Garvey.

National Organization of Women 1975. "Statement of Purpose." In Gayle Graham Yates, *What Women Want: The Ideas of the Movement*. Cambridge: Harvard University Press.

"New Brunswick, 24 Westmoreland, Moncton City" *Recensement du Canada, 1891*.

"New Brunswick, 33 Westmoreland, Moncton Town." *Recensement du Canada, 1881*.

Nielsen, J.M., P. Eberle, N. Thoennes, and L.E. Walker 1979. *Why Women Stay in Battering Relationships: Preliminary Results*. Paper presented at the annual meeting of the American Sociological Association, Boston.

Nietzsche, F. 1964 [1887]. *La Généalogie de la morale*. Paris: Gallimard.

Nimier, Jacques 1976. *Mathématiques et affectivité*. Paris: Stock.

Nolen-Hoeksema, S. 1987. "Sex Differences in Unipolar Depression: Evidence and Theory." *Psychological Bulletin* 101: 259–82.

North, Sadie 1969. "Boy or girl? Now you can choose." *Family Circle*, Oct.

Oakley, A. 1986. "Beyond the Yellow Wallpaper." In *Telling the Truth About Jerusalem*. Oxford: Blackwell, 131–48.

– 1984. *The Captured Womb*. Oxford: Basil Blackwell.

– 1981. "Interviewing Women: A Contradiction in Terms." In *Doing Feminist Research*. See Helen Roberts 1981a.

– 1980. *Women Confined: Toward a Sociology of Childbirth*. New York: Schocken Books.

– 1979. *Becoming a Mother*. Oxford: Martin Robertson.

– 1976. "Wisewoman and Medicine Man: Changes in the Management of Childbirth." In *The Rights and Wrongs of Women*. See Mitchell and Oakley 1976.

O'Brien, Mary 1983. "Feminism and Education: A Critical Review Essay." *Women and Education I/Les femmes et l'education I Resources for Feminist Research* 12 (3): 3–16.

– 1981. *The Politics of Reproduction*. London: Routledge and Kegan Paul.

– 1979. "Why Feminism? Why Women? Why Now?" Mimeographed.

O'Brien, Patricia 1982. "The Newfoundland Patriotic Association: the Administration of the War Effort 1914–1918." Master's thesis, Memorial University of Newfoundland.

Okun, L. 1986. *Woman Abuse: Facts Replacing Myths*. New York: State University of New York Press.

– 1984. *Termination or Resumption of Cohabitation in Woman-Battering Relationships: A Statistical Study*. Paper presented at the Second Conference of the National Family Violence Researchers, Durham, New Hampshire.

Ontario Law Reform Commission 1985. *Report of Human Artificial Reproduction and Related Matters*. 2 vols. Toronto: Ministry of the Attorney General.

Padesky, C.A., and C.L. Hammen 1981. "Sex Differences in Depressive Symptom Expression and Help-Seeking Among College Students." *Sex Roles* 7: 309–20.

Page, S. 1987. "On Gender Roles and Perception of Maladjustment." *Canadian Psychology* 28: 53–9.

Pagelow, M.D. 1981. *Woman-Battering: Victims and Their Experiences*. Beverley Hills: Sage.

Parr, Joy 1980. *Labouring Children: British Immigrant Apprentices to Canada 1869–1924*. Montreal: McGill-Queen's University Press.

Patterson, Elizabeth C. 1983. *Mary Sommerville and the Cultivation of Science: 1815–1840*. Boston: Kluwer Academic Publishers.

Pebley, A.R., and C.F. Westoff 1982. "Women's Sex Preferences in the United States." *Demography* 19: 177–89.

Pegano, Jo Anne 1986. *Teaching Toward Empowerment: Integrating Feminist Pedagogy into General Education*. Paper presented at the annual meeting of the American Educational Research Association in San Francisco.

Peiffer, Jeanne 1986. « La place réservée aux femmes en sciences exactes et appliquées: place aveugle ou non-lieu? » *Perspectives universitaires* 3 (1–2): 113–37.

Perl, Teri H. 1978. *Math Equals: Biographies of Women Mathematicians and Related Activities*. Addison-Wesley.

Perry, W.G. 1981. "Cognitive and Ethical Growth: The Making of Meaning." In *The Modern American College*. See Chickering 1981.

Petchesky, Rosalind P. 1981. "Anti-Abortion, Antifeminism and the Rise of the New Right." *Feminist Studies* 2: 206–46.

Peterat, L. ed, 1987. "Isabel Bevier: A Different Voice for Women's Education in the Mid-West." In *The Conversation and Company of Educated Women*. Edited by L. Peterat. Urbana-Champaign, Ill.: Illinois Teacher of Home Economics.

Peterson, C.C., and J.L. Peterson 1973. "Preference for Sex of Offspring as a Measure of Change in Sex Attitudes." *Psychology* 10: 3–5.

Piaget, J. 1970. *Genetic Epistemology*. New York: Columbia University Press.

Piercy, Marge 1976. *Woman on the Edge of Time*. Greenwich, Conn.: Fawcett.

Pilon, Debra 1985. "Conception Without Sex." *Healthsharing* 6 (4): 21–4.

Pohli, Carol 1983. "Church Closets and Back Doors: A Feminist View of Moral Majority Women." *Feminist Studies* 9 (3): 529–58.

Porter, Maureen, and Sally MacIntyre 1984. "What Is, Must Be Best: A Research Note on Conservative or Deferential Responses to Antenatal Care Provisions." *Social Science and Medicine* 19 (11): 197–200.

Prentice, Alison and Susan Trofimenkoff, eds. 1985. *The Neglected Majority.* 2 vols. Toronto: McClelland and Stewart.

Quéniart, Anne 1987a. « Le façonnement social de la grossesse: une analyse des diverses dimensions du vécu des femmes. » Thèse de doctorat en sociologie, Université du Québec a Montréal.

– 1987b. « La technologie: une réponse à l'insécurité des femmes? » Dans *Accoucher autrement.* Voir Saillant et O'Neill 1987, 213–35.

Randall, Melanie 1985. "Defining Feminism." *Resources for Feminist Research* 14 (3): 2–6.

« Rapport des commissaires chargés de faire une enquête sur le fonctionnement des moulins et fabriques du Canada, et sur la main-d'oeuvre qui est employée » 1882. *Documents de la Session* no. 42, 45 Vict. A.

Raymond, Janice 1985. "Women's Studies: A Knowledge of One's Own." In *Gendered Subjects.* See Culley and Portuges 1985, 49–63.

Recensement du Canada 1880–81, vols. 1, 2; 1890–91. vols. 1, 2, 3.

Reissman, Frank, 1976. "How Does Self-Help Work?" *Social Policy* (Sept./ Oct.): 41–52.

Renaud, Marc et al. 1987. « Regard médical et grossesse en Amérique du Nord: l'évolution de l'obstétrique prénatale au 20è siècle. » Dans *Accoucher autrement.* Voir Saillant et O'Neill 1987, 181–212.

Repetti, R.L., and F. Crosby 1984. "Gender and Depression: Exploring the Adult-Role Explanation." *Journal of Social and Clinical Psychology* 2: 57– 70.

Report of the Royal Commission on the Relations of Capital and Labour in Canada 1889a. Evidence-New Brunswick. Ottawa: Queen's Printer.

Report of the Royal Commission on the Relations of Capital and Labour in Canada 1889b. Ottawa: Queen's Printer.

"*Report on the Manufacturing Industries of Certain Sections of the Maritime Provinces* 1885. Documents de la Session no. 37, 48, Vict. A.

Rich, Adrienne 1979. *On Lies, Secrets and Silence.* New York: W.W. Norton.

– 1977. *Of Women Born.* New York: Bantam.

Ritter, Erika 1984. "A Renovated Doll's House." *City Woman* (Winter): 14.

Roberts, Barbara 1979. "A Work for Empire: Canadian Reformers and British Female Immigration." In *A Not Unreasonable Claim.* See Kealy 1979, 185–202.

Roberts, Helen, ed. 1981a. *Doing Feminist Research.* London: Routledge and Kegan Paul.

– 1981b. *Women, Health and Reproduction.* London: Routledge and Kegan Paul.

Roberts, Joan 1985. "A Deeper Way of Looking at Multiple Roles." *Journal of Thought* 20 (3): 65–73.

Robins, Elizabeth 1928. *Ibsen and the Actress*. London: Hogarth Press.

Rogers, Barbara 1980. *The Domestication of Women: Discrimination in Developing Societies*. London: Tavistock.

Roldan, Martha 1983. « Testimonio de las obreras agricolas de Sinaloa. Una trabaja más para quedarse igual. » *Fem* 8 (29): 21–3.

Rorvik, David M., and Landrum B. Shettles 1970. "How to Chose Your Baby's Sex." *Look* 24 (April): 89–98.

Rosenzweig, Saul, and Stuart Adelman 1976. "Parental Predetermination of the Sex of Offspring: The Attitudes of Young Married Couples with University Education." *Journal of Biosocial Science* 8: 122–30.

Rosser, Sue 1986. *Teaching Science and Health From a Feminist Perspective*. New York: Pergamon Press.

Rossi, Alice S. 1964. "Equality Between the Sexes: An Immodest Proposal." *Daedulus* 93 (Spring): 624–5.

Rossiter, Margaret 1982. *Women Scientists in America: Struggles and Strategies to 1940*. Baltimore: Johns Hopkins University Press.

Rothman, Barbara Katz 1982. *In Labour: Women and Power in the Birthplace*. New York: W.W. Norton.

Rothschild, Jean, ed. 1983. *Machina Ex Dea: Feminist Perspectives on Technology*. New York: Pergamon Press.

Rouillard, Jacques 1974. *Les travailleurs du coton au Québec 1900–1915*. Montréal: P.U.Q.

Rounsaville, B.J. 1978. "Theories in Marital Violence: Evidence from a Study of Battered Women." *Victimology* 3 (1–2): 11–31.

Roy, Michel 1978. *L'Acadie perdue*. Montréal: Québec-Amérique.

Royer, Jean 1972. « Un personnage universel qui prend ses racines dans l'enfance acadienne d'Antonine Maillet. » *Le Soleil* 14 oct.

Rubin, R. 1983. *Intimate Strangers: Men and Women Together*. New York: Harper and Row.

Ruskai, Mary Beth 1986. "Letter on Feminism and Women in Science." *Association for Women in Mathematics Newsletter* 16 (3): 4–6.

Russell, Diane 1984. *Sexual Exploitation*. Beverley Hills: Sage.

Ruzek, Sheryl Burt 1978. *The Women's Health Movement: Feminist Alternatives to Medical Control*. New York: Praeger.

Sabia, Laura 1978. "Women and Politics." In *Women on Women*. See Shteir 1978, 29–42.

Sacouman, J.R. 1980. "Semi-Proletarianization and Rural Underdevelopment in the Maritimes." *Canadian Review of Sociology and Anthropology* 17 (3): 232–45.

Saillant, F., and M. O'Neill, eds. 1987. *Accoucher autrement. Repères historiques, sociaux et culturels de la grossesse et de l'accouchement au Québec*. Montréal: St-Martin.

Sandmaier, M. 1982. *The Invisible Alcoholics*. New York: McGrawHill.

Sanford, N. 1967. *Learning After College*. CA: Jossey Bass.

Saunders, Trevor J., translator and editor. 1975. *Plato: The Laws*. Harmondsworth, UK: Penguin.

Sawicki, Jana 1986. "Foucault and Feminism: Toward a Politics of Difference." *Hypatia: A Journal of Feminist Philosophy* 1 (2).

Schildkamp-Kündiger, Erika, ed. 1982. *An International Review of Gender and Mathematics*. Columbus, Ohio: The ERIC Science, Mathematics and Environmental Education Clearinghouse, Ohio State University.

Scully, Diana, and Pauline Bart 1973. "A Funny Thing Happened on the Way to the Orifice: Women in Gynecology Textbooks." *American Journal of Sociology* 78 (1): 1045–50.

Sells, Lucy 1973. *High School Mathematics as the Critical Filter in the Job Market*. ERIC: ED 080–351.

Sénéchal, Brigitte 1982. « Mathématiques, féminité et langage. » *Mythematics. Maths et société*. Groupe Inter-IREM, 27–30.

Shaw, Nancy Stoller 1974. *Forced Labour: Maternity Care in the United States*. New York: Pergamon Press.

Shearer, M. 1983. "The Difficulty of Defining and Measuring Satisfactory Perinatal Care." *Birth* 10: 77.

Sherif, C.W. 1977. "Bias in Psychology." In *The Prism of Sex*. See Sherman and Beck 1977, 93–133.

Sherman, and Beck eds. 1977. *The Prism of Sex*. Minnesota: University of Wisconsin Press.

Shettles, Landrum, B. 1961. "Conception and Birth Sex Ratios: A Review." *Obstetrics and Gynecology* 18: 122–30.

Shields, N.M., and C.R. Hanneke 1983. "Attribution Processes in Violent Relationships: Perceptions of Violent Husbands and Their Wives." *Journal of Applied Social Psychology* 13 (6): 515–27.

Shteir, Ann B. ed., 1978. *Women on Women*. Toronto: York University.

Silverman, P.R. 1981. *Helping Women Cope with Grief*. Beverley Hills: Sage.

Sinclair, D. 1985. *Understanding Wife Assault: A Training Manual for Counsellors and Advocates*. Family Violence Program. Toronto: Ontario Ministry of Community and Social Services.

Sinclair, P. 1985. "From Traps to Draggers, Social and Economic Studies." *Institute of Social and Economic Research* 31 (Memorial University of Newfoundland).

Smallwood, Joseph 1937. "Industrial, Commercial and Financial Development." Vol. 1 of *Book of Newfoundland*. St. John's: Newfoundland Book Publishers.

Smith, Estelle, ed. 1977. *Those who Live from the Sea*. St. Paul: West.

Smith, P. 1984. *Breaking the Silence: Descriptive Report of a Follow-Up Study of Abused Women*. Regina: Regina Transition Women's Society.

Smith, P., and D.L. Chalmers 1984. "Does Sheltering Help Abused Women? Preliminary Survey Results: Regina Transition Follow-Up Study, a Shelter for the Physically and/or Emotionally Abused." Paper presented at the annual meeting of the Canadian Sociology and Anthropology Association, Guelph, Ontario.

Spender, Dale 1986. "Some Thoughts on the Power of Mathematics: What Is the Problem?" In *Girls into Math Can Go*. See Burton 1986, 58–60.

– 1984. *Time and Tide Wait for No Man*. London: Pandora Press.

– 1982. *Women of Ideas*. London: Routledge.

– 1981. *Men's Studies Modified: The Impact of Feminism on the Academic Disciplines*. Oxford: Pergamon Press.

Spivak, Gayatri 1979. "Explanation and Culture: Marginalia." *Humanities in Society* 2.

Stacey, W., and A. Shupe 1983. *The Family Secret: Domestic Violence in America*. Boston: Beacon.

Stark, E., A. Flitcraft, and W. Frazier 1979. "Medicine and Patriarchal Violence: The Social Construction of a 'Private' Event." *International Journal of Health Services* 9 (3): 461–93.

Stark-Adamec, C. 1981. "Is There a Double Standard in Mental Health Research Funding As Well As a Double Standard in Mental Health?" *Ontario Psychologist* 13: 5–16.

Staudt, Kathleen 1985. "Policy Strategies at the End of the Decade." *Africa Report* 30 (2): 71–5.

Stein, Dorothy 1985. *Ada: A Life and Legacy*. Cambridge, Mass.: MIT Press.

Stevens, Doris 1976 [1920]. *Jailed for Freedom*. New York: Schocken.

Stoppard, J.M. 1987. "An Evaluation of the Adequacy of Cognitive/Behavioural Theories and Treatments of Depression for Understanding Depression in Women." Paper presented at the Institutue of the Section on Women and Psychology, Canadian Psychological Association, Vancouver, British Columbia, 17 June.

Strindberg, August 1972 [1884, 1886]. "A Doll's House." *Getting Married Part I and II*. Edited and translated by Mary Sandbach. London: Victor Gollancz, 167–84.

Suler, John 1984. "The Role of Ideology in Self-Help Groups." *Social Policy* 14 (3): 29–36.

Tabet, Paola 1985. « Fertilité naturelle, reproduction forcée. » *L'arraisonnement des femmes*. Voir Mathieu et al. 1985, 61–131.

Thomas, Louis-Vincent 1978. *Mort et pouvoir*. Paris: Payot.

Thornton, Patricia A. 1985. "Problems of Out-Migration from Atlantic Canada 1871–1921: A New Look." *Acadiensis* 15 (Autumn).

"Towards a Canadian Feminist Party" 1979. *Atlantis* 5: 142–5.

Tremblay, Marielle 1985. « Un syndicalisme au masculin: la CEQ et la question des femmes. » Thèse de doctorat, Département de science politique, Université du Québec à Montréal.

Tulloch, Elspeth 1985. *Nous les soussignées: un aperçu historique du statut politique et légal des femmes du Nouveau-Brunswick 1784–1984*. Moncton: Conseil consultatif sur la condition de la femme du Nouveau-Brunswick, 95–105.

Vandelac, L., D. Belise, A. Gauthier, et V. Pinard 1985. *Du travail et de l'amour. Les dessous de la production domestique*. Montréal: St-Martin, Collection Femmes.

Verslinghuysen, Margaret Connor 1981. "Midwives, Medical Men and 'Poor Women Labouring of Child': Lying-In Hospitals in Eighteenth Century London." In *Women, Health and Reproduction*. See Helen Roberts 1981b.

Victoria Committee to Consider the Social, Ethical and Legal Issues Arising for In Vitro Fertilization 1983. *Report on Donor Gametes in IVF*.

Waldron, Ingrid 1967. "Why Do Women Live Longer than Men?" In *The Sociology of Health and Illness: Critical Perspectives*. See Conrad and Rochelle 1967, 45–67.

Walker, L.E. 1984. *The Battered Woman Syndrome*. New York: Springer.

– 1979. *The Battered Women*. New York: Harper and Row.

Warren, L.W. 1983. "Male Intolerance of Depression: A Review with Implications for Psychotherapy." *Clinical Psychology Review* 3: 147–56.

Weingourt, R. 1979. "Battered Women: The Grieving Process." *Journal of Psychiatric Nursing* 17: 40–7.

Weissman, M.M., and G.L. Klerman 1977. "Sex Differences and the Epidemiology of Depression." *Archives of General Psychiatry* 34: 98–111.

Weissman, M.M., P.J. Leaf, C.E. Holzer, J.K. Myers, and G.L. Tischler 1984. "The Epidemiology of Depression: An Update on Sex Differences in Rates." *Journal of Affective Disorders* 7: 179–88.

Wertz, Richard W., and Dorothy C. Wertz 1979. *Lying-In: A History of Childbirth in America*. New York: Schocken Books.

Whitfield, C. 1984. "Stress Management and Spirituality During Recovery: A Transpersonal Approach: Part III, Transforming." *Alcoholism Treatment Quarterly* 1 (4): 1–53.

Williamson, Nancy E. 1976a. *Sons or Daughters: A Cross-Cultural Survey of Parental Preferences*. Beverley Hills: Sage.

– 1976b. "Sex Preferences, Sex Control and the Status of Women." *Signs: Journal of Women and Culture in Society* 1 (4): 847–62.

Woolf, Virginia 1977 [1929]. *Une chambre à soi*. (Titre original. *A Room of One's Own*.) Traduit par by Clara Malraux. Paris: Deynoël-Gonthier.

Contributors
Collaboratrices-eurs

MARGUERITE ANDERSEN studied in Germany and France before obtaining her doctorate from the Université de Montréal. She has taught in Tunisia, France, Germany, the United States, and Canada. Since 1987, she has occupied the chair of Women's Studies at Mount St. Vincent University in Halifax. She has published several books including the novel *De mémoire de femme* (1982) which received the Journal de Montréal prize in 1983, and *Mother Was Not a Person* (1972).

MARIE-ANDRÉE BERTRAND a fait des études en service social et en criminologie à l'Université de Montréal, et a obtenu un doctorat en criminologie de l'Université de Californie (Berkeley) en 1967. Elle est professeure titulaire à l'Ecole de criminologie de l'Université de Montréal et l'auteure d'un livre *La femme et le crime* (Montréal: L'Aurore 1979) ainsi que plusieurs articles féministes sur la question des femmes et de la norme pénale.

JESSIE CHISHOLM is currently a Ph.D. student in History at Memorial University, Newfoundland, where, with the assistance of a SSHRC doctoral fellowship, she is working on her dissertation on "Working-Class Community, St. John's 1890-1914." Her working experience includes ten years as a contract researcher with a variety of agencies including government departments, the MicMac Indian Lands Claims, the Historical Atlas of Canada, and Memorial University.

OMER CHOUINARD est originaire de la péninsule gaspésienne. Il fut directement associé au regroupement des pêcheurs côtiers des provinces Maritimes, plus particulièrement dans la région acadienne du Nouveau-Brunswick, où il a mis sur pied l'Union des pêcheurs des

Maritimes. Il rédige en ce moment sa thèse de doctorat en sociologie, à l'Université du Québec à Montréal.

LORRAINE CODE is a SSHRC Canada Research Fellow, and assistant professor in the Department of Philosophy and the Women's Studies Research Group at York University. She is the author of *Epistemic Responsibility* (Brown University Press, 1987), and coeditor of *Feminist Perspectives: Philosophical Essays on Minds and Morals* (University of Toronto Press, 1988) and *Changing Patterns: Women in Canada* (McClelland and Stewart, 1988). She is currently writing a book on knowledge and gender.

TRACY C. DAVIS is a SSHRC Canada Research Fellow and assistant professor in the Department of Drama at Queen's University. She is currently combining her interest in Victorian theatre and social history in a book on the state as an employment alternative for Englishwomen in the nineteenth century.

MICHELINE DE SÈVE est professeure au département de science politique de l'Université du Québec à Montréal. Docteure en études politiques de l'Université de Paris I, elle est l'auteure de *Pour un féminisme libertaire* (Montréal: Boréal Express 1985). Ses principaux champs d'intérêt concernent les mouvements sociaux et surtout le mouvement des femmes, les pays de l'Europe de l'Est et la théorie politique féministe.

IRENE DEVINE obtained her Ph.D. from Case Western Reserve University and is an assistant professor of Management, and associate dean, Faculty of Commerce and Administration, Concordia University. Her research interests include organizational crisis, organizational change and development, and women and careers in organizations. She has published articles on the theoretical aspects of organizations in crisis, and on men and women working together in organizations.

HOLLY DEVOR is presently a doctoral candidate in sociology at the University of Washington, and she teaches women's studies in the Federal penitentiaries in British Columbia. Her research interests focus on the social construction of gender in everyday life. She is currently working on a book based on her MA thesis: "Gender Blending: When Two is Not Enough," to be published by Indiana University Press in 1988.

MARGRIT EICHLER is professor of Sociology at the Ontario Institute for Studies in Education. She has conducted research in the areas of feminist research, nonsexist research methods, and family policy. She is cofounder of *Resources for Feminist Research*, has been president of CRIAW, and is currently involved in the Canadian Coalition for a Royal Commission on New Reproductive Technologies, which she founded.

LORNA ERWIN teaches courses on women and on the sociology of education at York University. Her contribution to the present volume is adapted from a survey study she is completing on the pro-family movement in Canada.

NANCY FORESTELL is currently a Ph.D. candidate at the Ontario Institute for Studies in Education where her dissertation topic centers on women's wage employment in Canada during World War I. She has degrees in history and library science from the University of Western Ontario and Memorial University, Newfoundland.

MONIQUE GENUIST est professeure de français et de littérature québécoise à l'Université de la Saskatchewan. Ses publications comprennent *La Création romanesque chez Gabrielle Roy, Languirand et l'absurde*, plusieurs articles dans le *Dictionnaire des oeuvres littéraires du Québec* et différentes contributions à l'étude d'écrivains comme Anne Hébert, Marie Laberge, Madeleine Ferron et Marie-Anna Roy.

JANE GORDON is an associate professor in the Department of Sociology at Mount St. Vincent University in Halifax, where she also teaches in the Women's Studies Department. Her current research interests deal with the social management of childbirth, and other aspects of reproduction.

LINDA J. KLIMACK has been a student and researcher in the area of wife assault for eight years. She recently graduated from Carleton University with an MA in women's studies.

MARIE FRANCE LABRECQUE est détentrice d'un Ph.D. de City University of New York et professeure d'anthropologie à l'Université Laval. Elle s'intéresse actuellement à la problématique des femmes et du développement, particulièrement en Amérique latine. Ses autres travaux portent sur la paysannerie, la lutte des classes en milieu rural et les femmes amérindiennes du Québec.

GINETTE LAFLEUR est recherchiste pour « Action Education Femmes », organisme féministe pour lequel elle effectue actuellement une étude du profil socio-économique de la femme francophone au Nouveau-Brunswick. Elle s'intéresse depuis longtemps aux recherches féministes et a présenté plusieurs communications sur l'histoire des femmes. Elle est en rédaction de thèse au Département d'histoire de l'Université de Moncton.

COLLEEN LUNDY teaches in the School of Social Work at Carleton University. She has worked with alcohol and drug dependent women in both the US and Canada. She is currently conducting further research on women and alcohol.

ANGÉLINE M. MARTEL is a professor of Second Languages at the Télé-université du Québec in Montréal. She holds a Ph.D. in curriculum and an MA in French Literature from the University of Alberta. She is very active in advocating the recognition of minority rights, and has a keen interest in gender from the theoretical and pedagogical perspectives.

LANIE MELAMED did her graduate studies in adult education at the Ontario Institute for Studies in Education. Her eclectic research interests are in the areas of women's epistemology, feminist pedagogy, and play and peace studies. She teaches at Concordia and McGill Universities.

MARIA ELISA MONTEJO est candidate en anthropologie à l'Université Laval et ses recherches s'articulent principalement autour de la subordination idéologique des femmes en milieu rural dans le cadre du développement au Mexique et en Colombie. Elle a également effectué des recherches ethnolinguistiques en Amérique latine et au Manitoba.

ROBERTA MURA est née en Italie où elle a entrepris ses études de mathématique. Elle a complété sa formation à l'Université d'Alberta (Ph.D., 1974) et depuis 1976, travaille dans le domaine de la didactique. Elle est actuellement professeure titulaire au département de didactique de l'Université Laval. Elle s'intéresse depuis longtemps, à la relation femmes-mathématique.

LINDA PETERAT is an assistant professor in Home Economics Education at the University of British Columbia. She holds a Ph.D. in curriculum studies from the University of Alberta. Her current research interests and writings are on the history and philosophy of women's education, feminist theory, and curriculum.

ANNE QUÉNIART est professeure au département de sociologie de l'Université du Québec à Montréal. Elle enseigne dans les domaines de la culture, des politiques sociales et de la santé, et de la méthodologie, notamment qualitative. Elle a effectué plusieurs recherches dans le champ de la santé des femmes (avortement, maternité, santé au travail) et prépare actuellement un projet de recherche sur la clientèle des médecines « douces » (représentations de la santé, de la maladie, du corps etc.).

JANET M. STOPPARD immigrated to Canada from England in 1971 and has worked as a clinical psychologist in Halifax, Kingston, Vancouver, and Fredericton. She completed her Ph.D. at Queen's University in 1976. Since 1979, she has been on the faculty of the Psychology Department at the University of New Brunswick, where she is currently coordinator of the Women's Studies program and is carrying out research on gender and depression.

PETA TANCRED-SHERIFF teaches sociology at McMaster University and has recently held the position of adjunct fellow at the Simone de Beauvoir Institute, Concordia University. Her feminist research interests centre around the position of women in organizations on which she is currently co-editing a book. She is also completing a study of selected Québec and Ontario universities, and of the position of women within them.

MARTIN THOMAS is a member of the Department of Political Science at York University, where he teaches courses in research methods and health policy. His current research interests include some political aspects of changes in reproductive behaviour, attitudes toward midwifery, and issue-avoidance on the part of elected representatives.

DOROTHY ZABORSZKY is an associate professor in the English Department, Laurentian University. She has written articles on Caroline Norton and the Infant Custody Bill, on Victorian feminism and George Robert Gissing's *The Odd Women*. Her main interests include women and politics, and women and work in the 1920s and 1930s. She was a founding member of the Feminist Party of Canada.